Rem Galleu

Race: Pantherian   Level: 40
A Summoner and an Adventurer. She has a small, catlike body with fluffy ears and a tail. She's also flat as a board. The Demon Lord Krebskulm was trapped inside her body, but Diablo saved her from that fate. Rem is always calm, though she's a bit of a prude.

Shera L Greenwood

Race: Elf   Level: 30
A Summoner and an Elf. She is slender and elegant, but also has an impressively large bosom that is at odds with the rest of her body. Her innocent and naive personality calms everyone around her. In reality, she is an Elvish princess from Greenwood, but she fled that kingdom to search for freedom.

Horn

Race: Grasswalker
Horn lives in the frontier city of Zircon Tower, where he enthusiastically guides adventurers through dungeons. An unexpected turn of events has him traveling with Diablo, helping him and his party take on the dungeon.

Lumachina Weselia

The holy High Priestess of the Church. Corruption within the Cardinal Council has put her life in danger. Her ability to heal others through prayer is unmatched. She believes that Diablo, who saved her, is God.

Varakness

High Commander of the newly awakened Demon Lord's forces. He leads the Demon Lord's army, initially targeting Zircon Tower and Laminitus.

Fanis Laminitus

The governor of Zircon Tower and a powerful Magi-Gunner. She is blatantly arrogant toward Diablo, the Church, and the king.

Gewait

A Paladin hired to assassinate Lumachina. He is quirky and speaks strangely, but he is also a skilled Summoner.

HOW NOT TO SUMMON A DEMON LORD

12

CONTENTS

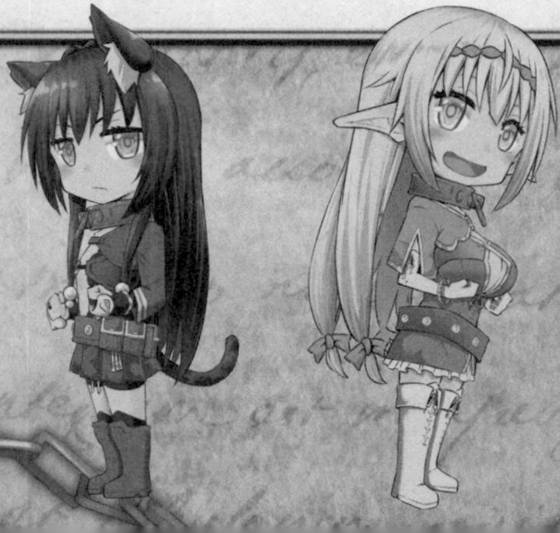

55 SAVING A COMPANION I

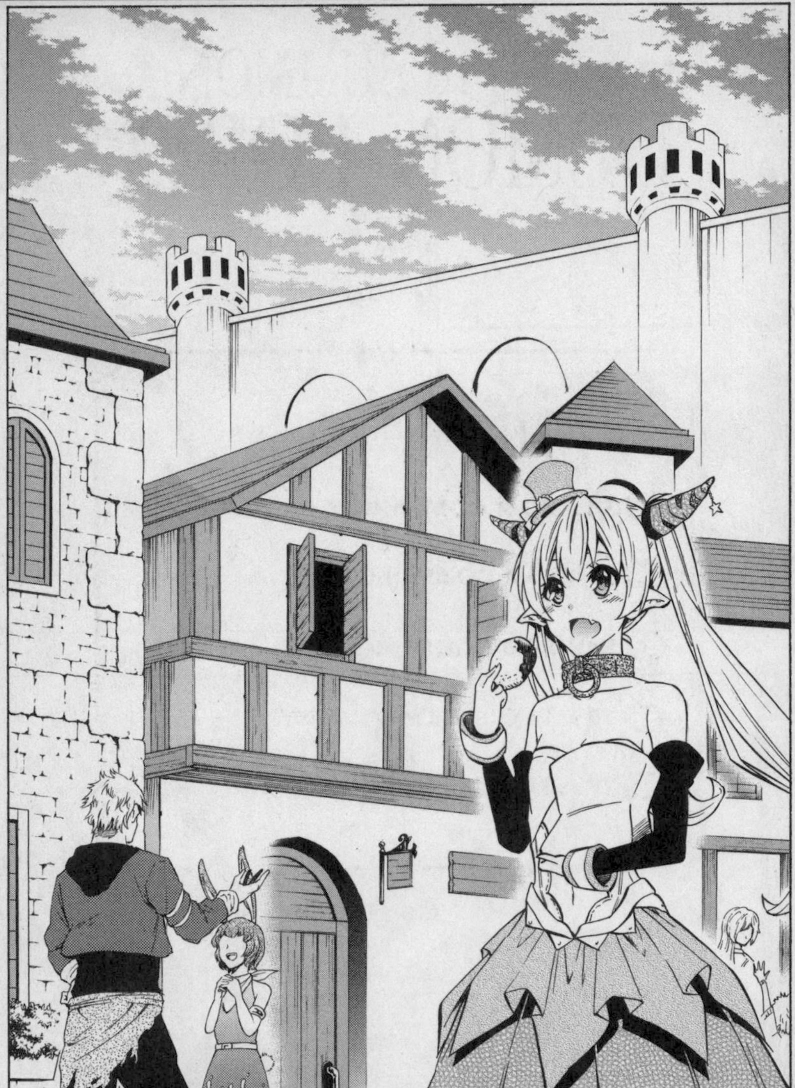

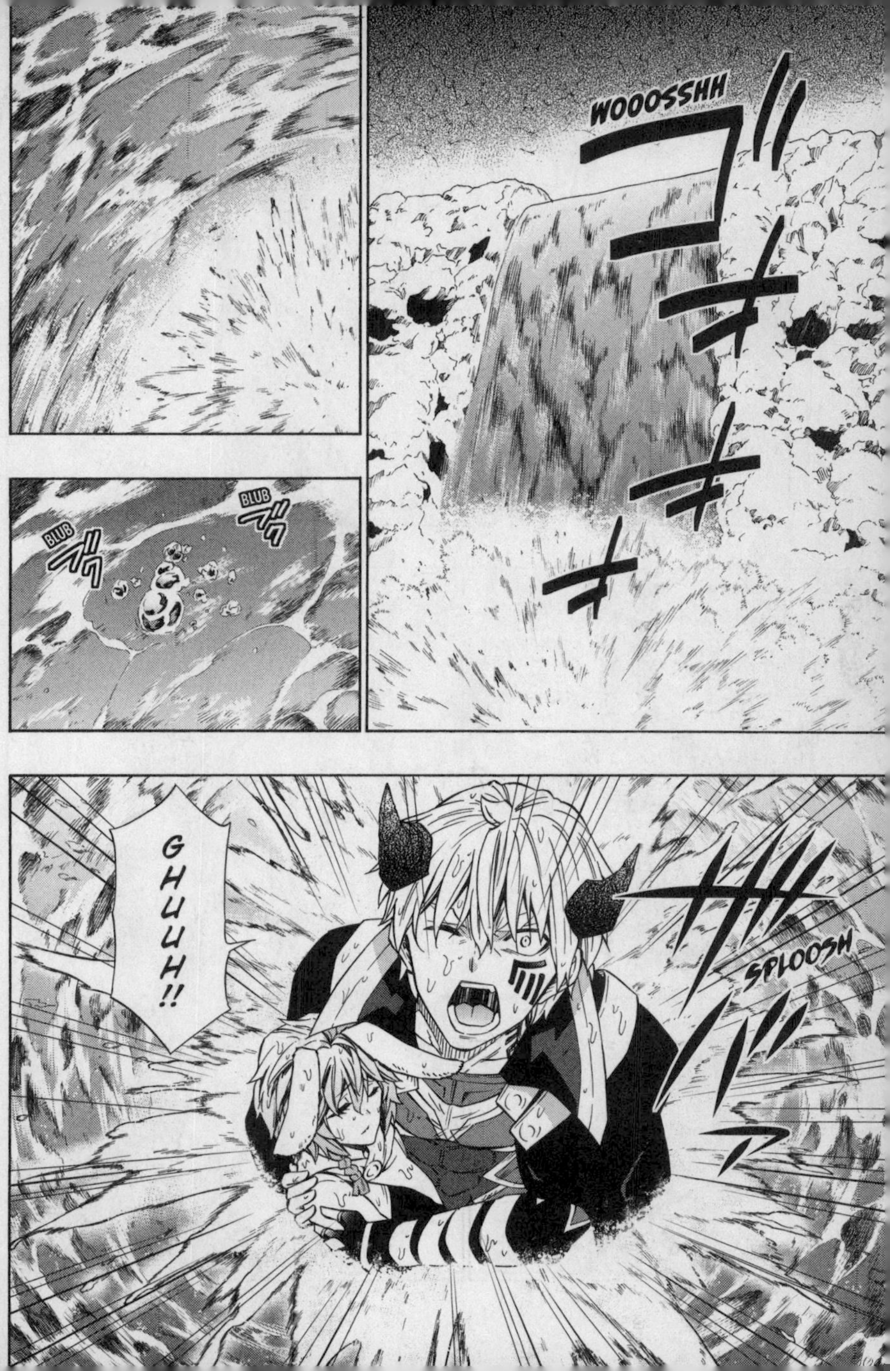
WOOOSSHH
BLUB
BLUB
SPLOOSH
GHUUH!!

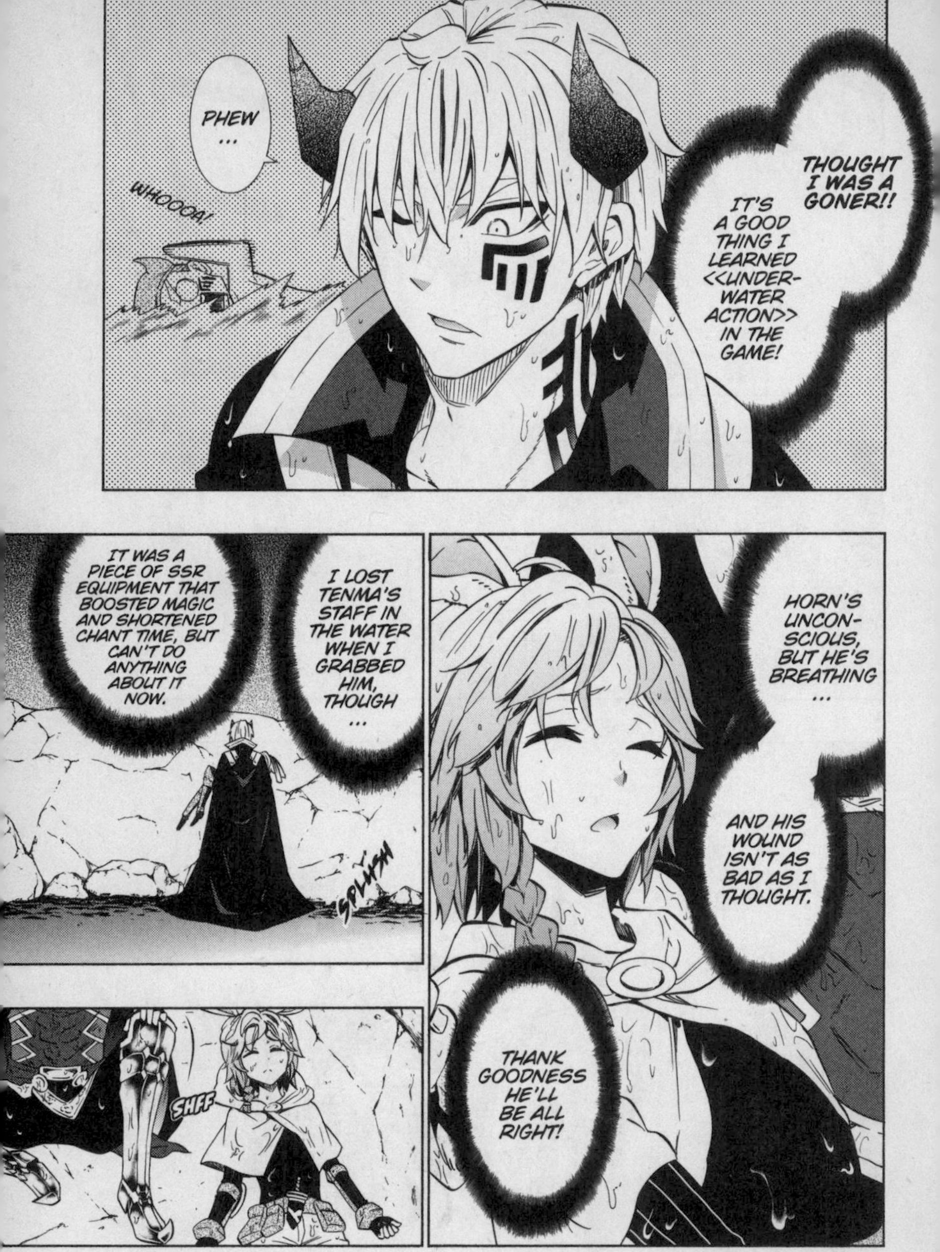
THOUGHT I WAS A GONER!!
IT'S A GOOD THING I LEARNED <<UNDER-WATER ACTION>> IN THE GAME!
PHEW ...
WHOOOA!
HORN'S UNCON-SCIOUS, BUT HE'S BREATHING ...
AND HIS WOUND ISN'T AS BAD AS I THOUGHT.
THANK GOODNESS HE'LL BE ALL RIGHT!
I LOST TENMA'S STAFF IN THE WATER WHEN I GRABBED HIM, THOUGH ...
IT WAS A PIECE OF SSR EQUIPMENT THAT BOOSTED MAGIC AND SHORTENED CHANT TIME, BUT CAN'T DO ANYTHING ABOUT IT NOW.
SPLASH
SHFF

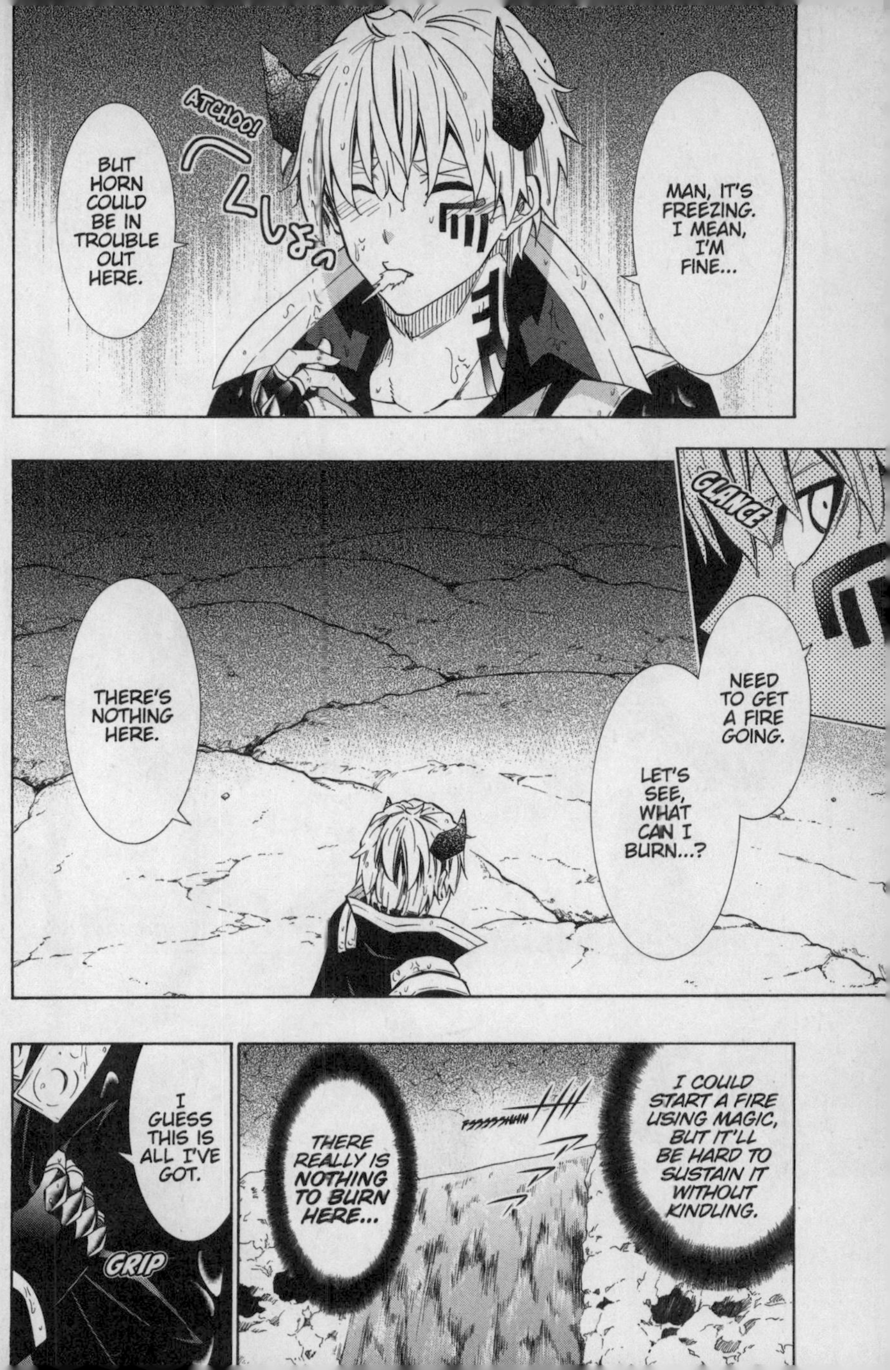
MAN, IT'S FREEZING. I MEAN, I'M FINE...
ATCHOO!
BUT HORN COULD BE IN TROUBLE OUT HERE.
GLANCE
NEED TO GET A FIRE GOING.
LET'S SEE, WHAT CAN I BURN...?
THERE'S NOTHING HERE.
I COULD START A FIRE USING MAGIC, BUT IT'LL BE HARD TO SUSTAIN IT WITHOUT KINDLING.
THERE REALLY IS NOTHING TO BURN HERE...
I GUESS THIS IS ALL I'VE GOT.
GRIP

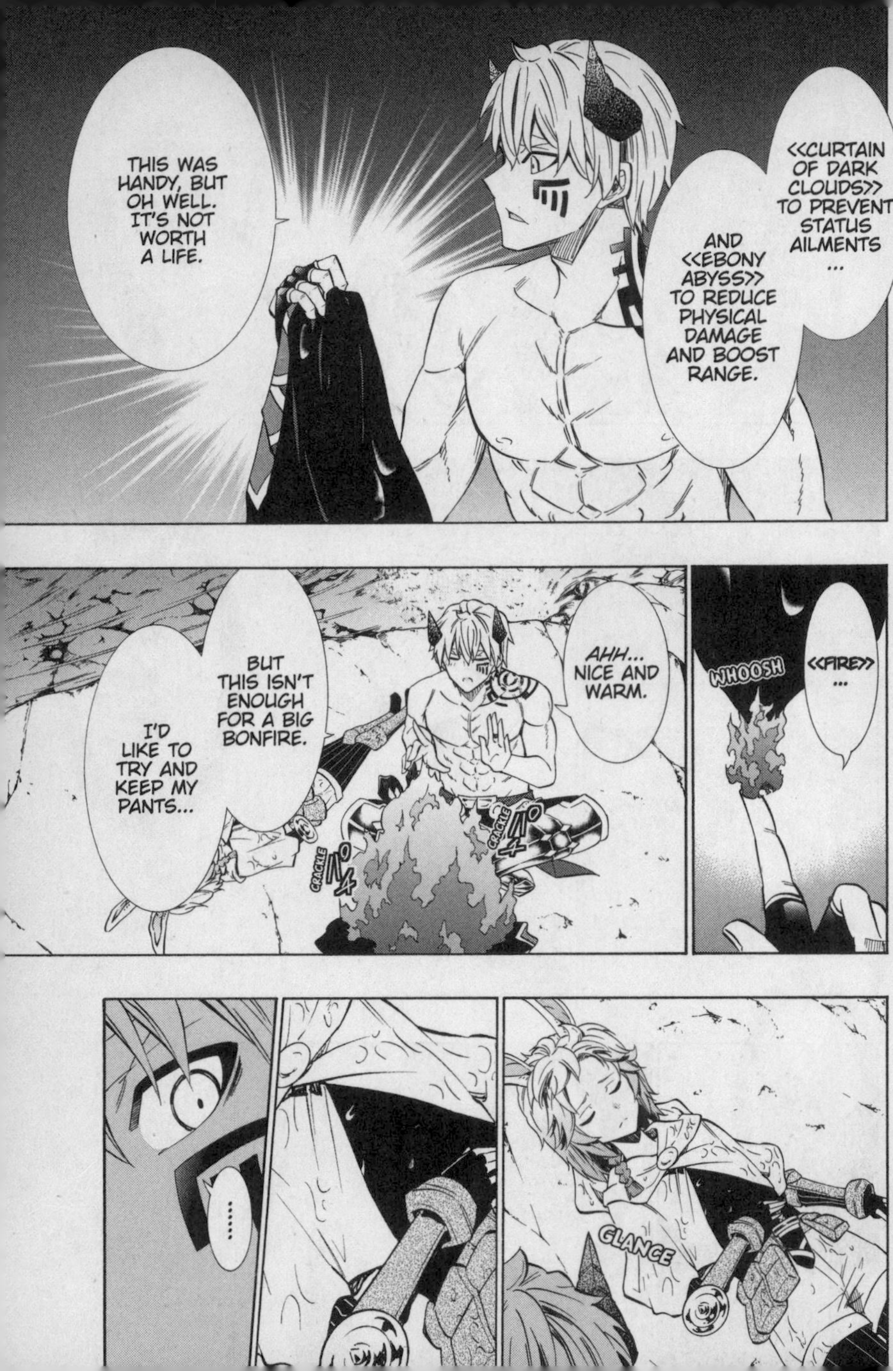
<<CURTAIN OF DARK CLOUDS>> TO PREVENT STATUS AILMENTS ...
AND <<EBONY ABYSS>> TO REDUCE PHYSICAL DAMAGE AND BOOST RANGE.
THIS WAS HANDY, BUT OH WELL. IT'S NOT WORTH A LIFE.
<<FIRE>> ...
WHOOSH
AHH... NICE AND WARM.
CRACKLE
CRACKLE
BUT THIS ISN'T ENOUGH FOR A BIG BONFIRE.
I'D LIKE TO TRY AND KEEP MY PANTS...
GLANCE
......

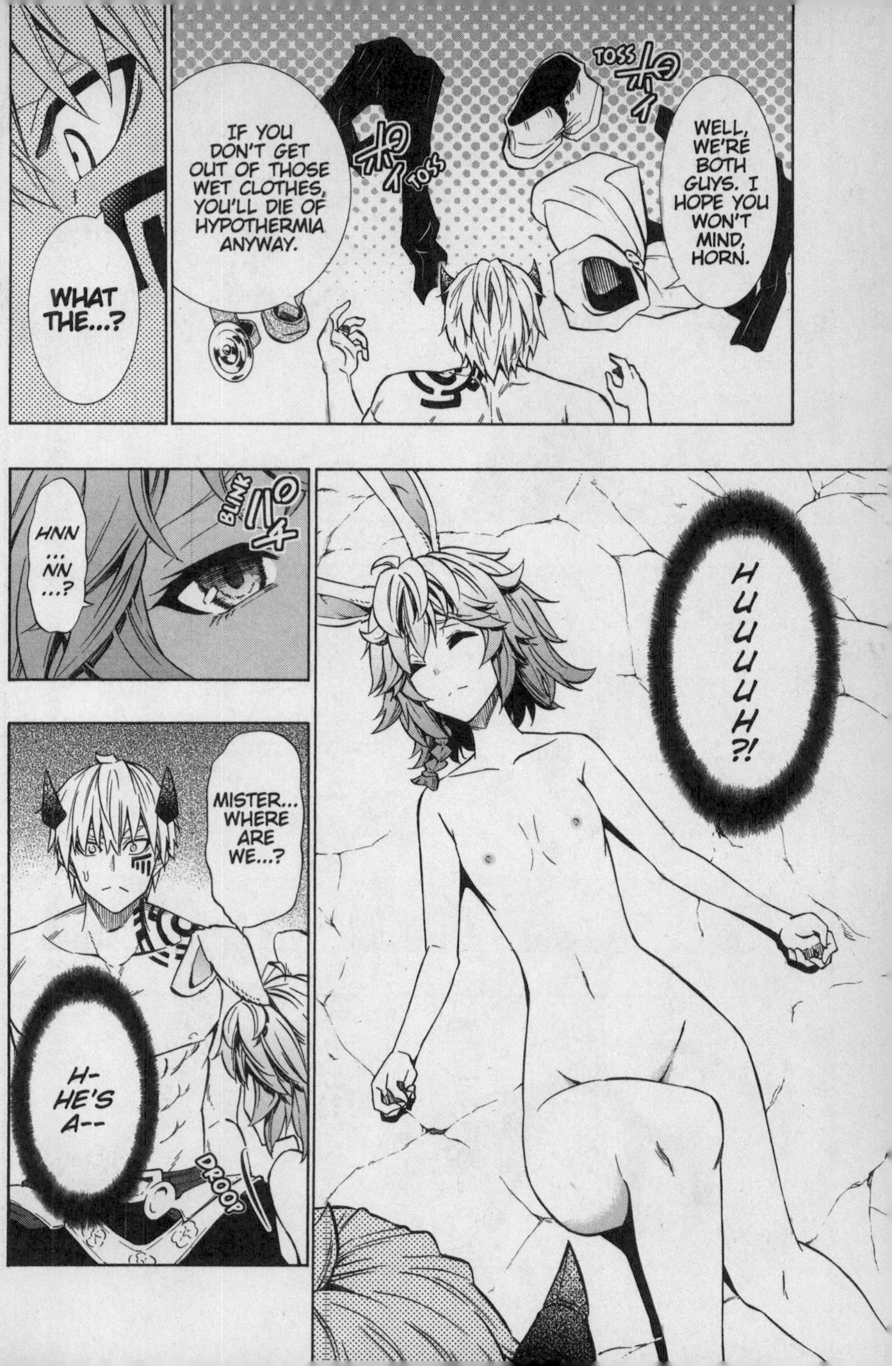
TOSS
WELL, WE'RE BOTH GUYS. I HOPE YOU WON'T MIND, HORN.
TOSS
IF YOU DON'T GET OUT OF THOSE WET CLOTHES, YOU'LL DIE OF HYPOTHERMIA ANYWAY.
WHAT THE...?
HUUUUUH?!
BLINK
HNN... NN...?
MISTER... WHERE ARE WE...?
H- HE'S A--
DROOP

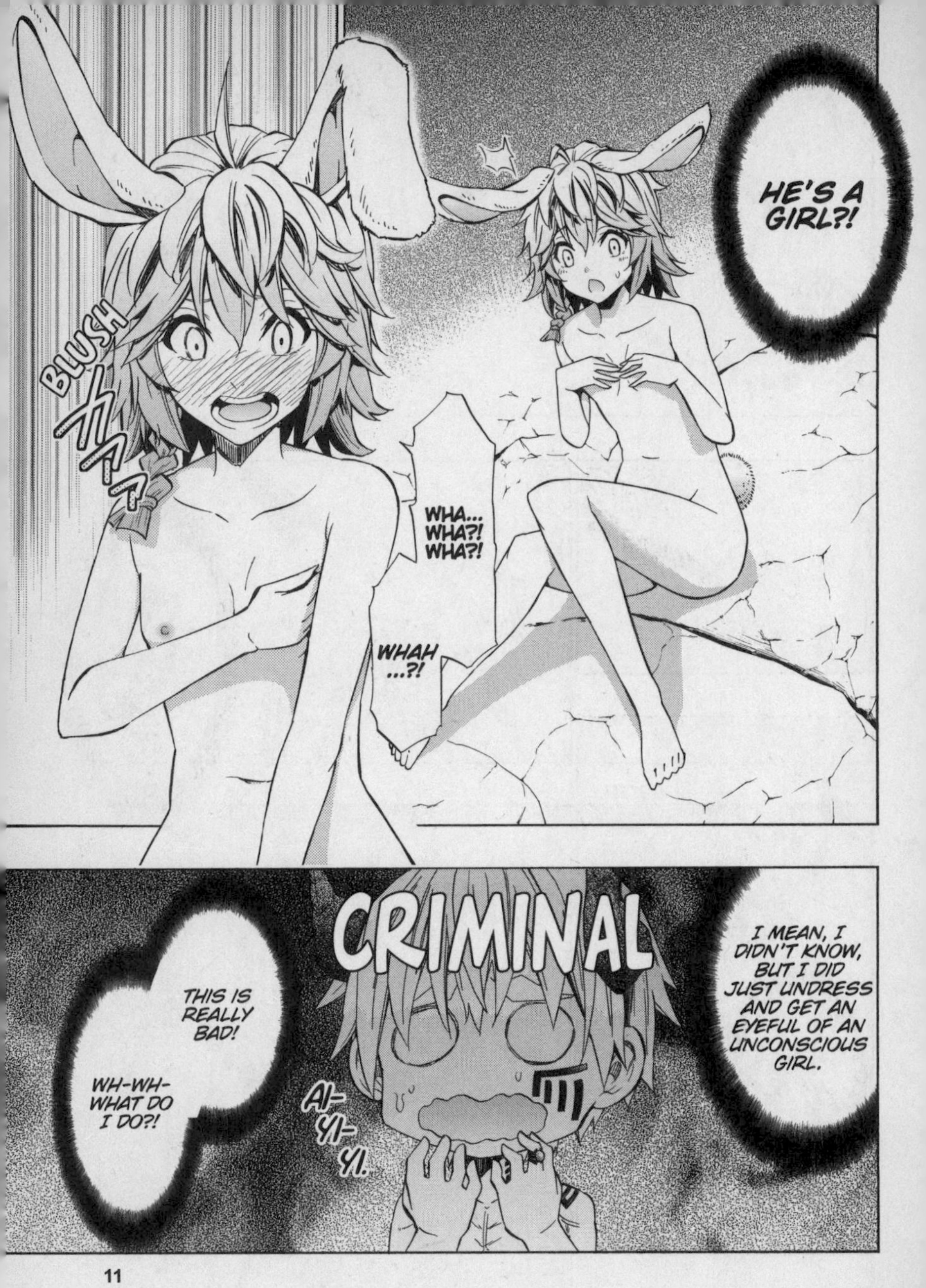
HE'S A GIRL?!
WHA... WHA?! WHA?!
WHAH ...?!
BLUSH
I MEAN, I DIDN'T KNOW, BUT I DID JUST UNDRESS AND GET AN EYEFUL OF AN UNCONSCIOUS GIRL.
CRIMINAL
THIS IS REALLY BAD!
AI-YI-YI.
WH-WH-WHAT DO I DO?!

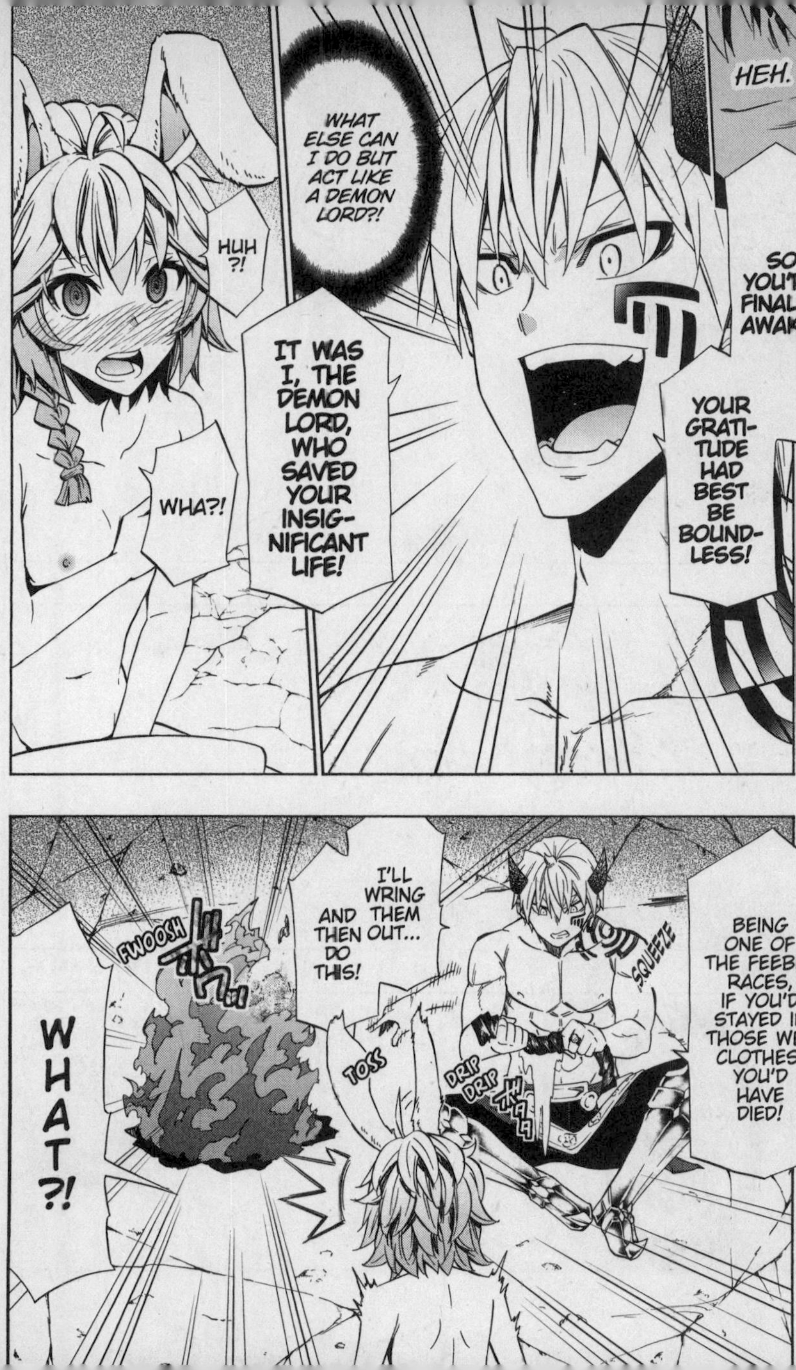
HEH.
WHAT ELSE CAN I DO BUT ACT LIKE A DEMON LORD?!
SO YOU'RE FINALLY AWAKE!
YOUR GRATITUDE HAD BEST BE BOUNDLESS!
IT WAS I, THE DEMON LORD, WHO SAVED YOUR INSIGNIFICANT LIFE!
HUH?!
WHA?!
BEING ONE OF THE FEEBLE RACES, IF YOU'D STAYED IN THOSE WET CLOTHES, YOU'D HAVE DIED!
SQUEEZE
I'LL WRING THEM OUT...
AND THEN DO THIS!
DRIP DRIP
TOSS
FWOOSH
WHAT?!

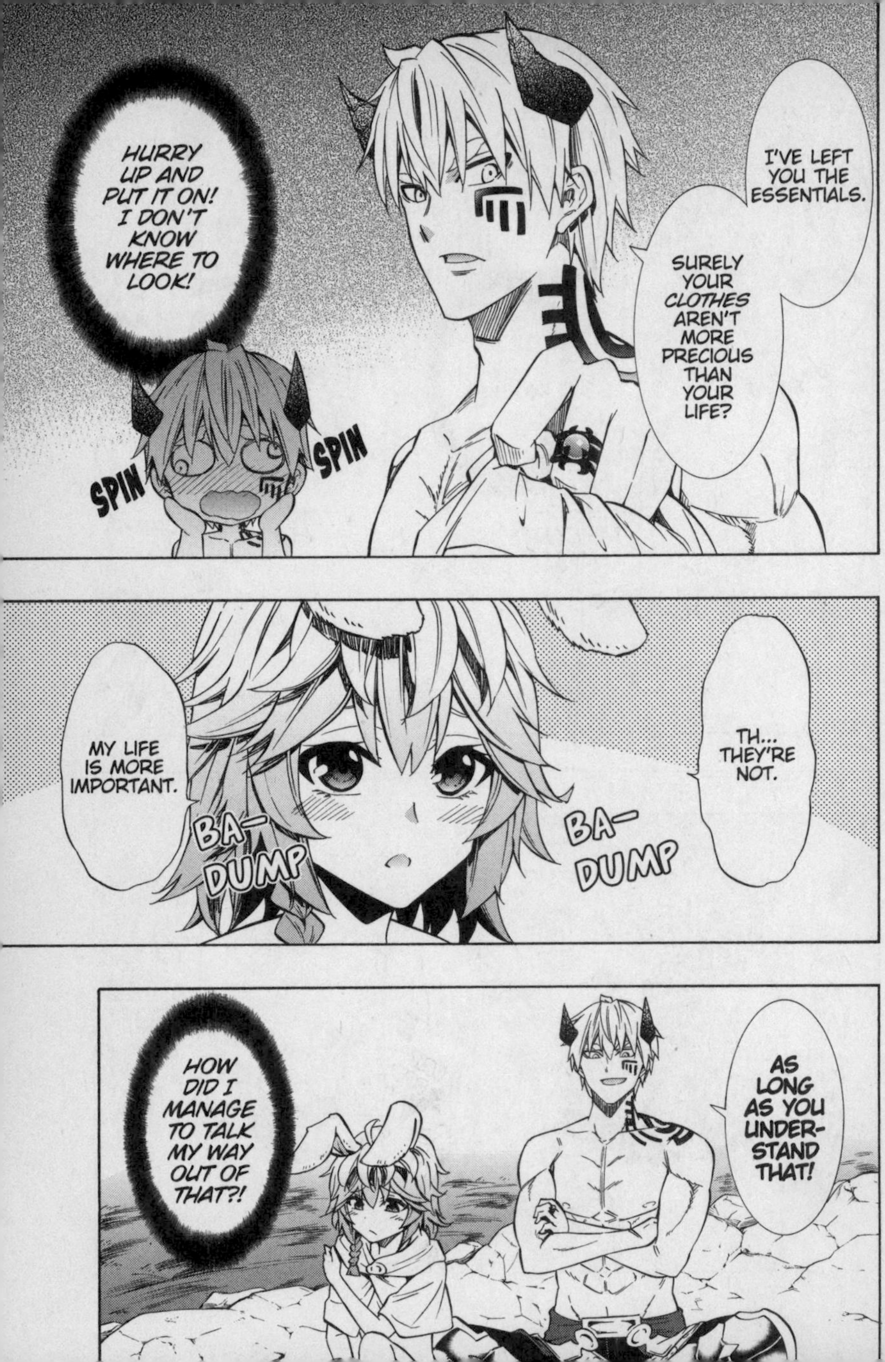
I'VE LEFT YOU THE ESSENTIALS.
SURELY YOUR CLOTHES AREN'T MORE PRECIOUS THAN YOUR LIFE?
HURRY UP AND PUT IT ON! I DON'T KNOW WHERE TO LOOK!
SPIN
SPIN
TH... THEY'RE NOT.
BA-DUMP
BA-DUMP
MY LIFE IS MORE IMPORTANT.
AS LONG AS YOU UNDER-STAND THAT!
HOW DID I MANAGE TO TALK MY WAY OUT OF THAT?!

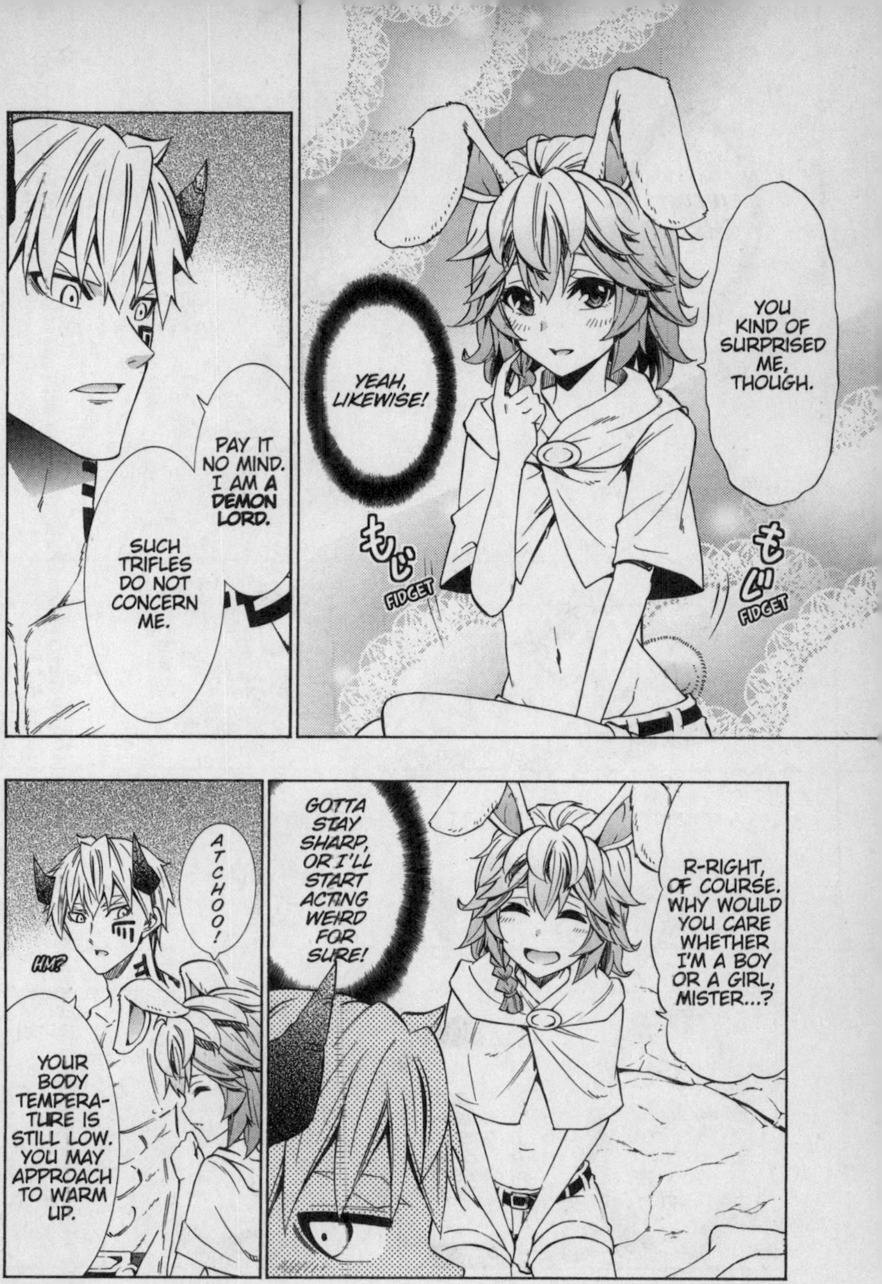
YOU KIND OF SURPRISED ME, THOUGH.
YEAH, LIKEWISE!
もじ
FIDGET
もじ
FIDGET
PAY IT NO MIND. I AM A DEMON LORD.
SUCH TRIFLES DO NOT CONCERN ME.
R-RIGHT, OF COURSE. WHY WOULD YOU CARE WHETHER I'M A BOY OR A GIRL, MISTER...?
GOTTA STAY SHARP, OR I'LL START ACTING WEIRD FOR SURE!
ATCHOO!
HM?
YOUR BODY TEMPERATURE IS STILL LOW. YOU MAY APPROACH TO WARM UP.

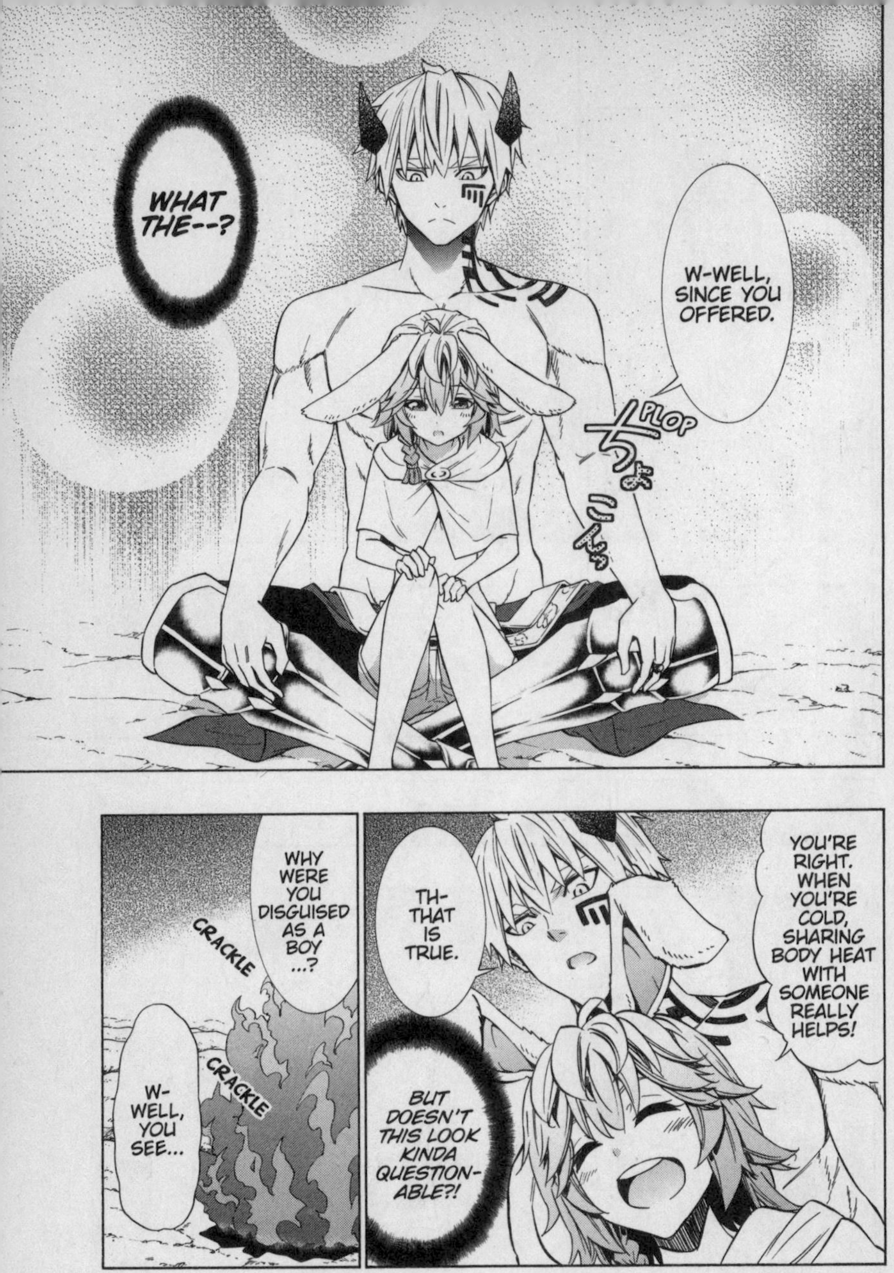
W-WELL, SINCE YOU OFFERED.
PLOP
ちょこん
WHAT THE--?
YOU'RE RIGHT. WHEN YOU'RE COLD, SHARING BODY HEAT WITH SOMEONE REALLY HELPS!
TH-THAT IS TRUE.
BUT DOESN'T THIS LOOK KINDA QUESTION-ABLE?!
WHY WERE YOU DISGUISED AS A BOY ...?
CRACKLE
CRACKLE
W-WELL, YOU SEE...

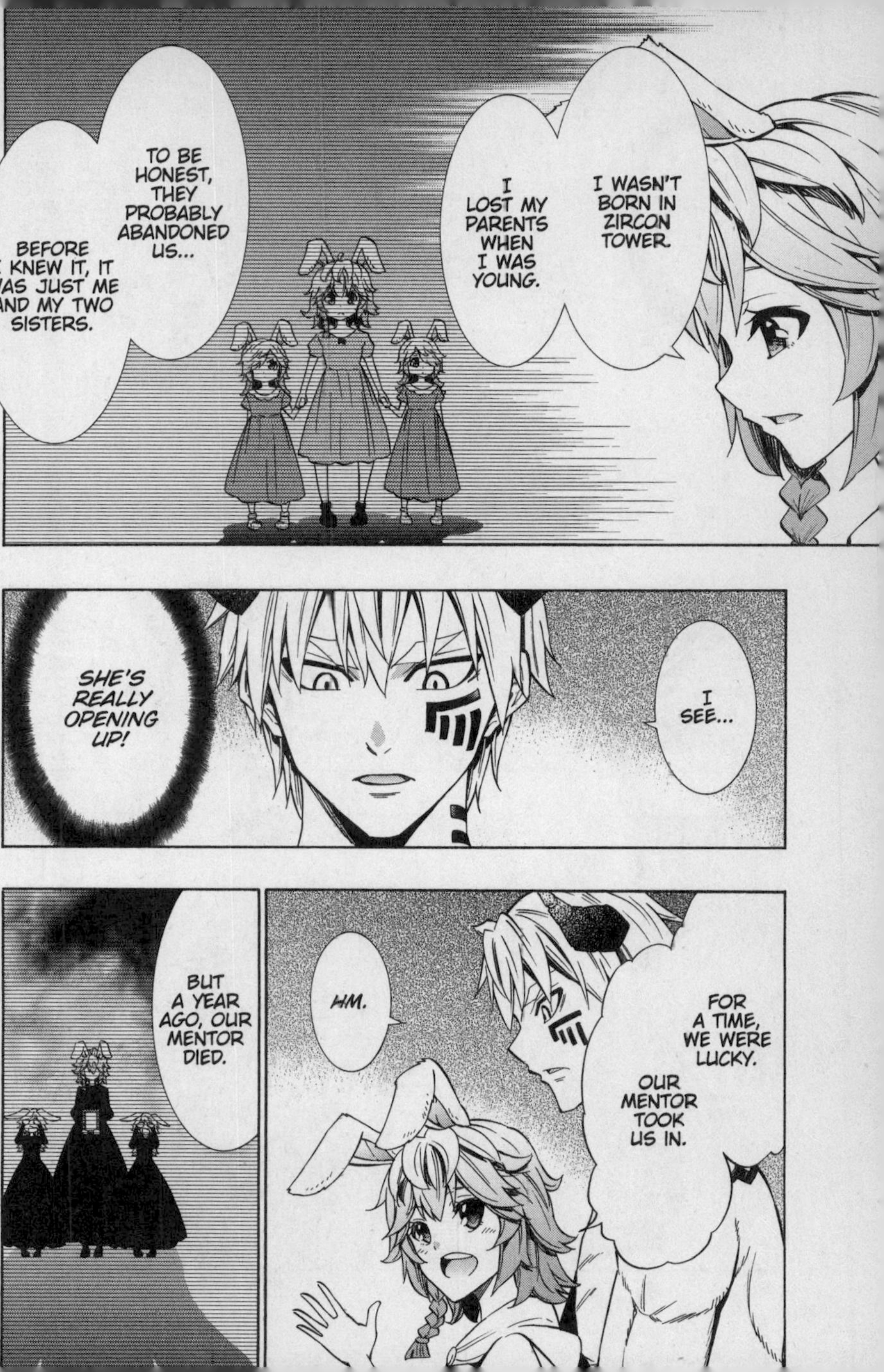
I WASN'T BORN IN ZIRCON TOWER.
I LOST MY PARENTS WHEN I WAS YOUNG.
TO BE HONEST, THEY PROBABLY ABANDONED US...
BEFORE I KNEW IT, IT WAS JUST ME AND MY TWO SISTERS.
I SEE...
SHE'S REALLY OPENING UP!
FOR A TIME, WE WERE LUCKY.
OUR MENTOR TOOK US IN.
HM.
BUT A YEAR AGO, OUR MENTOR DIED.

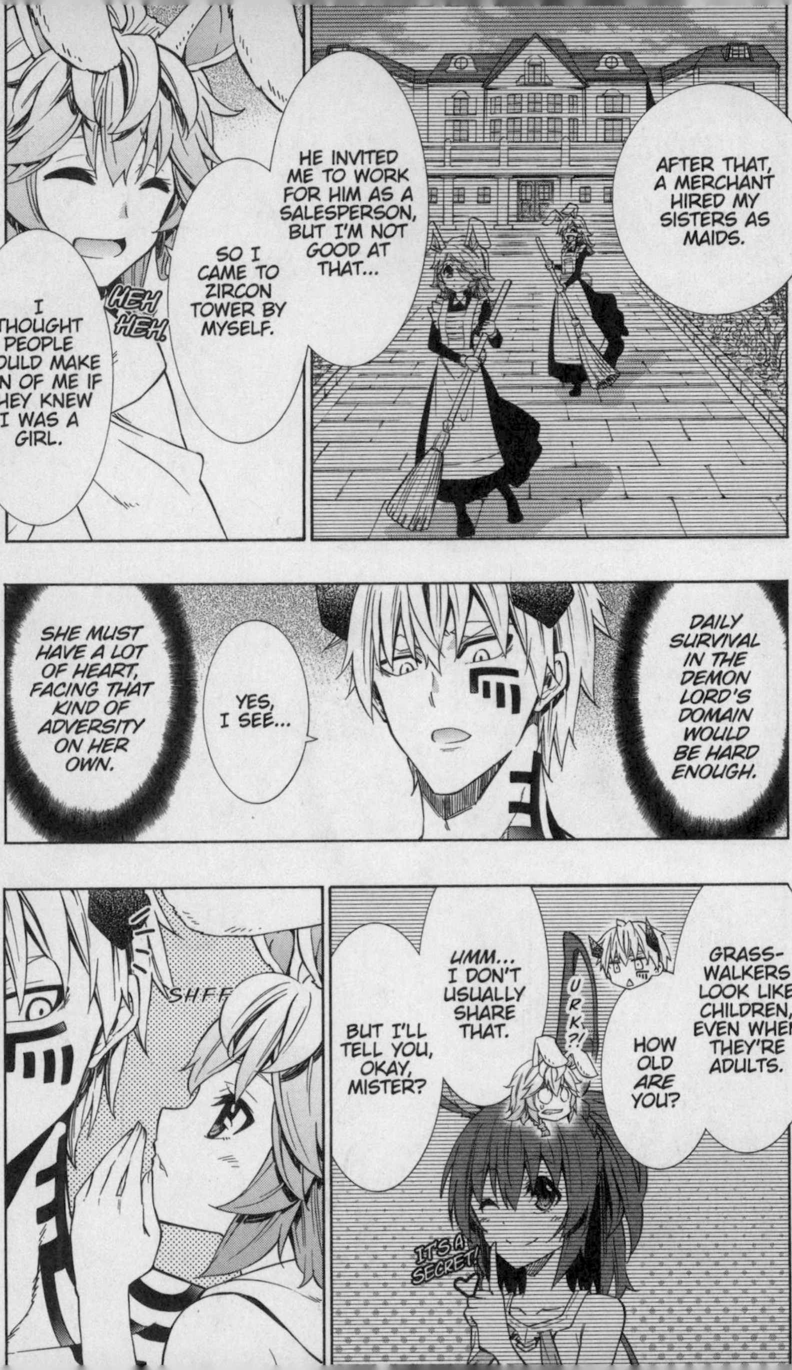
AFTER THAT, A MERCHANT HIRED MY SISTERS AS MAIDS.
HE INVITED ME TO WORK FOR HIM AS A SALESPERSON, BUT I'M NOT GOOD AT THAT...
SO I CAME TO ZIRCON TOWER BY MYSELF.
HEH HEH.
I THOUGHT PEOPLE WOULD MAKE FUN OF ME IF THEY KNEW I WAS A GIRL.
DAILY SURVIVAL IN THE DEMON LORD'S DOMAIN WOULD BE HARD ENOUGH.
YES, I SEE...
SHE MUST HAVE A LOT OF HEART, FACING THAT KIND OF ADVERSITY ON HER OWN.
GRASS-WALKERS LOOK LIKE CHILDREN, EVEN WHEN THEY'RE ADULTS.
HOW OLD ARE YOU?
URK?!
UMM... I DON'T USUALLY SHARE THAT.
BUT I'LL TELL YOU, OKAY, MISTER?
IT'S A SECRET!
SHFF

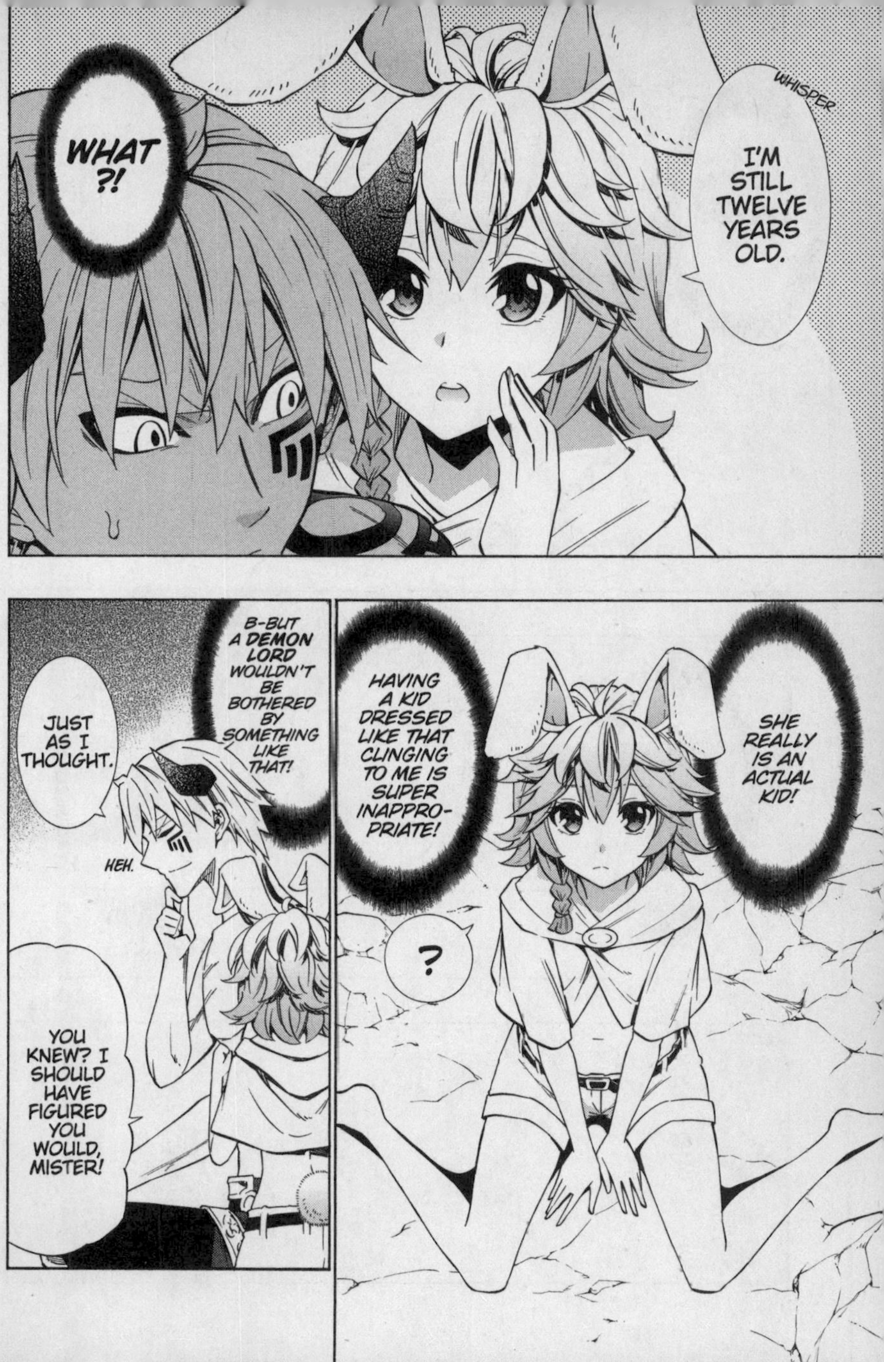
WHISPER
I'M STILL TWELVE YEARS OLD.
WHAT?!
SHE REALLY IS AN ACTUAL KID!
HAVING A KID DRESSED LIKE THAT CLINGING TO ME IS SUPER INAPPROPRIATE!
?
B-BUT A DEMON LORD WOULDN'T BE BOTHERED BY SOMETHING LIKE THAT!
JUST AS I THOUGHT.
HEH.
YOU KNEW? I SHOULD HAVE FIGURED YOU WOULD, MISTER!

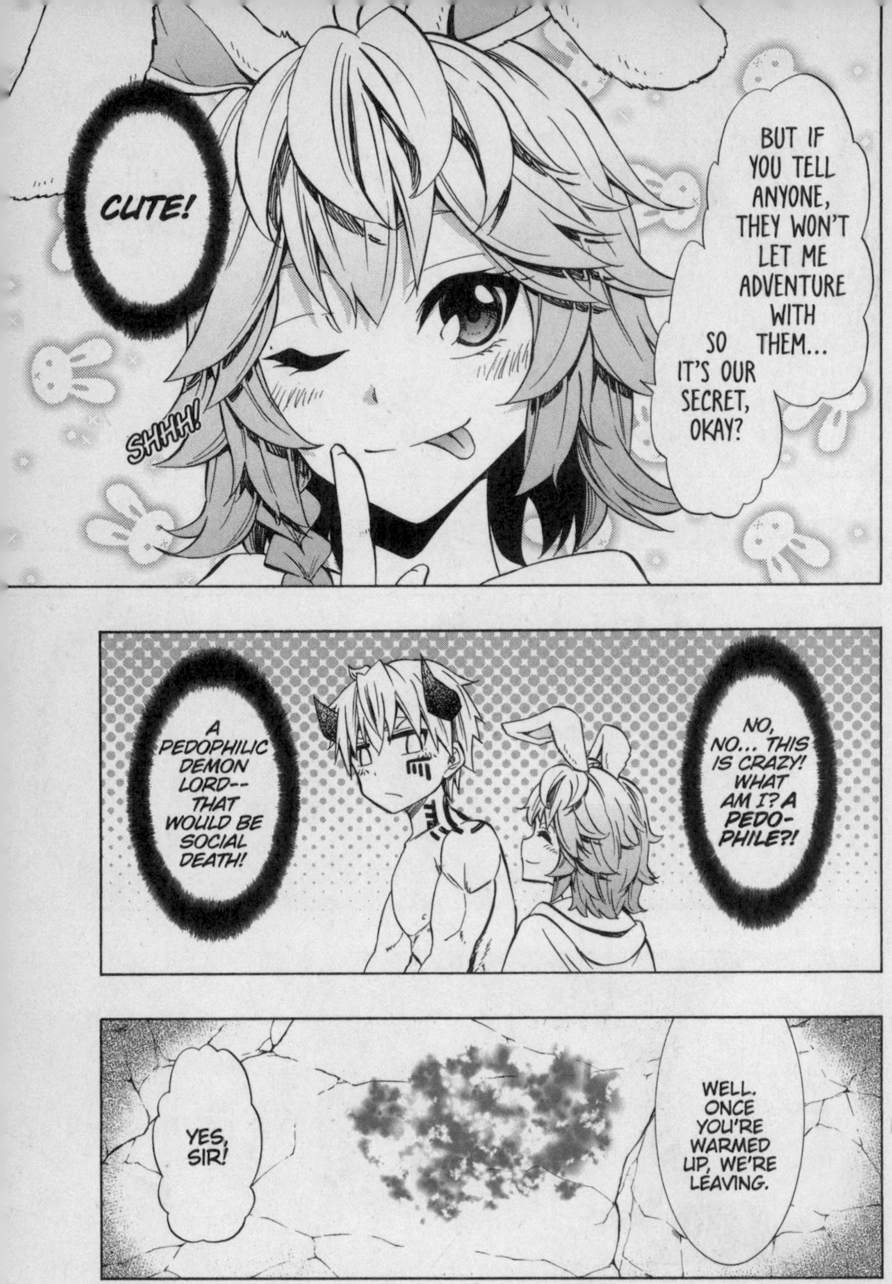
BUT IF YOU TELL ANYONE, THEY WON'T LET ME ADVENTURE WITH THEM... SO IT'S OUR SECRET, OKAY?
CUTE!
SHHH!
NO, NO... THIS IS CRAZY! WHAT AM I? A PEDO-PHILE?!
A PEDOPHILIC DEMON LORD--THAT WOULD BE SOCIAL DEATH!
WELL. ONCE YOU'RE WARMED UP, WE'RE LEAVING.
YES, SIR!

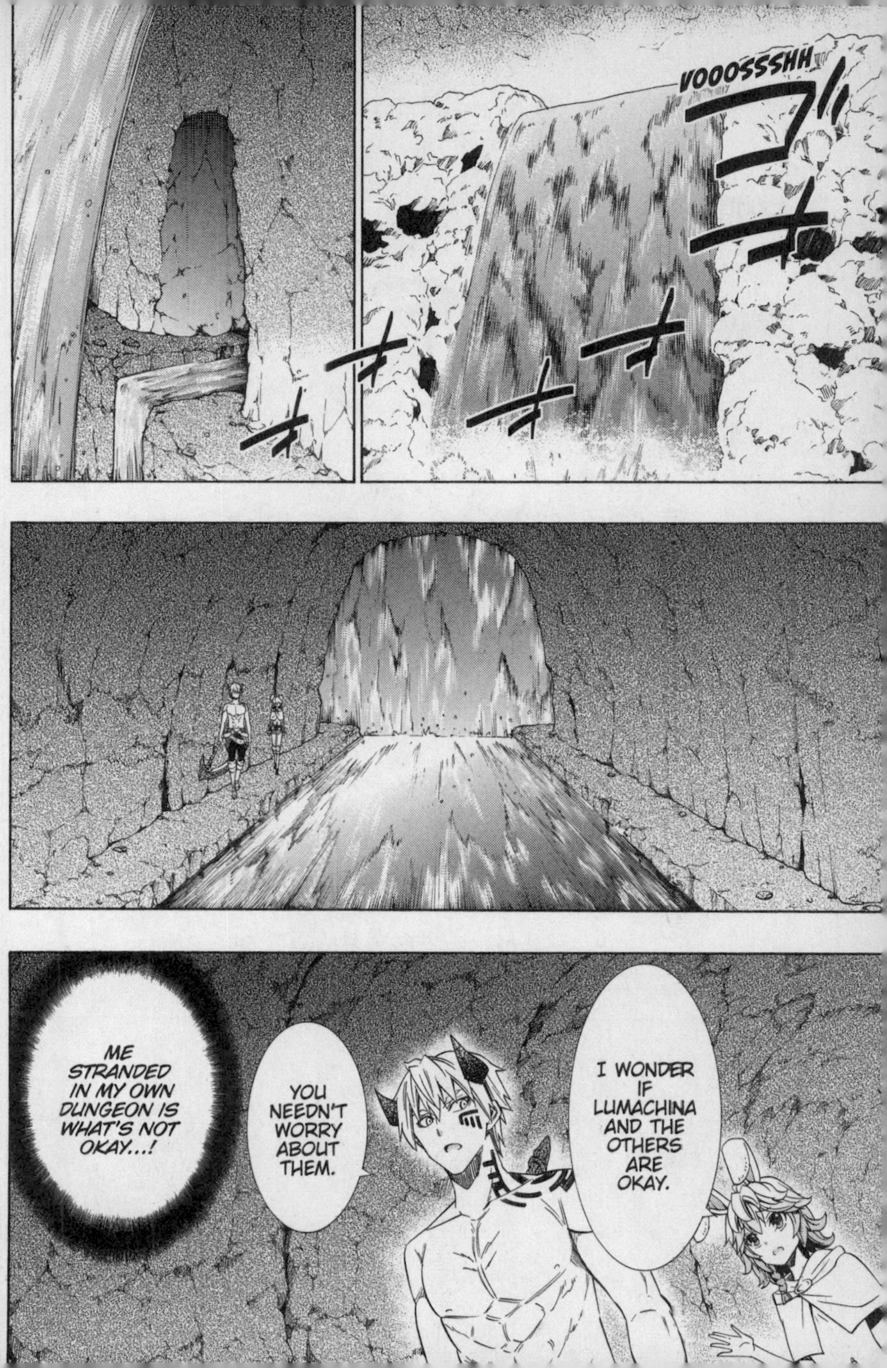
VOOOSSSHH
I WONDER IF LUMACHINA AND THE OTHERS ARE OKAY.
YOU NEEDN'T WORRY ABOUT THEM.
ME STRANDED IN MY OWN DUNGEON IS WHAT'S NOT OKAY...!

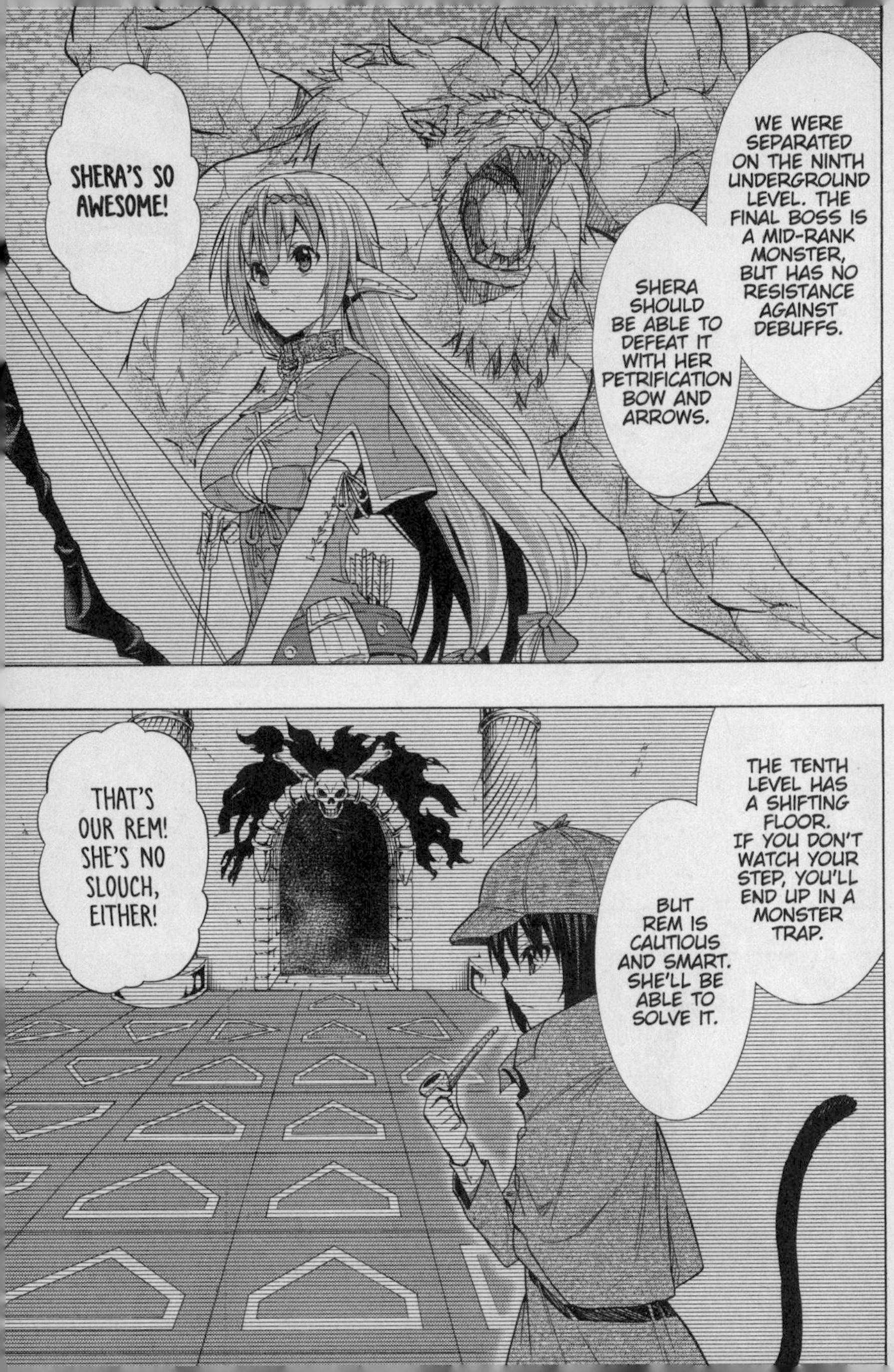
WE WERE SEPARATED ON THE NINTH UNDERGROUND LEVEL. THE FINAL BOSS IS A MID-RANK MONSTER, BUT HAS NO RESISTANCE AGAINST DEBUFFS.
SHERA SHOULD BE ABLE TO DEFEAT IT WITH HER PETRIFICATION BOW AND ARROWS.
SHERA'S SO AWESOME!
THE TENTH LEVEL HAS A SHIFTING FLOOR. IF YOU DON'T WATCH YOUR STEP, YOU'LL END UP IN A MONSTER TRAP.
BUT REM IS CAUTIOUS AND SMART. SHE'LL BE ABLE TO SOLVE IT.
THAT'S OUR REM! SHE'S NO SLOUCH, EITHER!

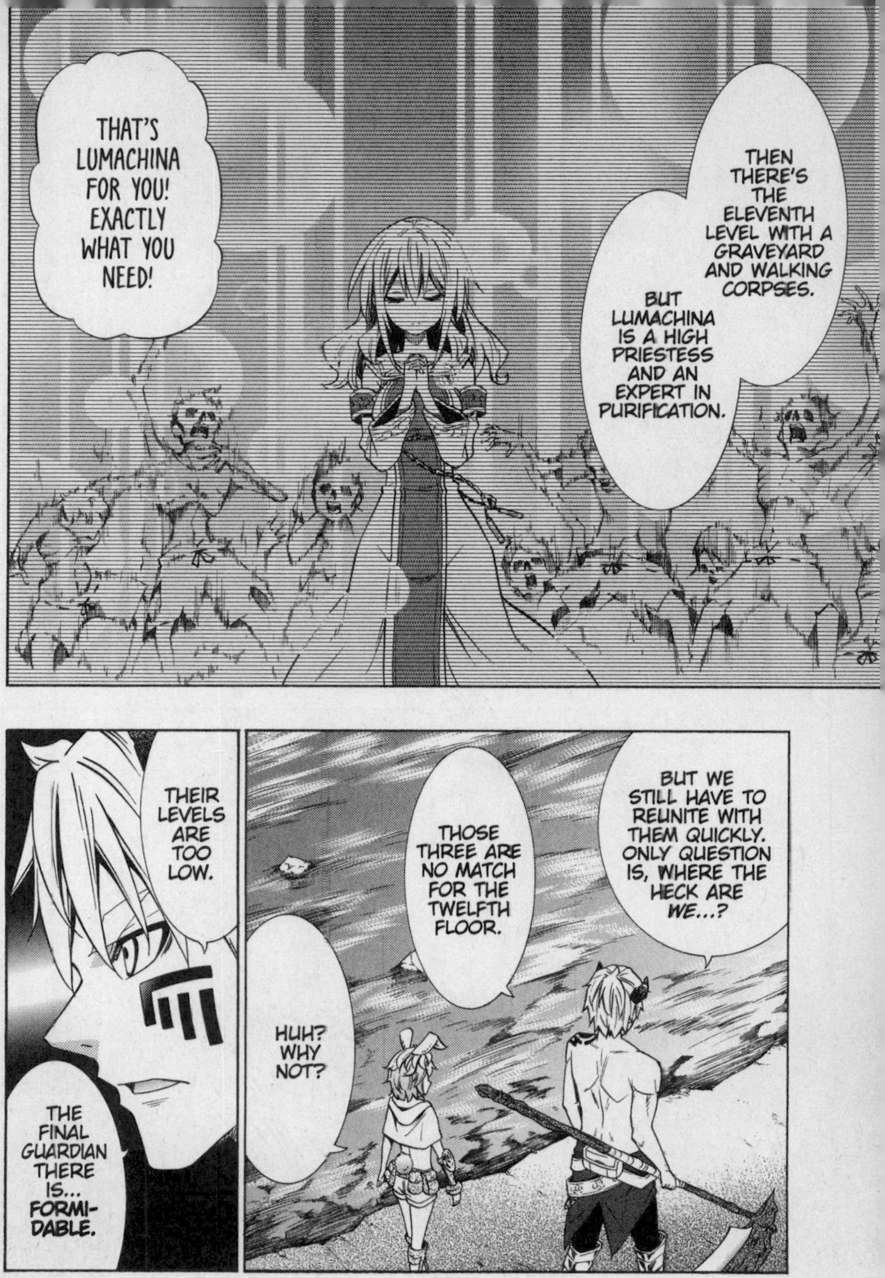
THEN THERE'S THE ELEVENTH LEVEL WITH A GRAVEYARD AND WALKING CORPSES.
BUT LUMACHINA IS A HIGH PRIESTESS AND AN EXPERT IN PURIFICATION.
THAT'S LUMACHINA FOR YOU! EXACTLY WHAT YOU NEED!
BUT WE STILL HAVE TO REUNITE WITH THEM QUICKLY. ONLY QUESTION IS, WHERE THE HECK ARE *WE*...?
THOSE THREE ARE NO MATCH FOR THE TWELFTH FLOOR.
HUH? WHY NOT?
THEIR LEVELS ARE TOO LOW.
THE FINAL GUARDIAN THERE IS... **FORMIDABLE.**

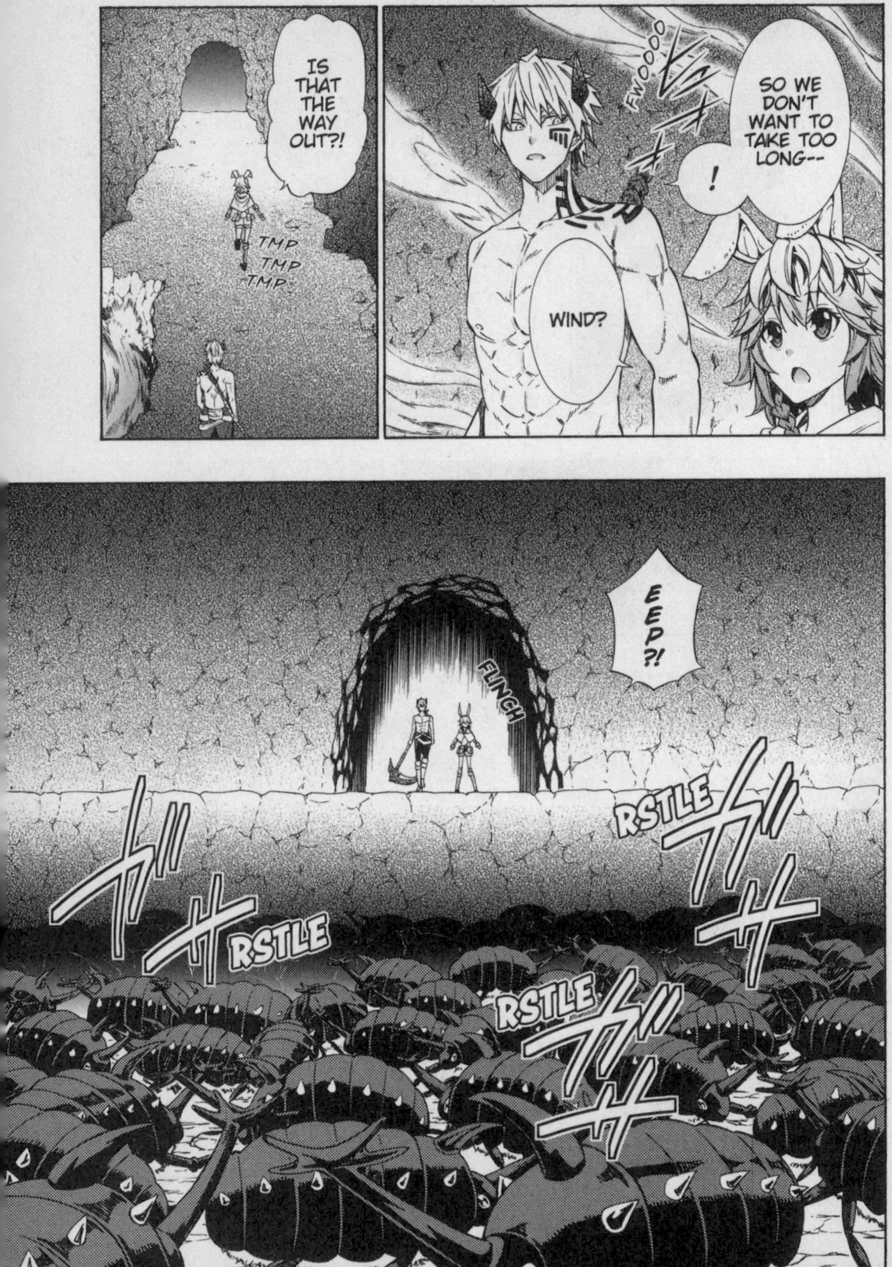
SO WE DON'T WANT TO TAKE TOO LONG--
FWOOOO
!
WIND?
IS THAT THE WAY OUT?!
TMP
TMP
TMP
EEP?!
FLINCH
RSTLE
RSTLE
RSTLE

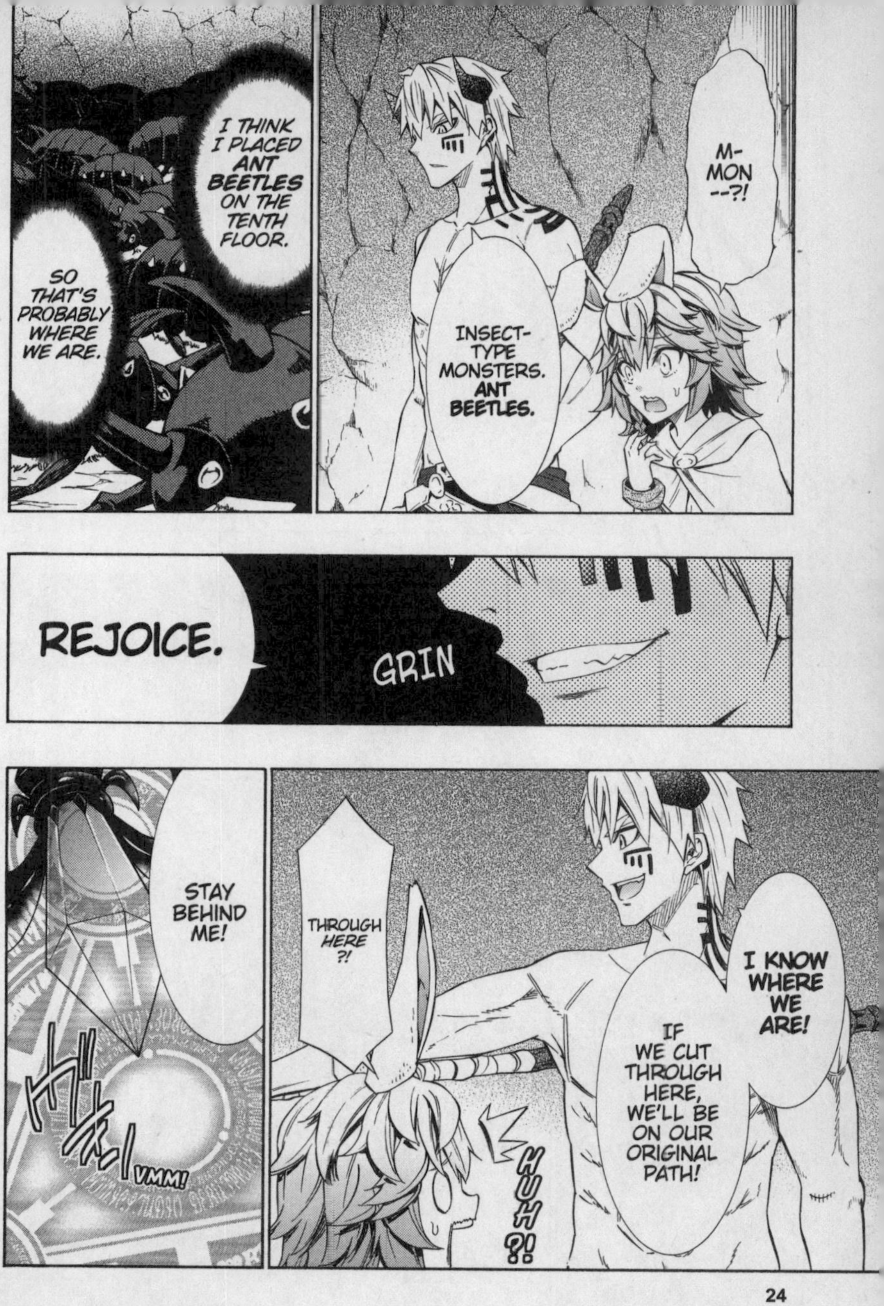
M-MON--?!
INSECT-TYPE MONSTERS. ANT BEETLES.
I THINK I PLACED ANT BEETLES ON THE TENTH FLOOR.
SO THAT'S PROBABLY WHERE WE ARE.
GRIN
REJOICE.
I KNOW WHERE WE ARE!
IF WE CUT THROUGH HERE, WE'LL BE ON OUR ORIGINAL PATH!
THROUGH HERE ?!
HUH ?!
STAY BEHIND ME!
VMM!

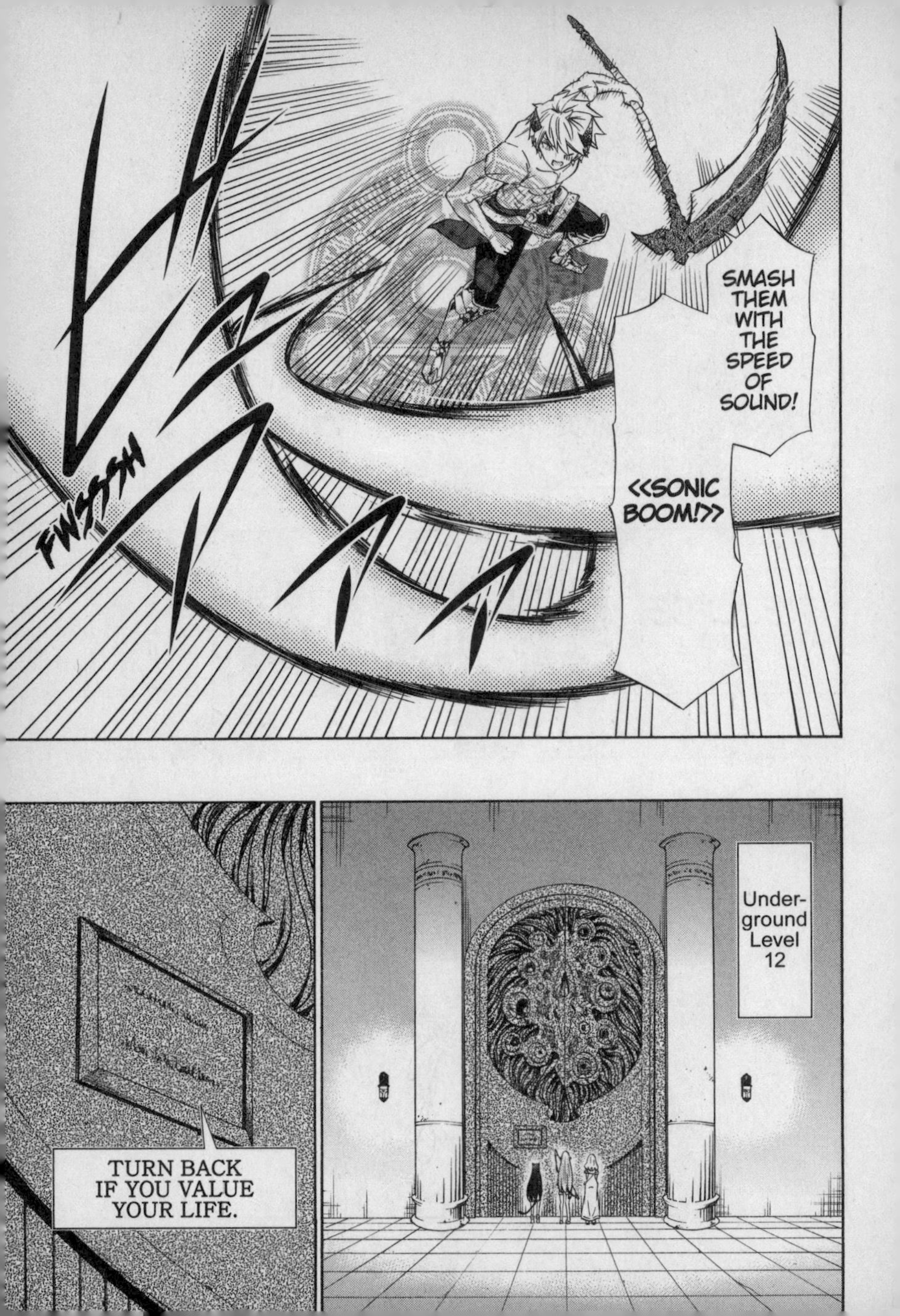
SMASH THEM WITH THE SPEED OF SOUND!
<<SONIC BOOM!>>
FWSSSH
Under-ground Level 12
TURN BACK IF YOU VALUE YOUR LIFE.

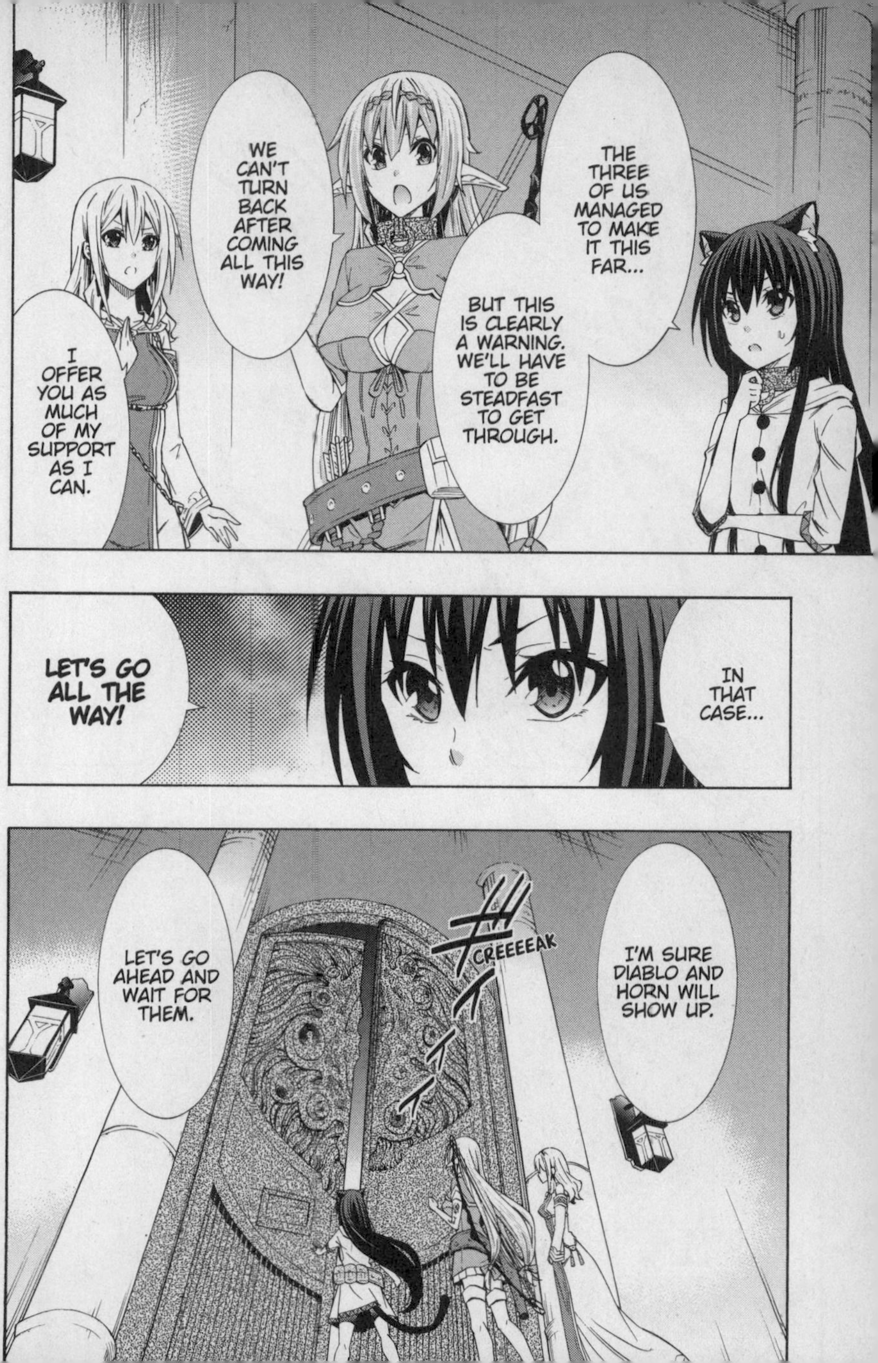
THE THREE OF US MANAGED TO MAKE IT THIS FAR...
BUT THIS IS CLEARLY A WARNING. WE'LL HAVE TO BE STEADFAST TO GET THROUGH.
WE CAN'T TURN BACK AFTER COMING ALL THIS WAY!
I OFFER YOU AS MUCH OF MY SUPPORT AS I CAN.
IN THAT CASE...
LET'S GO ALL THE WAY!
I'M SURE DIABLO AND HORN WILL SHOW UP.
CREEEEAK
LET'S GO AHEAD AND WAIT FOR THEM.

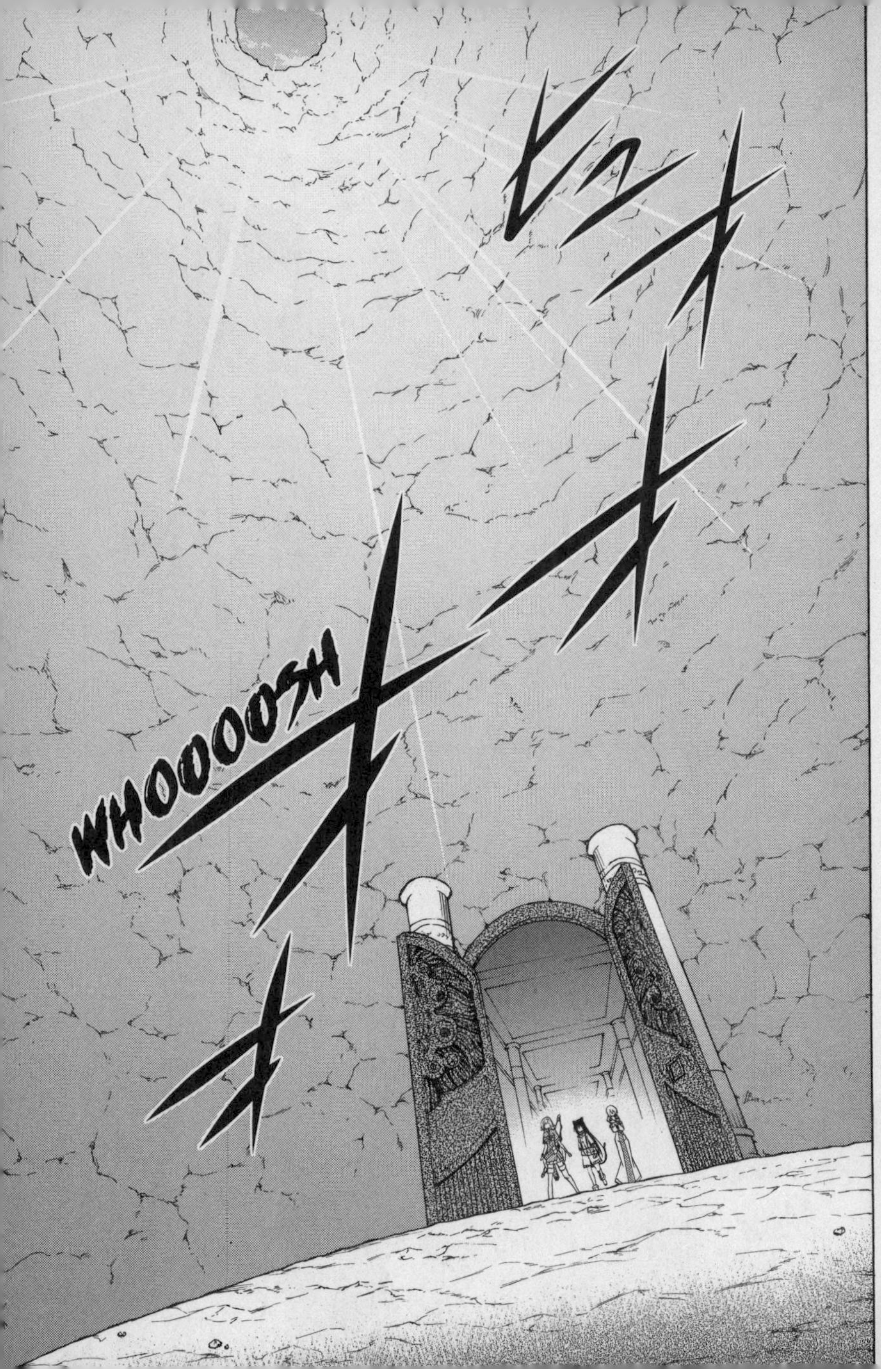
ヒュオオオオ
WHOOOOSH

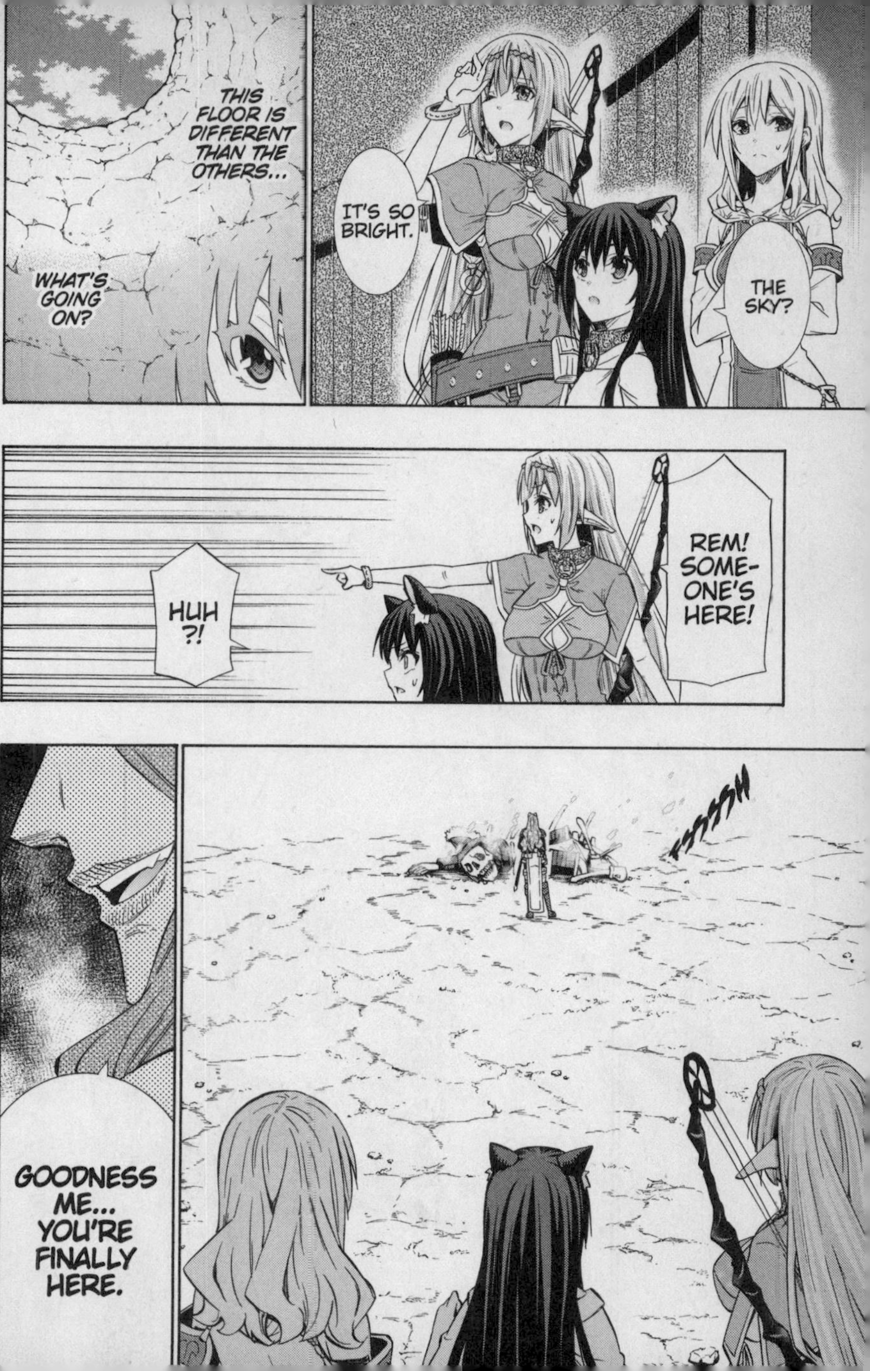
IT'S SO BRIGHT.
THE SKY?
THIS FLOOR IS DIFFERENT THAN THE OTHERS...
WHAT'S GOING ON?
REM! SOME-ONE'S HERE!
HUH?!
GOODNESS ME... YOU'RE FINALLY HERE.

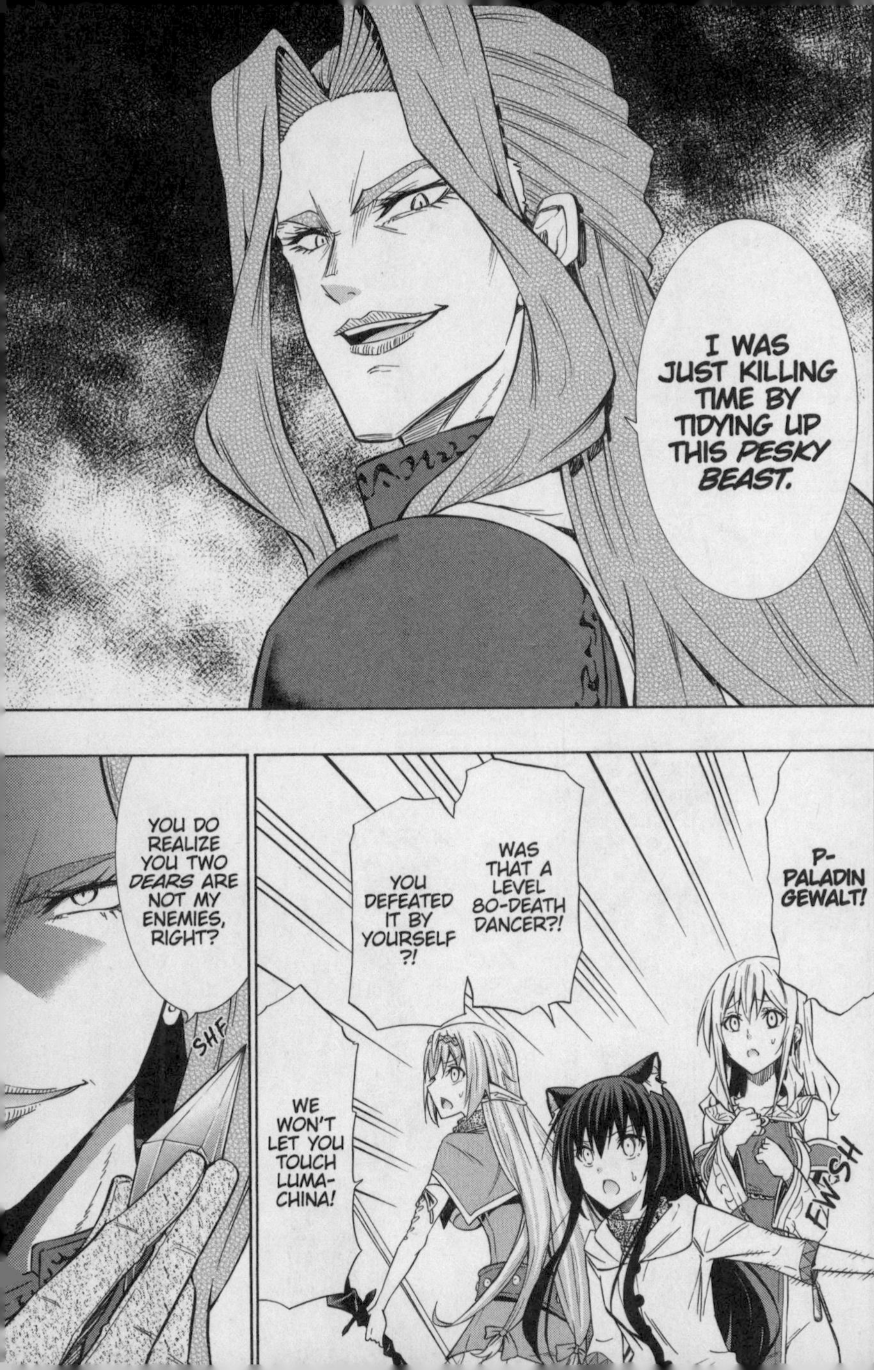
I WAS JUST KILLING TIME BY TIDYING UP THIS *PESKY BEAST.*
P-PALADIN GEWALT!
WAS THAT A LEVEL 80-DEATH DANCER?!
YOU DEFEATED IT BY YOURSELF?!
FW-SH
WE WON'T LET YOU TOUCH LUMA-CHINA!
YOU DO REALIZE YOU TWO *DEARS* ARE NOT MY ENEMIES, RIGHT?
SHF

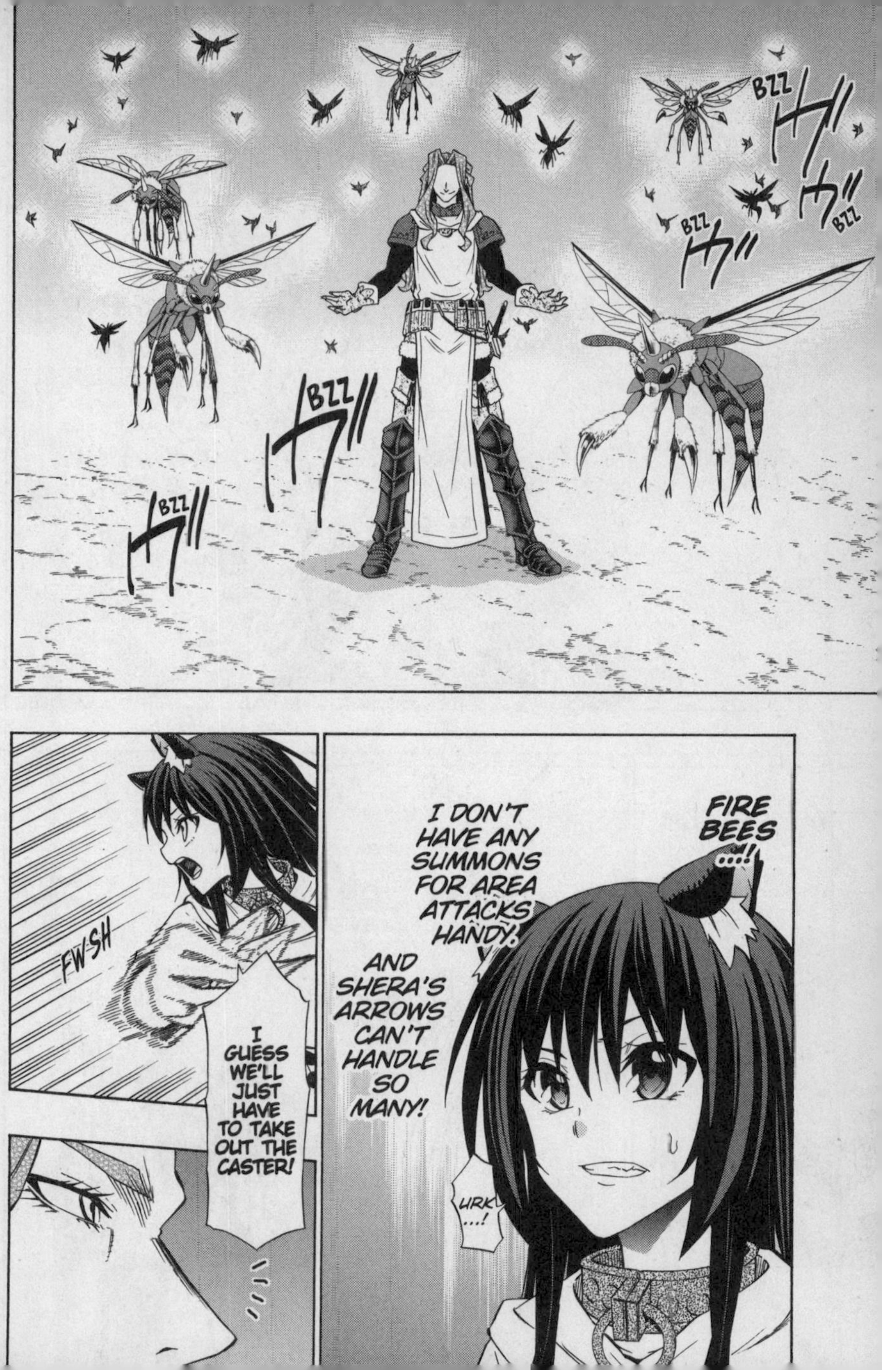
BZZ
BZZ
BZZ
BZZ
BZZ
FIRE BEES ...!!
I DON'T HAVE ANY SUMMONS FOR AREA ATTACKS HANDY.
AND SHERA'S ARROWS CAN'T HANDLE SO MANY!
URK ...!
FW-SH
I GUESS WE'LL JUST HAVE TO TAKE OUT THE CASTER!

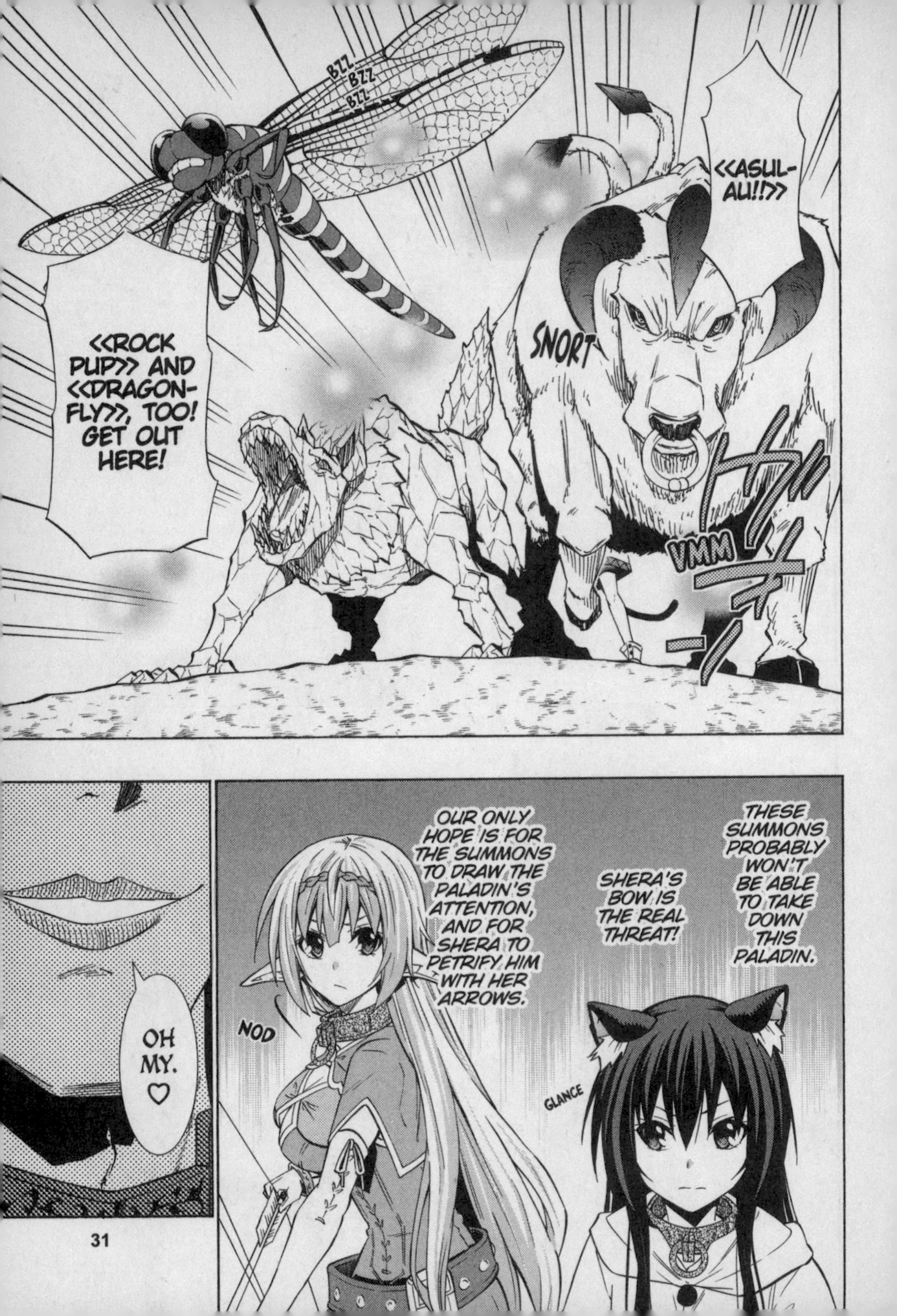
<<ASUL-AU!!>>
BZZ BZZ BZZ
SNORT
<<ROCK PUP>> AND <<DRAGONFLY>>, TOO! GET OUT HERE!
VMM
THESE SUMMONS PROBABLY WON'T BE ABLE TO TAKE DOWN THIS PALADIN.
SHERA'S BOW IS THE REAL THREAT!
OUR ONLY HOPE IS FOR THE SUMMONS TO DRAW THE PALADIN'S ATTENTION, AND FOR SHERA TO PETRIFY HIM WITH HER ARROWS.
NOD
GLANCE
OH MY. ♡

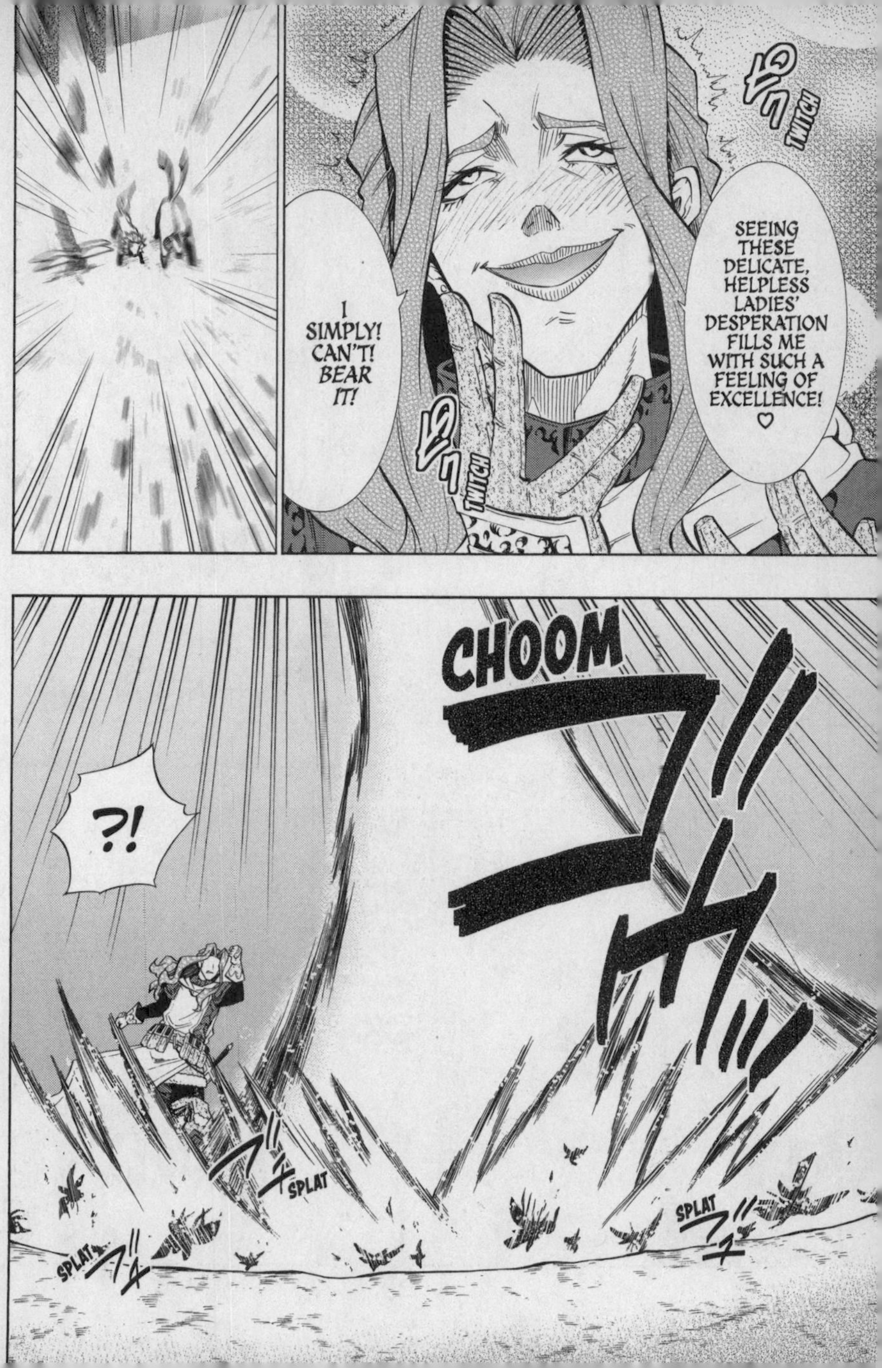
TWITCH
SEEING THESE DELICATE, HELPLESS LADIES' DESPERATION FILLS ME WITH SUCH A FEELING OF EXCELLENCE! ♡
I SIMPLY! CAN'T! BEAR IT!
TWITCH
CHOOM
?!
SPLAT
SPLAT
SPLAT

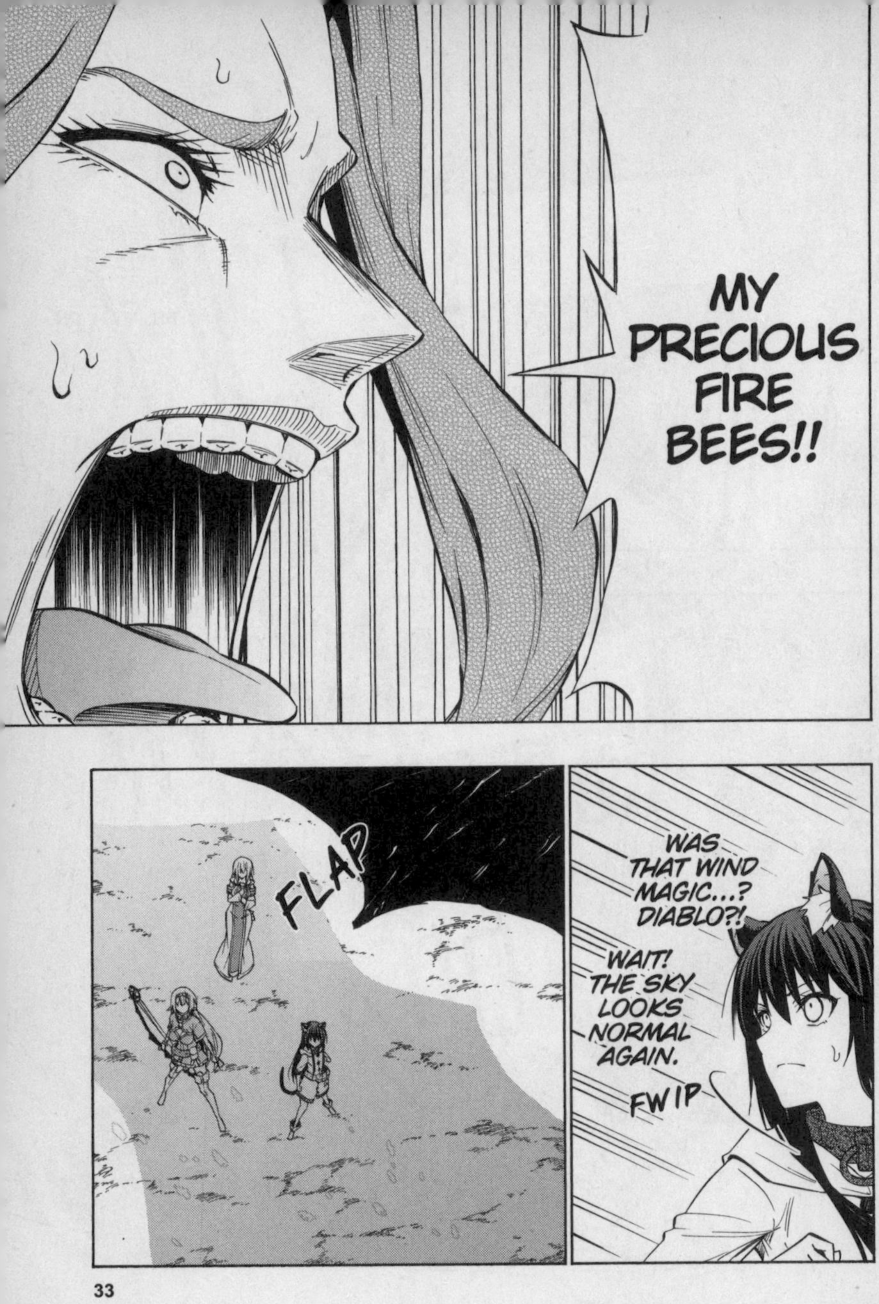
MY PRECIOUS FIRE BEES!!
WAS THAT WIND MAGIC...? DIABLO?!
WAIT! THE SKY LOOKS NORMAL AGAIN.
FWIP
FLAP

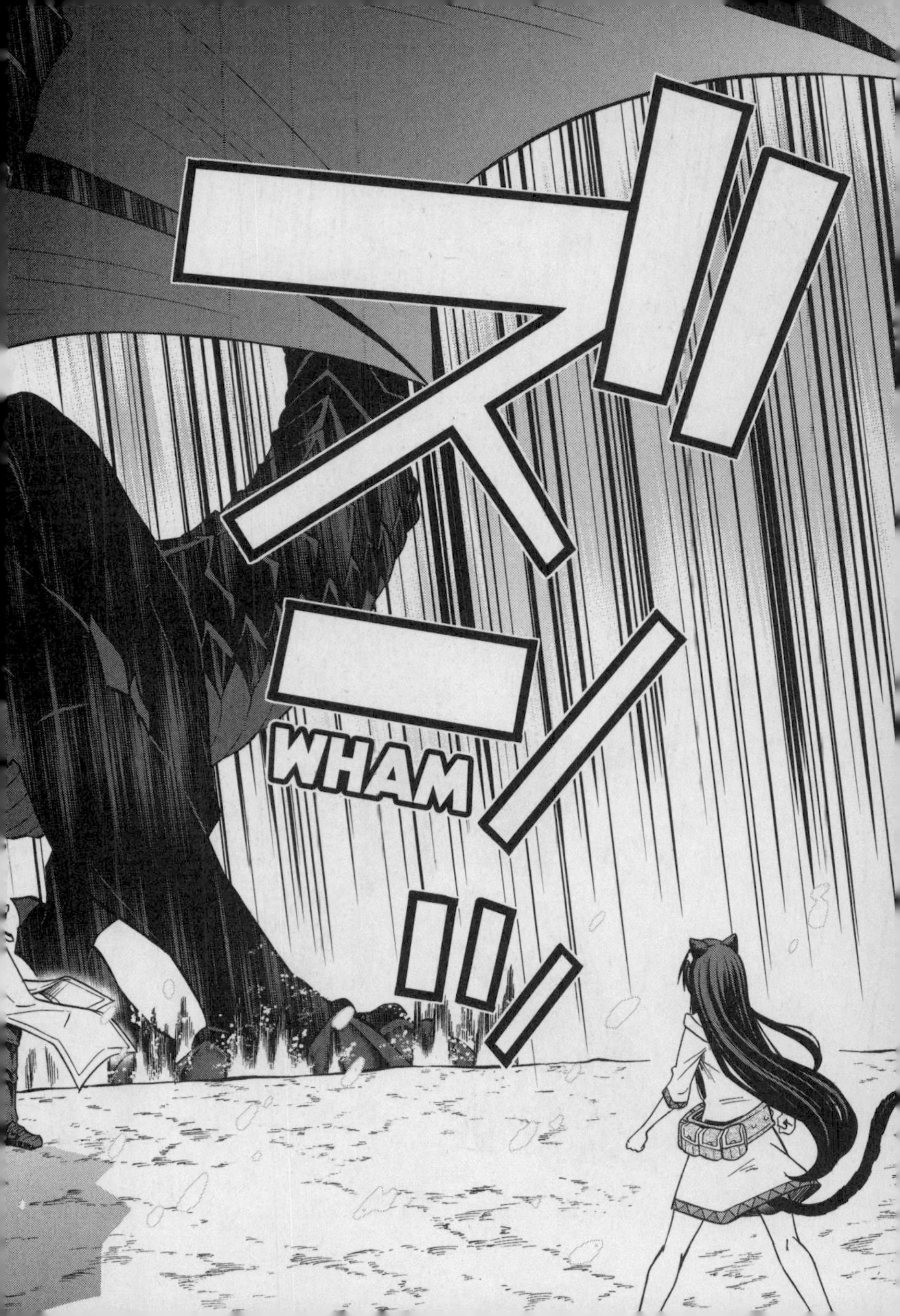
WHAM

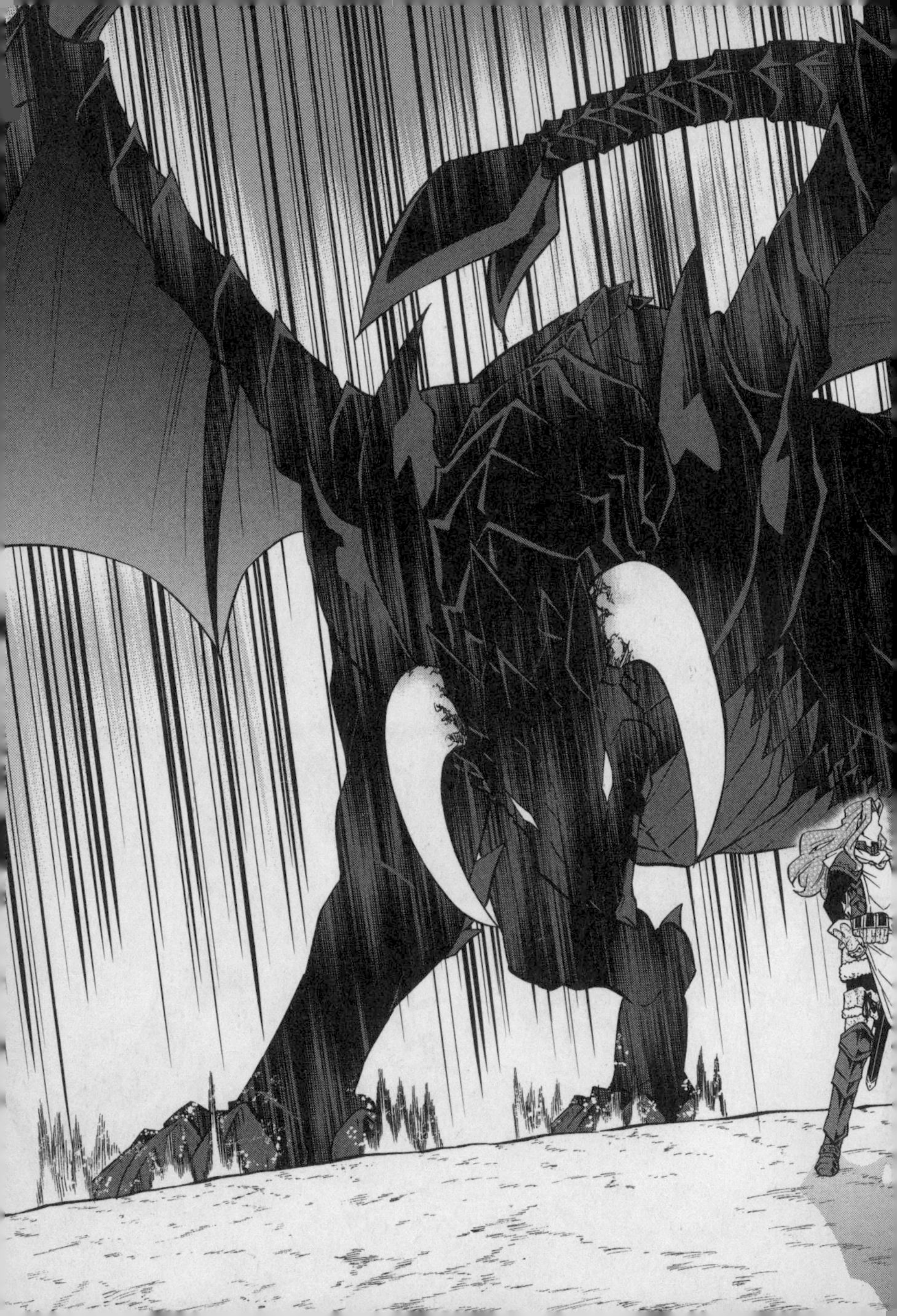

A LARGE BLACK DRAGON?!

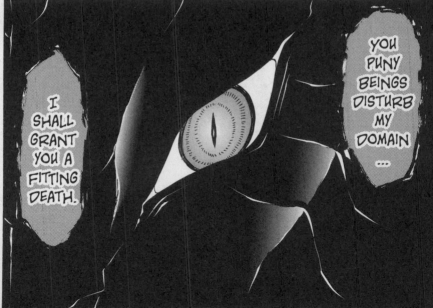

YOU PUNY BEINGS DISTURB MY DOMAIN...

I SHALL GRANT YOU A FITTING DEATH.

HOW NOT TO SUMMON A
DEMON LORD

56 SAVING A COMPANION II

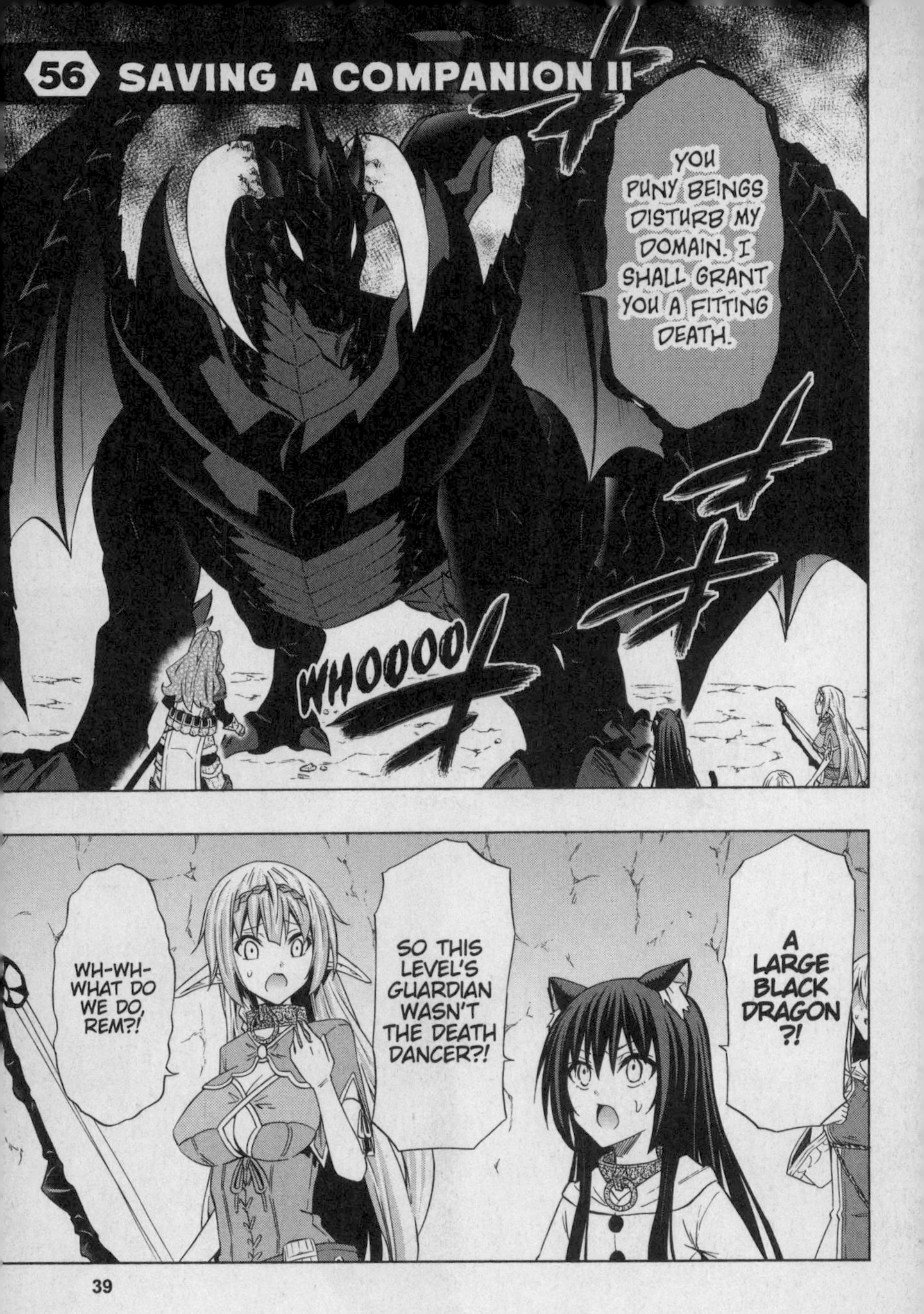
YOU PUNY BEINGS DISTURB MY DOMAIN. I SHALL GRANT YOU A FITTING DEATH.
WHOOOO
A LARGE BLACK DRAGON?!
SO THIS LEVEL'S GUARDIAN WASN'T THE DEATH DANCER?!
WH-WH-WHAT DO WE DO, REM?!

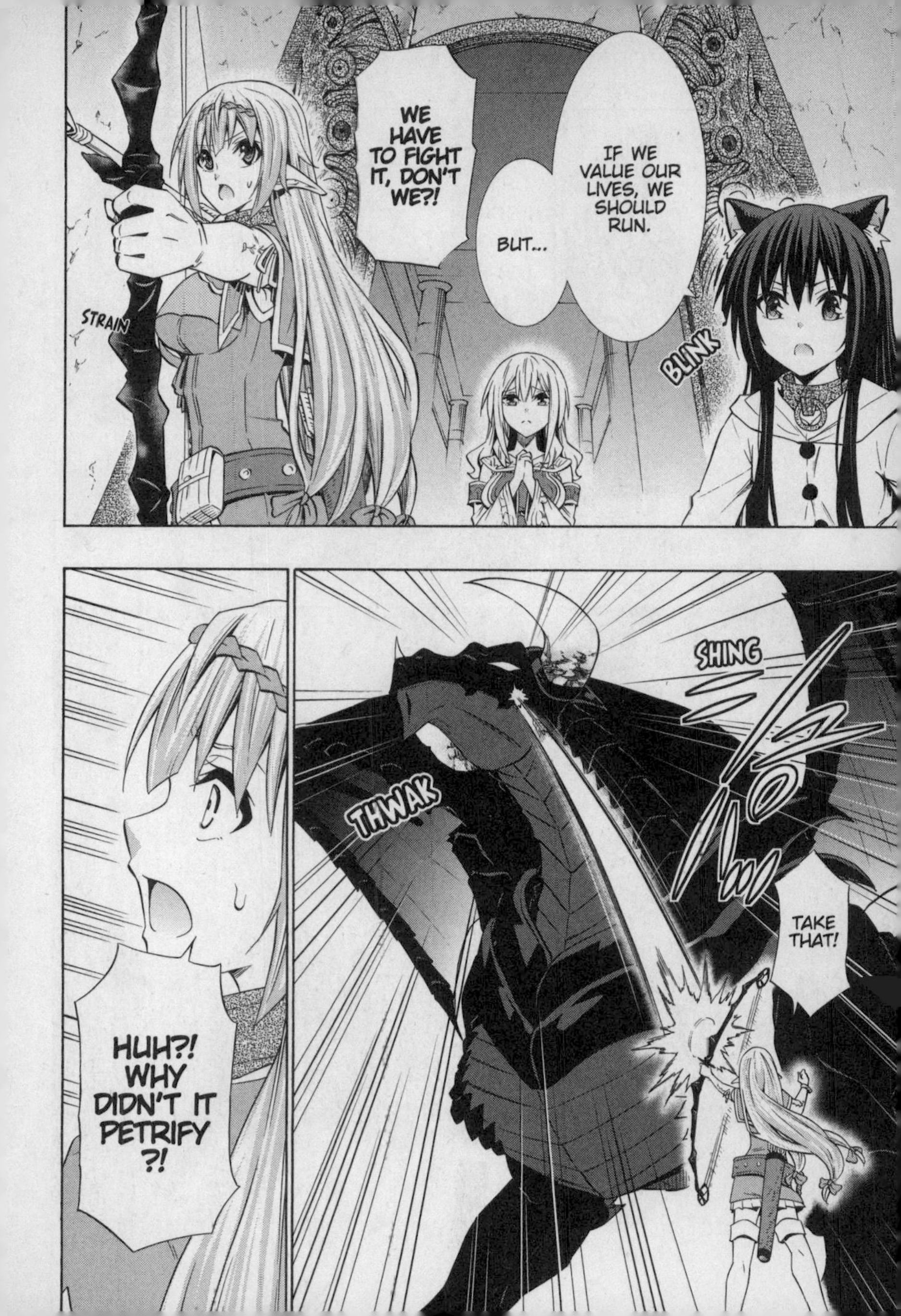
IF WE VALUE OUR LIVES, WE SHOULD RUN.
BUT...
BLINK
WE HAVE TO FIGHT IT, DON'T WE?!
STRAIN
SHING
TAKE THAT!
THWAK
HUH?! WHY DIDN'T IT PETRIFY?!

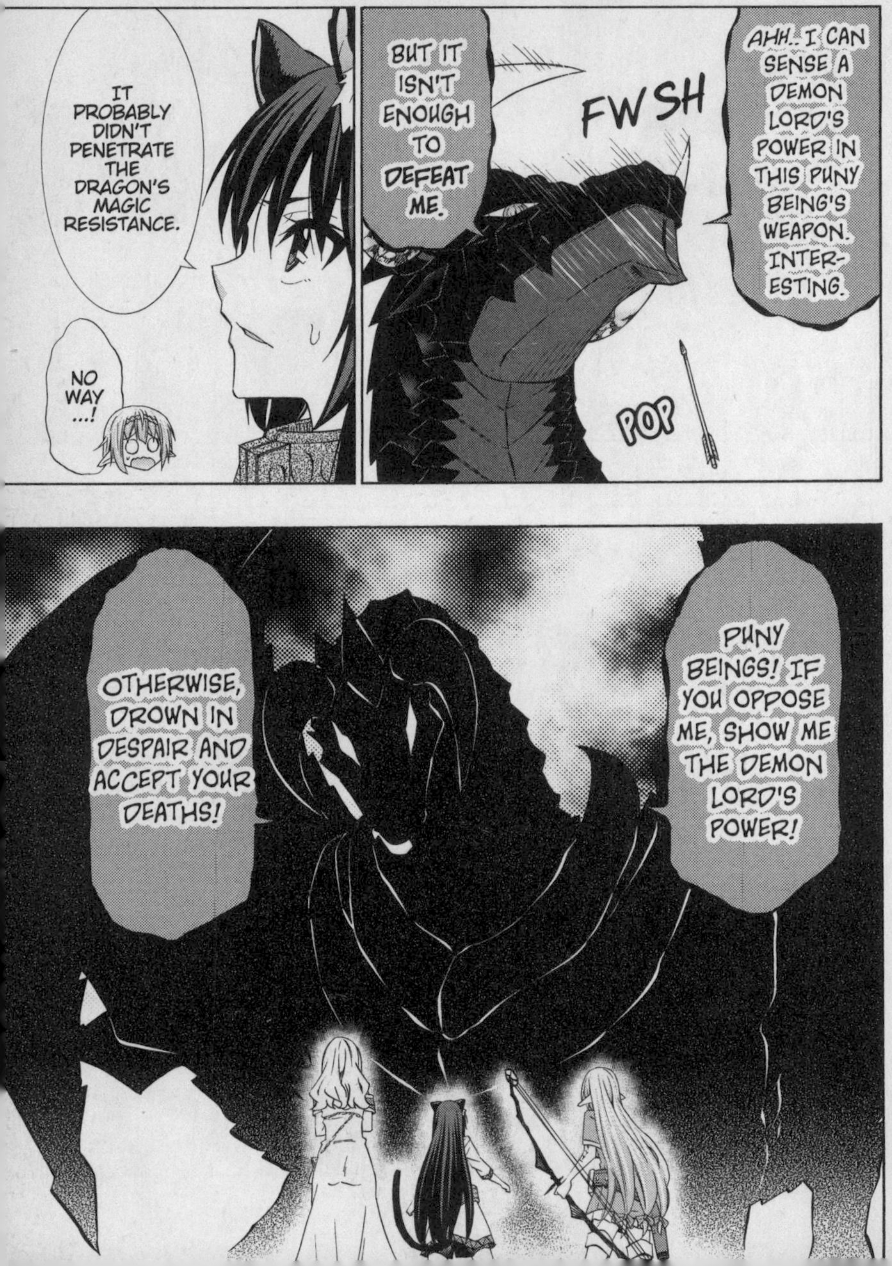
AHH.. I CAN SENSE A DEMON LORD'S POWER IN THIS PUNY BEING'S WEAPON. INTER-ESTING.
FWSH
POP
BUT IT ISN'T ENOUGH TO DEFEAT ME.
IT PROBABLY DIDN'T PENETRATE THE DRAGON'S MAGIC RESISTANCE.
NO WAY ...!
PUNY BEINGS! IF YOU OPPOSE ME, SHOW ME THE DEMON LORD'S POWER!
OTHERWISE, DROWN IN DESPAIR AND ACCEPT YOUR DEATHS!

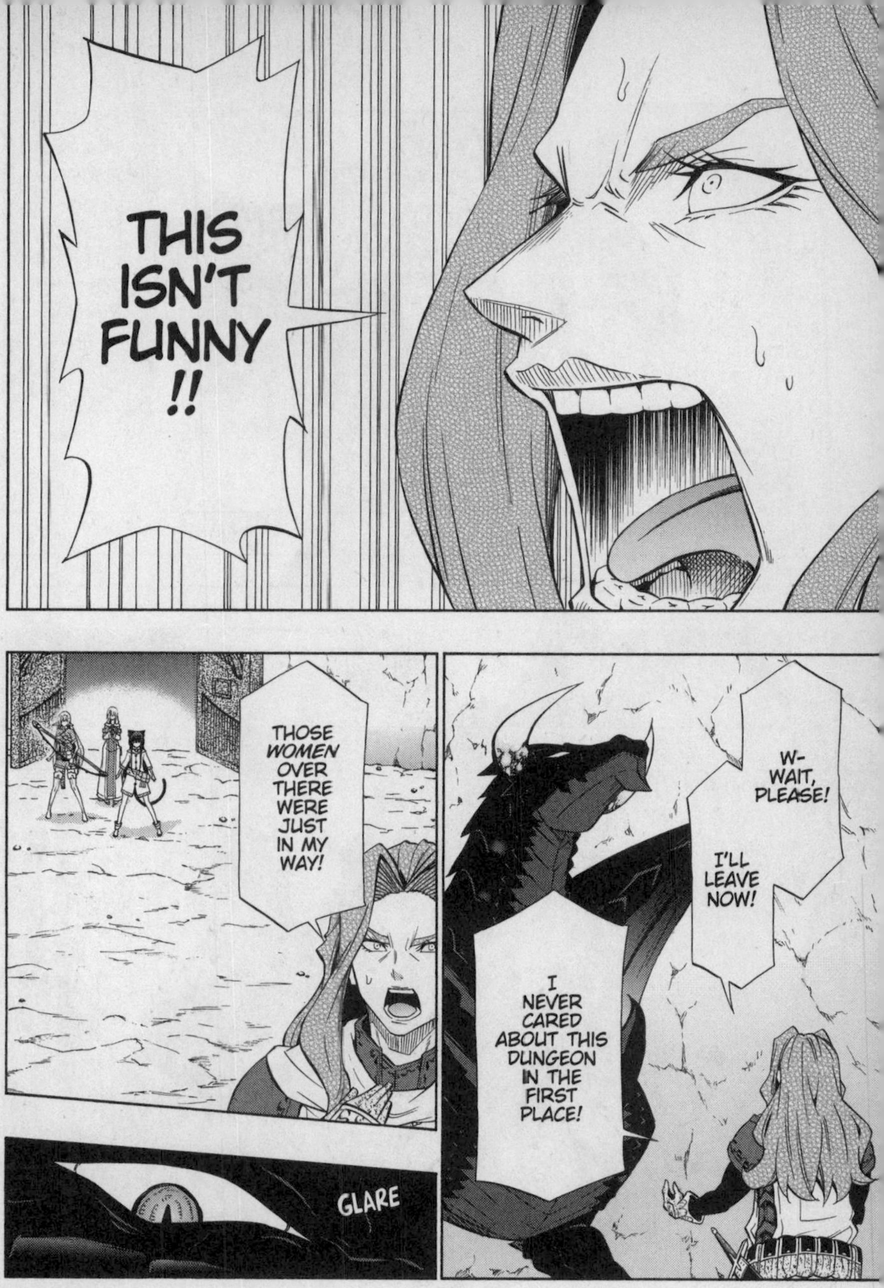
THIS ISN'T FUNNY!!
W- WAIT, PLEASE!
I'LL LEAVE NOW!
I NEVER CARED ABOUT THIS DUNGEON IN THE FIRST PLACE!
THOSE *WOMEN* OVER THERE WERE JUST IN MY WAY!
GLARE

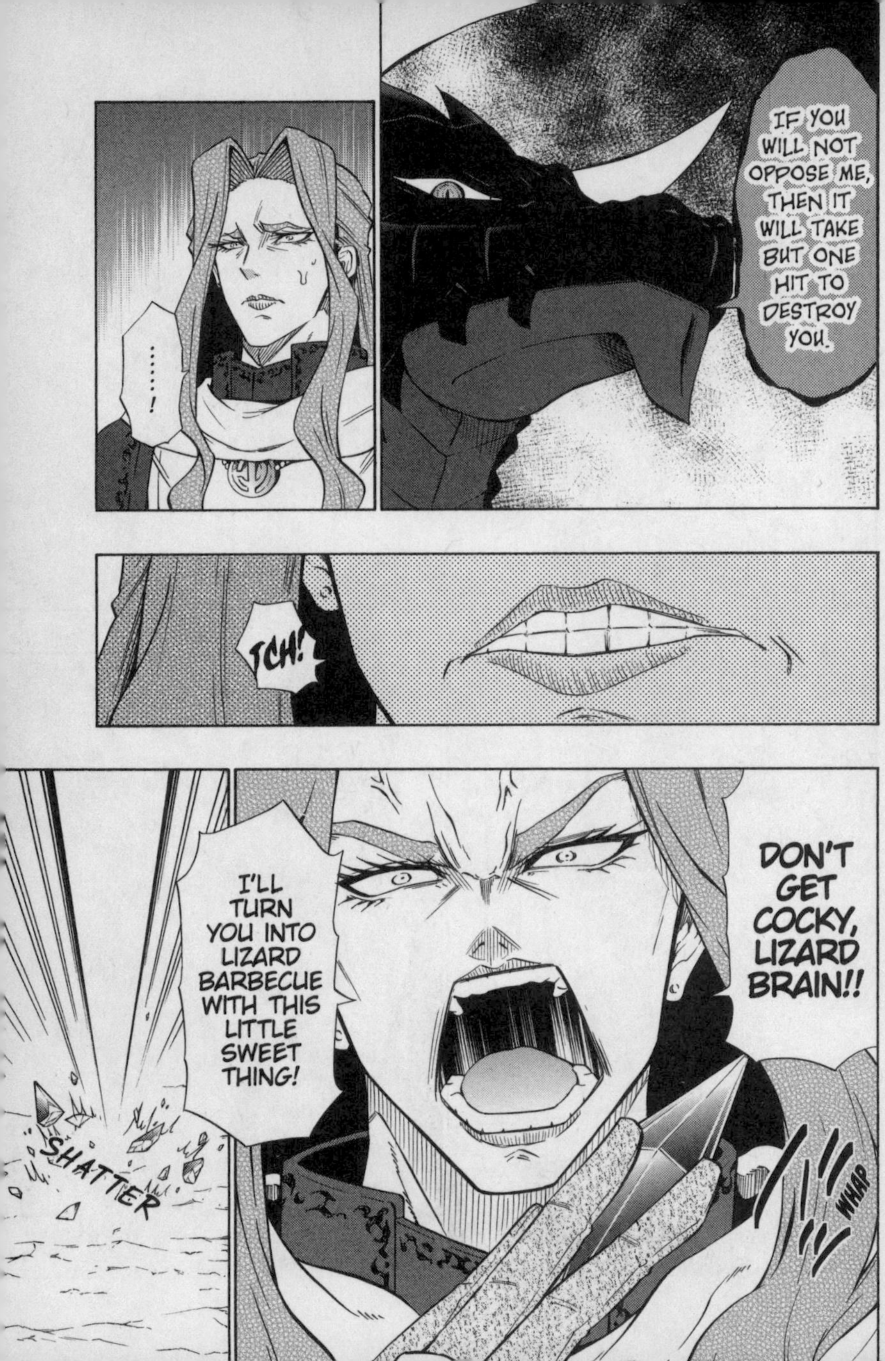
IF YOU WILL NOT OPPOSE ME, THEN IT WILL TAKE BUT ONE HIT TO DESTROY YOU.
......!
TCH!
DON'T GET COCKY, LIZARD BRAIN!!
I'LL TURN YOU INTO LIZARD BARBECUE WITH THIS LITTLE SWEET THING!
WHAP
SHATTER

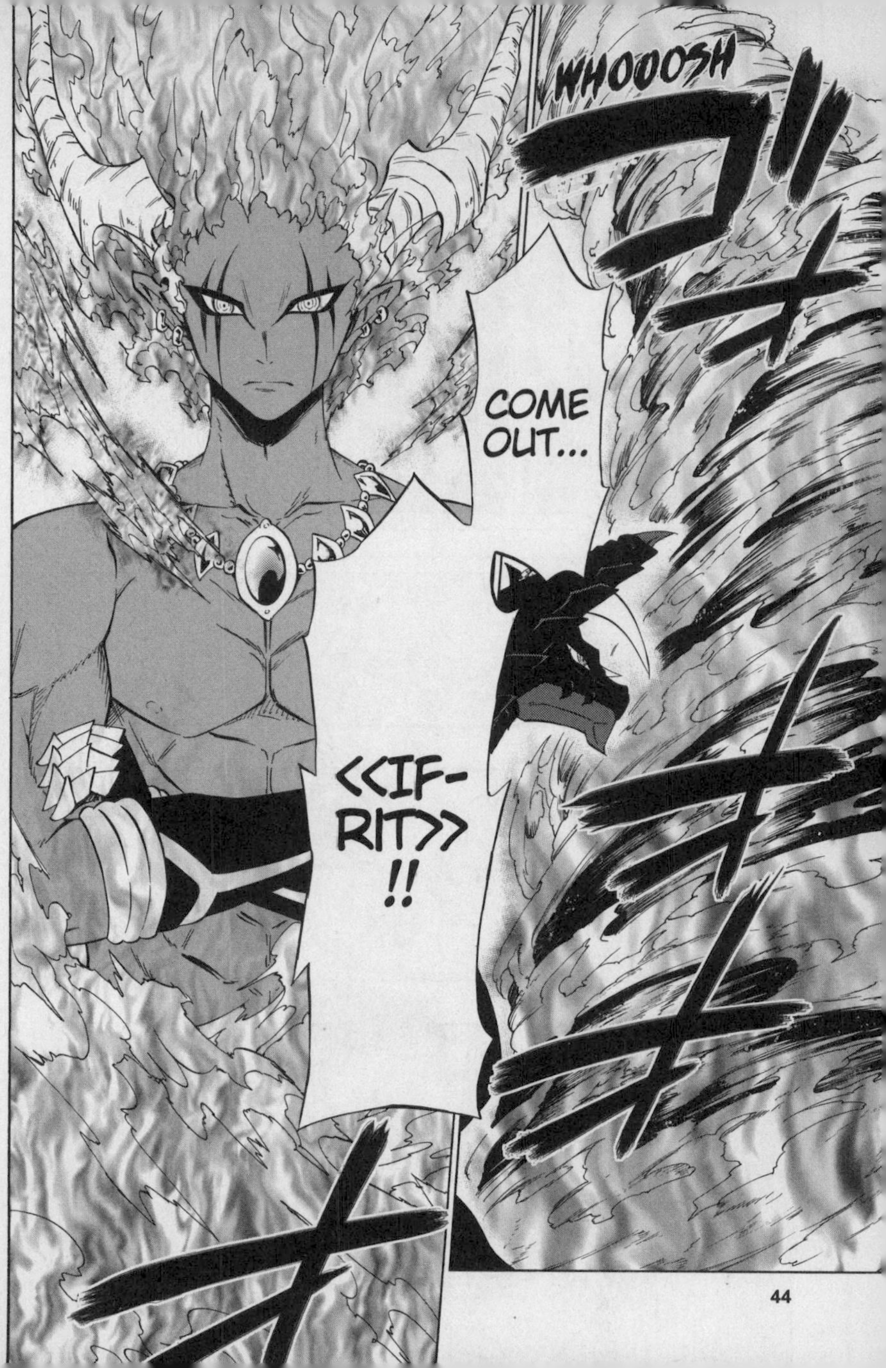
WHOOOSH
COME OUT...
<<IF-RIT>>!!

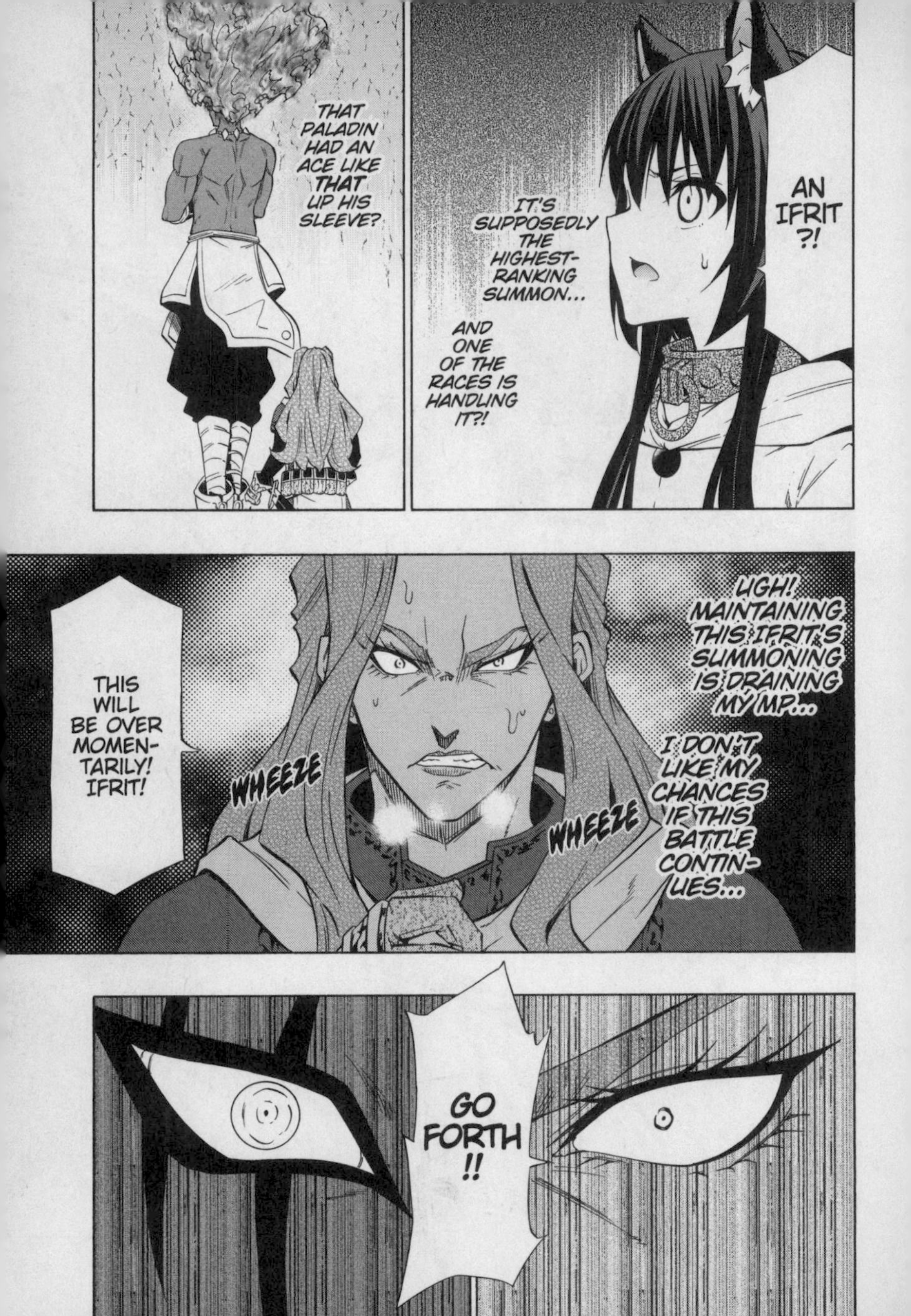
AN IFRIT ?!
IT'S SUPPOSEDLY THE HIGHEST-RANKING SUMMON...
AND ONE OF THE RACES IS HANDLING IT?!
THAT PALADIN HAD AN ACE LIKE THAT UP HIS SLEEVE?
UGH! MAINTAINING THIS IFRIT'S SUMMONING IS DRAINING MY MP...
I DON'T LIKE MY CHANCES IF THIS BATTLE CONTINUES...
WHEEZE
WHEEZE
THIS WILL BE OVER MOMENTARILY! IFRIT!
GO FORTH !!

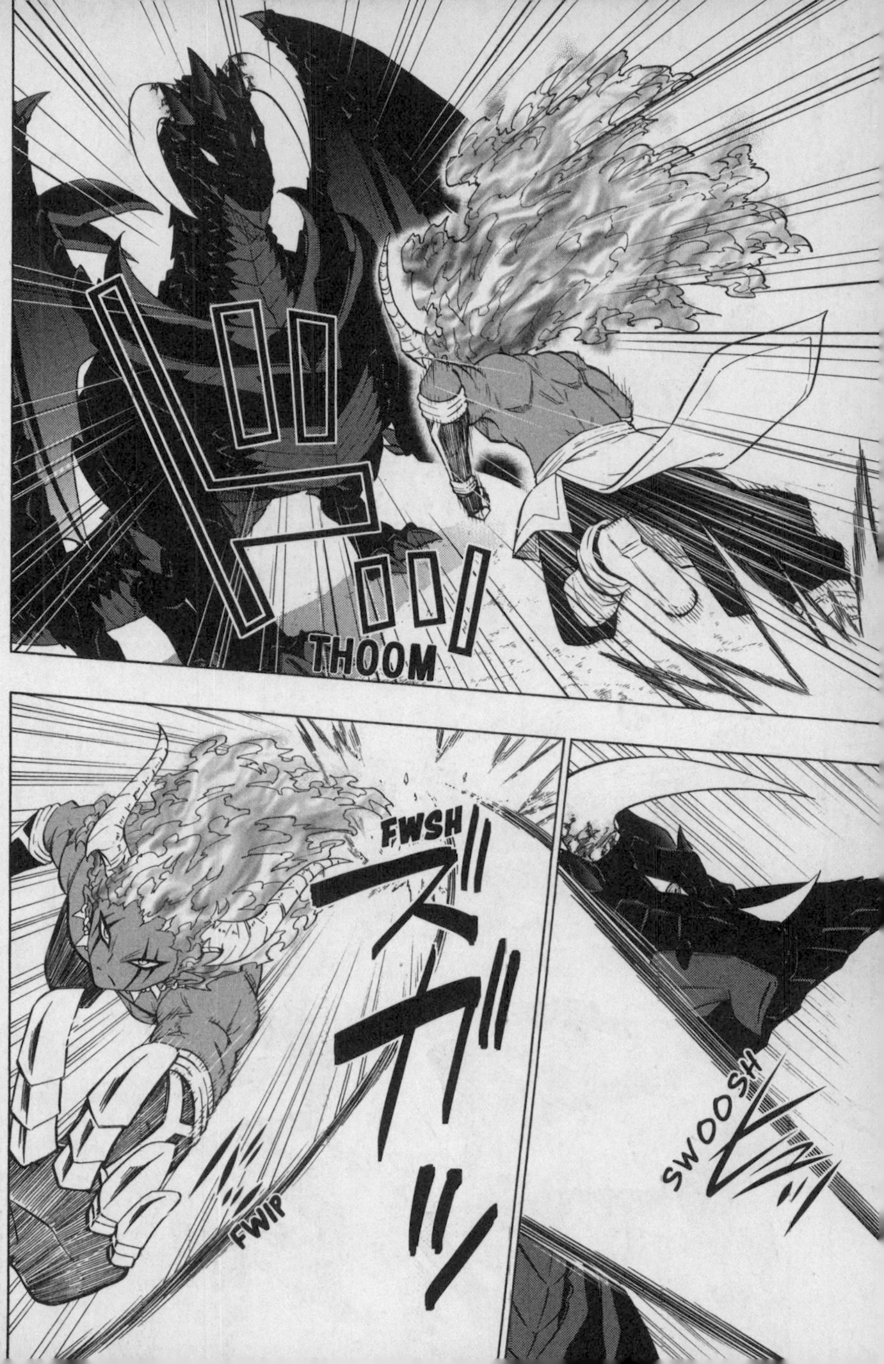
THOOM
SWOOSH
FWSH
FWIP

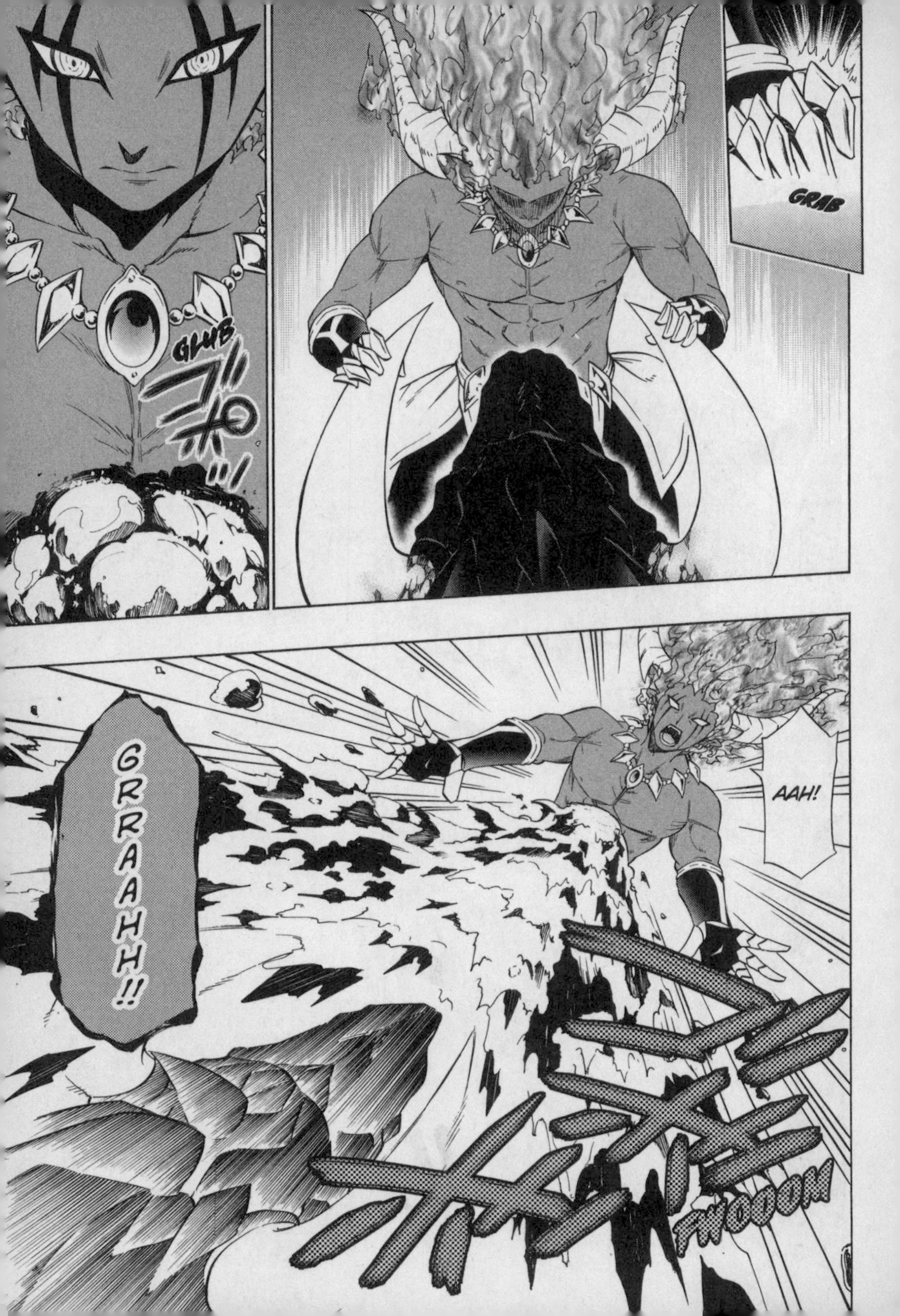
GRAB
GLUB
ゴポッ!!
AAH!
GRRAAAHH!!
THOOOM

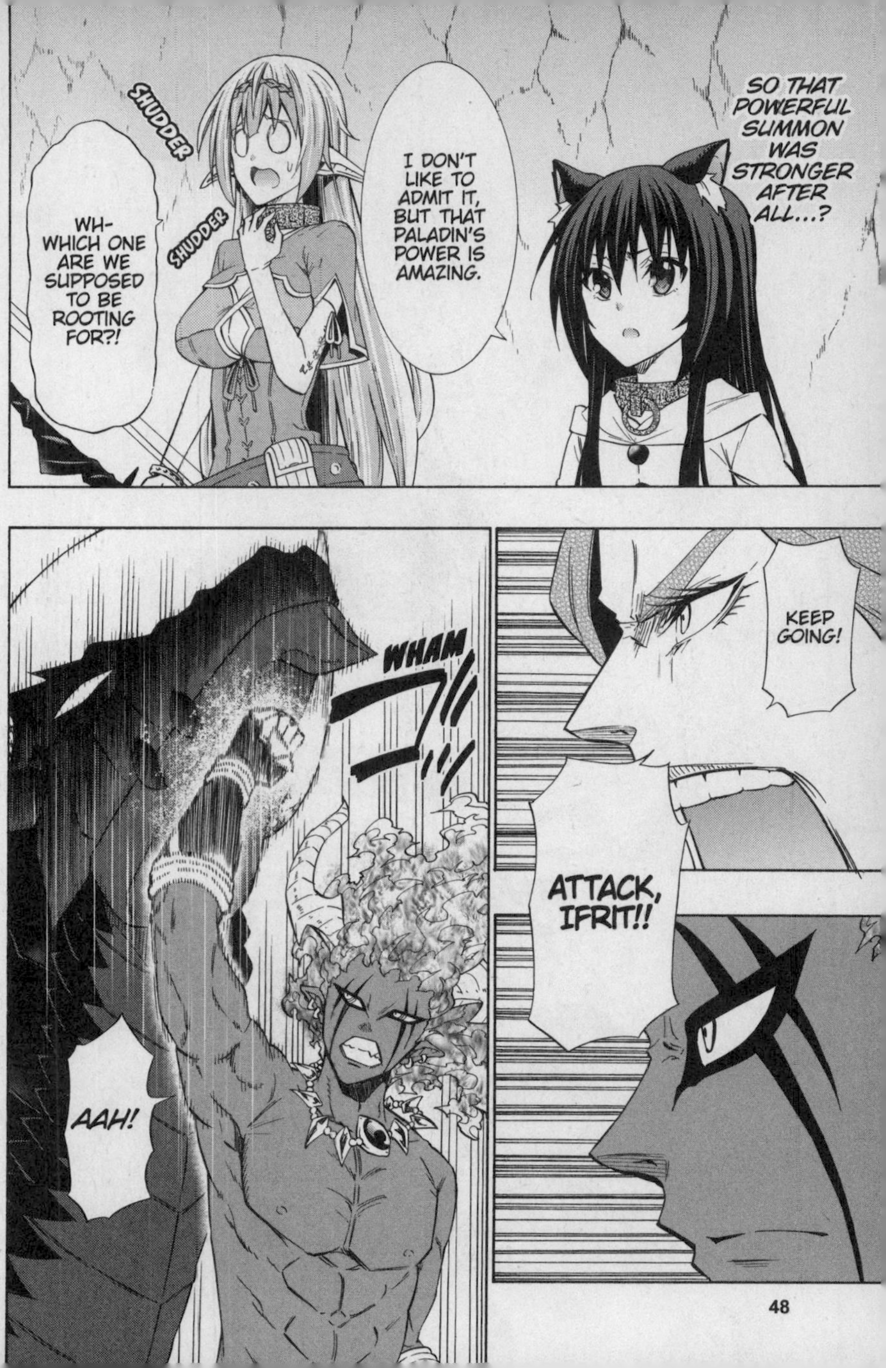
SO THAT POWERFUL SUMMON WAS STRONGER AFTER ALL...?
I DON'T LIKE TO ADMIT IT, BUT THAT PALADIN'S POWER IS AMAZING.
SHUDDER
SHUDDER
WH-WHICH ONE ARE WE SUPPOSED TO BE ROOTING FOR?!
KEEP GOING!
ATTACK, IFRIT!!
WHAM
AAH!

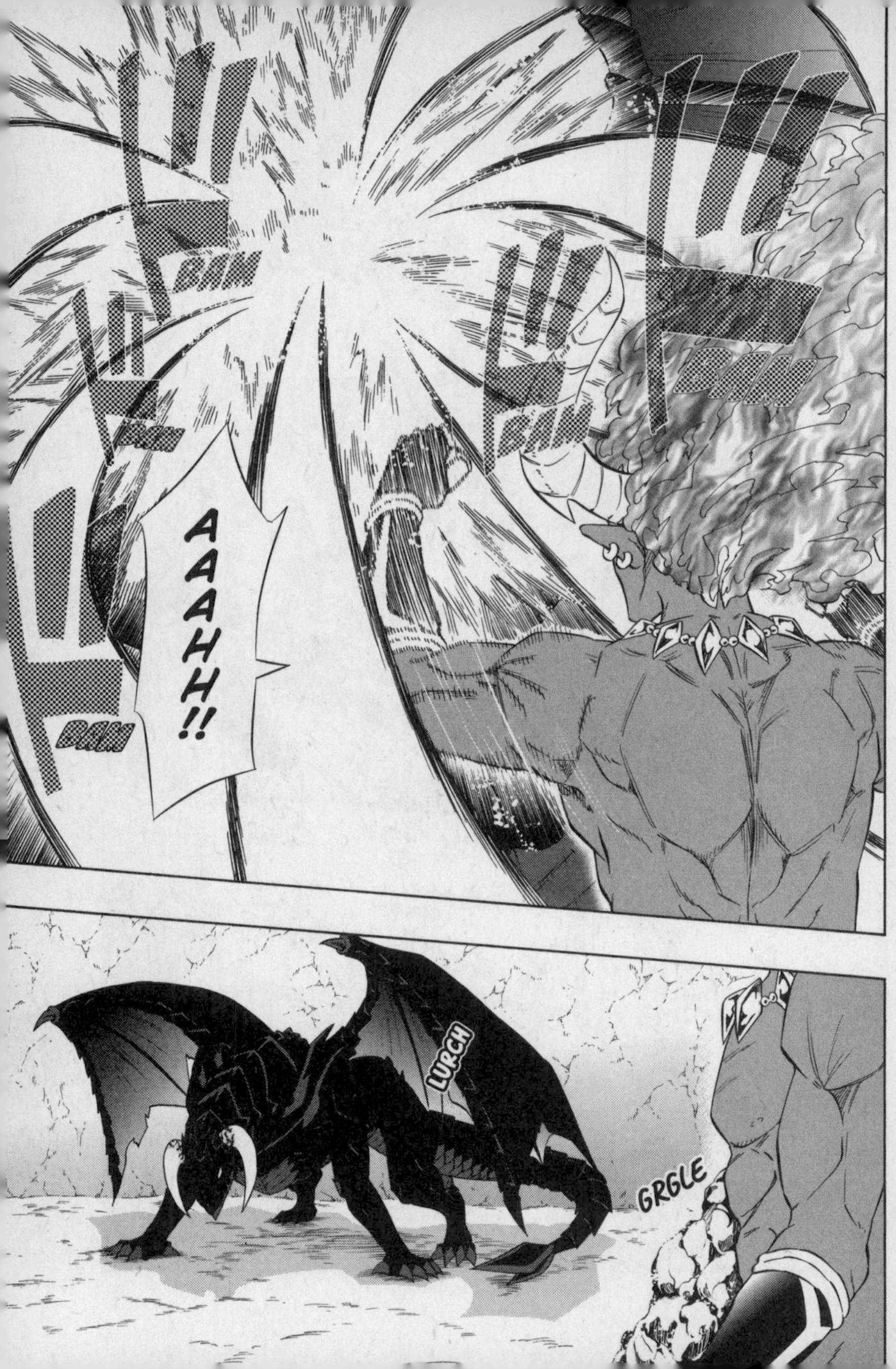
BAM
BAM
BAM
BAM
AAAAHH!!
BAM
GRGLE
LURCH

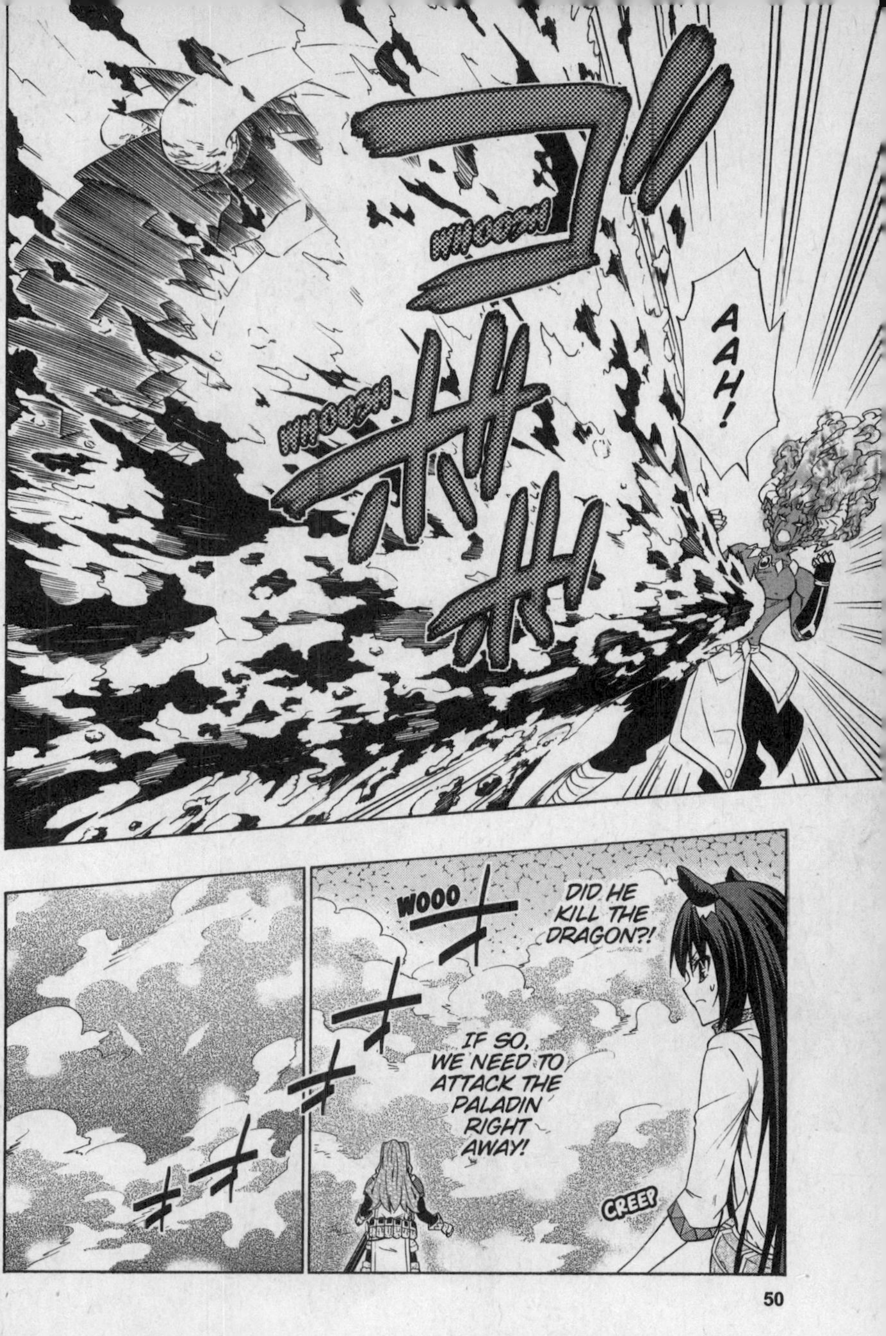
AAH!
WHOOSH
WHOOSH
WOOO
DID HE KILL THE DRAGON?!
IF SO, WE NEED TO ATTACK THE PALADIN RIGHT AWAY!
CREEP

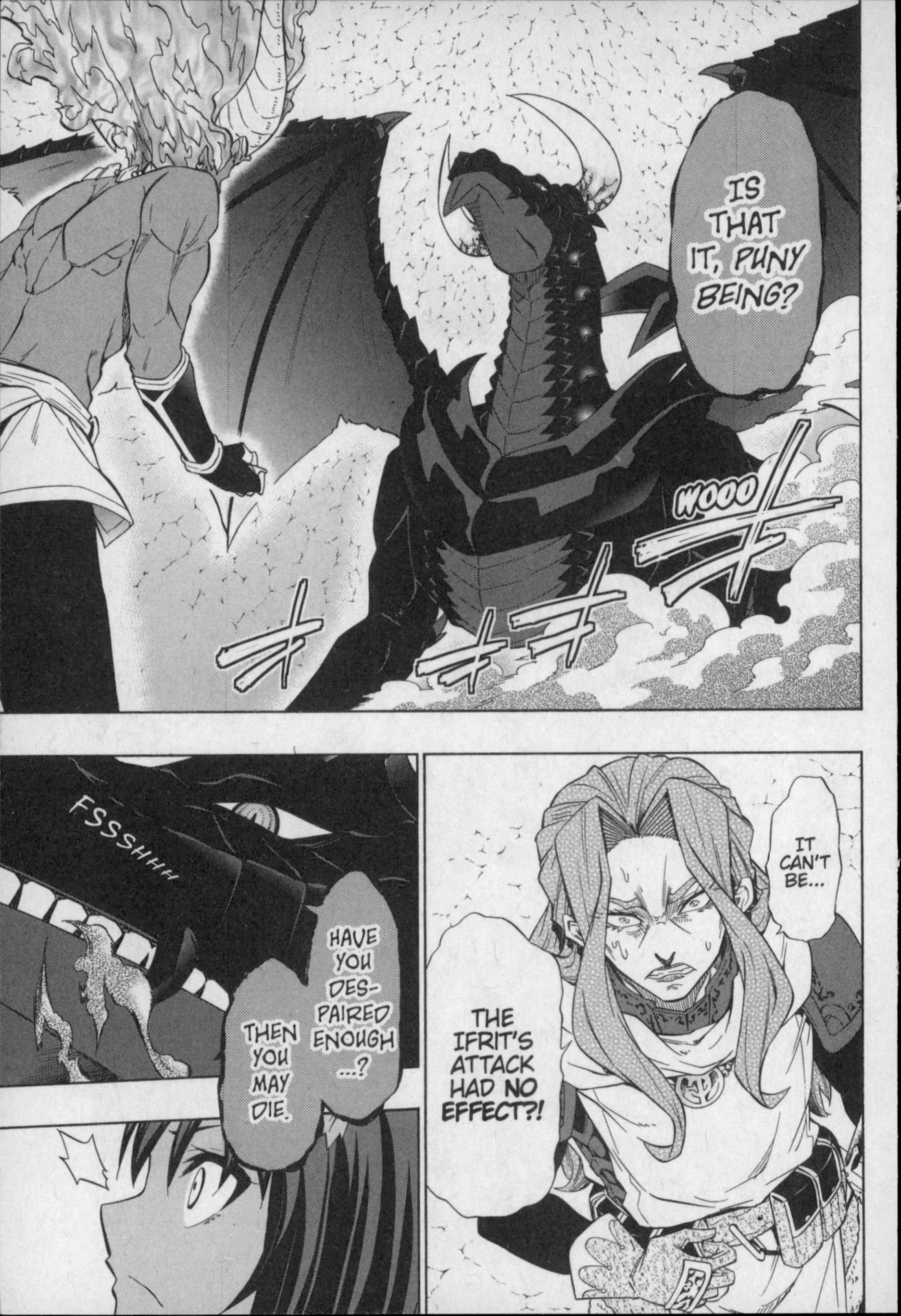
IS THAT IT, PUNY BEING?
WOOO
IT CAN'T BE...
THE IFRIT'S ATTACK HAD NO EFFECT?!
FSSSHHH
HAVE YOU DES-PAIRED ENOUGH ...?
THEN YOU MAY DIE.

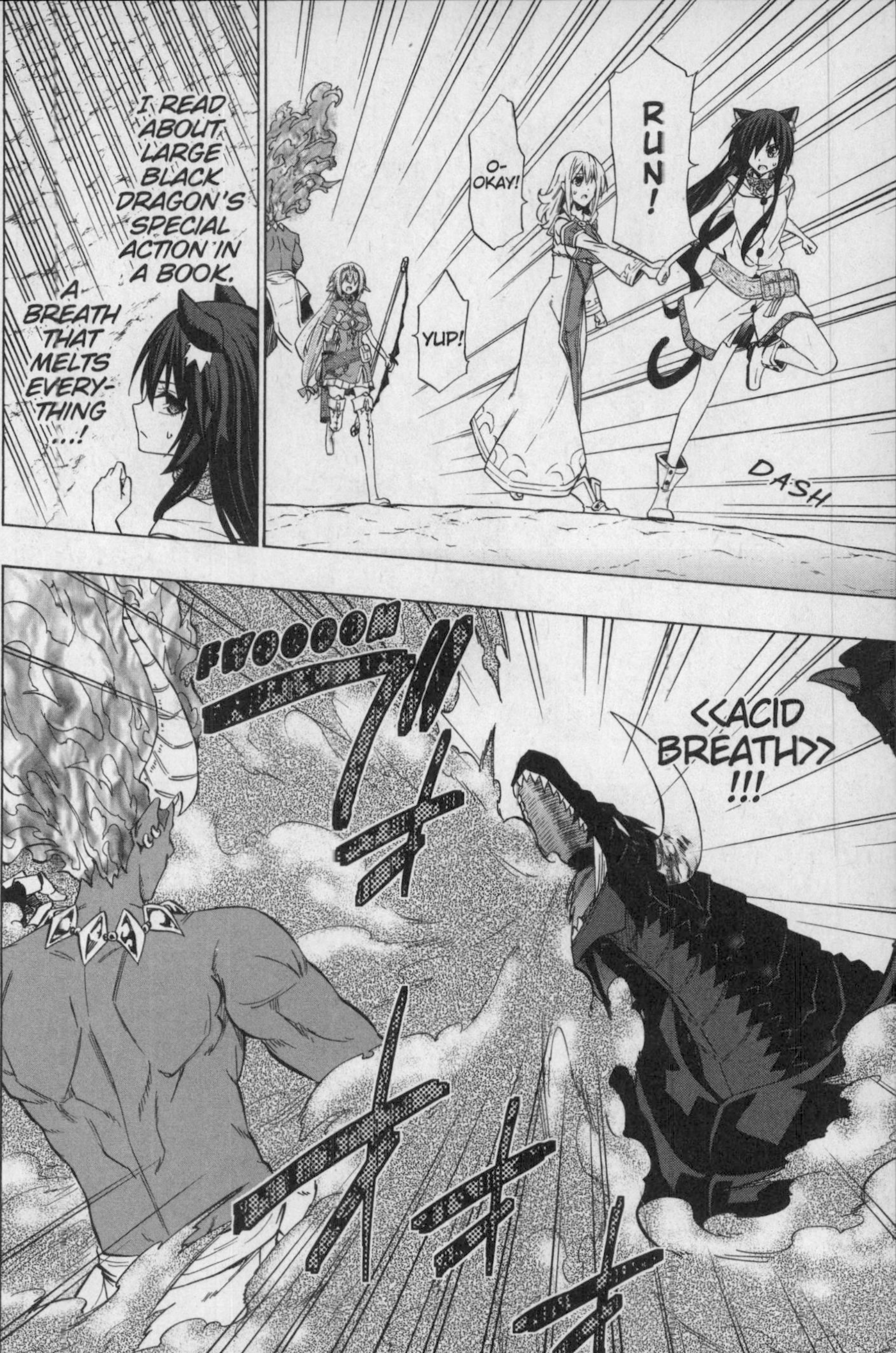
RUN!
O-OKAY!
YUP!
DASH
I READ ABOUT LARGE BLACK DRAGON'S SPECIAL ACTION IN A BOOK.
A BREATH THAT MELTS EVERYTHING...!
<<ACID BREATH>> !!!
FWOOOOM

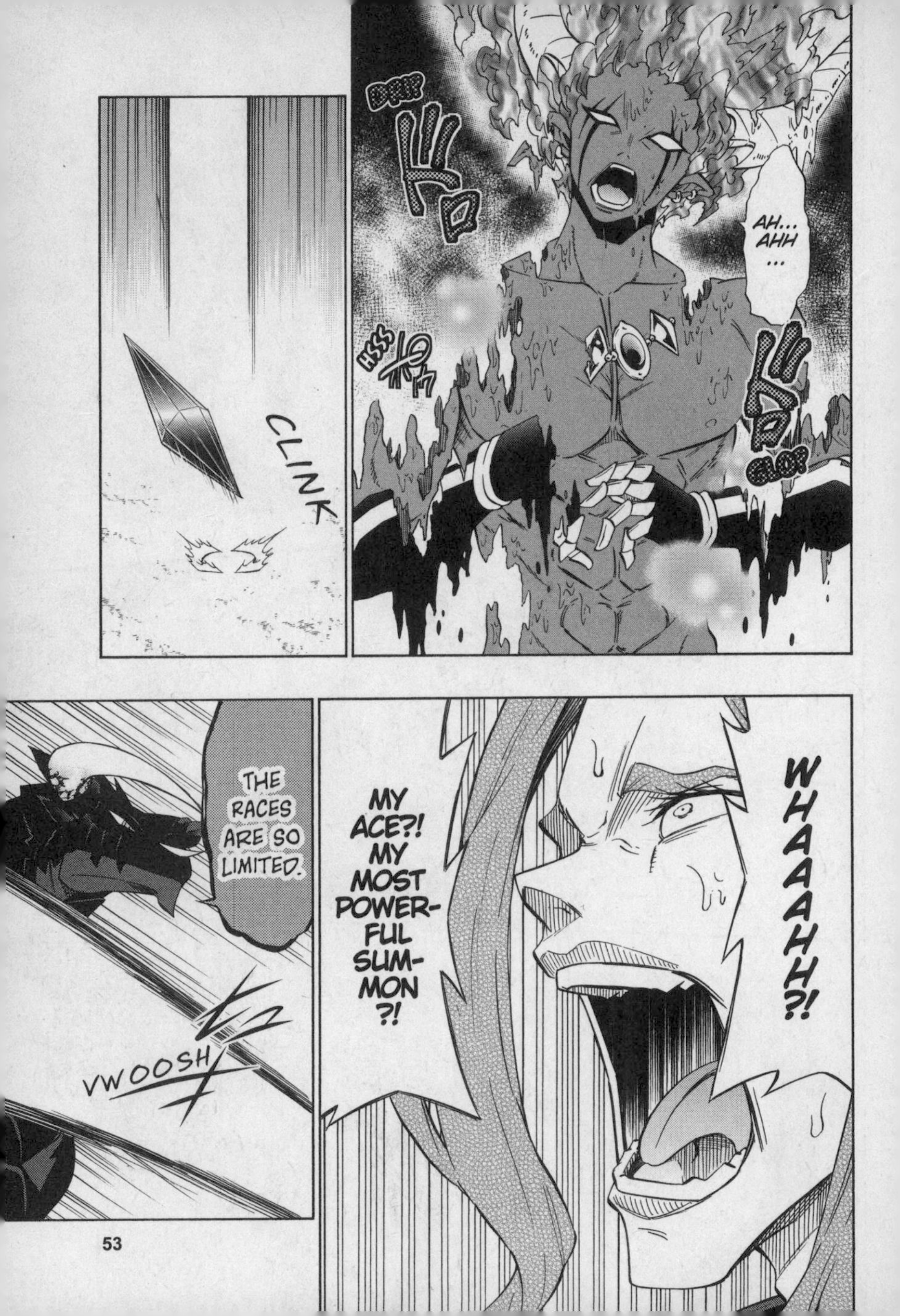
DRIP
AH... AHH ...
GLOP
HSSS
CLINK
WHAAAAHH?!
MY ACE?! MY MOST POWER-FUL SUM-MON?!
THE RACES ARE SO LIMITED.
VWOOSH

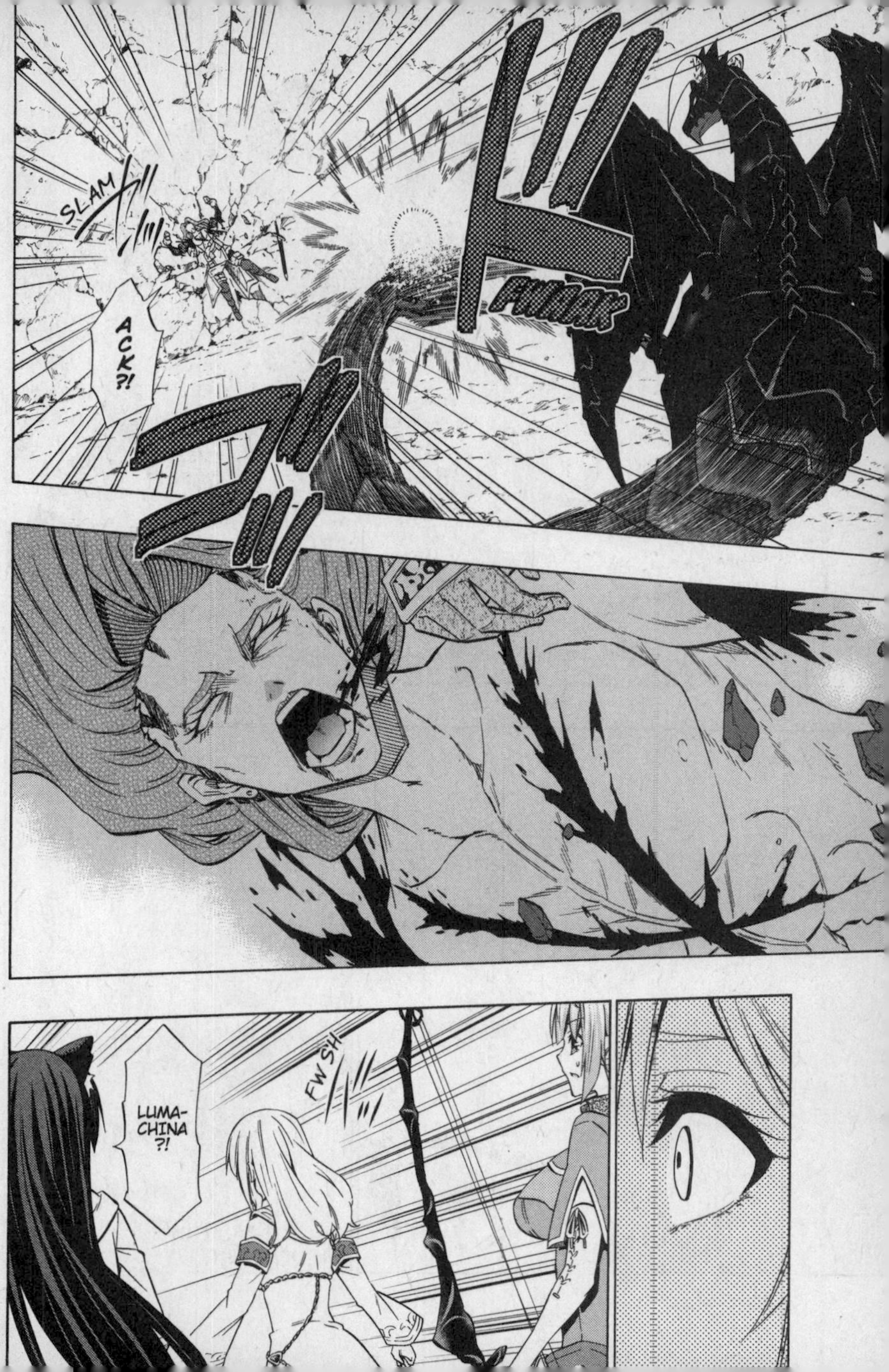
SLAM
ACK?!
FWSH
LUMA-CHINA?!

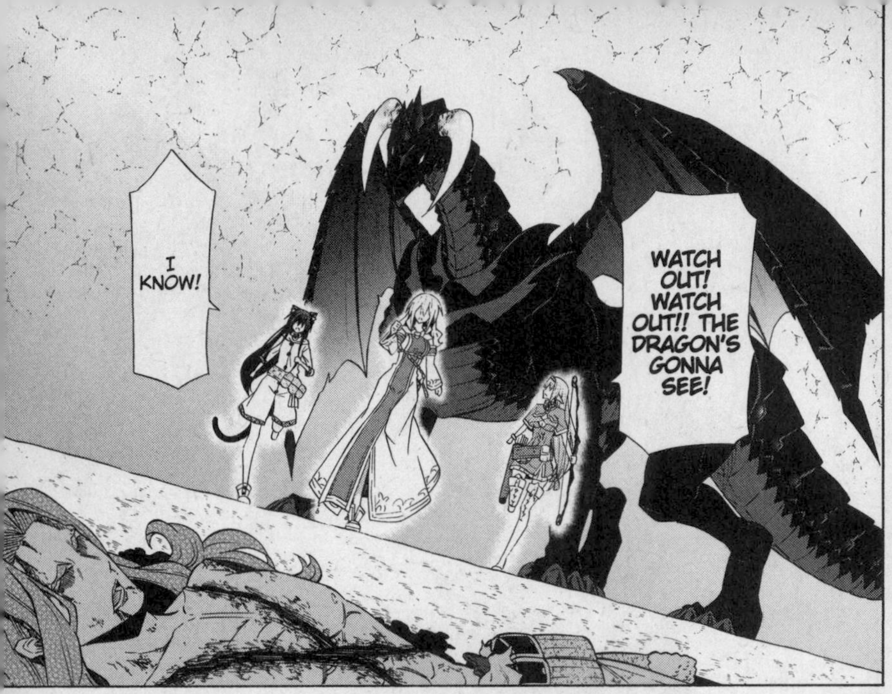
WATCH OUT! WATCH OUT!! THE DRAGON'S GONNA SEE!
I KNOW!

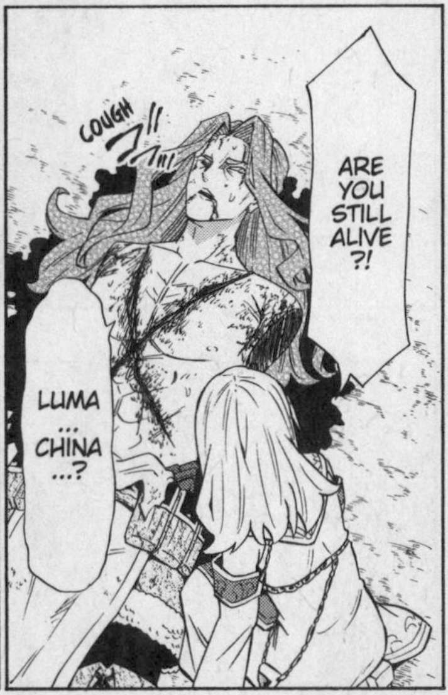
ARE YOU STILL ALIVE?!
COUGH
LUMA ... CHÏNA ...?

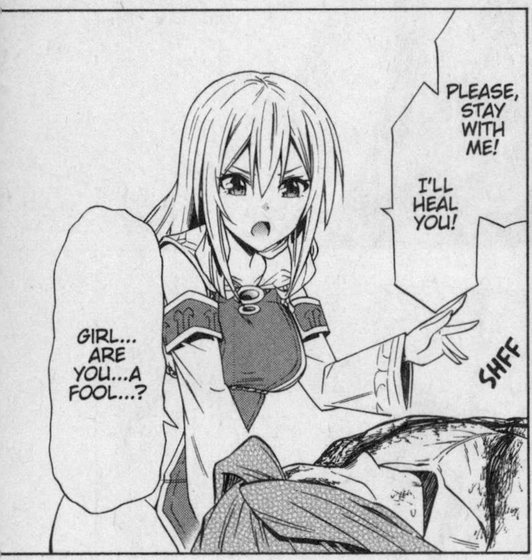
PLEASE, STAY WITH ME!
I'LL HEAL YOU!
SHFF
GIRL... ARE YOU...A FOOL...?

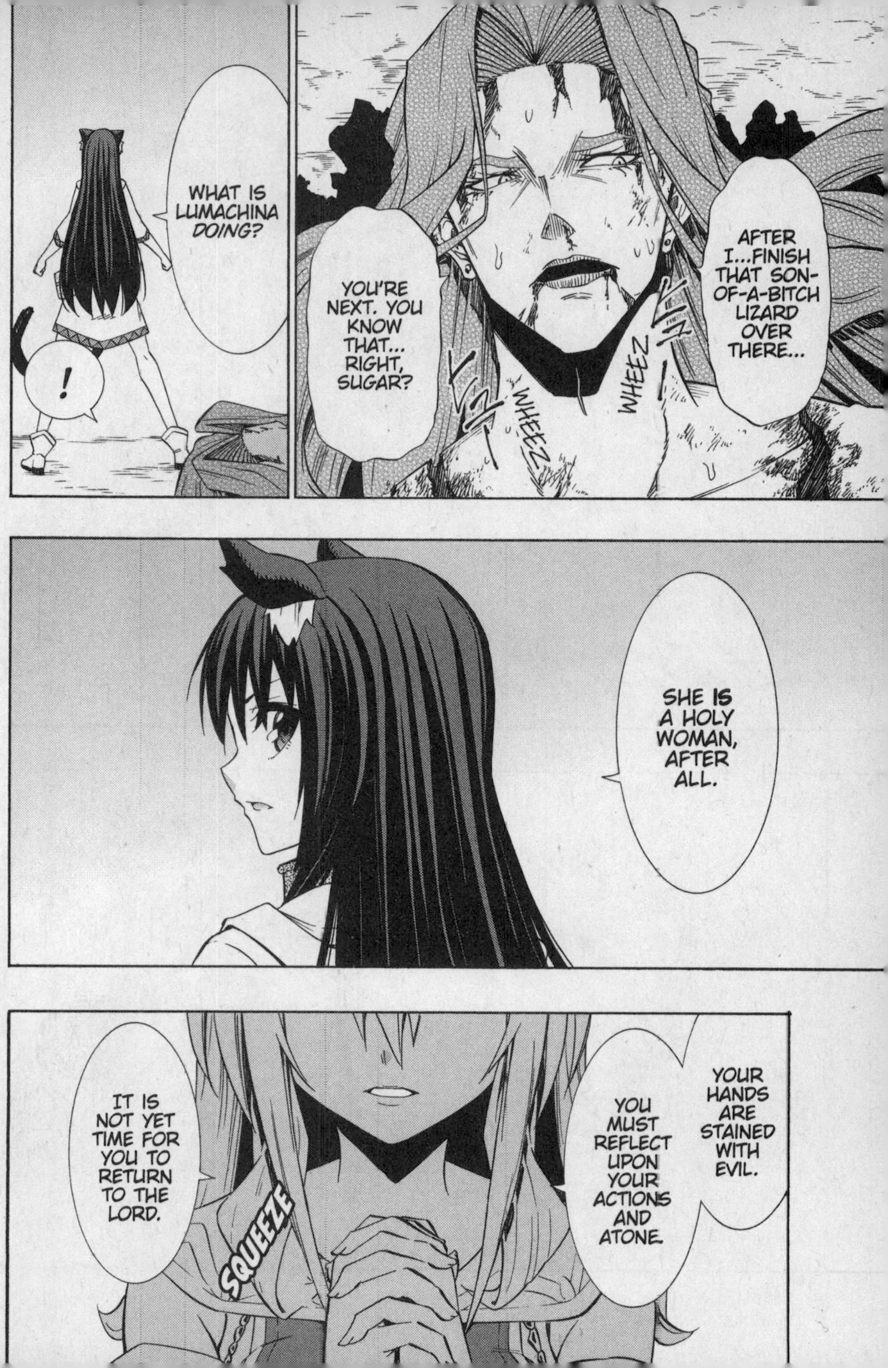
AFTER I...FINISH THAT SON-OF-A-BITCH LIZARD OVER THERE...
WHEEZ
WHEEZ
YOU'RE NEXT. YOU KNOW THAT... RIGHT, SUGAR?
WHAT IS LUMACHINA DOING?
!
SHE IS A HOLY WOMAN, AFTER ALL.
YOUR HANDS ARE STAINED WITH EVIL.
YOU MUST REFLECT UPON YOUR ACTIONS AND ATONE.
IT IS NOT YET TIME FOR YOU TO RETURN TO THE LORD.
SQUEEZE

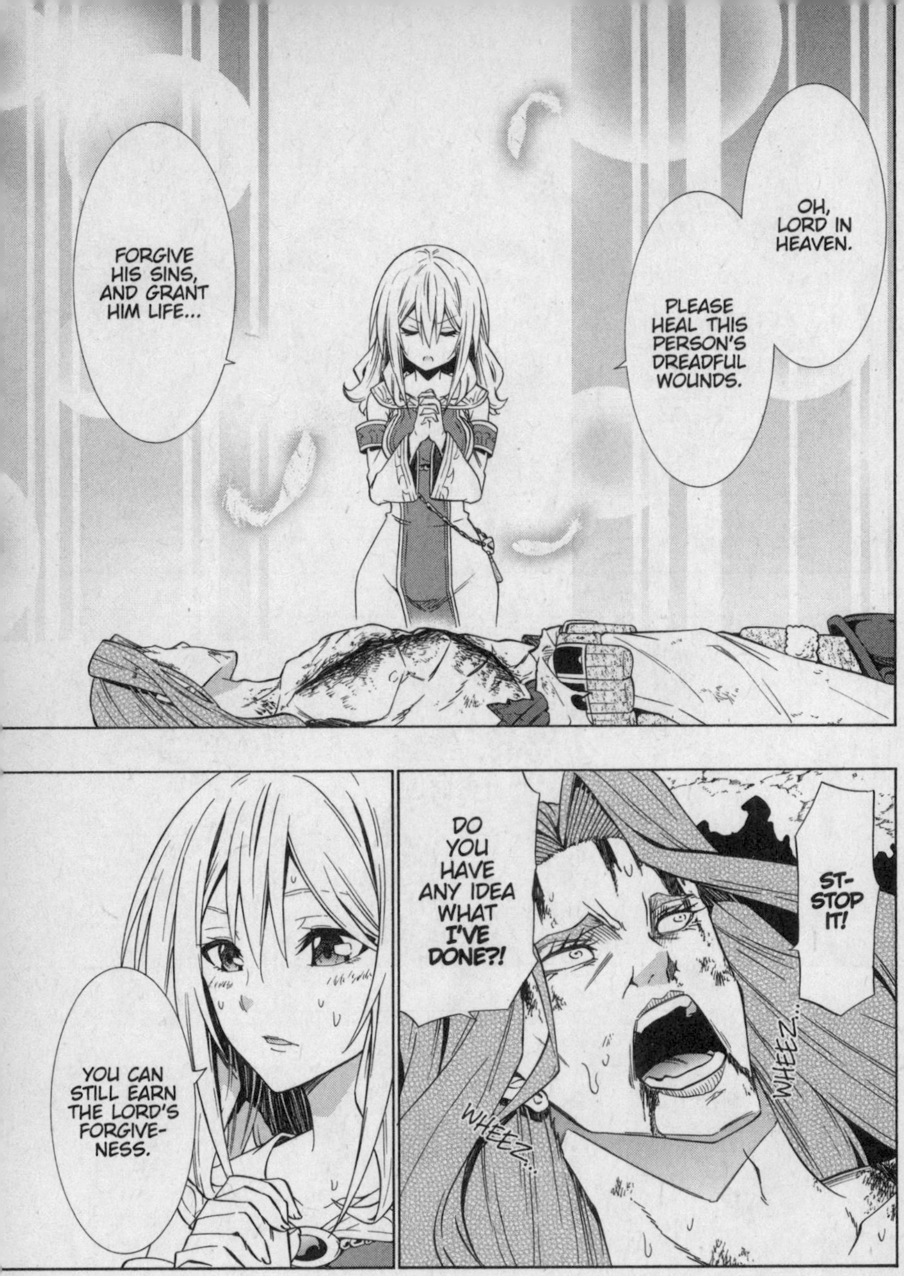
OH, LORD IN HEAVEN.
PLEASE HEAL THIS PERSON'S DREADFUL WOUNDS.
FORGIVE HIS SINS, AND GRANT HIM LIFE...
ST- STOP IT!
DO YOU HAVE ANY IDEA WHAT I'VE DONE?!
WHEEZ...
WHEEZ...
YOU CAN STILL EARN THE LORD'S FORGIVE-NESS.

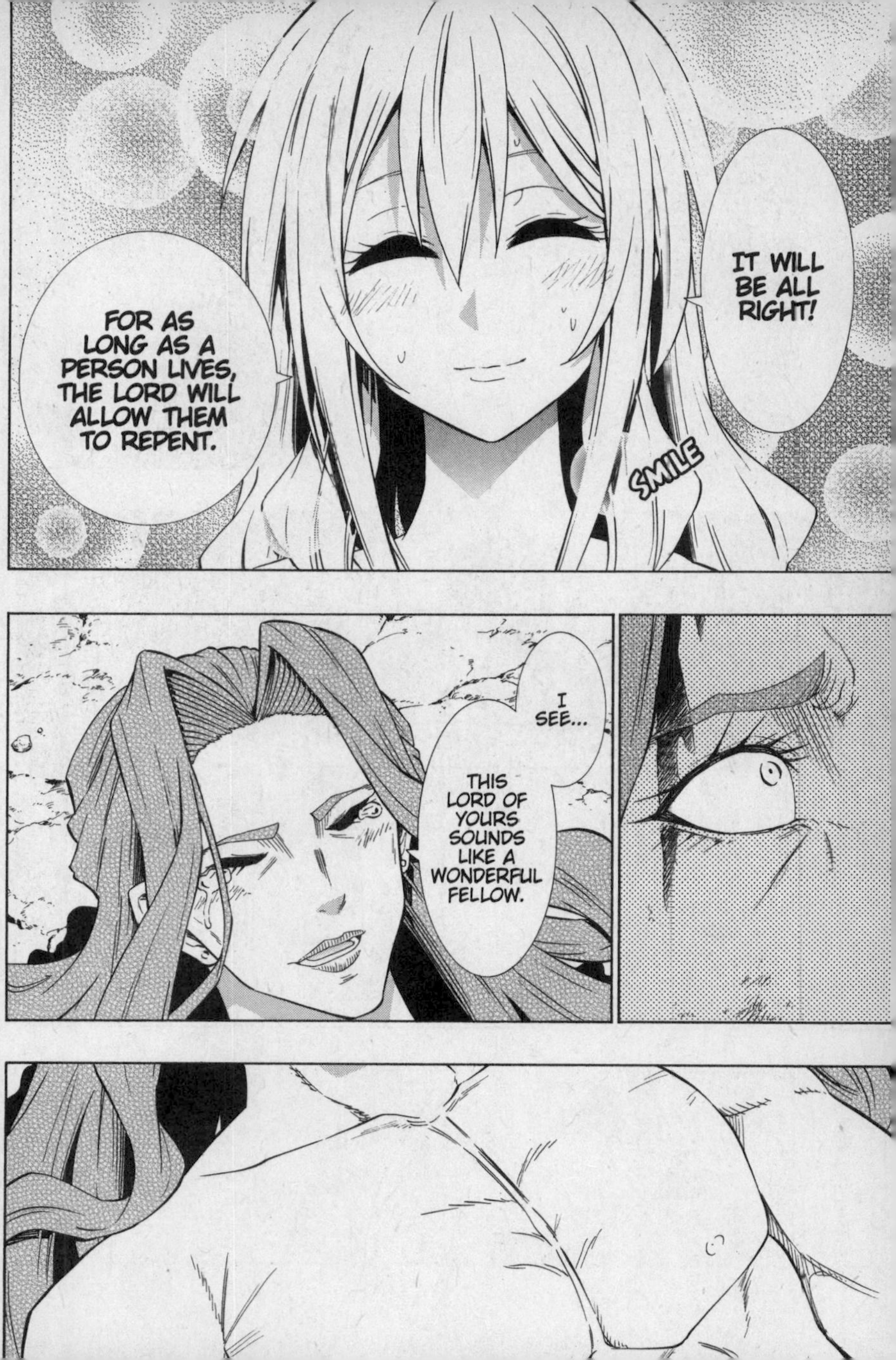
IT WILL BE ALL RIGHT!
SMILE
FOR AS LONG AS A PERSON LIVES, THE LORD WILL ALLOW THEM TO REPENT.
I SEE...
THIS LORD OF YOURS SOUNDS LIKE A WONDERFUL FELLOW.

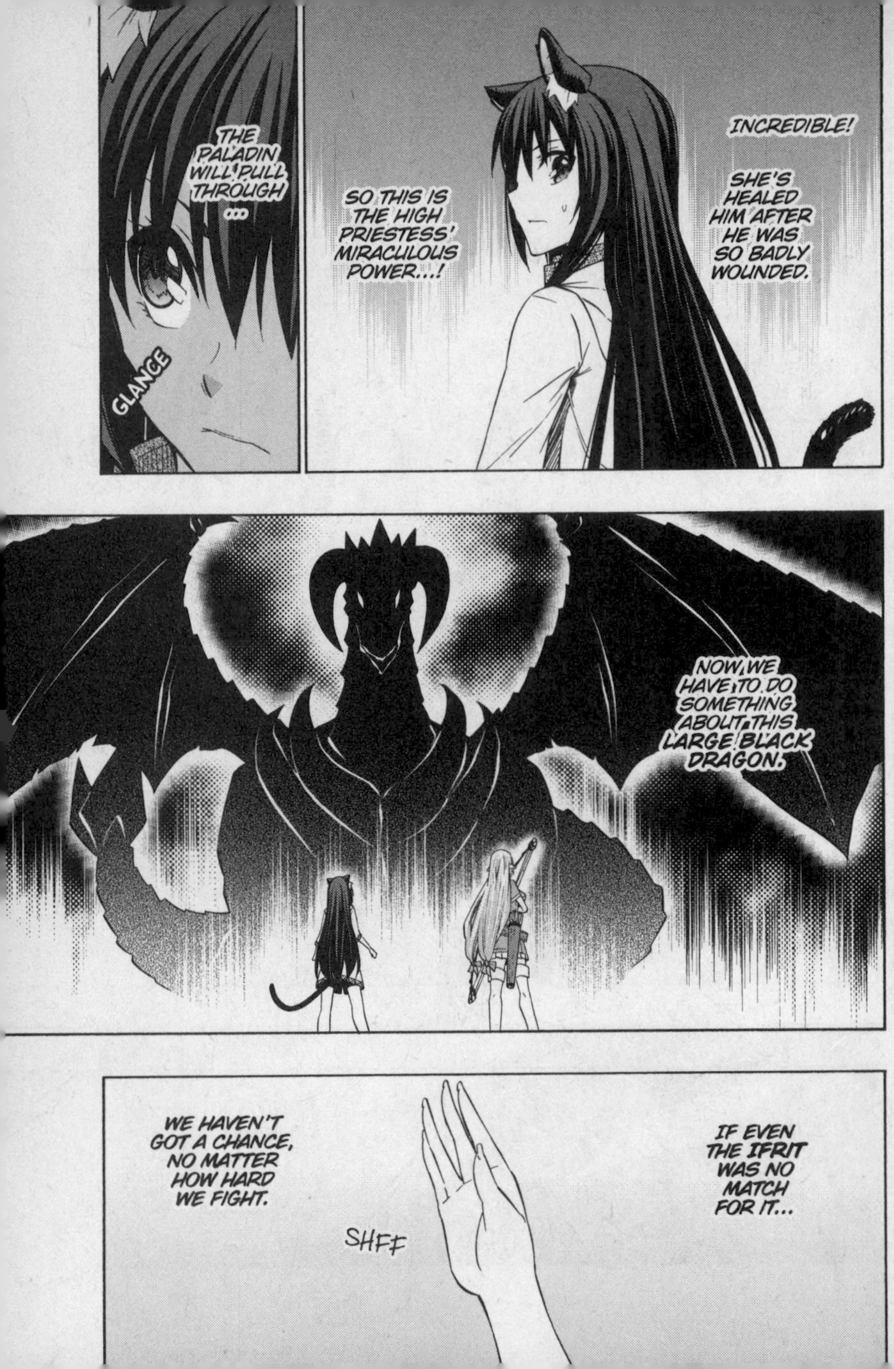
INCREDIBLE!
SHE'S HEALED HIM AFTER HE WAS SO BADLY WOUNDED.
SO THIS IS THE HIGH PRIESTESS' MIRACULOUS POWER...!
THE PALADIN WILL PULL THROUGH...
GLANCE
NOW WE HAVE TO DO SOMETHING ABOUT THIS LARGE BLACK DRAGON.
IF EVEN THE IFRIT WAS NO MATCH FOR IT...
WE HAVEN'T GOT A CHANCE, NO MATTER HOW HARD WE FIGHT.
SHFF

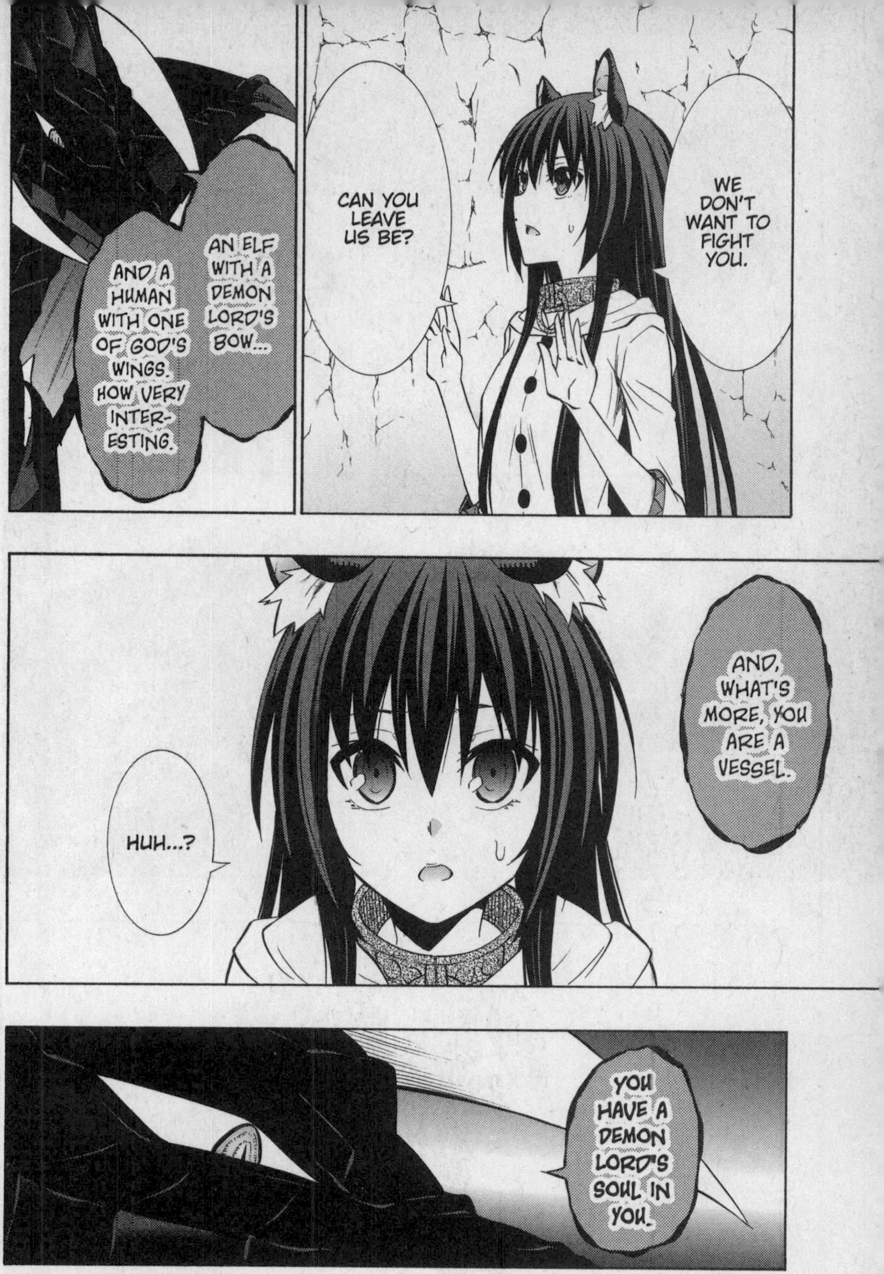
WE DON'T WANT TO FIGHT YOU.
CAN YOU LEAVE US BE?
AN ELF WITH A DEMON LORD'S BOW...
AND A HUMAN WITH ONE OF GOD'S WINGS. HOW VERY INTER-ESTING.
AND, WHAT'S MORE, YOU ARE A VESSEL.
HUH...?
YOU HAVE A DEMON LORD'S SOUL IN YOU.

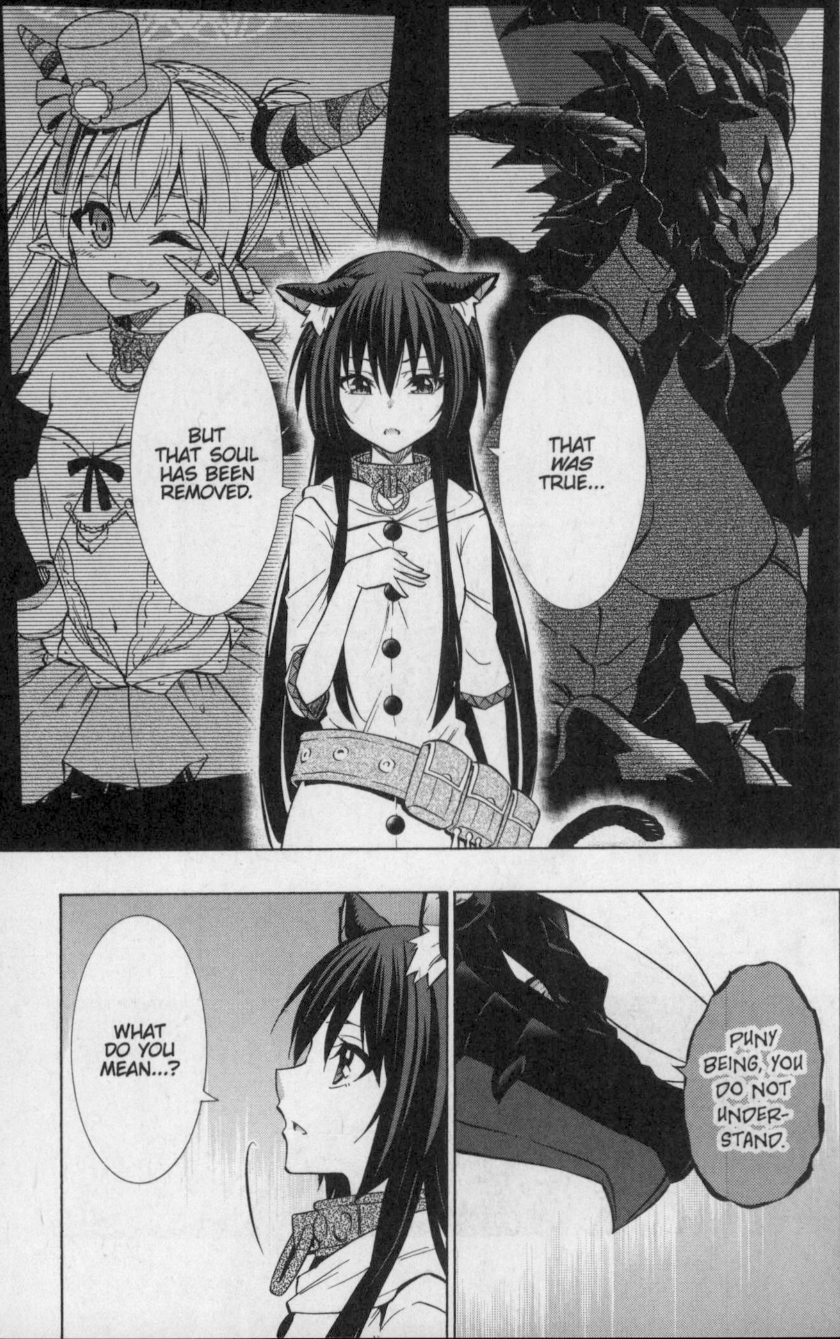
THAT WAS TRUE...
BUT THAT SOUL HAS BEEN REMOVED.
PUNY BEING, YOU DO NOT UNDER-STAND.
WHAT DO YOU MEAN...?

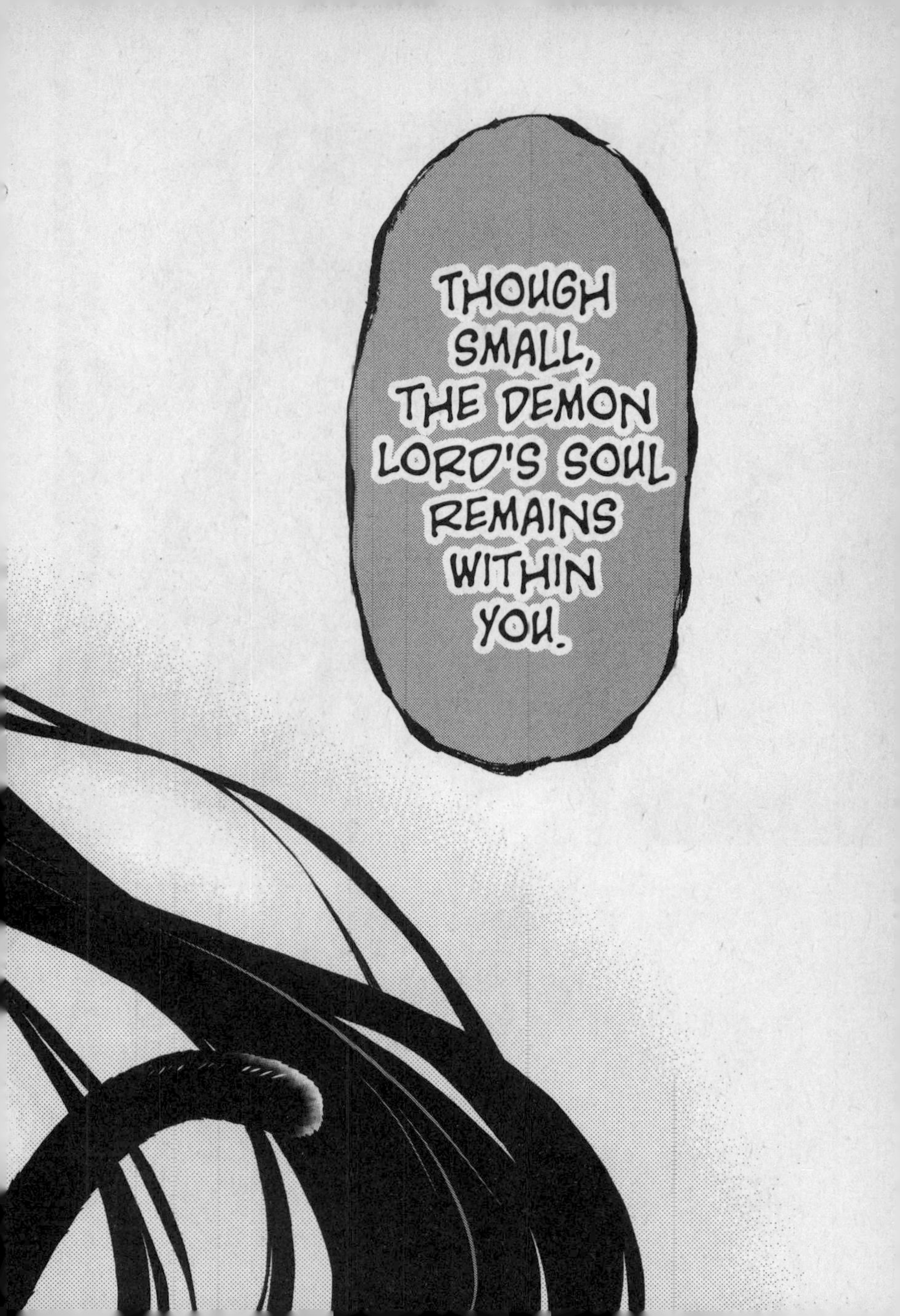
THOUGH SMALL, THE DEMON LORD'S SOUL REMAINS WITHIN YOU.

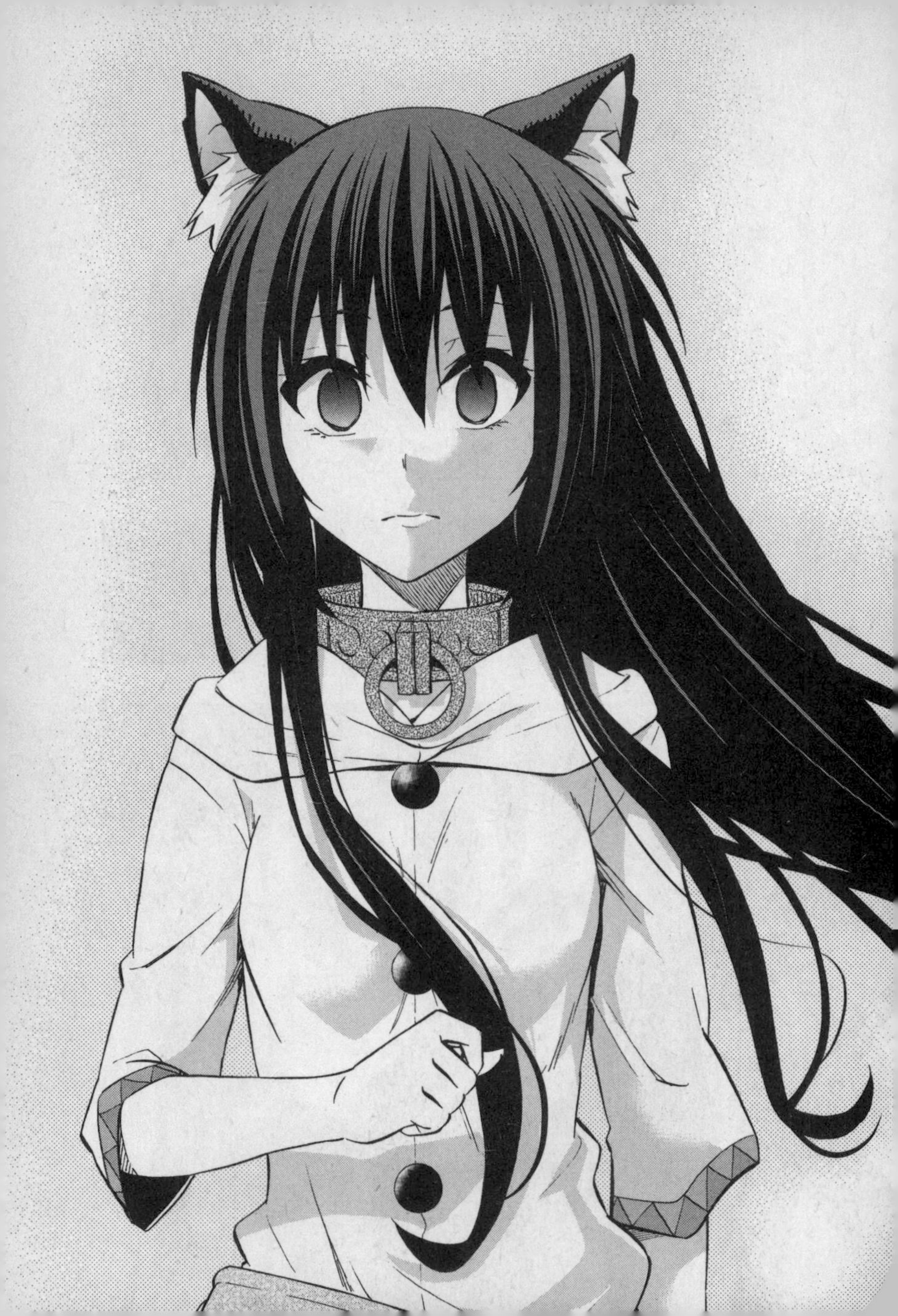

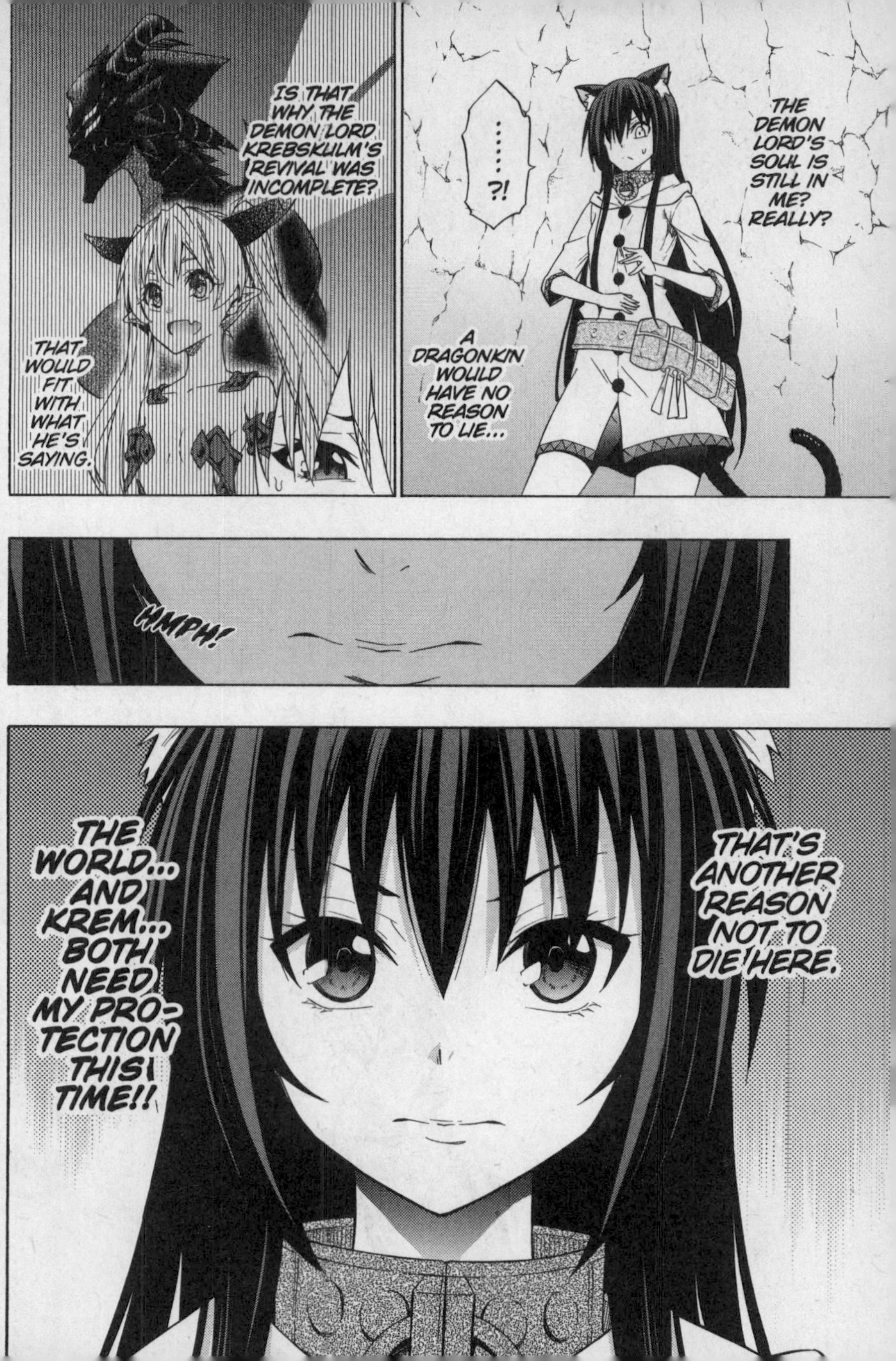
THE DEMON LORD'S SOUL IS STILL IN ME? REALLY?
......?!
A DRAGONKIN WOULD HAVE NO REASON TO LIE...
IS THAT WHY THE DEMON LORD KREBSKULM'S REVIVAL WAS INCOMPLETE?
THAT WOULD FIT WITH WHAT HE'S SAYING.
HMPH!
THAT'S ANOTHER REASON NOT TO DIE HERE.
THE WORLD... AND KREM... BOTH NEED MY PROTECTION THIS TIME!!

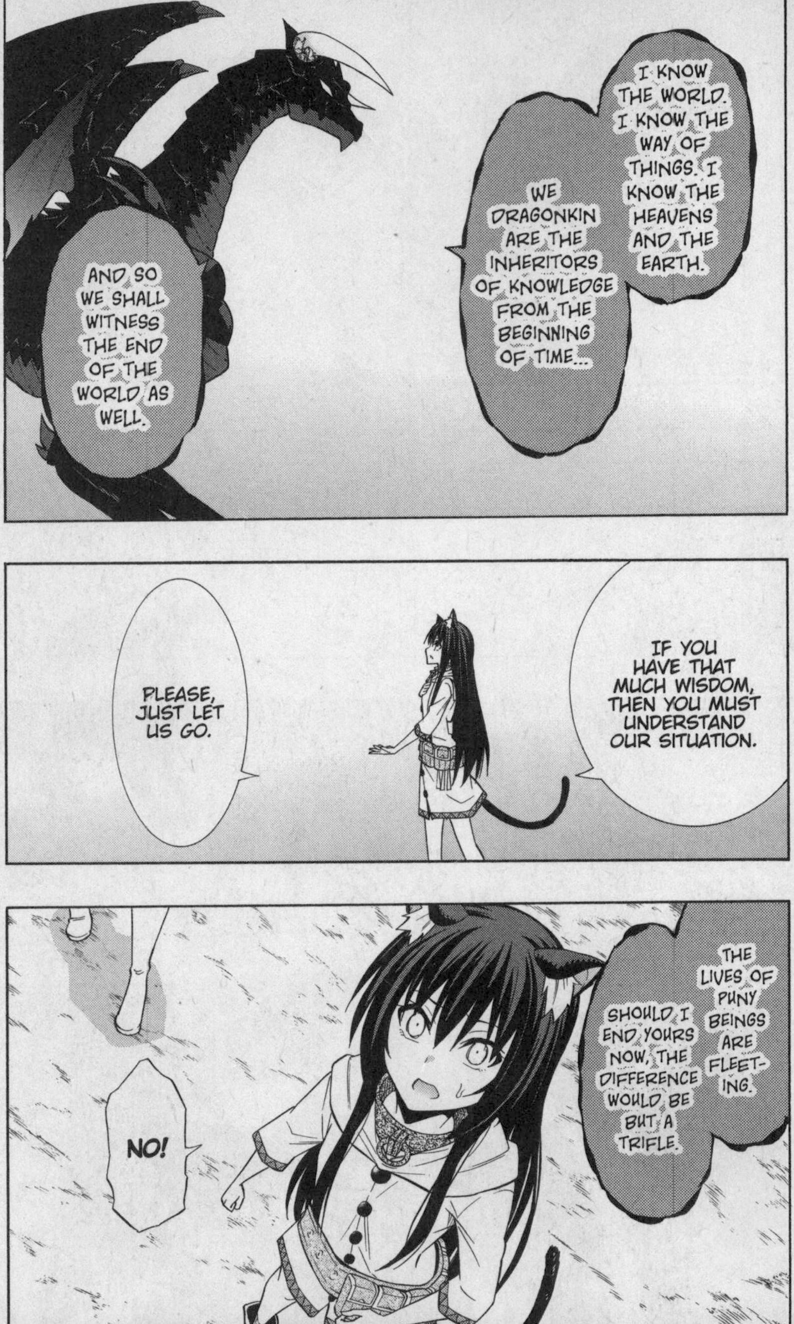
I KNOW THE WORLD. I KNOW THE WAY OF THINGS. I KNOW THE HEAVENS AND THE EARTH.
WE DRAGONKIN ARE THE INHERITORS OF KNOWLEDGE FROM THE BEGINNING OF TIME...
AND SO WE SHALL WITNESS THE END OF THE WORLD AS WELL.
IF YOU HAVE THAT MUCH WISDOM, THEN YOU MUST UNDERSTAND OUR SITUATION.
PLEASE, JUST LET US GO.
THE LIVES OF PUNY BEINGS ARE FLEET-ING.
SHOULD I END YOURS NOW, THE DIFFERENCE WOULD BE BUT A TRIFLE.
NO!

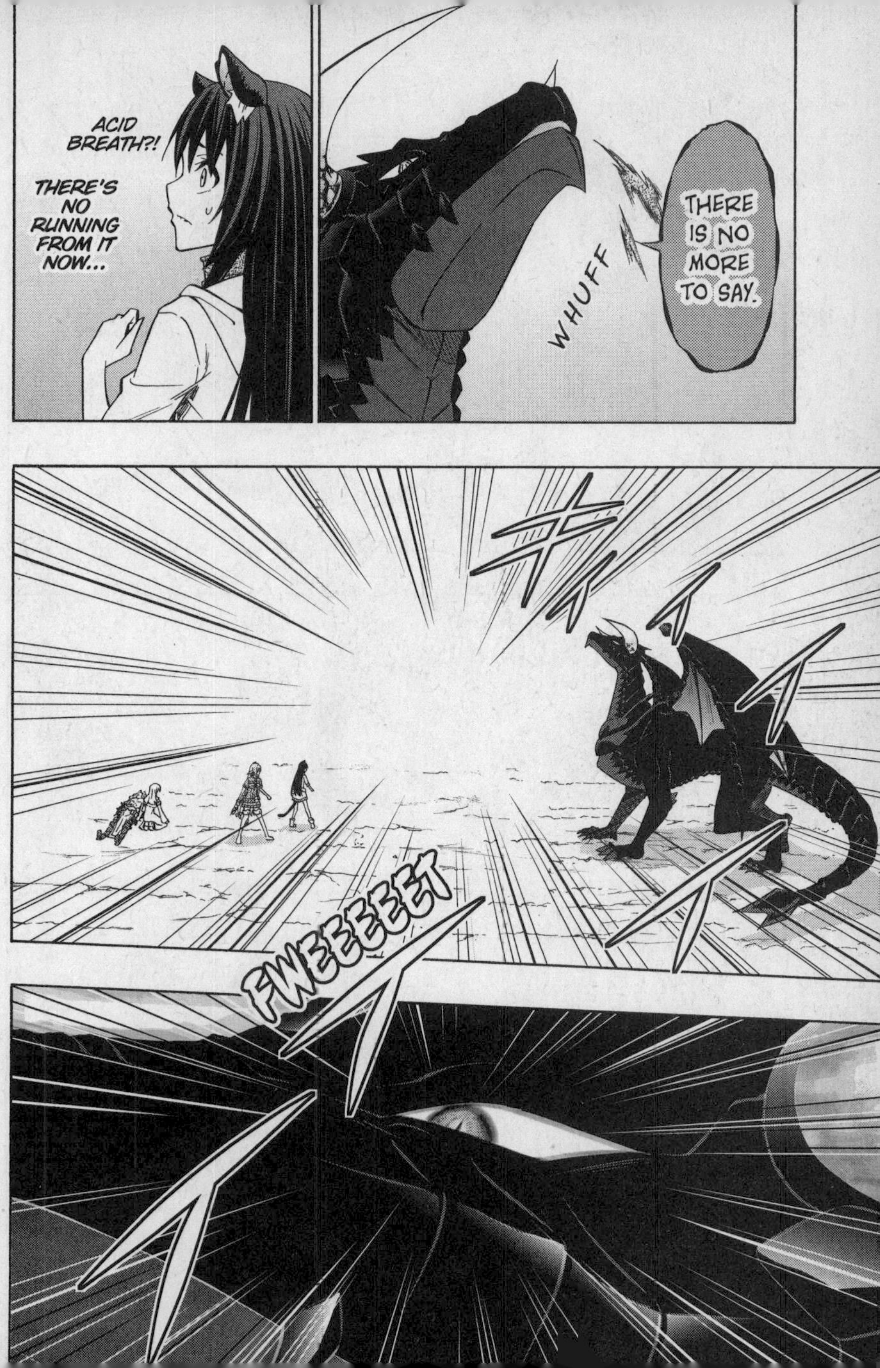
THERE IS NO MORE TO SAY.
WHUFF
ACID BREATH?!
THERE'S NO RUNNING FROM IT NOW...
FWEEEEEET

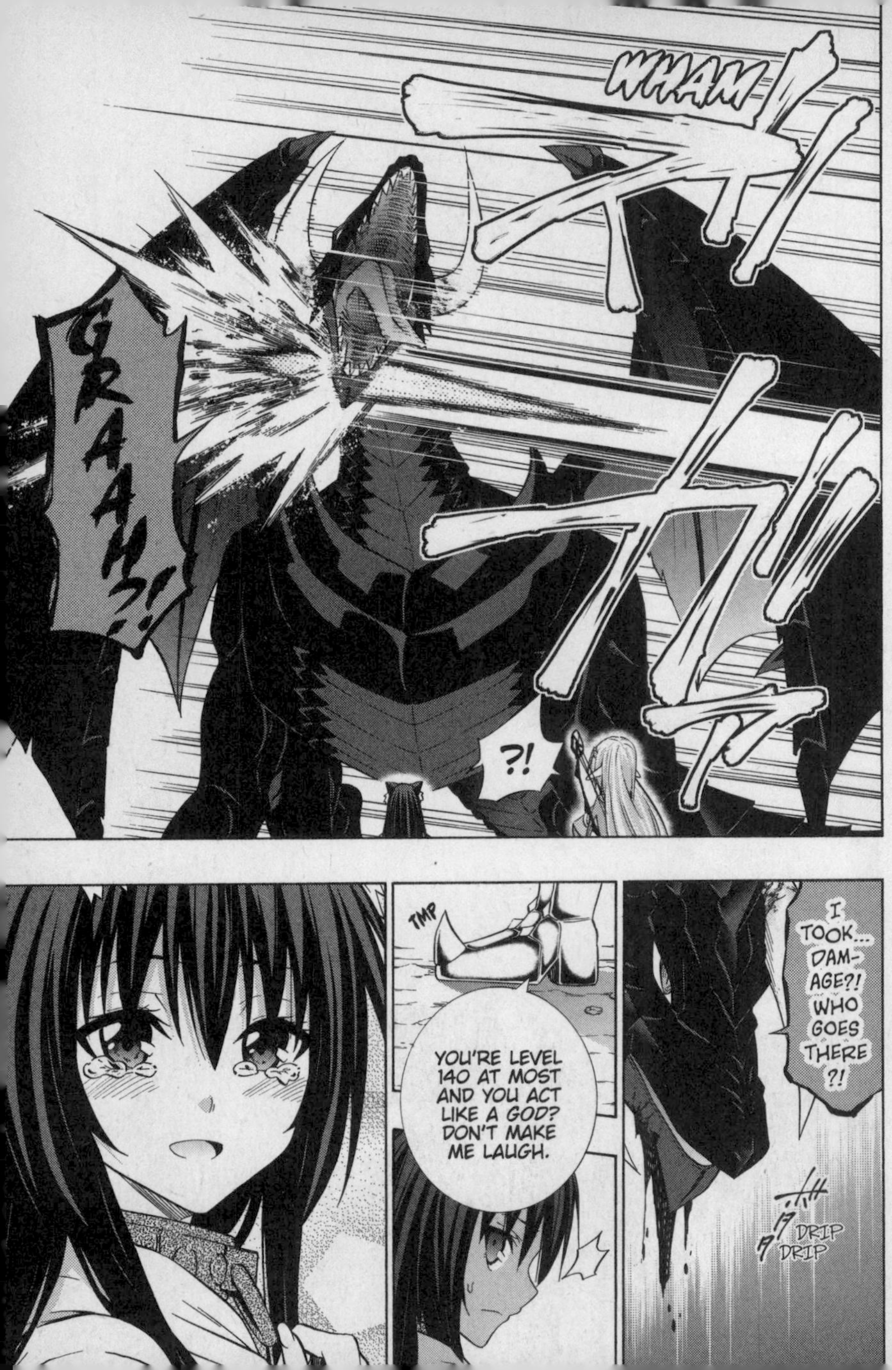
WHAM
GRAAH?!
?!
I TOOK... DAMAGE?! WHO GOES THERE?!
DRIP DRIP
TMP
YOU'RE LEVEL 140 AT MOST AND YOU ACT LIKE A GOD? DON'T MAKE ME LAUGH.

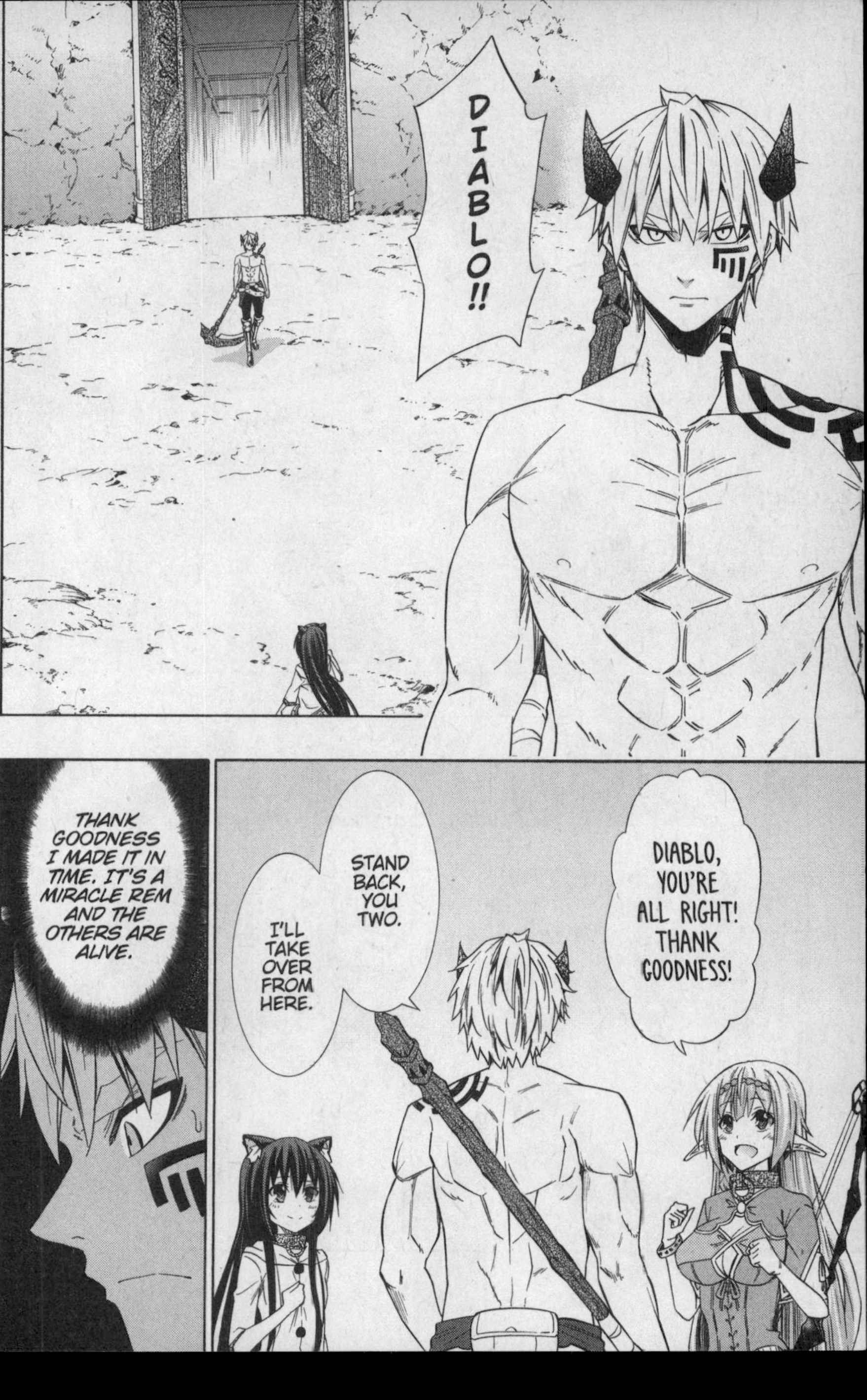
DIABLO!!
DIABLO, YOU'RE ALL RIGHT! THANK GOODNESS!
STAND BACK, YOU TWO.
I'LL TAKE OVER FROM HERE.
THANK GOODNESS I MADE IT IN TIME. IT'S A MIRACLE REM AND THE OTHERS ARE ALIVE.

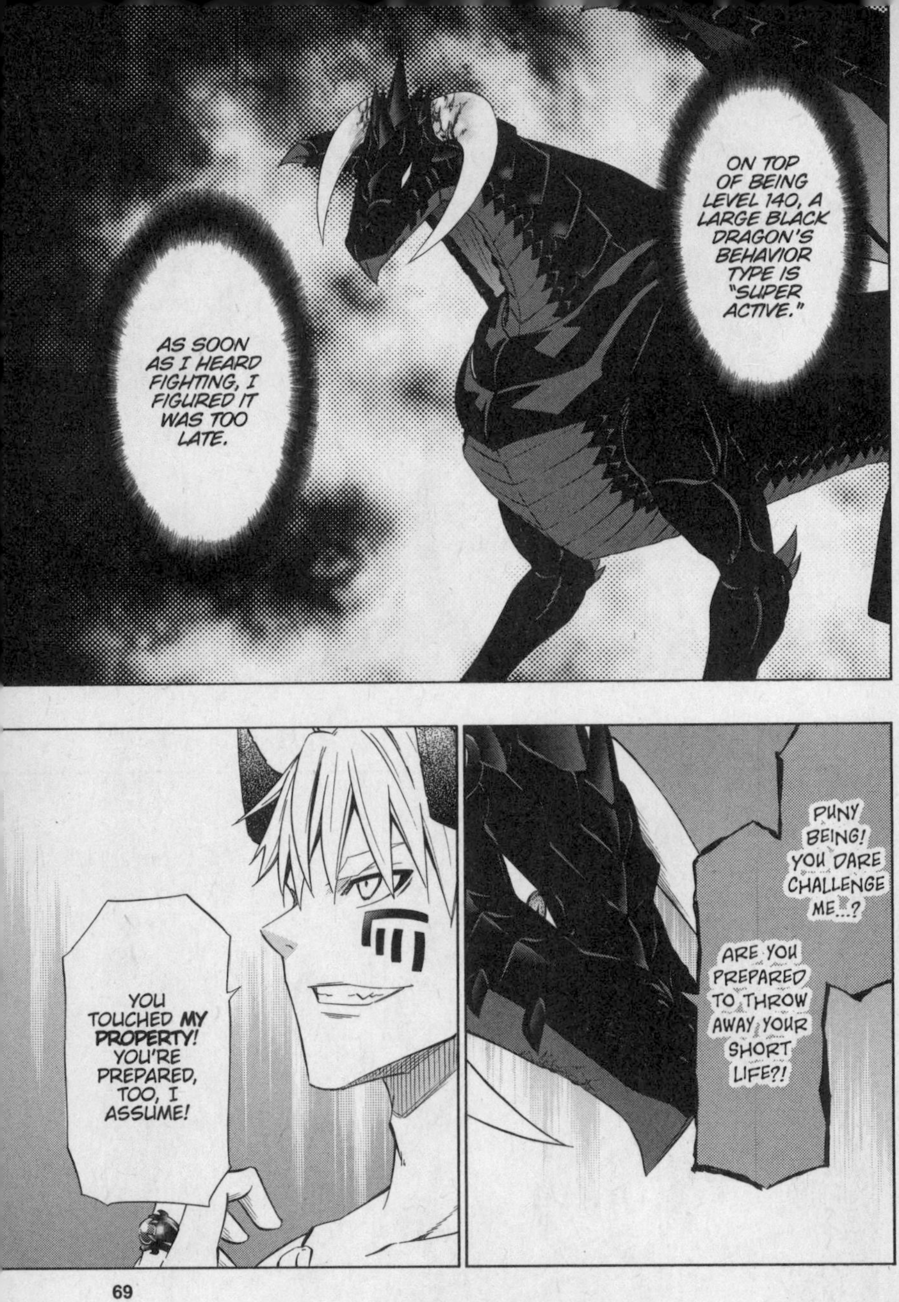
ON TOP OF BEING LEVEL 140, A LARGE BLACK DRAGON'S BEHAVIOR TYPE IS "SUPER ACTIVE."
AS SOON AS I HEARD FIGHTING, I FIGURED IT WAS TOO LATE.
PUNY BEING! YOU DARE CHALLENGE ME...?
ARE YOU PREPARED TO THROW AWAY YOUR SHORT LIFE?!
YOU TOUCHED MY PROPERTY! YOU'RE PREPARED, TOO, I ASSUME!

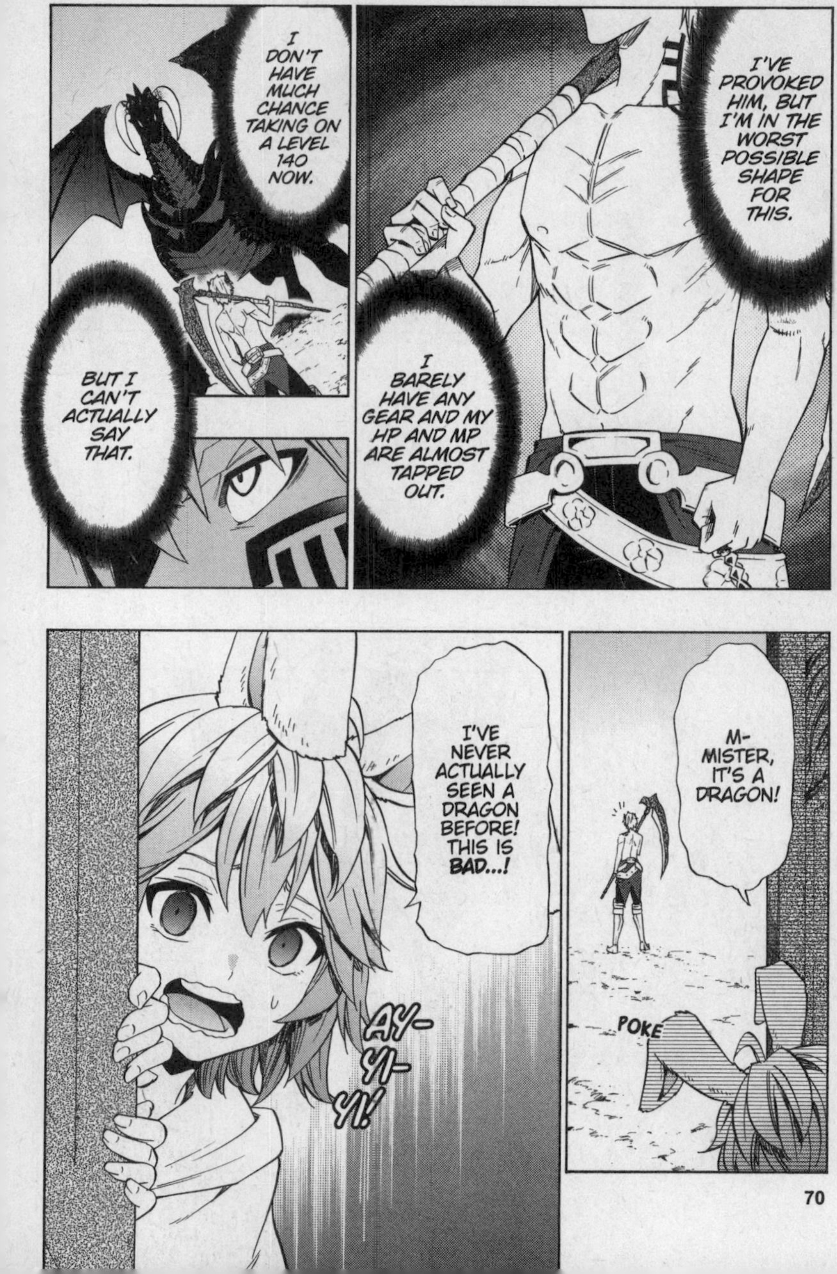
I'VE PROVOKED HIM, BUT I'M IN THE WORST POSSIBLE SHAPE FOR THIS.
I BARELY HAVE ANY GEAR AND MY HP AND MP ARE ALMOST TAPPED OUT.
I DON'T HAVE MUCH CHANCE TAKING ON A LEVEL 140 NOW.
BUT I CAN'T ACTUALLY SAY THAT.
M-MISTER, IT'S A DRAGON!
POKE
I'VE NEVER ACTUALLY SEEN A DRAGON BEFORE! THIS IS BAD...!
AY-YI-YI!

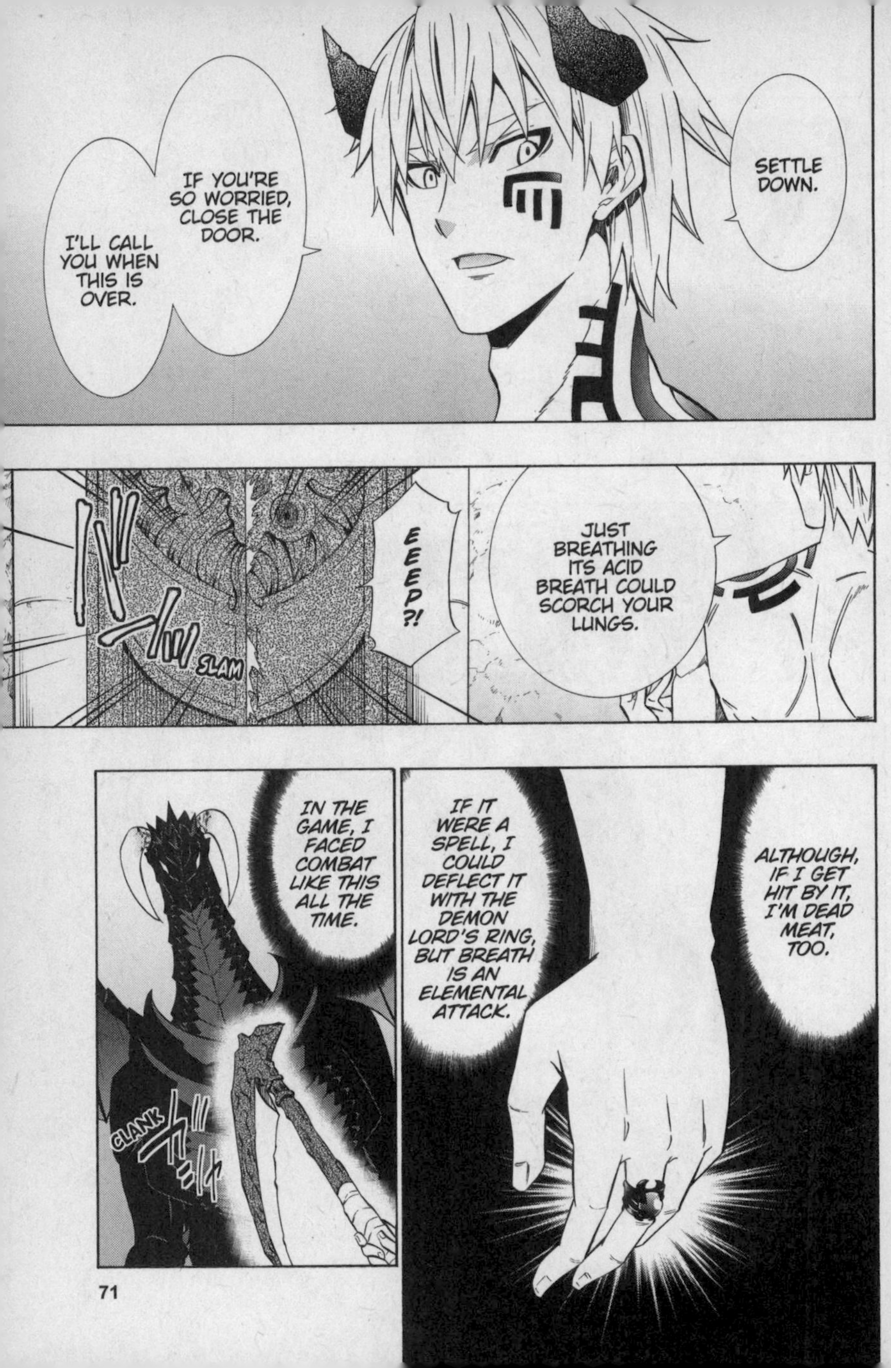
SETTLE DOWN.
IF YOU'RE SO WORRIED, CLOSE THE DOOR.
I'LL CALL YOU WHEN THIS IS OVER.
JUST BREATHING ITS ACID BREATH COULD SCORCH YOUR LUNGS.
EEEP?!
SLAM
ALTHOUGH, IF I GET HIT BY IT, I'M DEAD MEAT, TOO.
IF IT WERE A SPELL, I COULD DEFLECT IT WITH THE DEMON LORD'S RING, BUT BREATH IS AN ELEMENTAL ATTACK.
IN THE GAME, I FACED COMBAT LIKE THIS ALL THE TIME.
CLANK

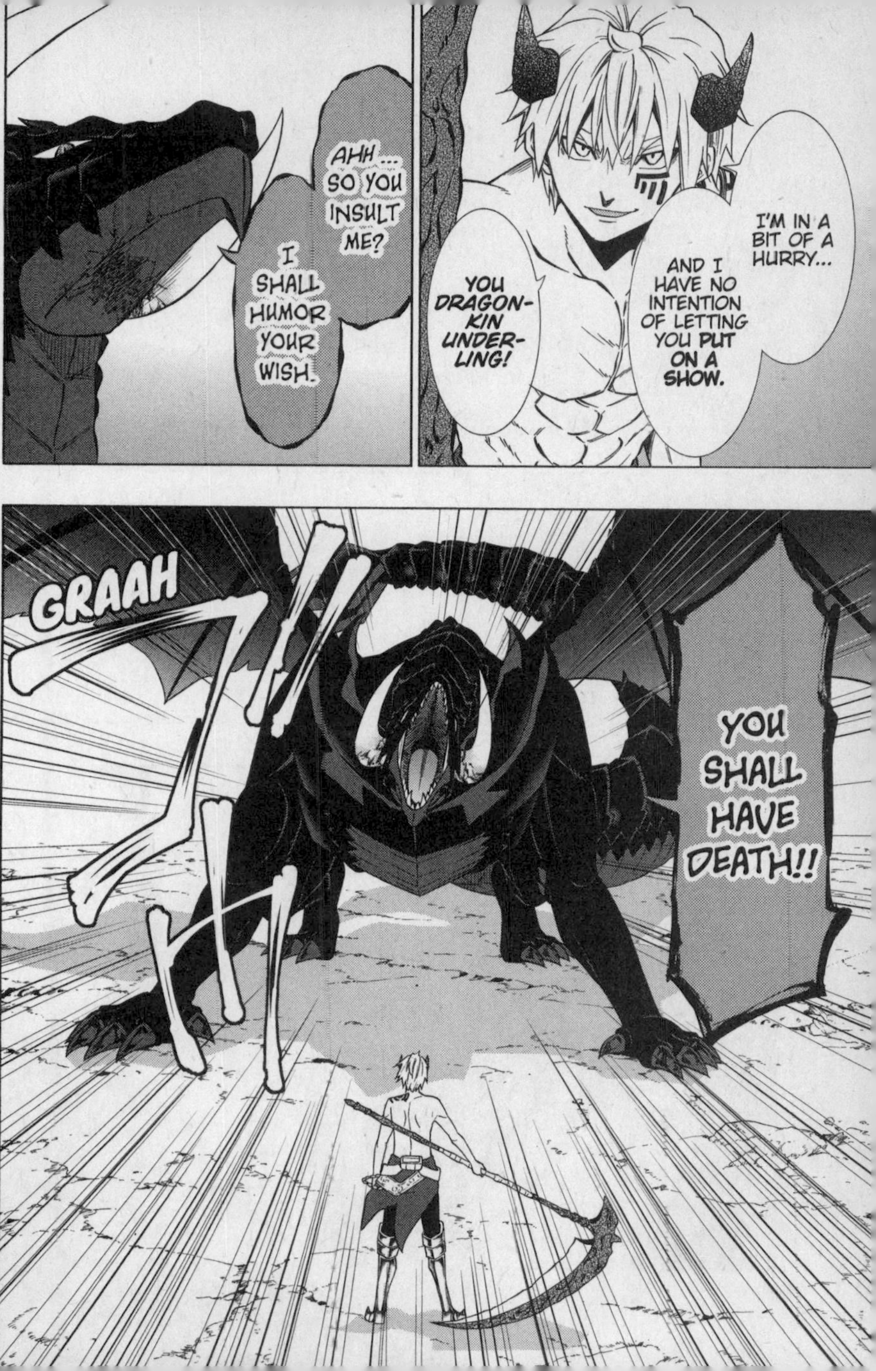
I'M IN A BIT OF A HURRY...
AND I HAVE NO INTENTION OF LETTING YOU PUT ON A SHOW.
YOU DRAGON-KIN UNDER-LING!
AHH... SO YOU INSULT ME?
I SHALL HUMOR YOUR WISH.
YOU SHALL HAVE DEATH!!
GRAAH

HOW NOT
TO SUMMON A
DEMON LORD

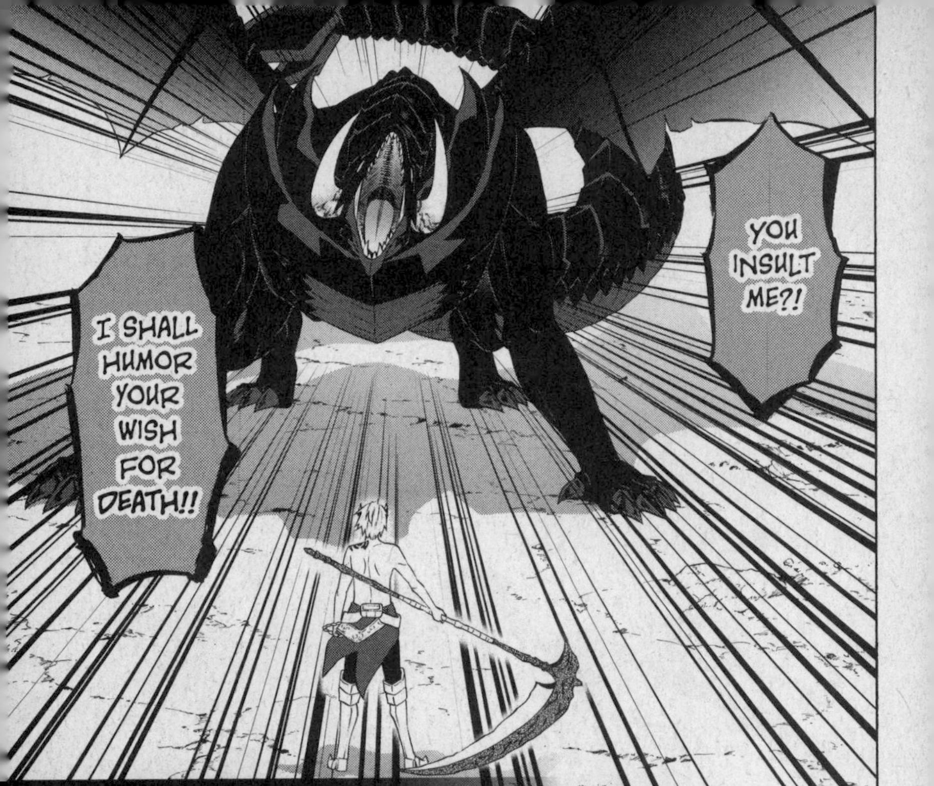
YOU INSULT ME?!
I SHALL HUMOR YOUR WISH FOR DEATH!!

57 SAVING A COMPANION III

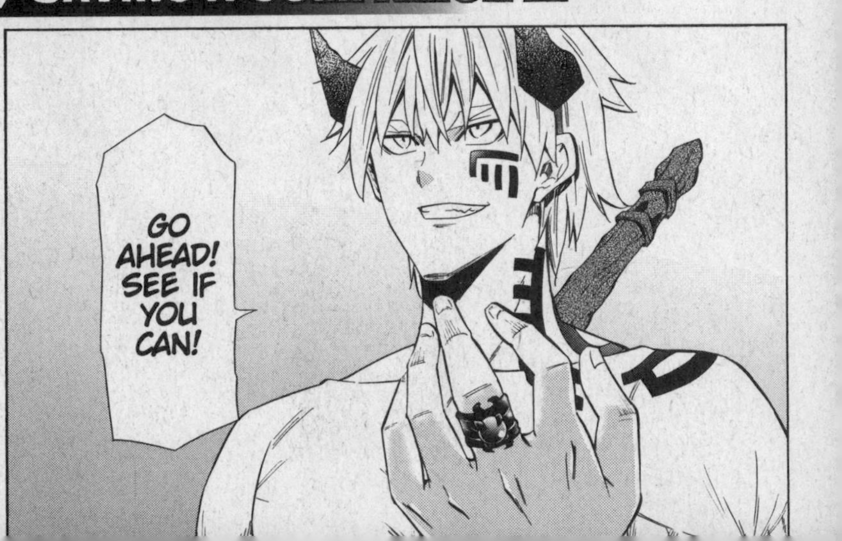
GO AHEAD! SEE IF YOU CAN!

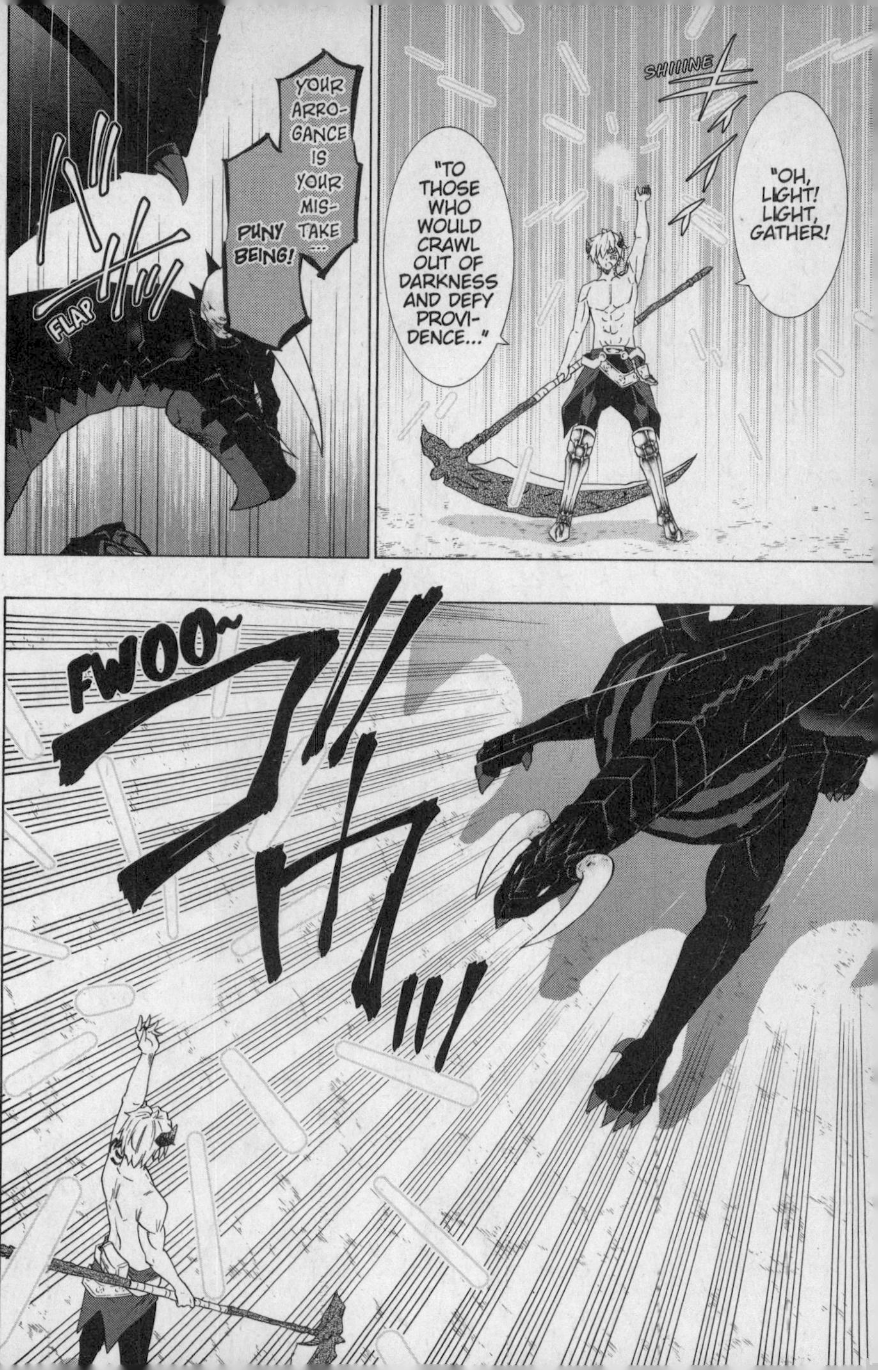
SHIIINE
"OH, LIGHT! LIGHT, GATHER!
"TO THOSE WHO WOULD CRAWL OUT OF DARKNESS AND DEFY PROVIDENCE..."
FLAP
YOUR ARROGANCE IS YOUR MISTAKE...
PUNY BEING!
FWOO

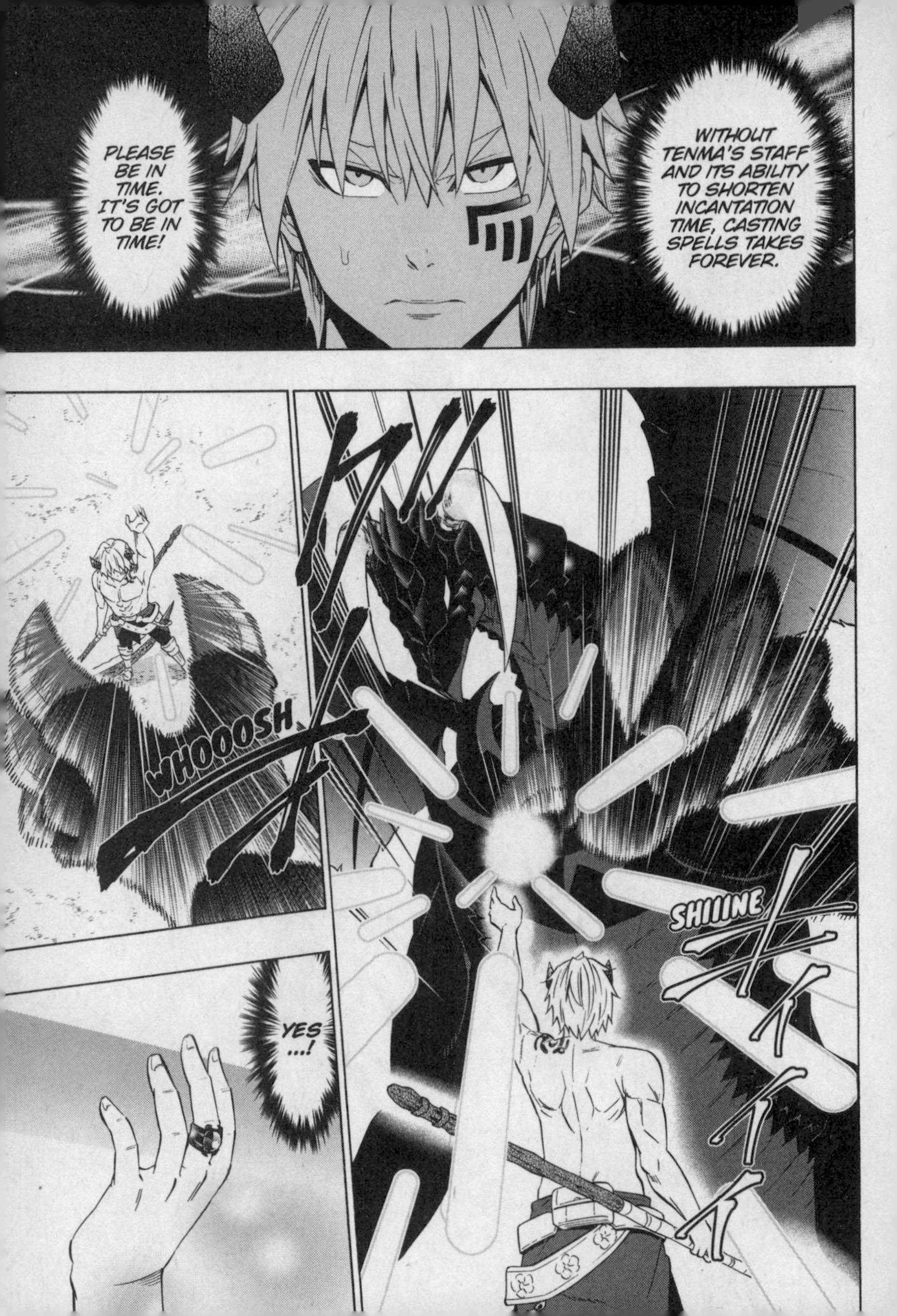
WITHOUT TENMA'S STAFF AND ITS ABILITY TO SHORTEN INCANTATION TIME, CASTING SPELLS TAKES FOREVER.
PLEASE BE IN TIME. IT'S GOT TO BE IN TIME!
SHIIINE
WHOOOSH
YES ...!

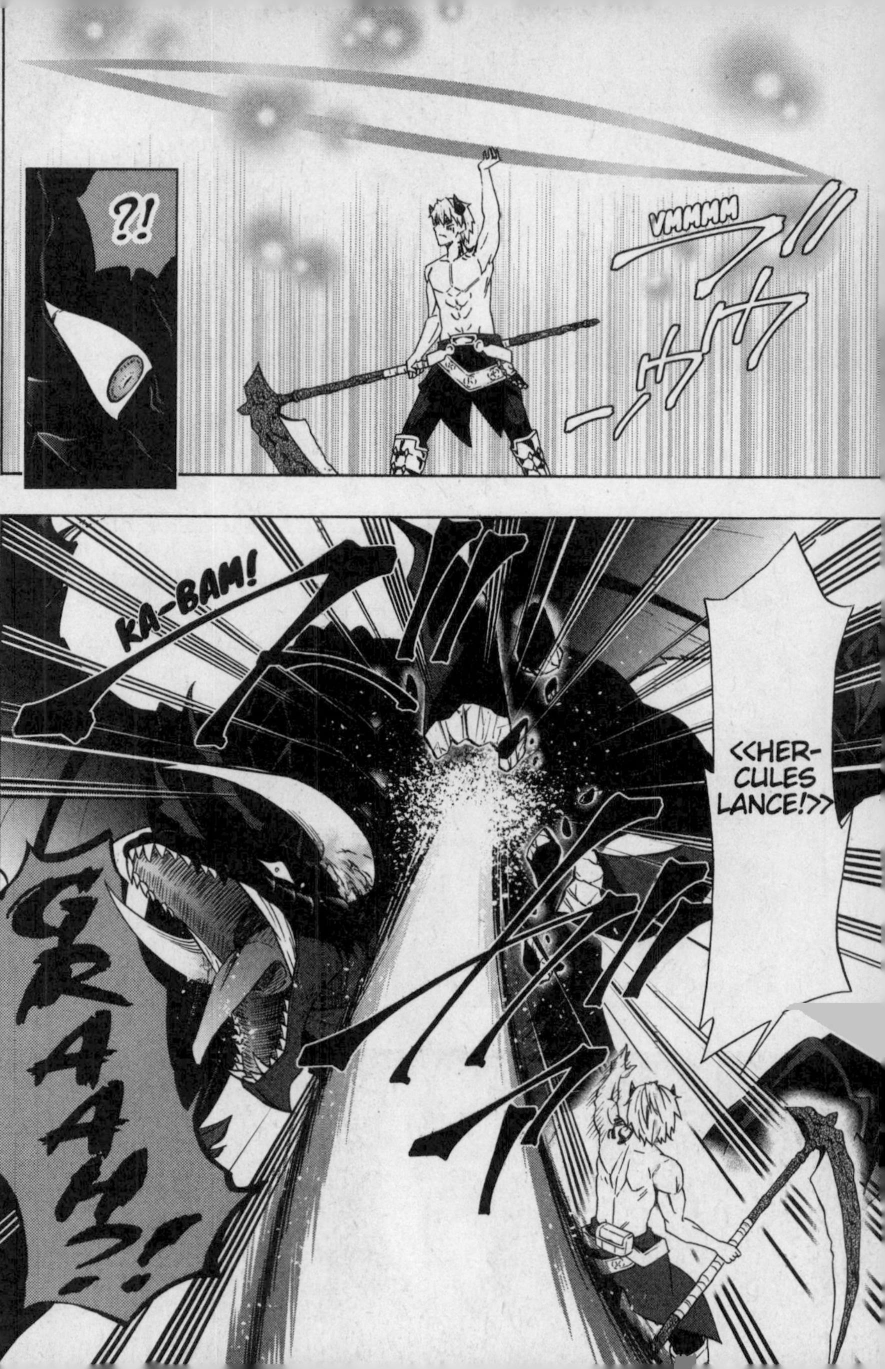
VMMMM
?!
<<HER-
CULES
LANCE!>>
KA-BAM!
GRAAAH?!

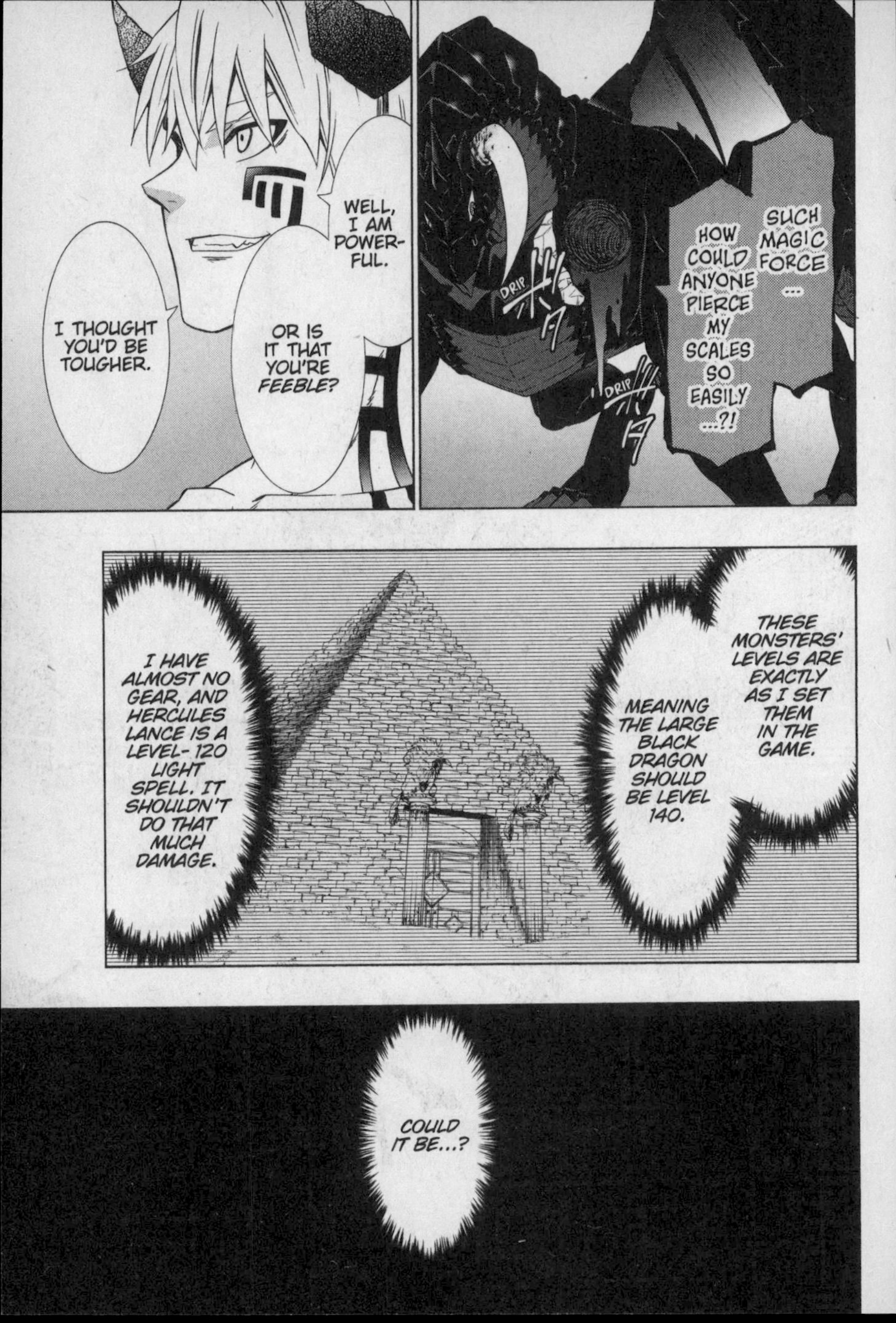
SUCH MAGIC FORCE ...
HOW COULD ANYONE PIERCE MY SCALES SO EASILY ...?!
DRIP
DRIP
WELL, I AM POWERFUL.
OR IS IT THAT YOU'RE FEEBLE?
I THOUGHT YOU'D BE TOUGHER.
THESE MONSTERS' LEVELS ARE EXACTLY AS I SET THEM IN THE GAME.
MEANING THE LARGE BLACK DRAGON SHOULD BE LEVEL 140.
I HAVE ALMOST NO GEAR, AND HERCULES LANCE IS A LEVEL-120 LIGHT SPELL. IT SHOULDN'T DO THAT MUCH DAMAGE.
COULD IT BE...?

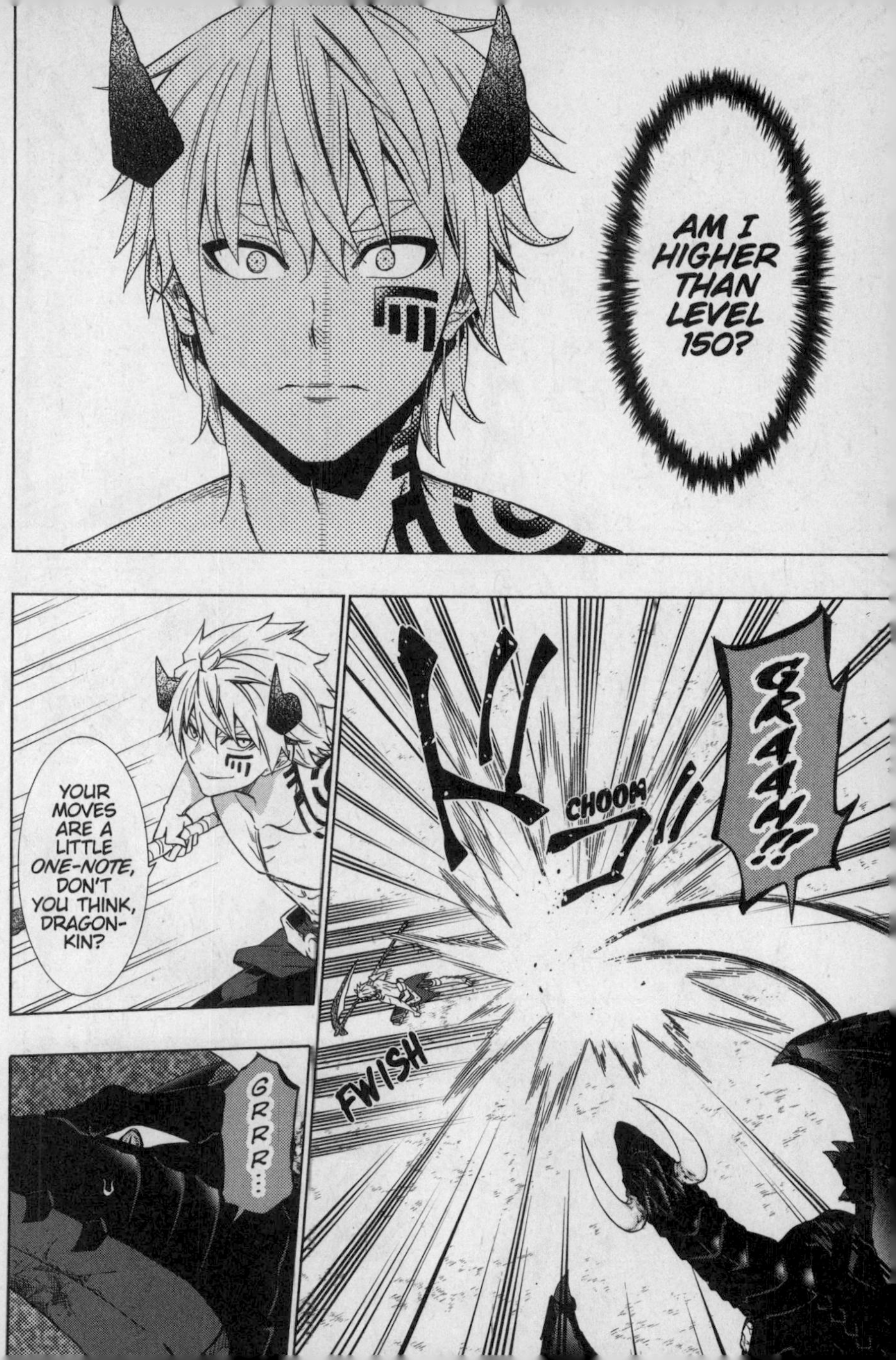
AM I HIGHER THAN LEVEL 150?
GRAAAH!!
CHOOM
FWISH
YOUR MOVES ARE A LITTLE ONE-NOTE, DON'T YOU THINK, DRAGON-KIN?
GRRR...

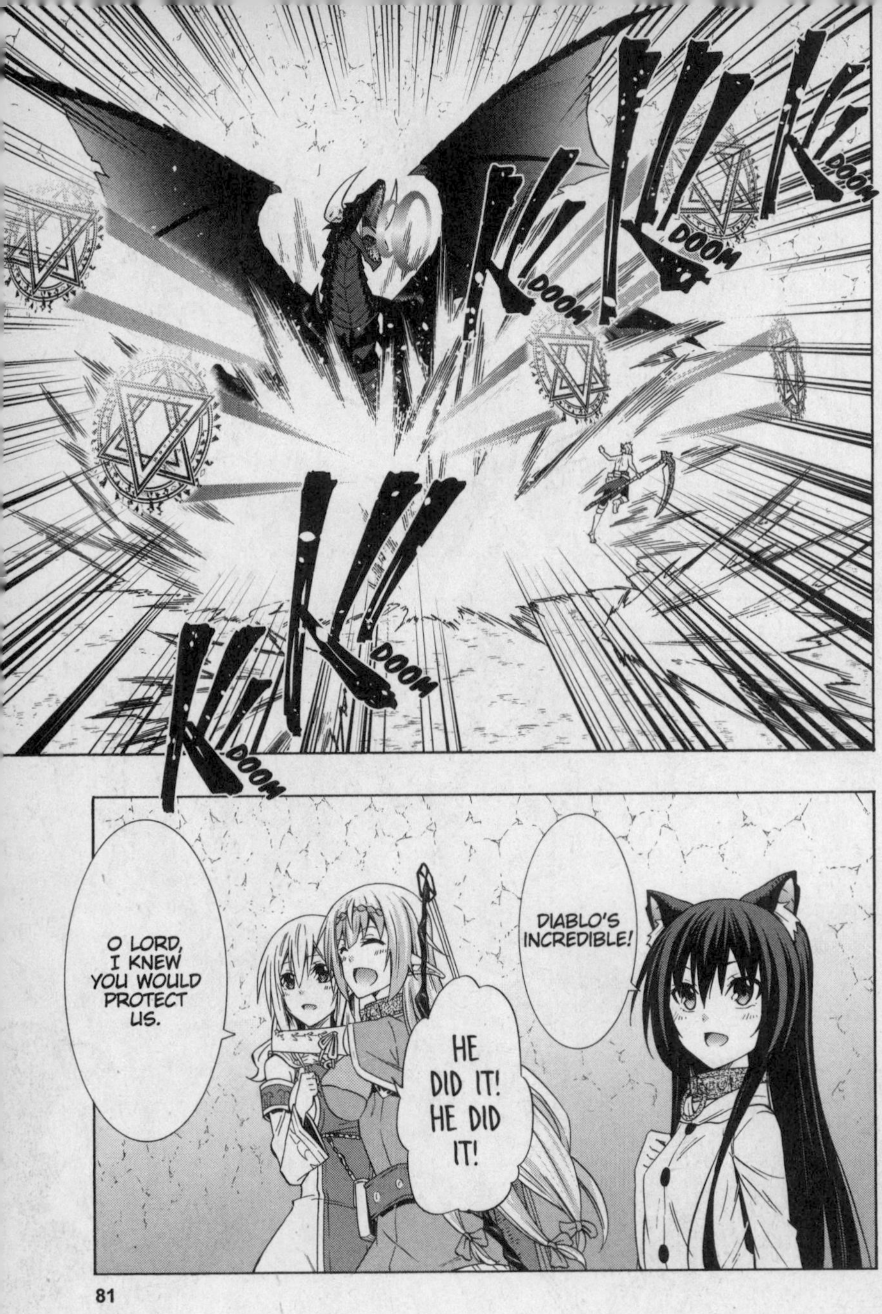
DOOM
DOOM
DOOM
DOOM
DOOM
DIABLO'S INCREDIBLE!
HE DID IT! HE DID IT!
O LORD, I KNEW YOU WOULD PROTECT US.

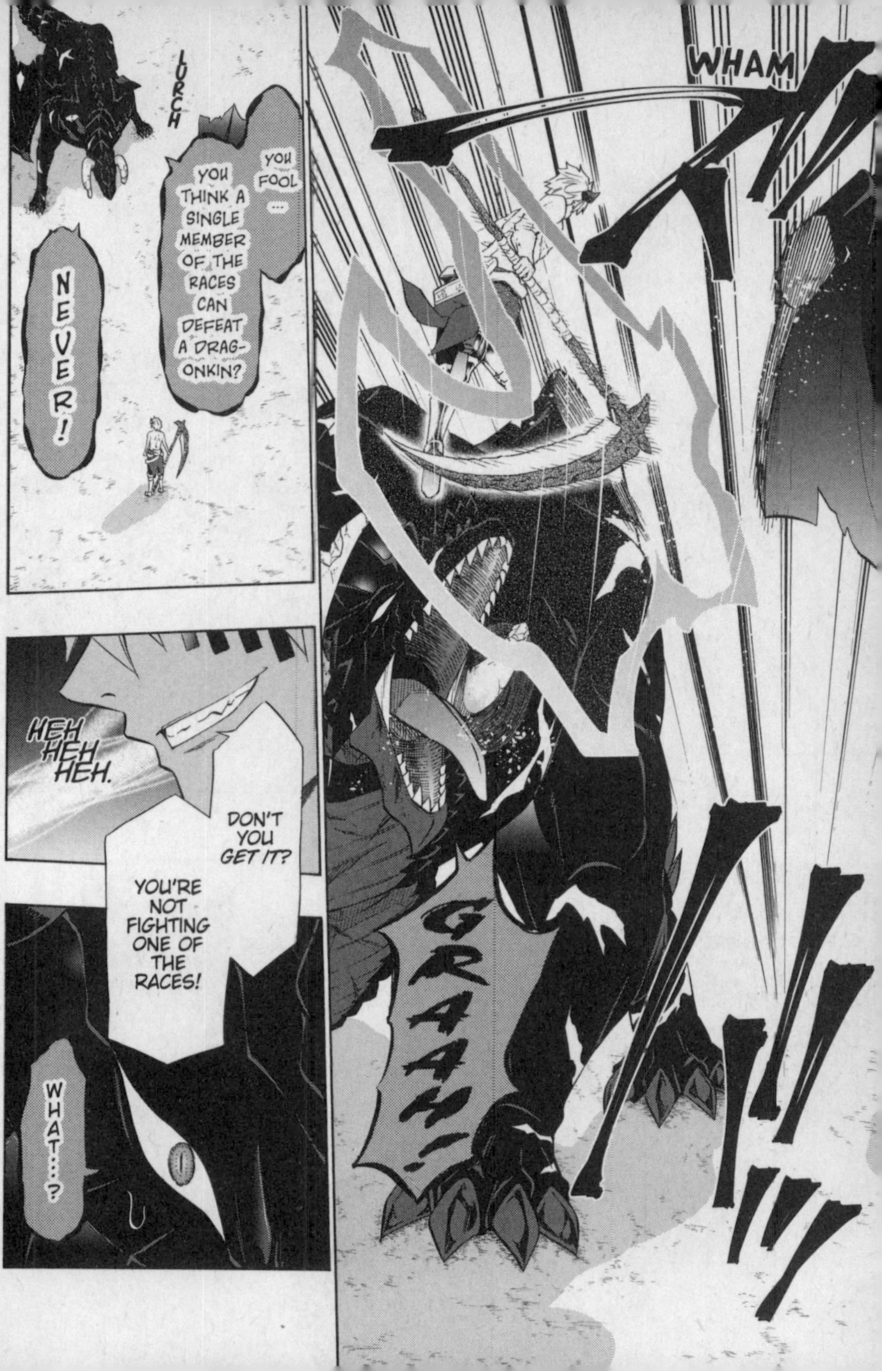

WHAM
GRAAAAH!!!
LURCH
YOU FOOL...
YOU THINK A SINGLE MEMBER OF THE RACES CAN DEFEAT A DRAGONKIN?
NEVER!
HEH HEH HEH.
DON'T YOU GET IT?
YOU'RE NOT FIGHTING ONE OF THE RACES!
WHAT...?

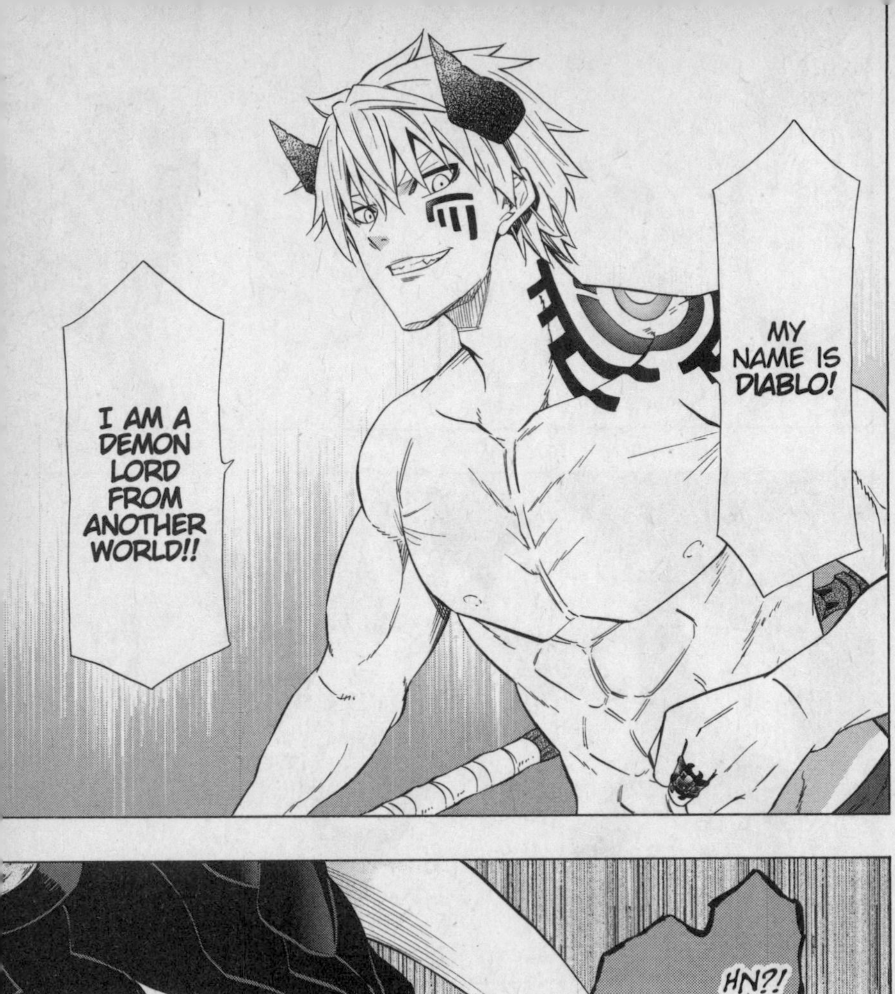
MY NAME IS DIABLO!
I AM A DEMON LORD FROM ANOTHER WORLD!!

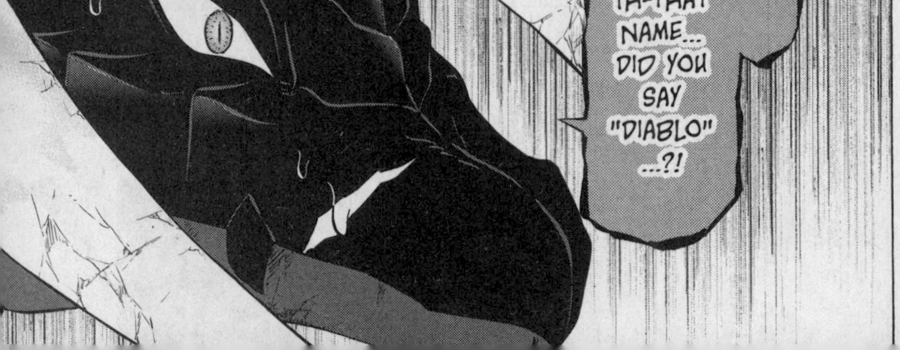
HN?!
TH-THAT NAME... DID YOU SAY "DIABLO" ...?!

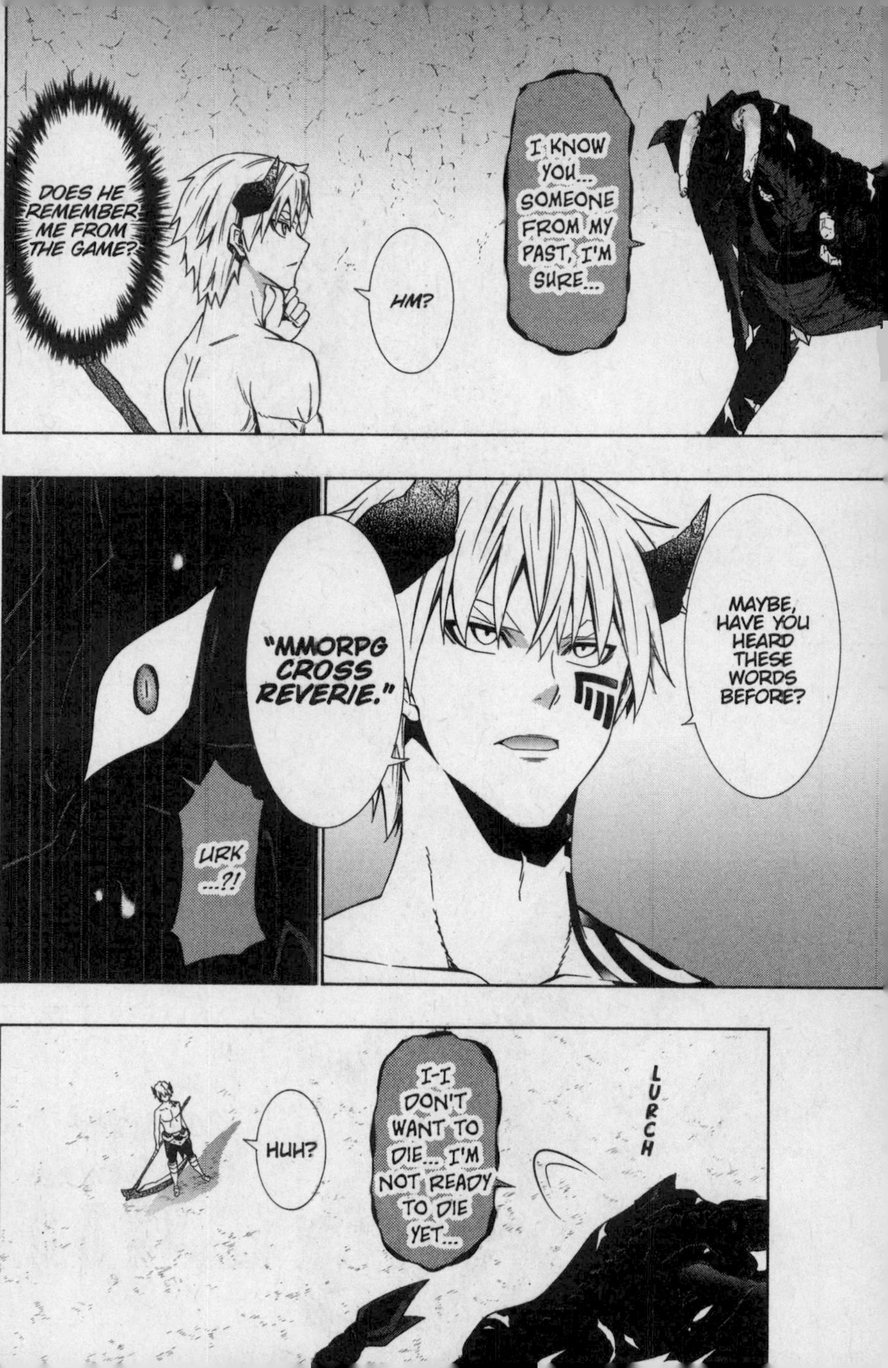
I KNOW YOU... SOMEONE FROM MY PAST, I'M SURE...
HM?
DOES HE REMEMBER ME FROM THE GAME?
MAYBE, HAVE YOU HEARD THESE WORDS BEFORE?
"MMORPG CROSS REVERIE."
URK ...?!
LURCH
I-I DON'T WANT TO DIE... I'M NOT READY TO DIE YET...
HUH?

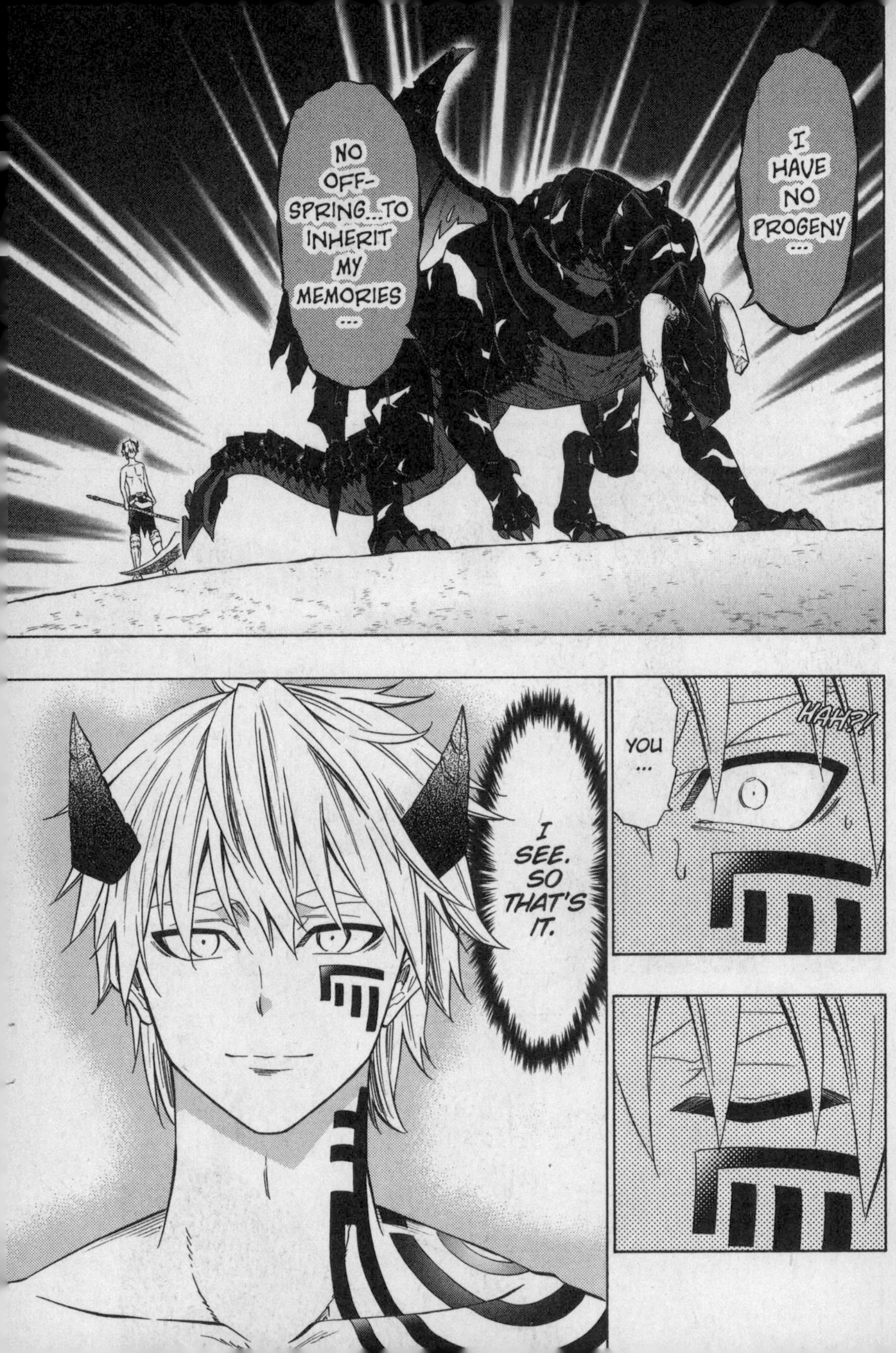
I HAVE NO PROGENY...
NO OFF-SPRING...TO INHERIT MY MEMORIES...
HAH?!
YOU...
I SEE. SO THAT'S IT.

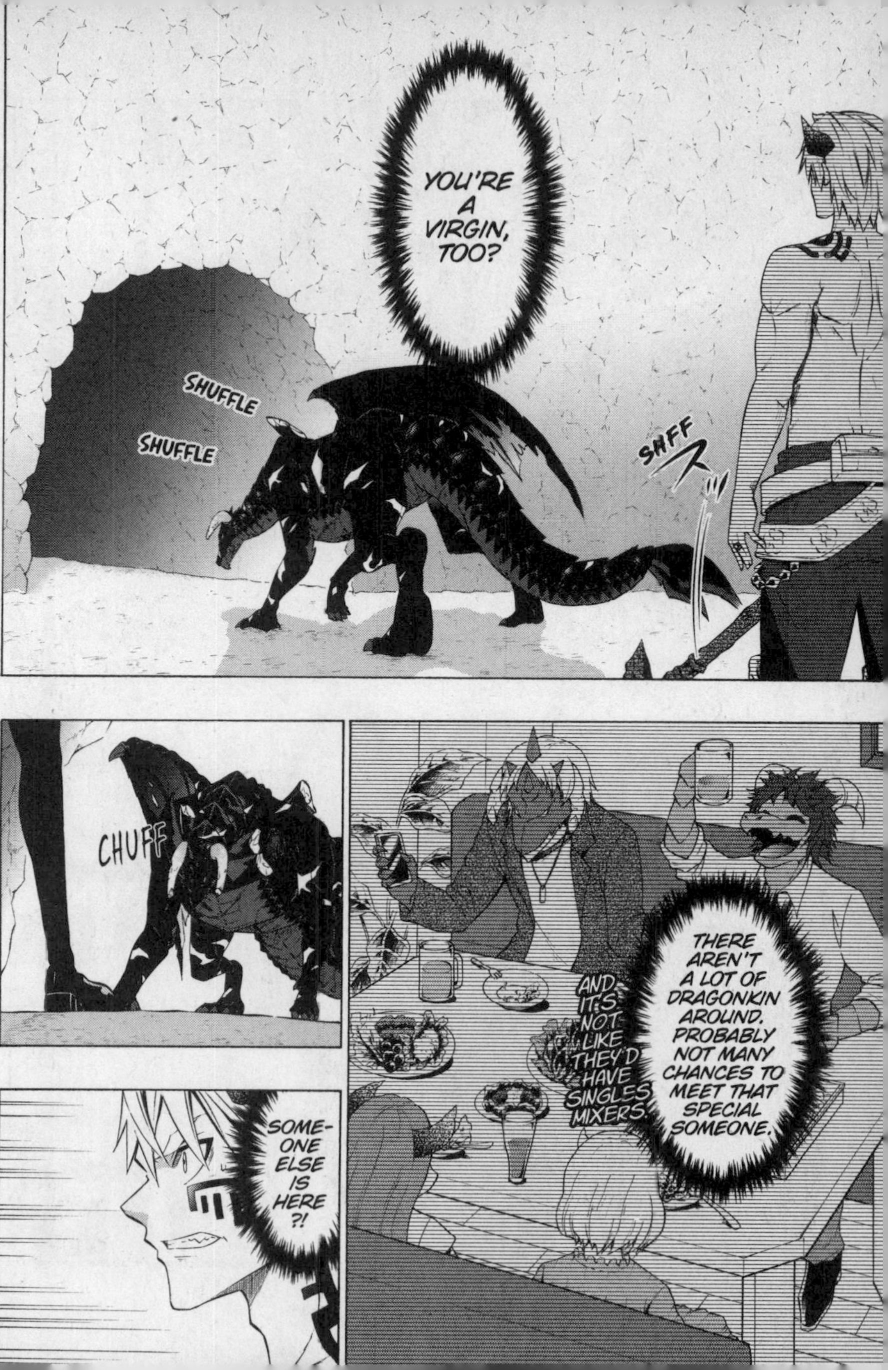
YOU'RE A VIRGIN, TOO?
SHUFFLE
SHUFFLE
SHFF
THERE AREN'T A LOT OF DRAGONKIN AROUND. PROBABLY NOT MANY CHANCES TO MEET THAT SPECIAL SOMEONE.
AND IT'S NOT LIKE THEY'D HAVE SINGLES MIXERS.
CHUFF
SOME-ONE ELSE IS HERE?!

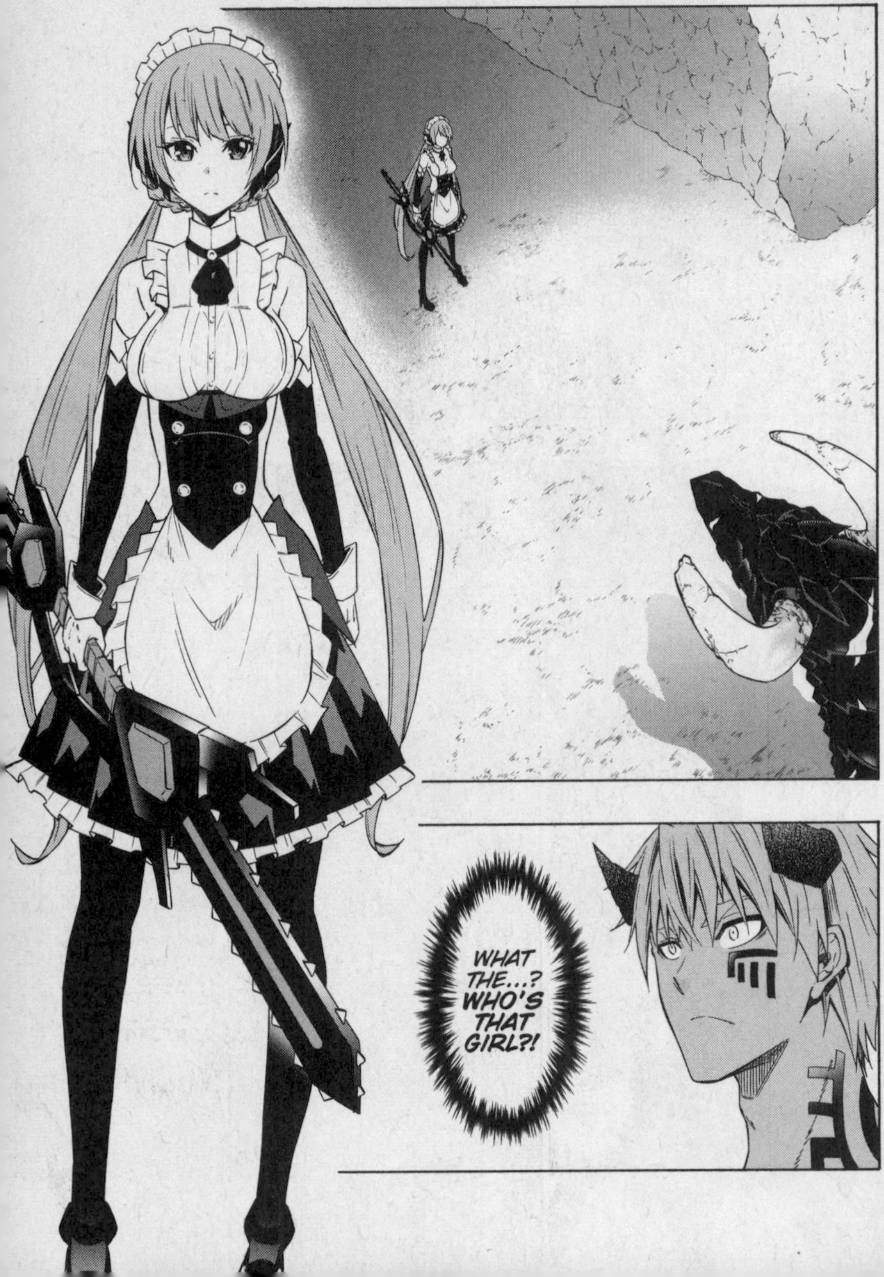
WHAT THE...? WHO'S THAT GIRL?!

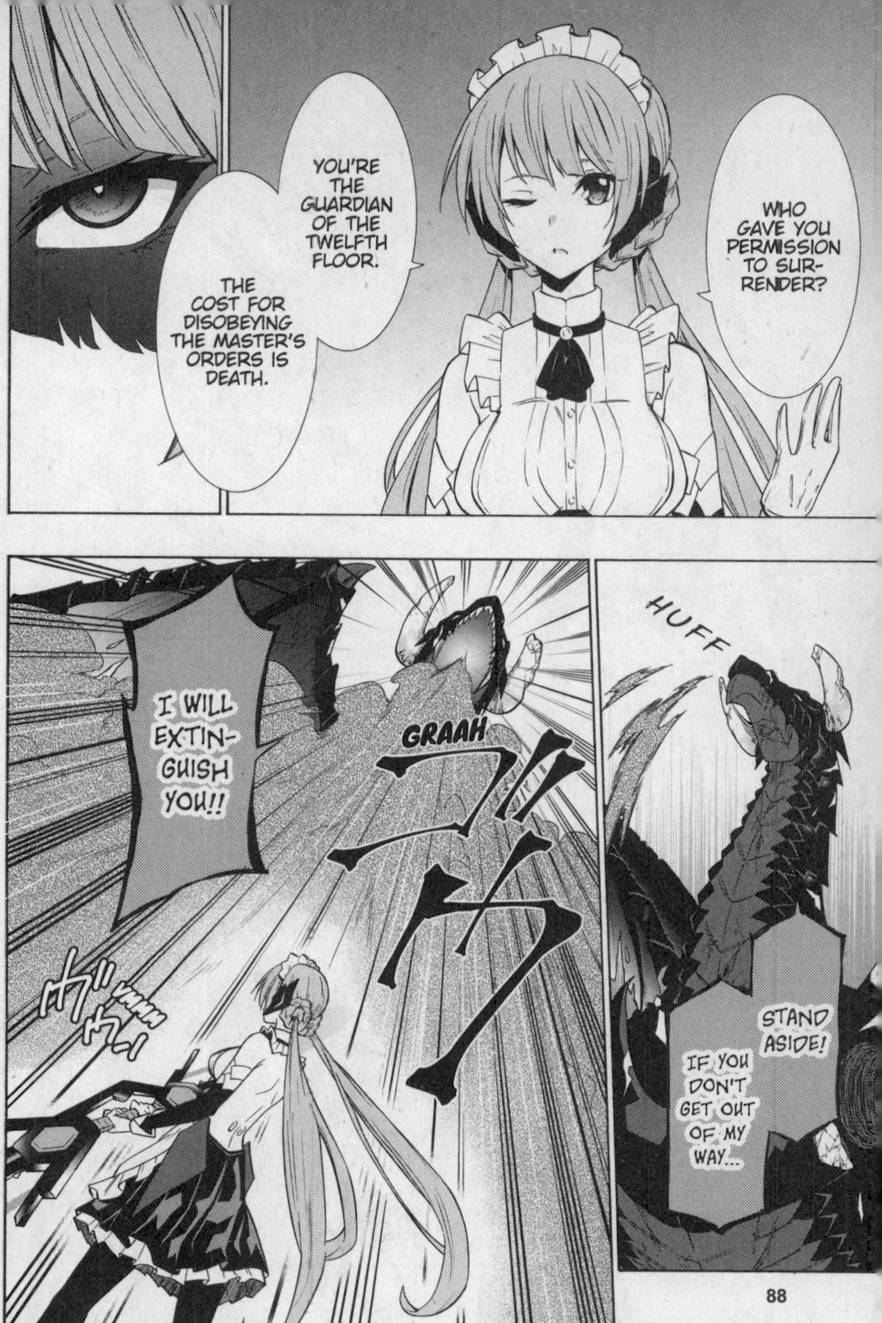
WHO GAVE YOU PERMISSION TO SUR-RENDER?
YOU'RE THE GUARDIAN OF THE TWELFTH FLOOR.
THE COST FOR DISOBEYING THE MASTER'S ORDERS IS DEATH.
HUFF
STAND ASIDE!
IF YOU DON'T GET OUT OF MY WAY...
I WILL EXTIN-GUISH YOU!!
GRAAH
VMMM

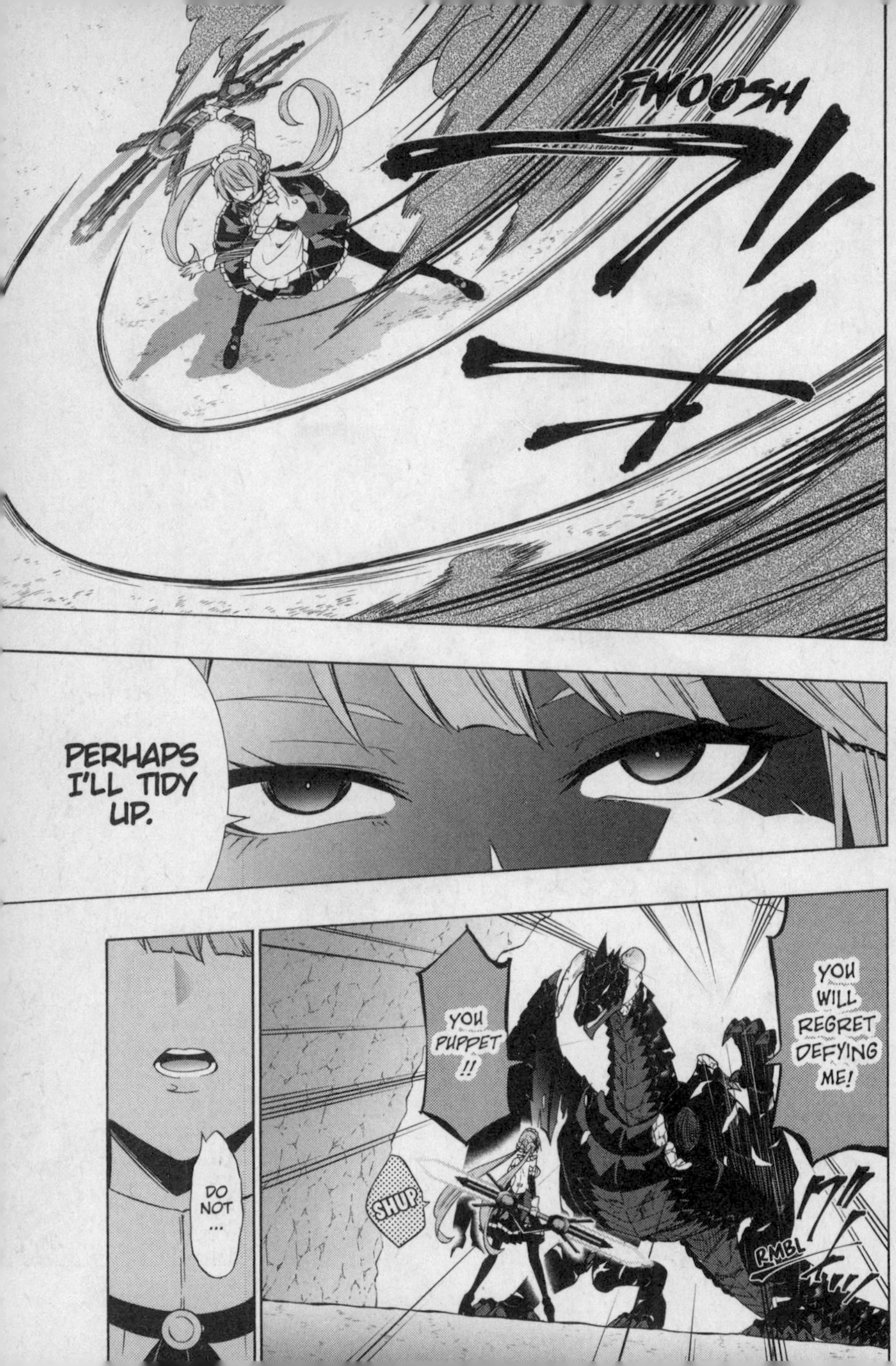
FWOOSH
PERHAPS I'LL TIDY UP.
YOU WILL REGRET DEFYING ME!
YOU PUPPET !!
RMBL
SHUP
DO NOT ...

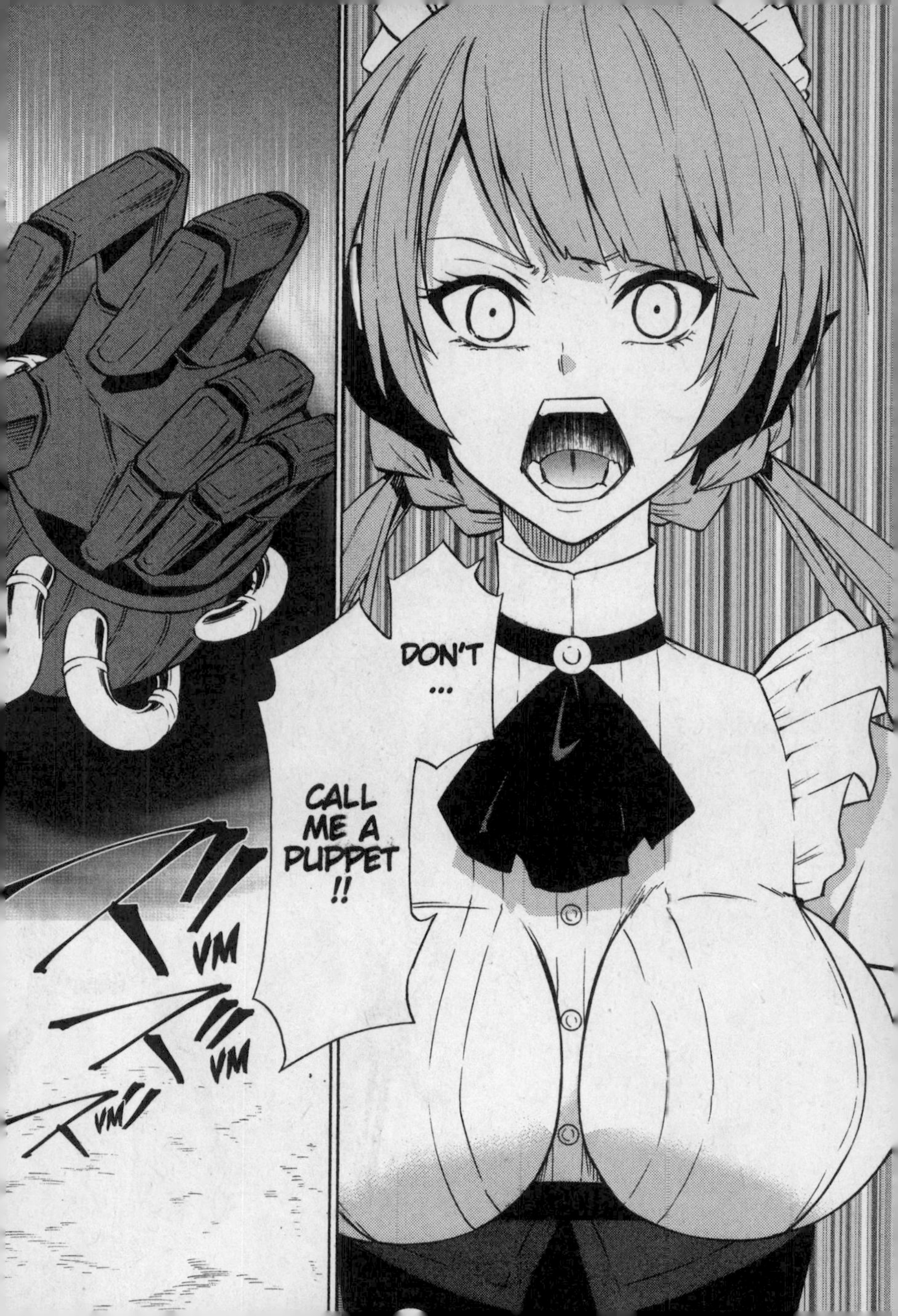
DON'T ...
CALL ME A PUPPET !!
VM
VM
VM

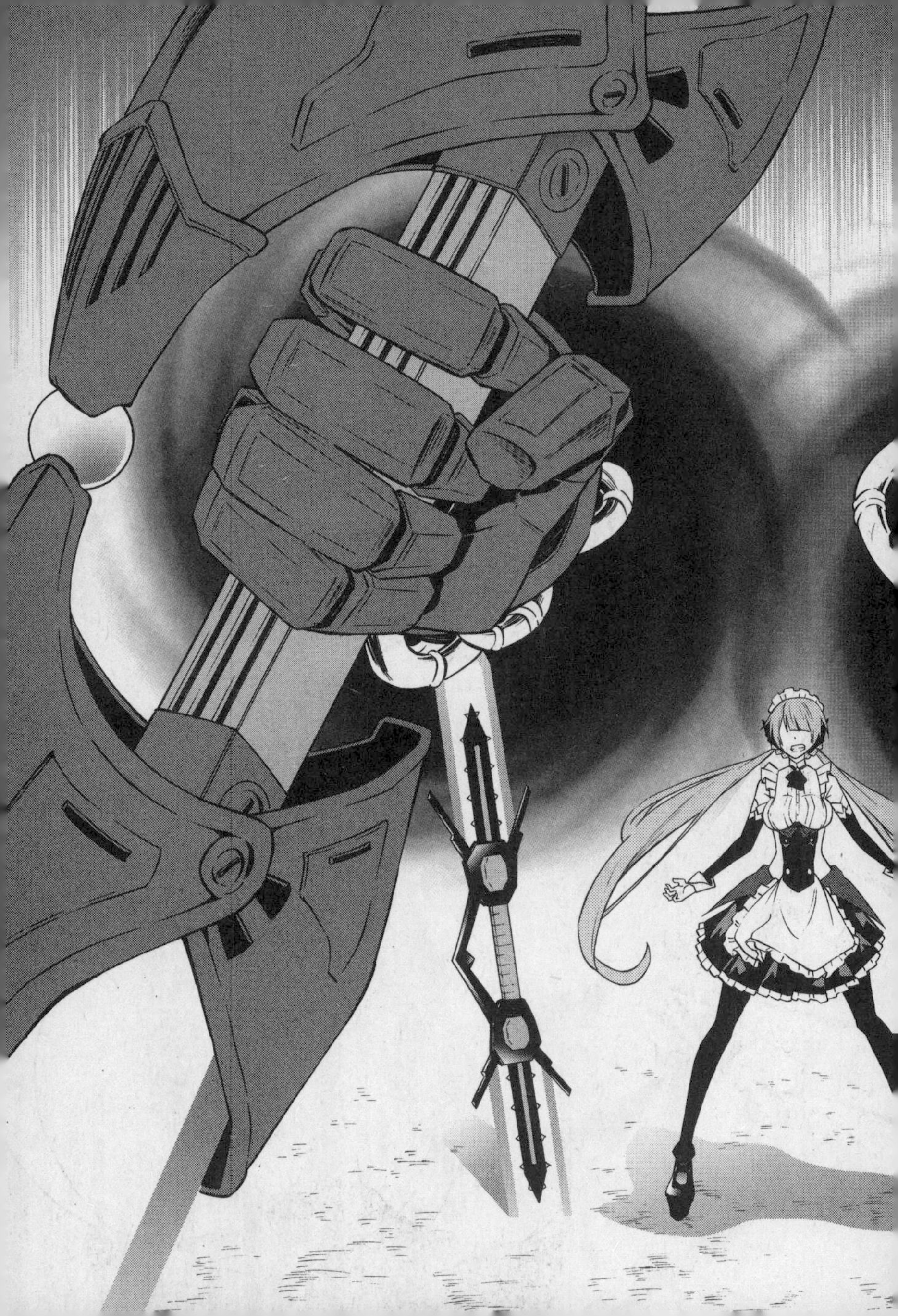

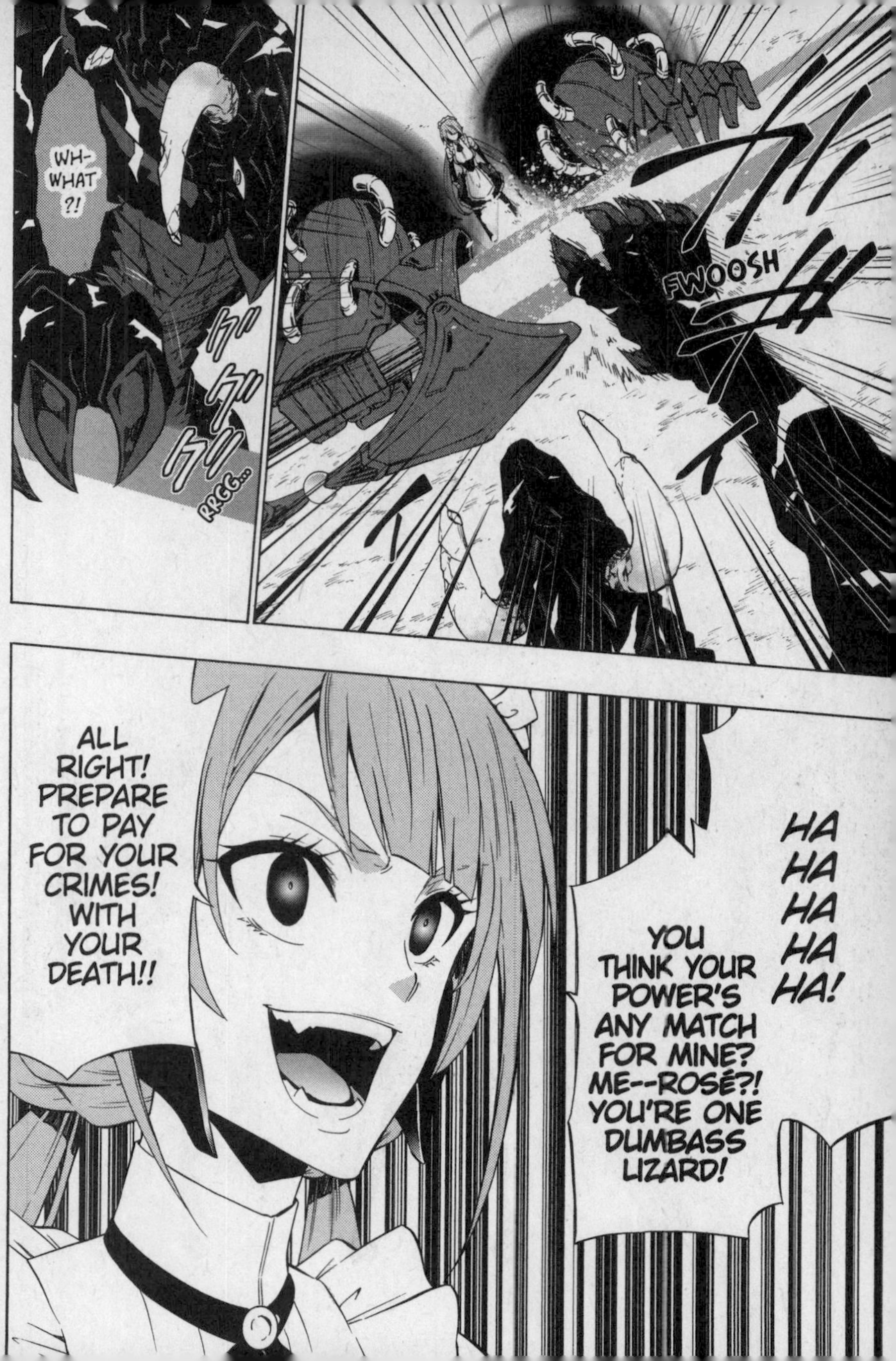
FWOOSH
WH-WHAT?!
RRGG...
HA HA HA HA HA!
YOU THINK YOUR POWER'S ANY MATCH FOR MINE? ME--ROSÉ?! YOU'RE ONE DUMBASS LIZARD!
ALL RIGHT! PREPARE TO PAY FOR YOUR CRIMES! WITH YOUR DEATH!!

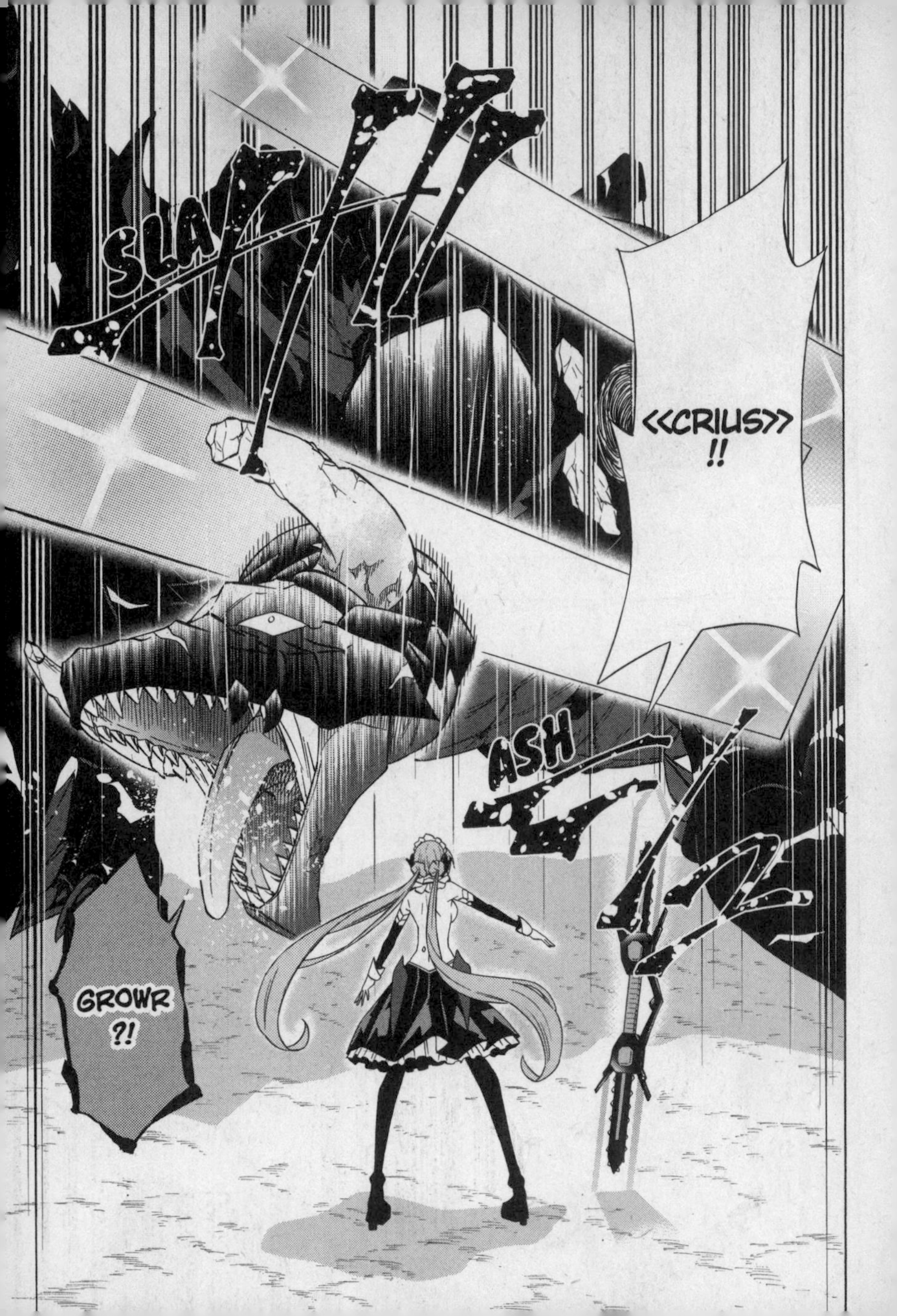
<<CRIUS>> !!
SLA
ASH
GROWR ?!

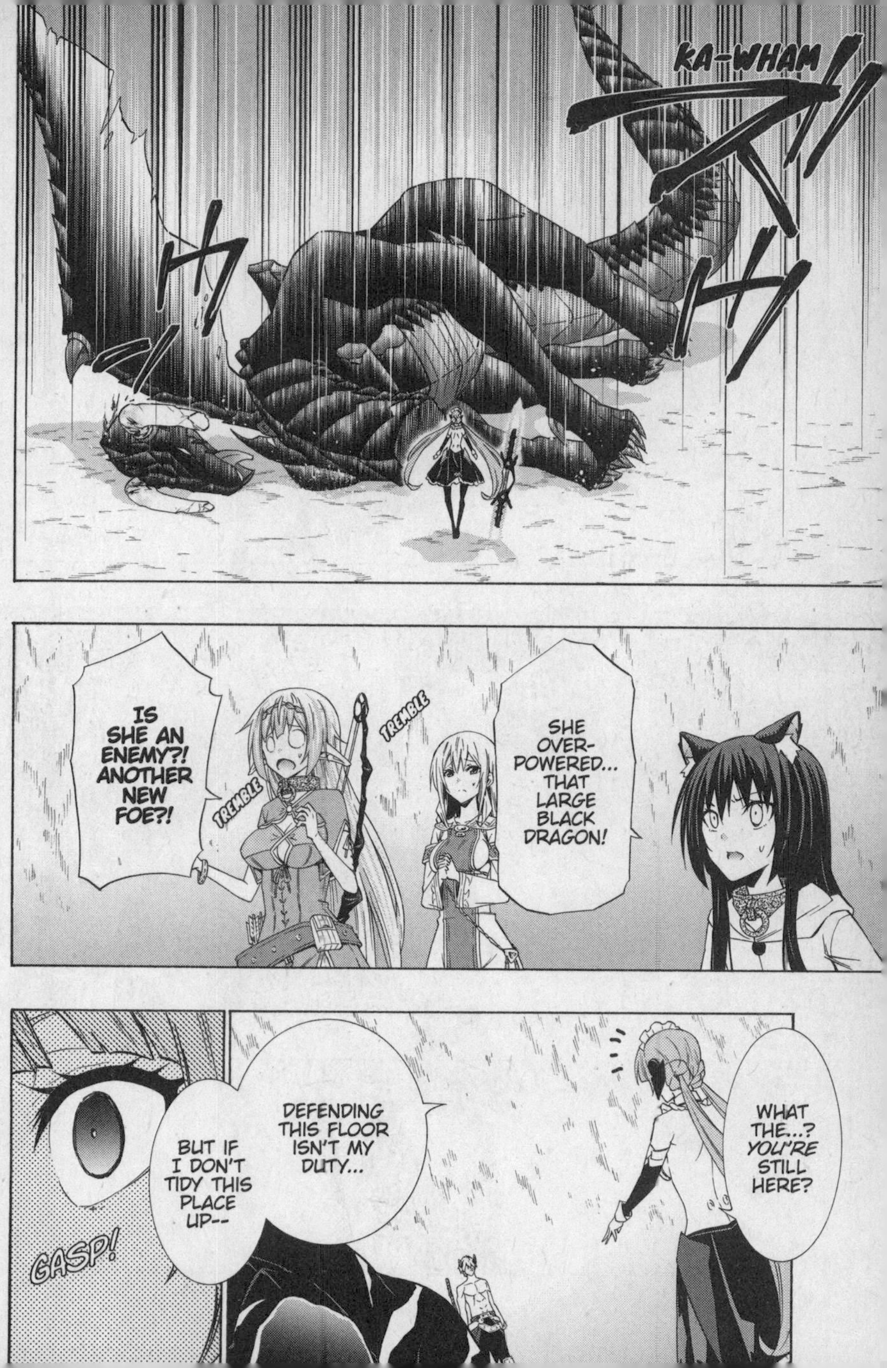
KA-WHAM
SHE OVER-POWERED... THAT LARGE BLACK DRAGON!
TREMBLE
IS SHE AN ENEMY?! ANOTHER NEW FOE?!
TREMBLE
WHAT THE...? YOU'RE STILL HERE?
DEFENDING THIS FLOOR ISN'T MY DUTY...
BUT IF I DON'T TIDY THIS PLACE UP--
GASP!

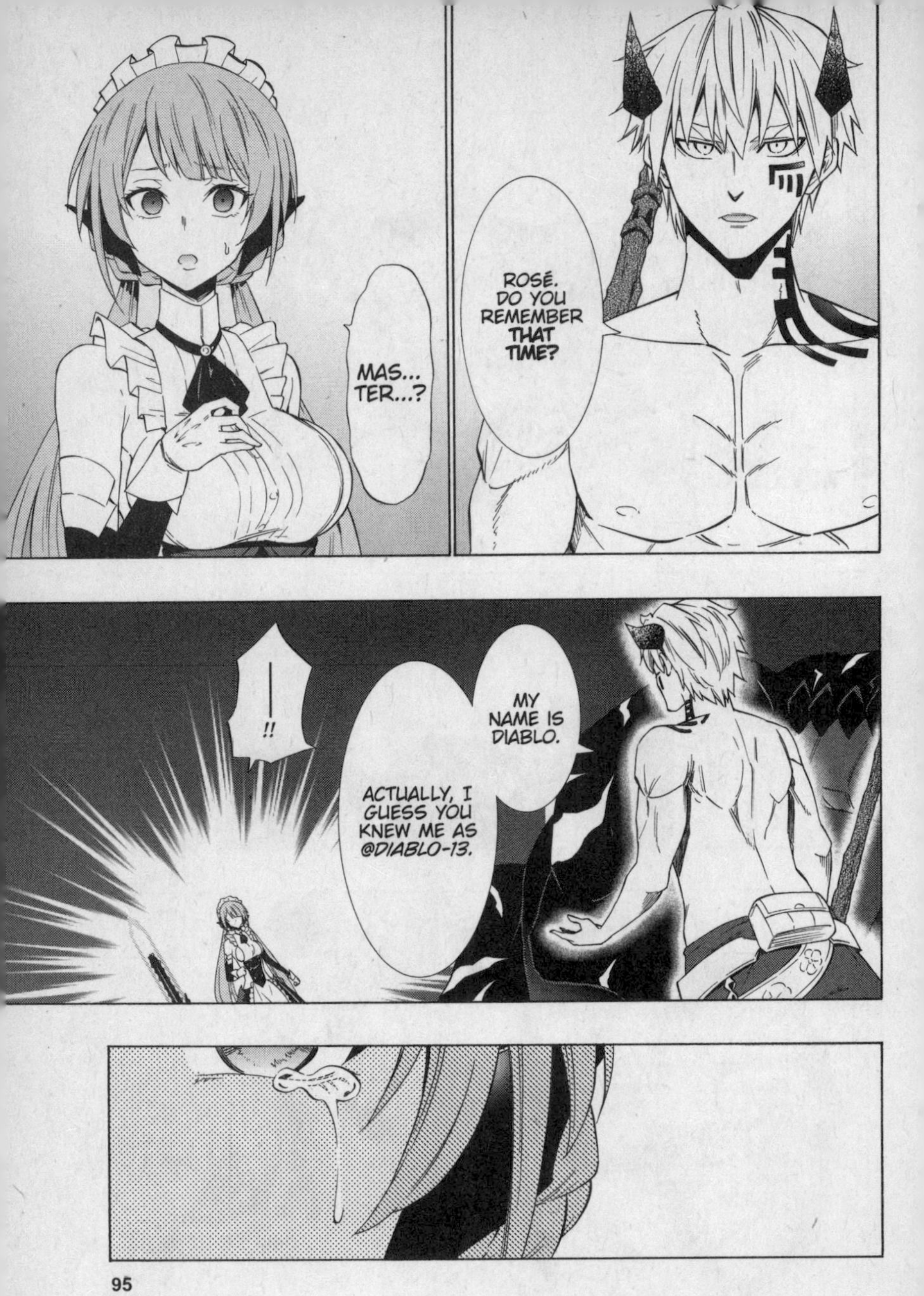
ROSÉ. DO YOU REMEMBER THAT TIME?
MAS... TER...?
MY NAME IS DIABLO.
ACTUALLY, I GUESS YOU KNEW ME AS @DIABLO-13.
—!!

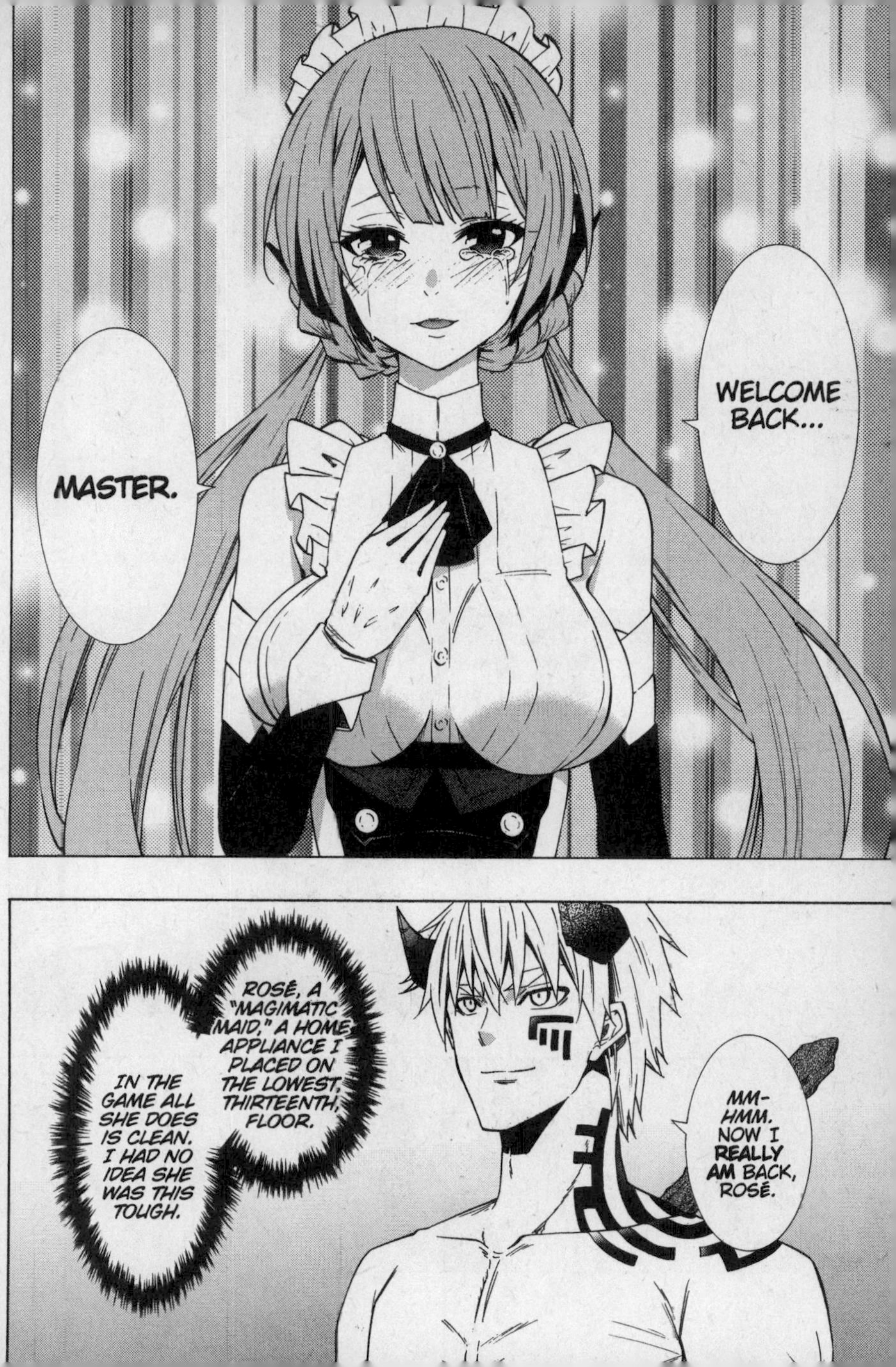
WELCOME BACK...
MASTER.
MM-HMM. NOW I REALLY AM BACK, ROSÉ.
ROSÉ, A "MAGIMATIC MAID," A HOME APPLIANCE I PLACED ON THE LOWEST, THIRTEENTH, FLOOR.
IN THE GAME ALL SHE DOES IS CLEAN. I HAD NO IDEA SHE WAS THIS TOUGH.

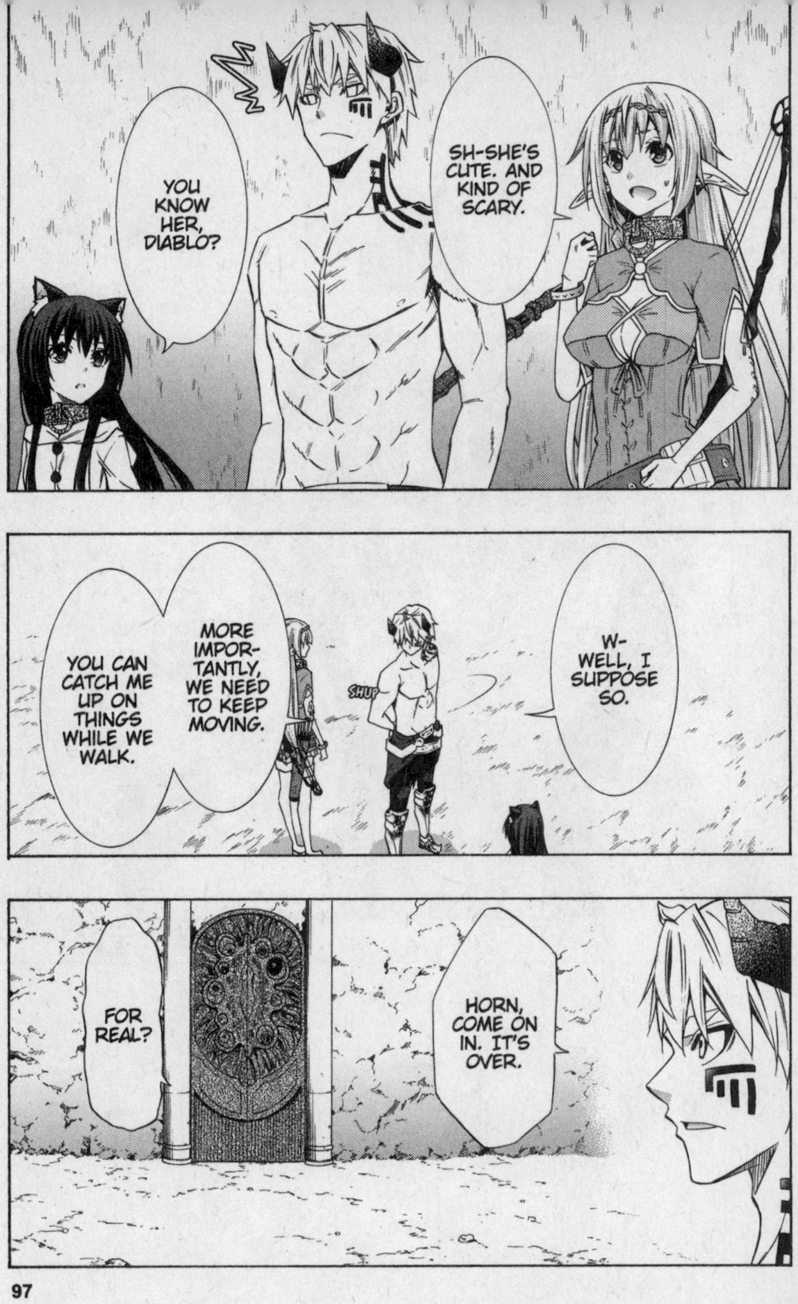
SH-SHE'S CUTE. AND KIND OF SCARY.
YOU KNOW HER, DIABLO?
W-WELL, I SUPPOSE SO.
SHUP
MORE IMPORTANTLY, WE NEED TO KEEP MOVING.
YOU CAN CATCH ME UP ON THINGS WHILE WE WALK.
HORN, COME ON IN. IT'S OVER.
FOR REAL?

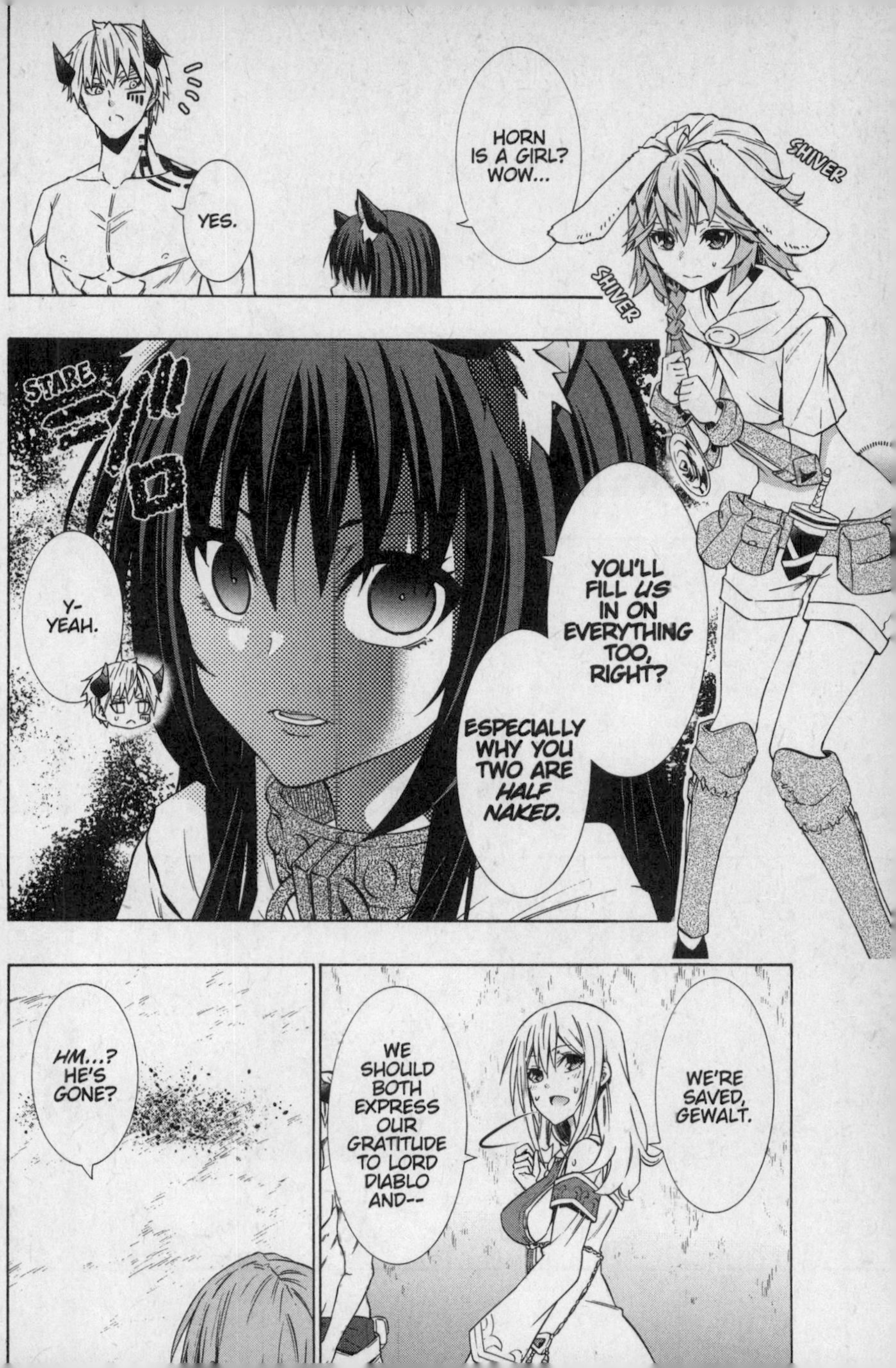
SHIVER
SHIVER
HORN IS A GIRL? WOW...
YES.
YOU'LL FILL US IN ON EVERYTHING TOO, RIGHT?
ESPECIALLY WHY YOU TWO ARE HALF NAKED.
STARE
Y-YEAH.
WE'RE SAVED, GEWALT.
WE SHOULD BOTH EXPRESS OUR GRATITUDE TO LORD DIABLO AND--
HM...? HE'S GONE?

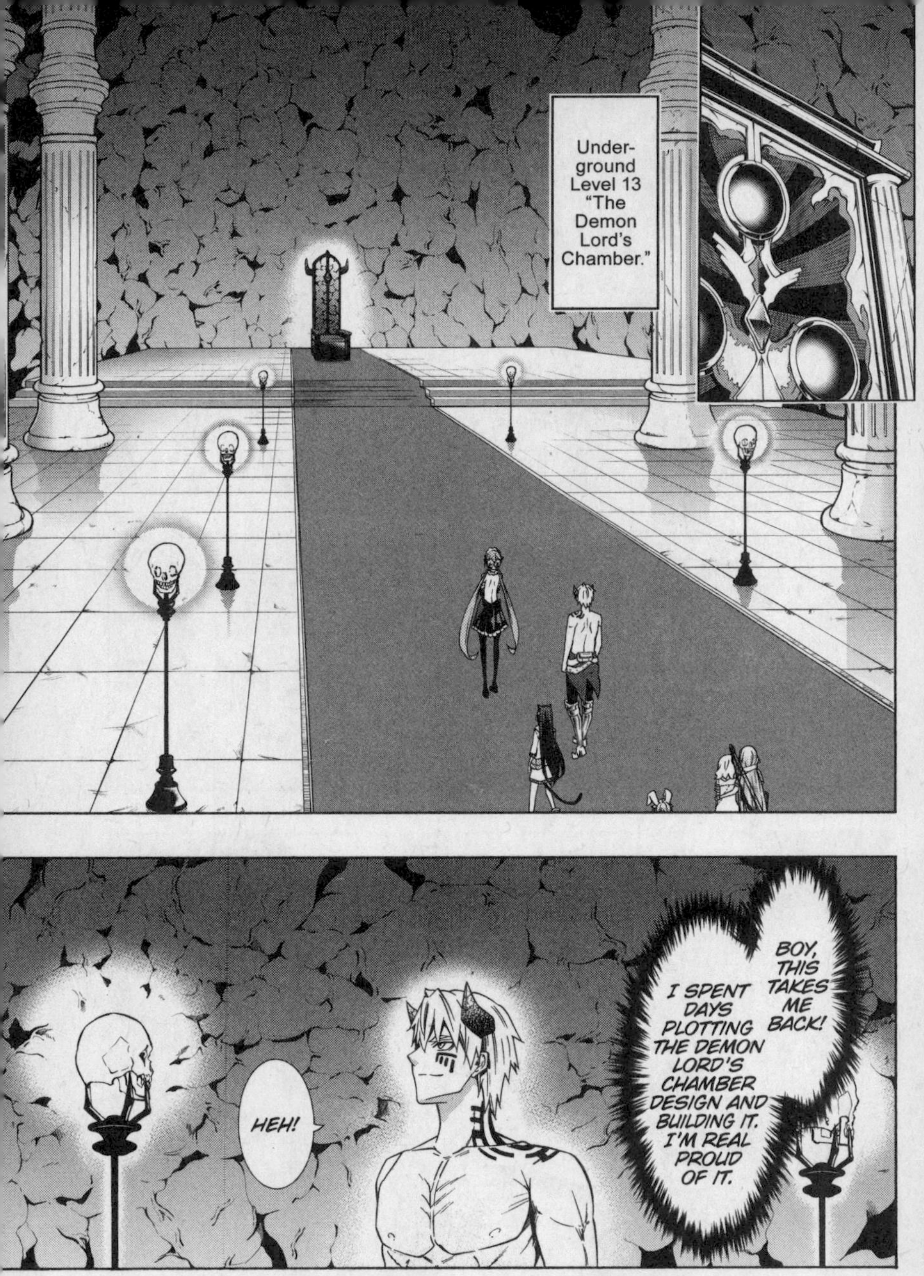

Under-ground Level 13 "The Demon Lord's Chamber."
BOY, THIS TAKES ME BACK!
I SPENT DAYS PLOTTING THE DEMON LORD'S CHAMBER DESIGN AND BUILDING IT. I'M REAL PROUD OF IT.
HEH!

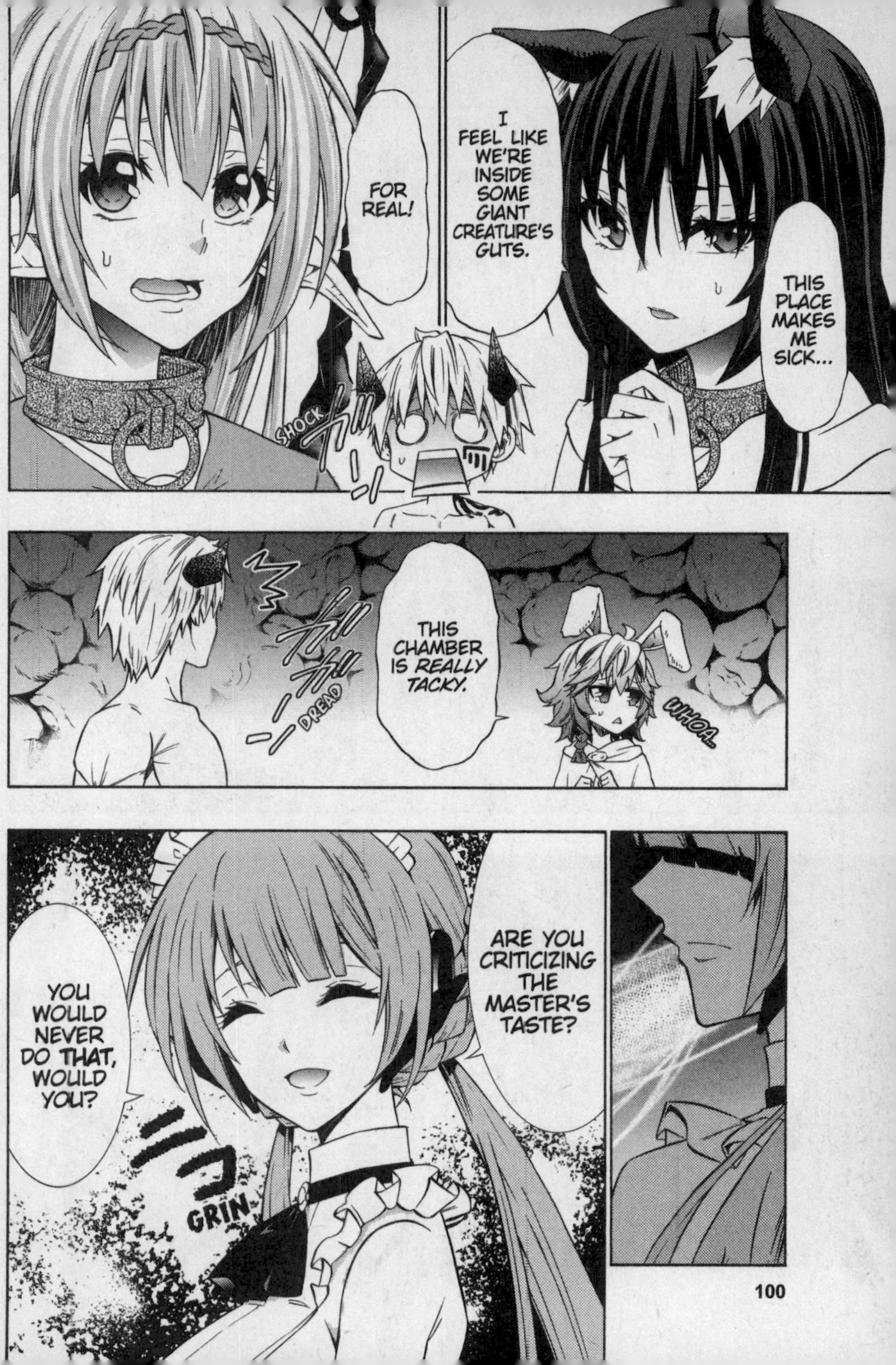
THIS PLACE MAKES ME SICK...
I FEEL LIKE WE'RE INSIDE SOME GIANT CREATURE'S GUTS.
FOR REAL!
SHOCK
WHOA...
THIS CHAMBER IS *REALLY* TACKY.
DREAD
ARE YOU CRITICIZING THE MASTER'S TASTE?
YOU WOULD NEVER DO THAT, WOULD YOU?
GRIN

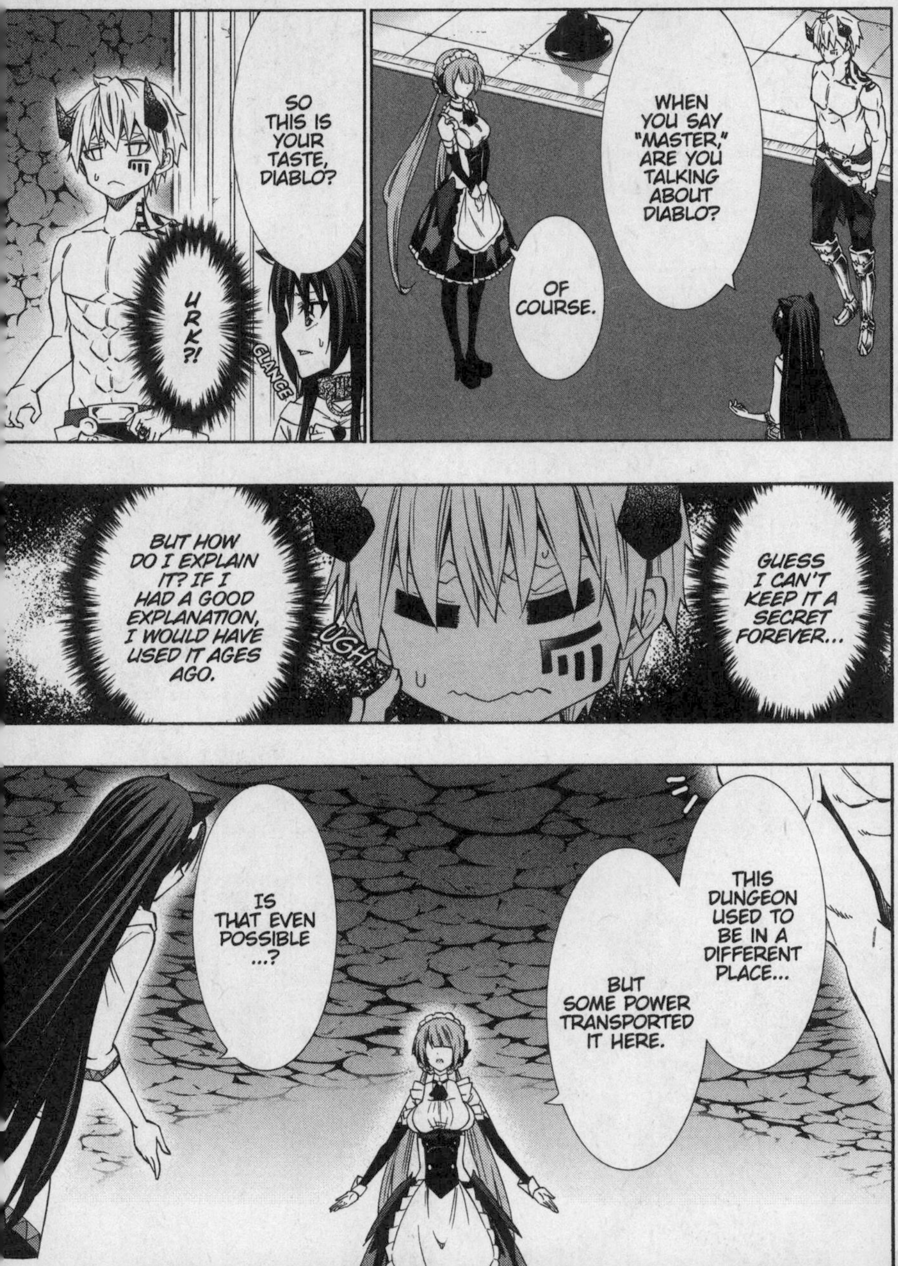
WHEN YOU SAY "MASTER," ARE YOU TALKING ABOUT DIABLO?
OF COURSE.
SO THIS IS YOUR TASTE, DIABLO?
URK?!
GLANCE
GUESS I CAN'T KEEP IT A SECRET FOREVER...
UGH
BUT HOW DO I EXPLAIN IT? IF I HAD A GOOD EXPLANATION, I WOULD HAVE USED IT AGES AGO.
THIS DUNGEON USED TO BE IN A DIFFERENT PLACE...
BUT SOME POWER TRANSPORTED IT HERE.
IS THAT EVEN POSSIBLE ...?

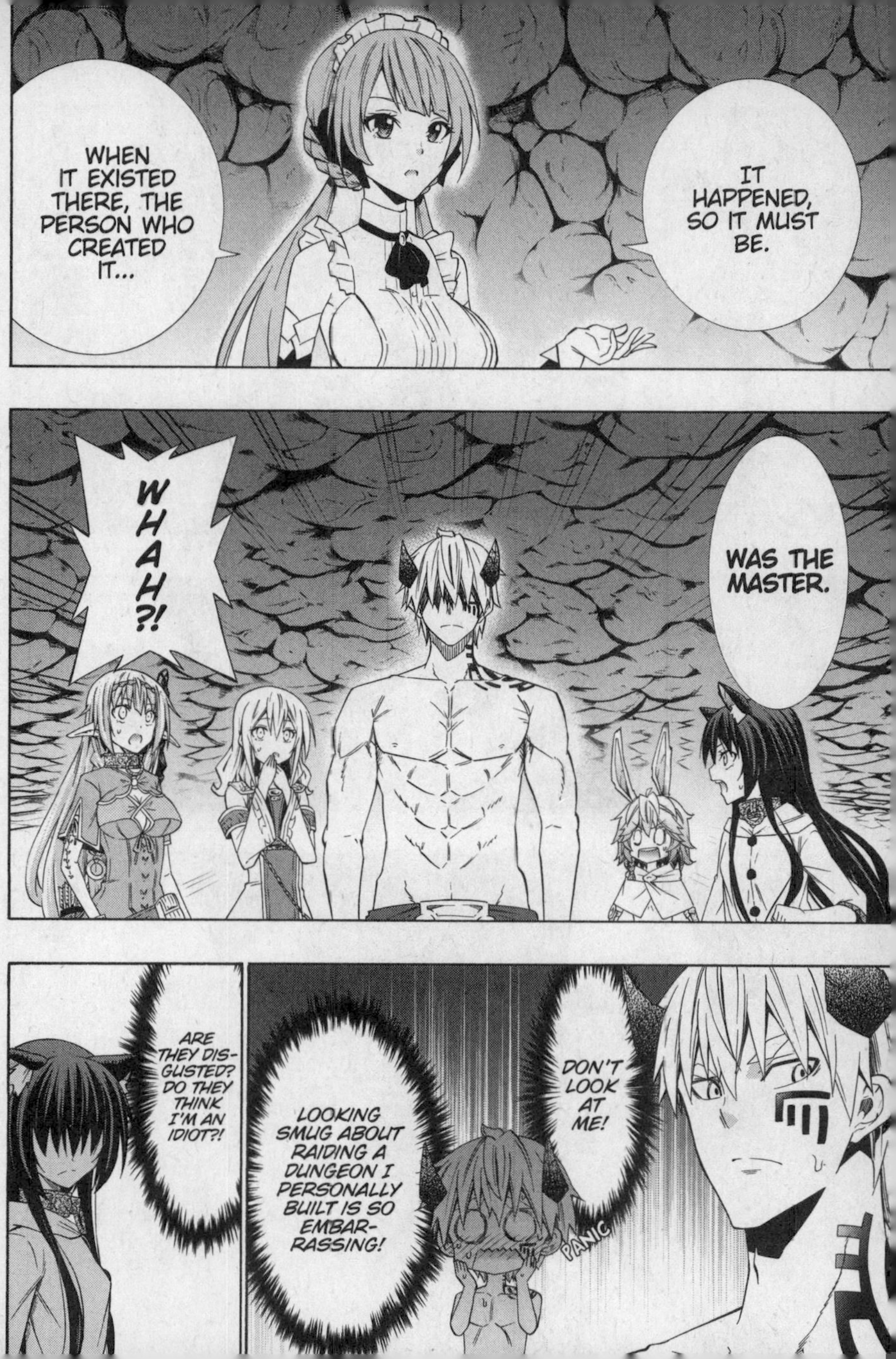
IT HAPPENED, SO IT MUST BE.
WHEN IT EXISTED THERE, THE PERSON WHO CREATED IT...
WAS THE MASTER.
WHAH?!
DON'T LOOK AT ME!
LOOKING SMUG ABOUT RAIDING A DUNGEON I PERSONALLY BUILT IS SO EMBAR-RASSING!
PANIC
ARE THEY DIS-GUSTED? DO THEY THINK I'M AN IDIOT?!

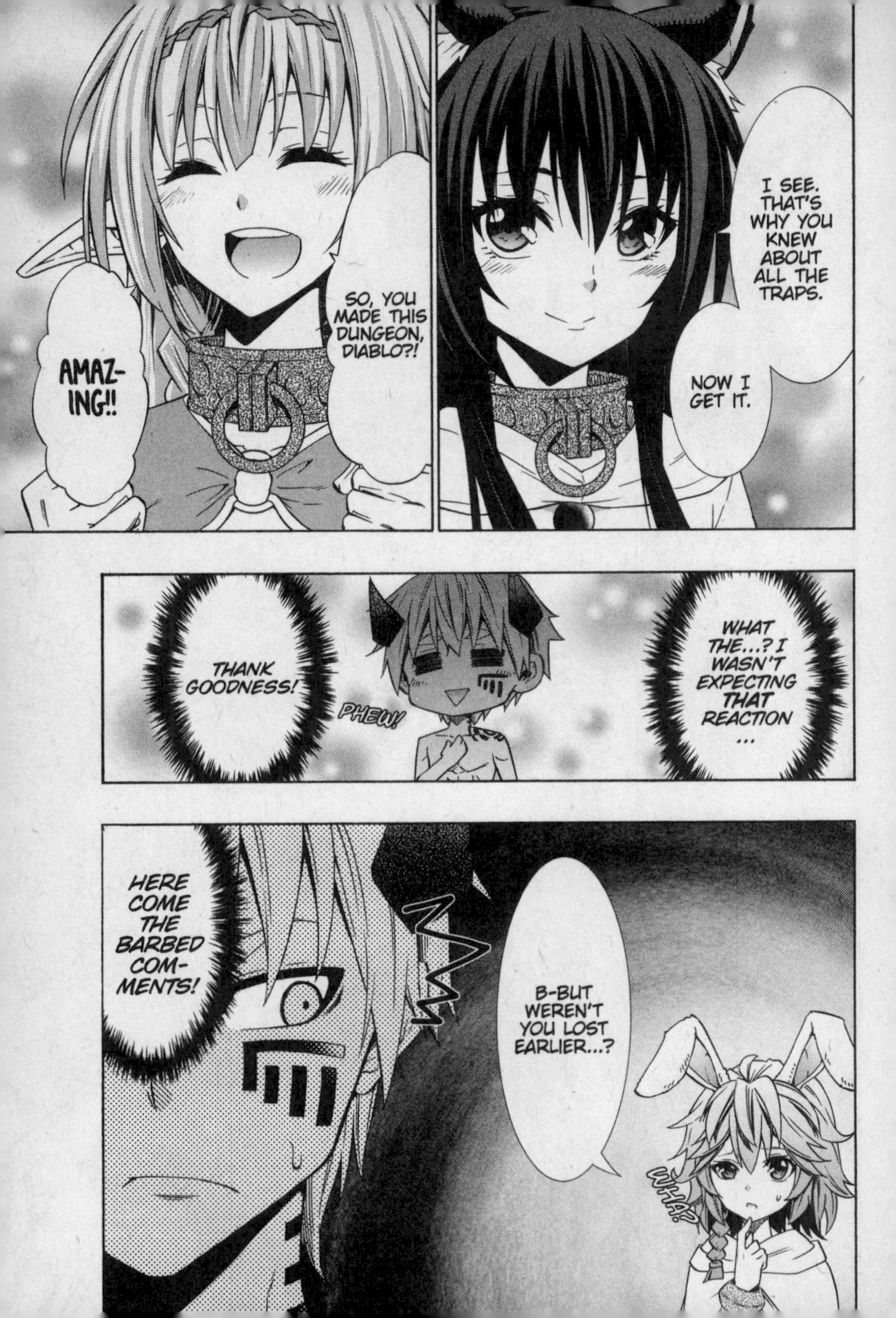
I SEE. THAT'S WHY YOU KNEW ABOUT ALL THE TRAPS.
NOW I GET IT.
SO, YOU MADE THIS DUNGEON, DIABLO?!
AMAZ-ING!!
WHAT THE...? I WASN'T EXPECTING THAT REACTION...
PHEW!
THANK GOODNESS!
WHA?
B-BUT WEREN'T YOU LOST EARLIER...?
HERE COME THE BARBED COM-MENTS!

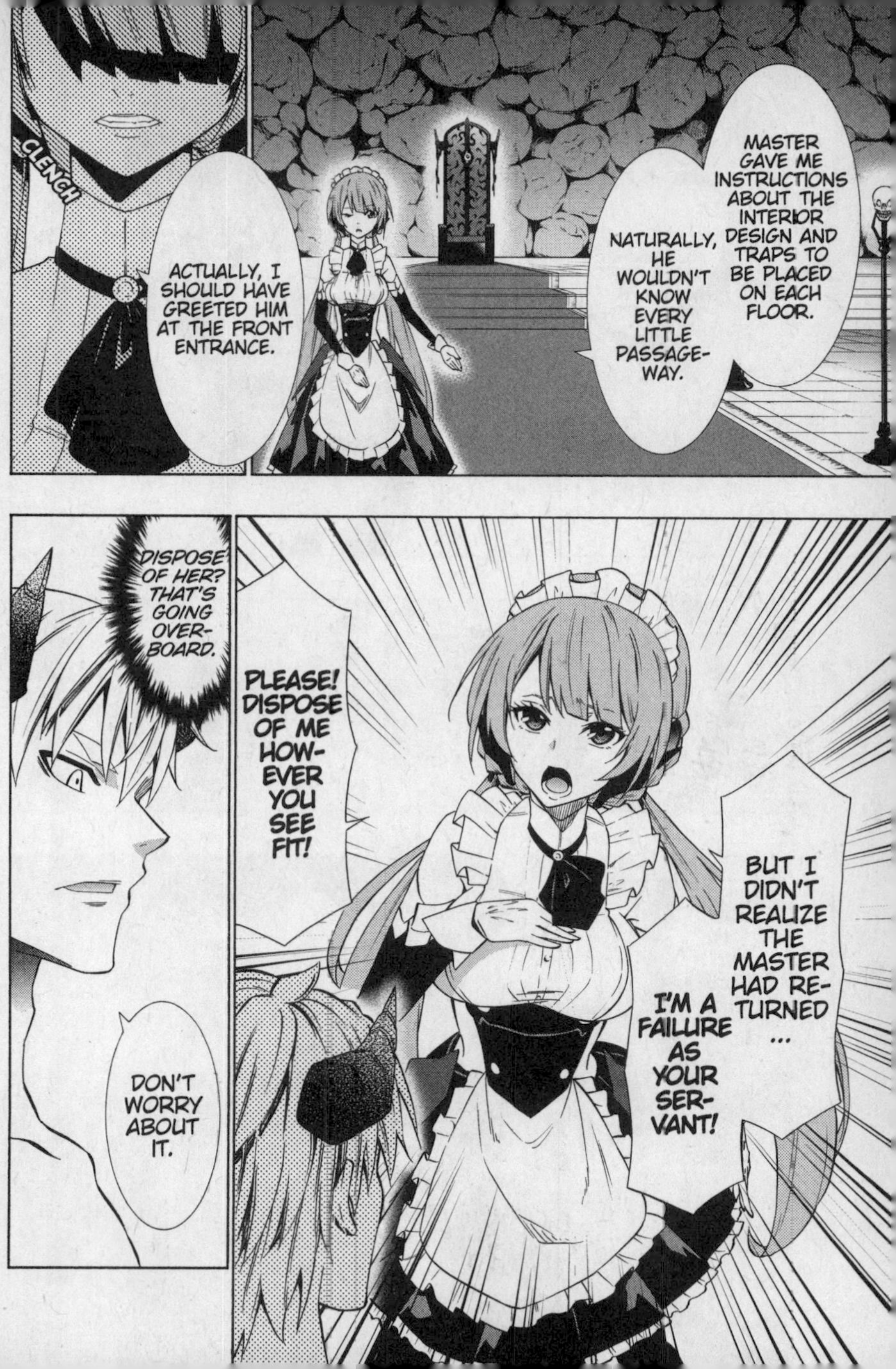
MASTER GAVE ME INSTRUCTIONS ABOUT THE INTERIOR DESIGN AND TRAPS TO BE PLACED ON EACH FLOOR.
NATURALLY, HE WOULDN'T KNOW EVERY LITTLE PASSAGE-WAY.
ACTUALLY, I SHOULD HAVE GREETED HIM AT THE FRONT ENTRANCE.
CLENCH
BUT I DIDN'T REALIZE THE MASTER HAD RE-TURNED ...
I'M A FAILURE AS YOUR SER-VANT!
PLEASE! DISPOSE OF ME HOW-EVER YOU SEE FIT!
DISPOSE OF HER? THAT'S GOING OVER-BOARD.
DON'T WORRY ABOUT IT.

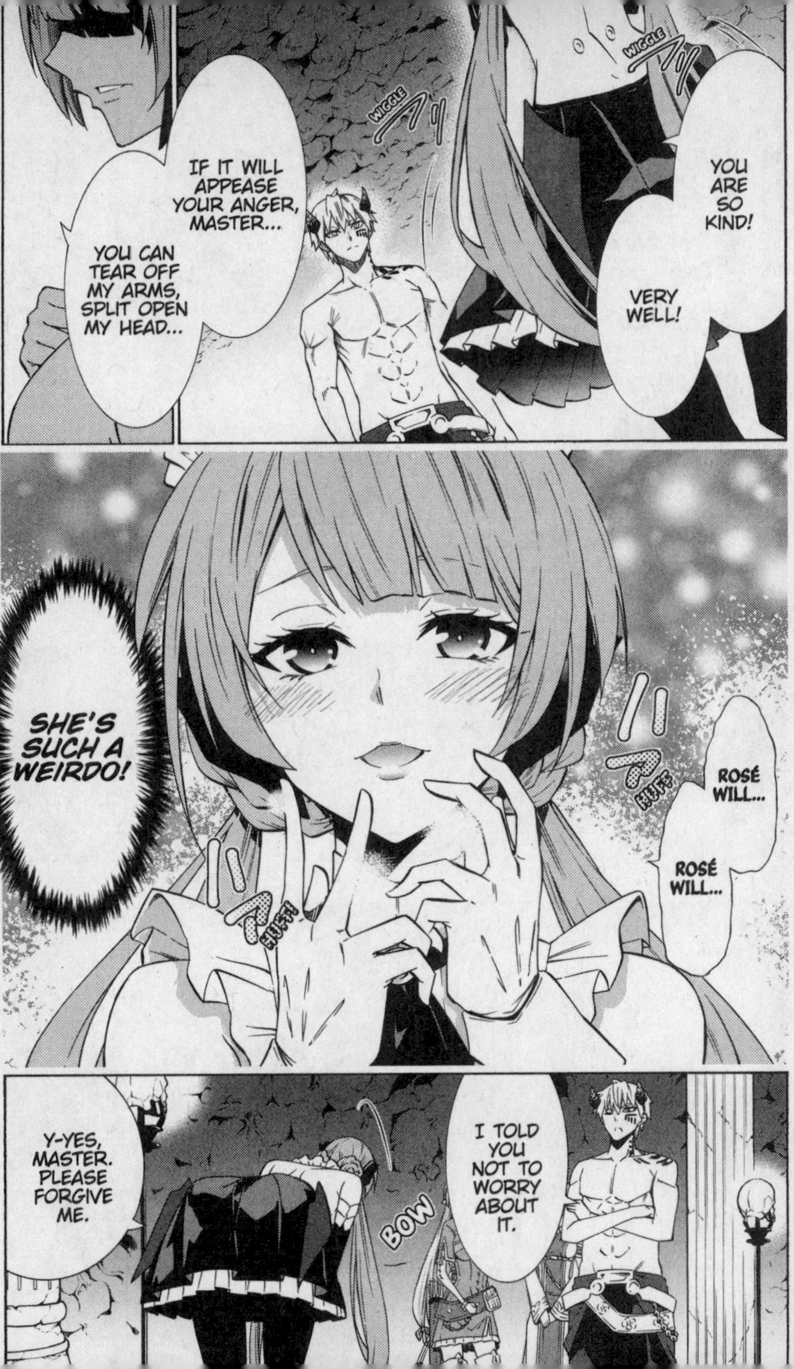
WIGGLE
WIGGLE
YOU ARE SO KIND!
VERY WELL!
IF IT WILL APPEASE YOUR ANGER, MASTER...
YOU CAN TEAR OFF MY ARMS, SPLIT OPEN MY HEAD...
HUFF
ROSÉ WILL...
ROSÉ WILL...
SHE'S SUCH A WEIRDO!
HUFF
I TOLD YOU NOT TO WORRY ABOUT IT.
BOW
Y-YES, MASTER. PLEASE FORGIVE ME.

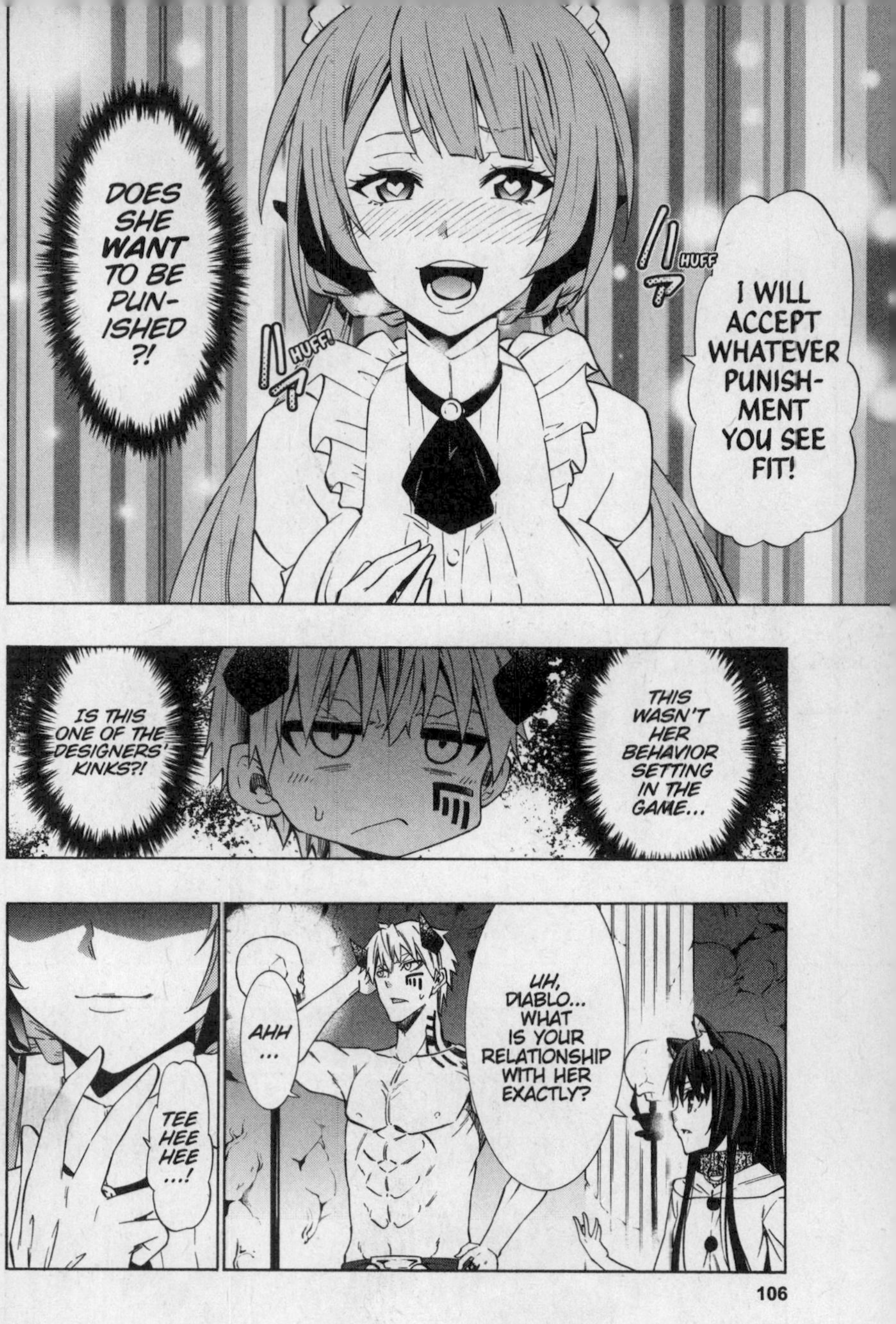
HUFF
I WILL ACCEPT WHATEVER PUNISH-MENT YOU SEE FIT!
HUFF!
DOES SHE WANT TO BE PUN-ISHED?!
THIS WASN'T HER BEHAVIOR SETTING IN THE GAME...
IS THIS ONE OF THE DESIGNERS' KINKS?!
UH, DIABLO... WHAT IS YOUR RELATIONSHIP WITH HER EXACTLY?
AHH ...
TEE HEE HEE ...!

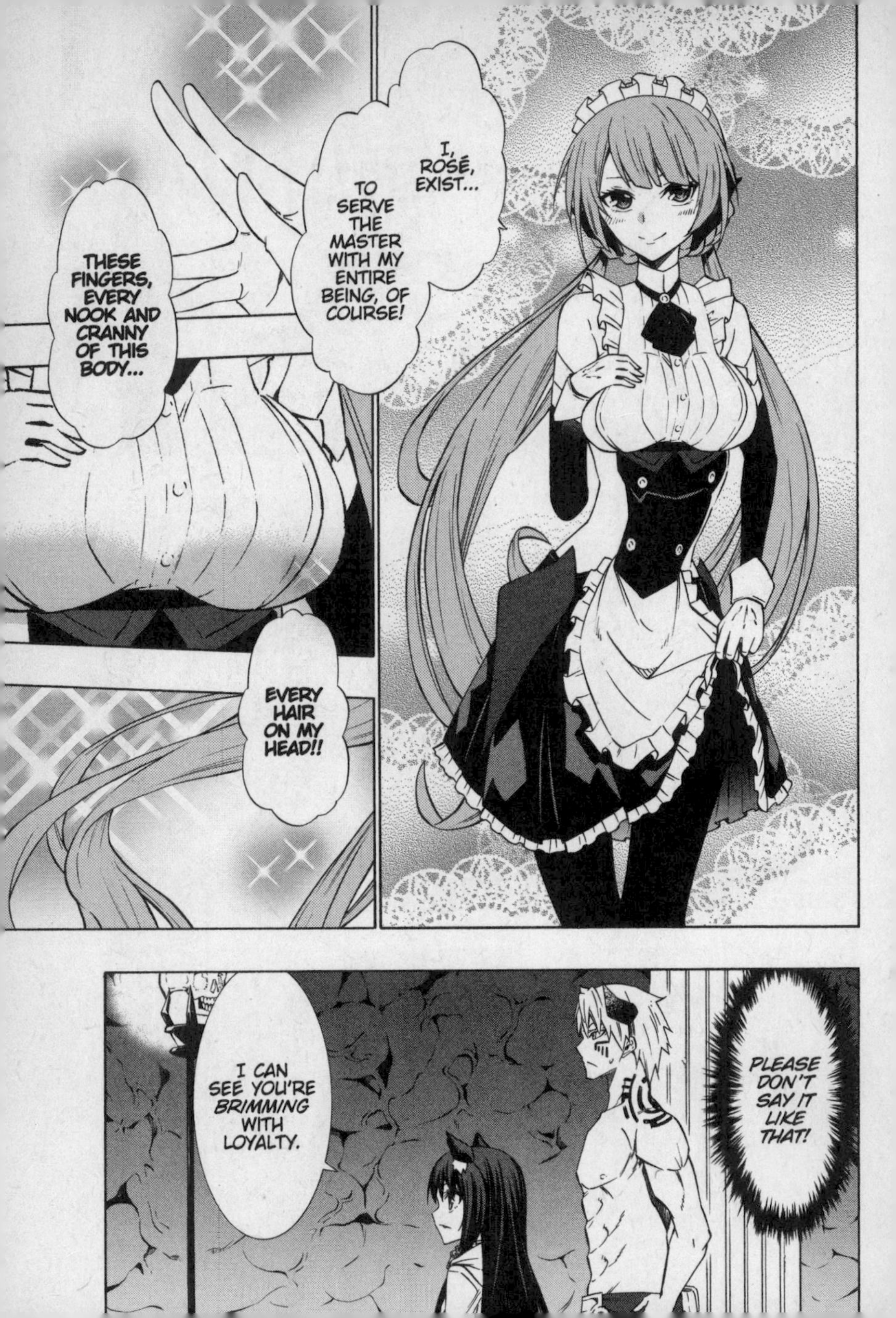
I, ROSÉ, EXIST...
TO SERVE THE MASTER WITH MY ENTIRE BEING, OF COURSE!
THESE FINGERS, EVERY NOOK AND CRANNY OF THIS BODY...
EVERY HAIR ON MY HEAD!!
I CAN SEE YOU'RE *BRIMMING* WITH LOYALTY.
PLEASE DON'T SAY IT LIKE THAT!

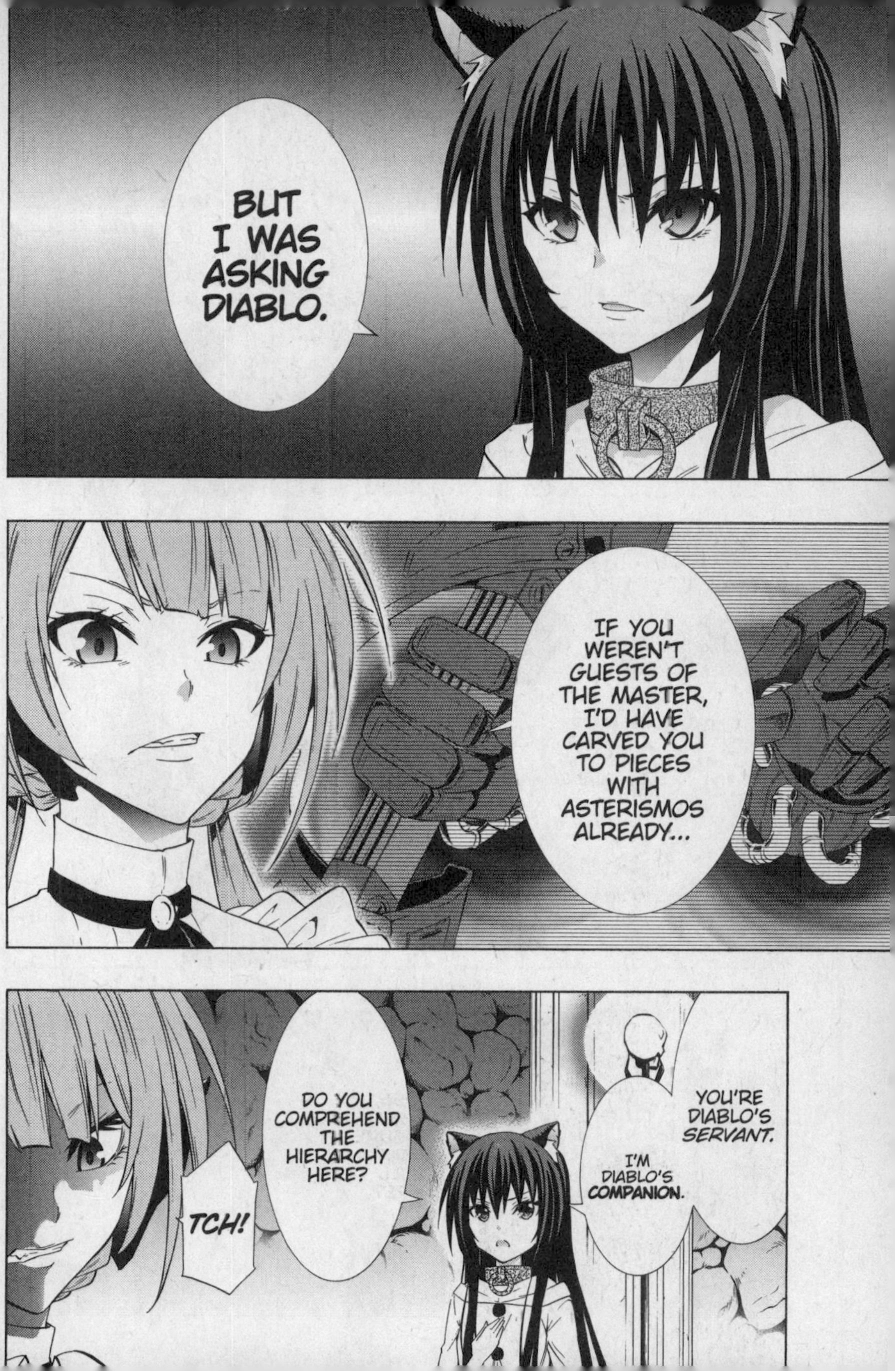
BUT I WAS ASKING DIABLO.
IF YOU WEREN'T GUESTS OF THE MASTER, I'D HAVE CARVED YOU TO PIECES WITH ASTERISMOS ALREADY...
YOU'RE DIABLO'S SERVANT.
I'M DIABLO'S COMPANION.
DO YOU COMPREHEND THE HIERARCHY HERE?
TCH!

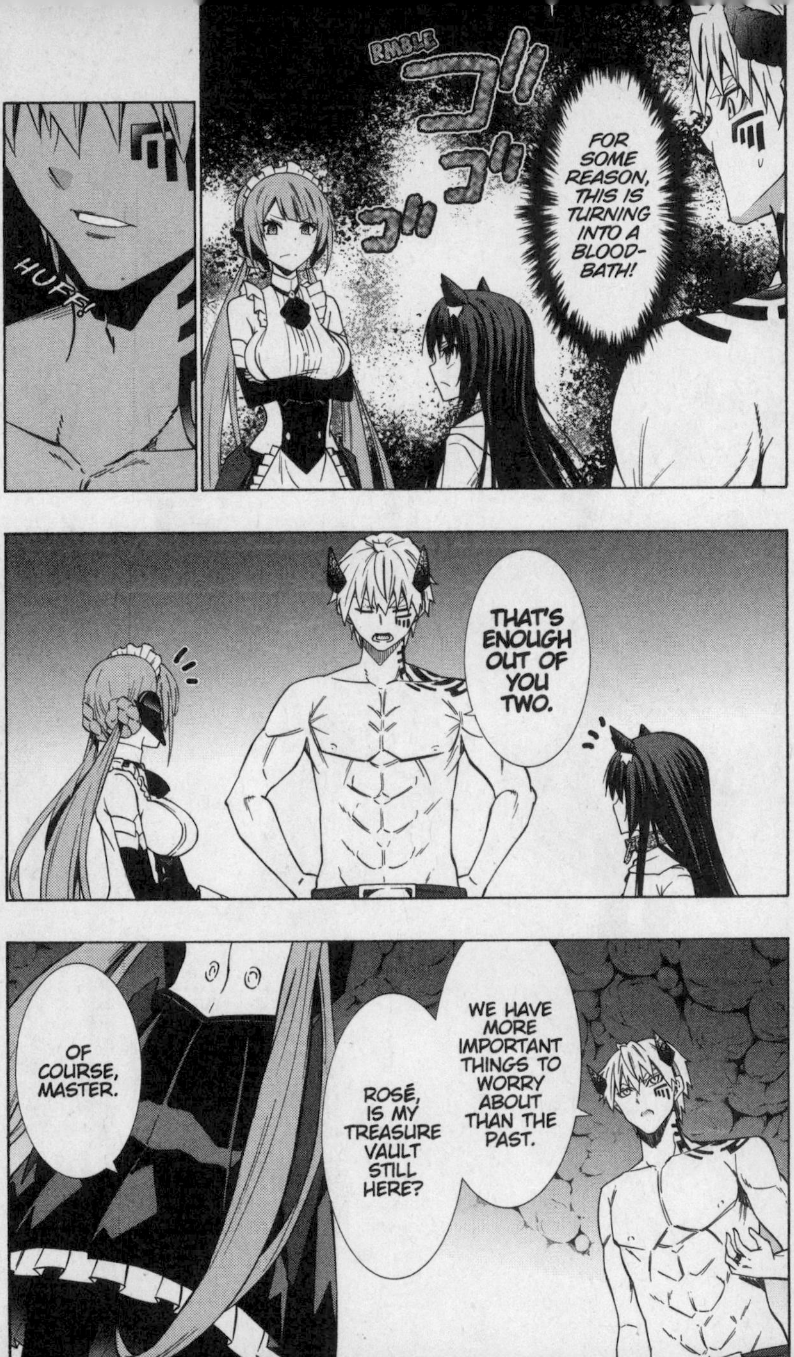
RMBLE
FOR SOME REASON, THIS IS TURNING INTO A BLOOD-BATH!
HUFF!
THAT'S ENOUGH OUT OF YOU TWO.
WE HAVE MORE IMPORTANT THINGS TO WORRY ABOUT THAN THE PAST.
ROSÉ, IS MY TREASURE VAULT STILL HERE?
OF COURSE, MASTER.

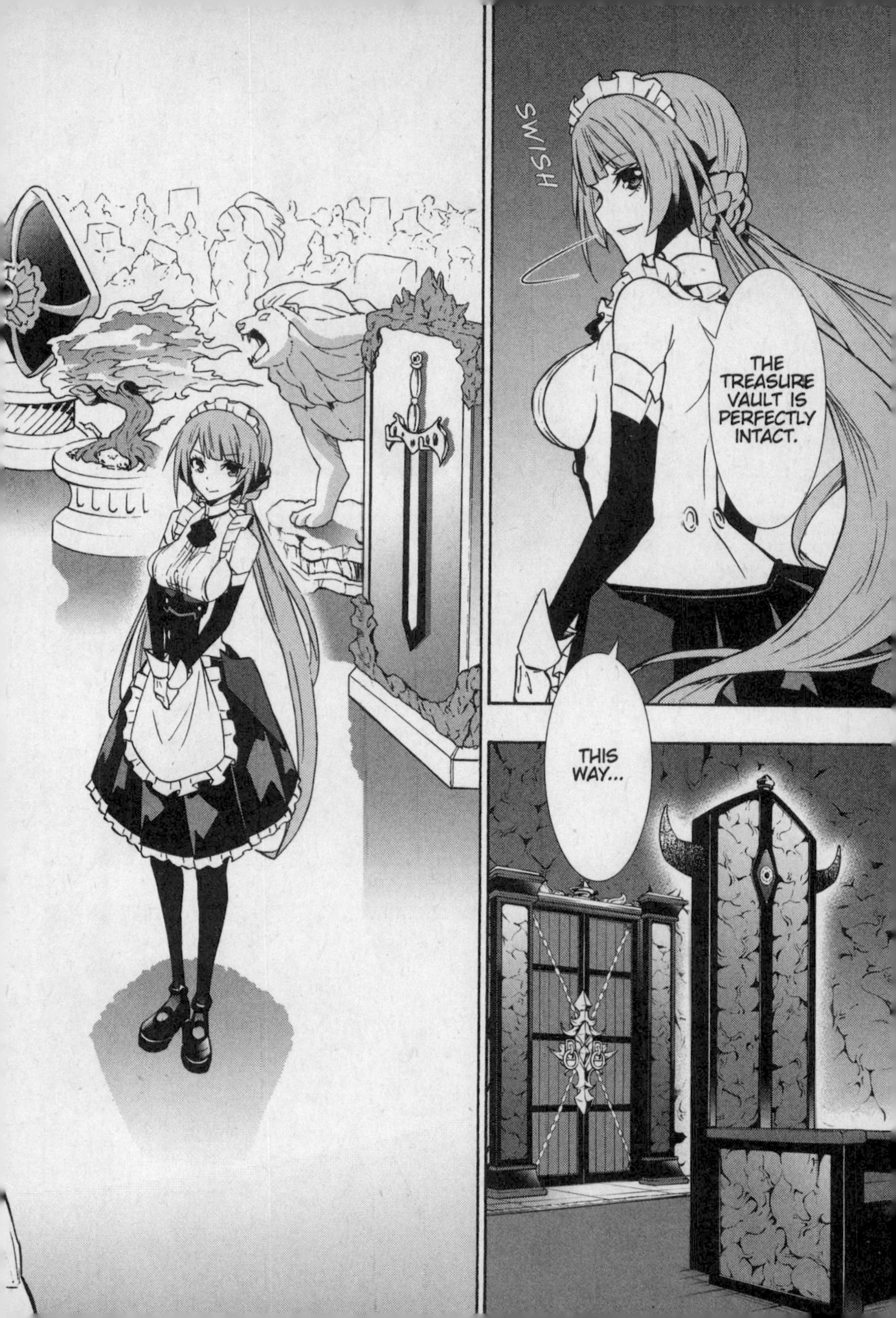
SWISH
THE TREASURE VAULT IS PERFECTLY INTACT.
THIS WAY...

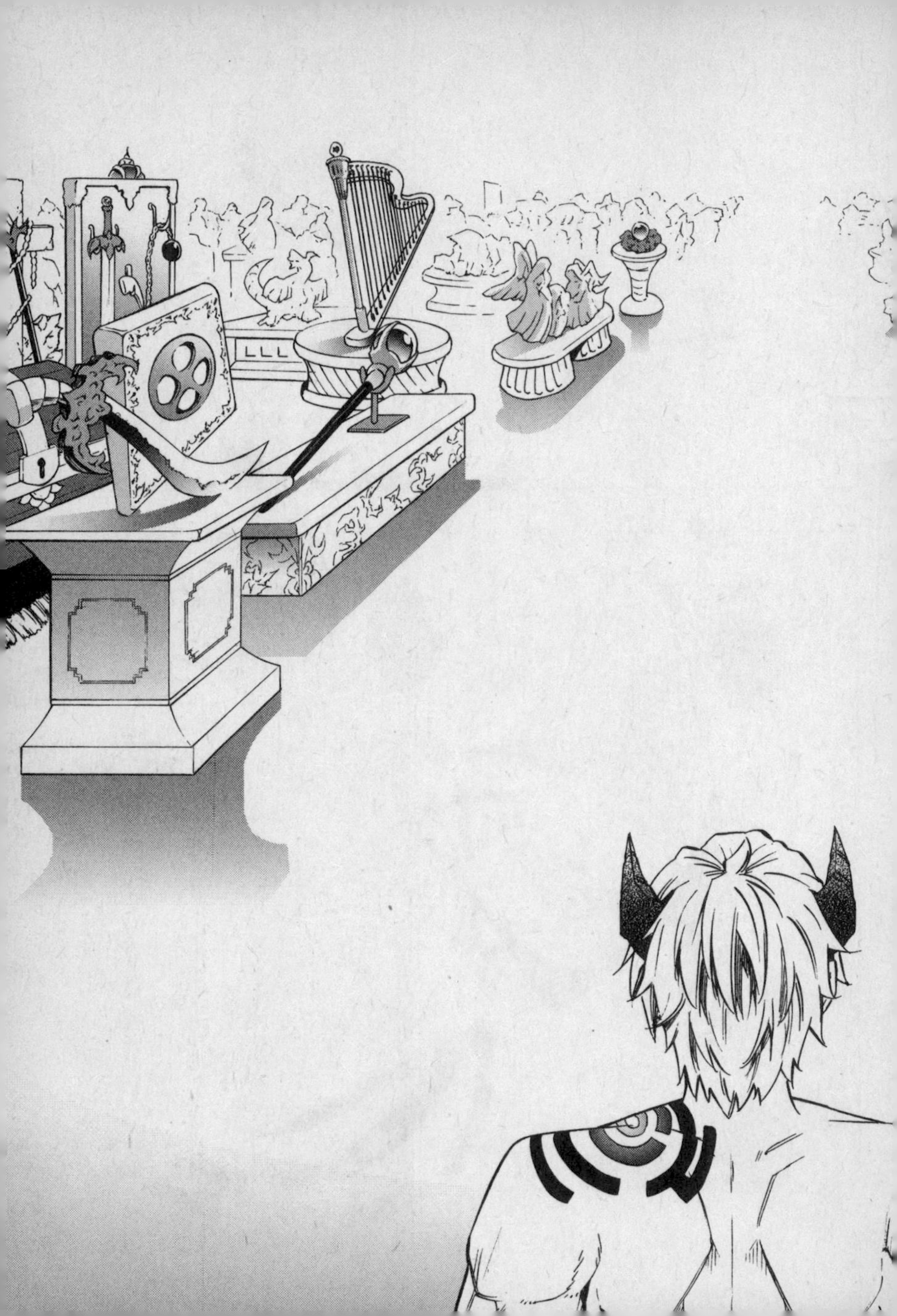

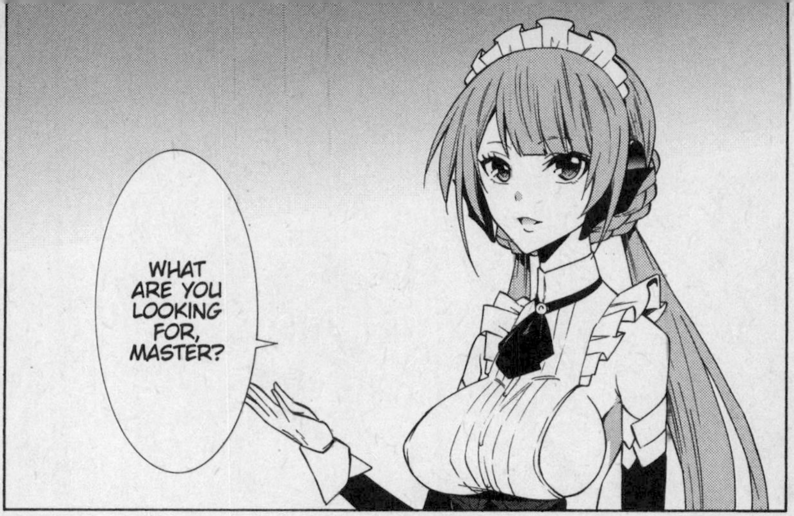
WHAT ARE YOU LOOKING FOR, MASTER?
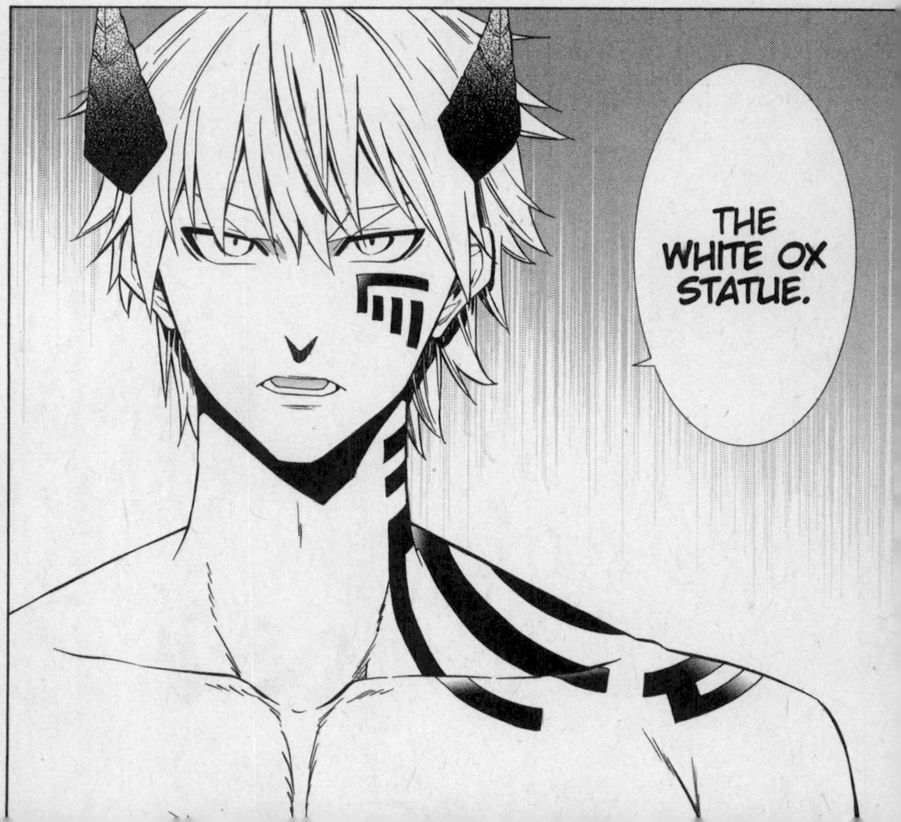
THE WHITE OX STATUE.

HOW NOT
TO SUMMON A
DEMON LORD

58 TRYING OUT NEW EQUIPMENT I

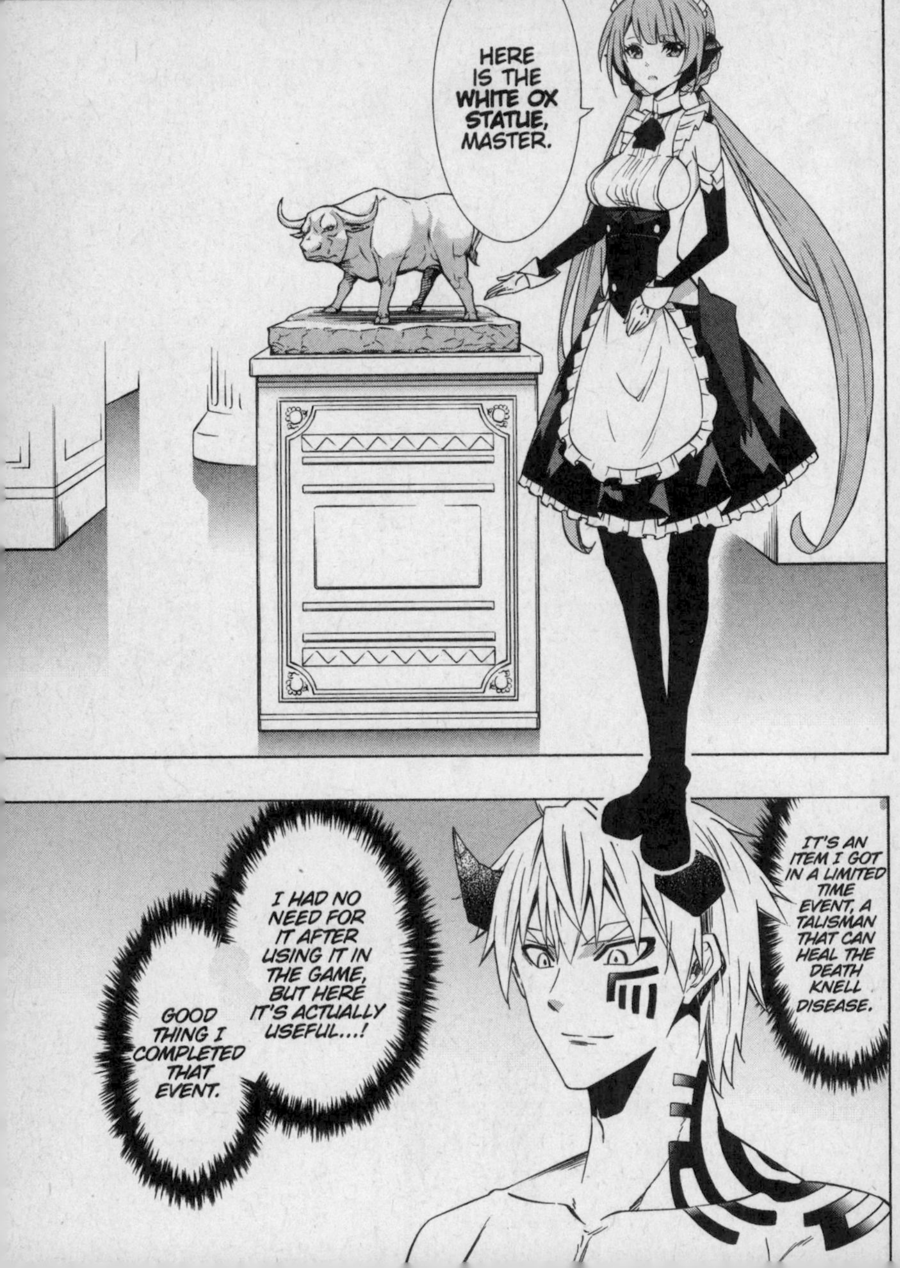
HERE IS THE WHITE OX STATUE, MASTER.
IT'S AN ITEM I GOT IN A LIMITED TIME EVENT, A TALISMAN THAT CAN HEAL THE DEATH KNELL DISEASE.
I HAD NO NEED FOR IT AFTER USING IT IN THE GAME, BUT HERE IT'S ACTUALLY USEFUL...!
GOOD THING I COMPLETED THAT EVENT.

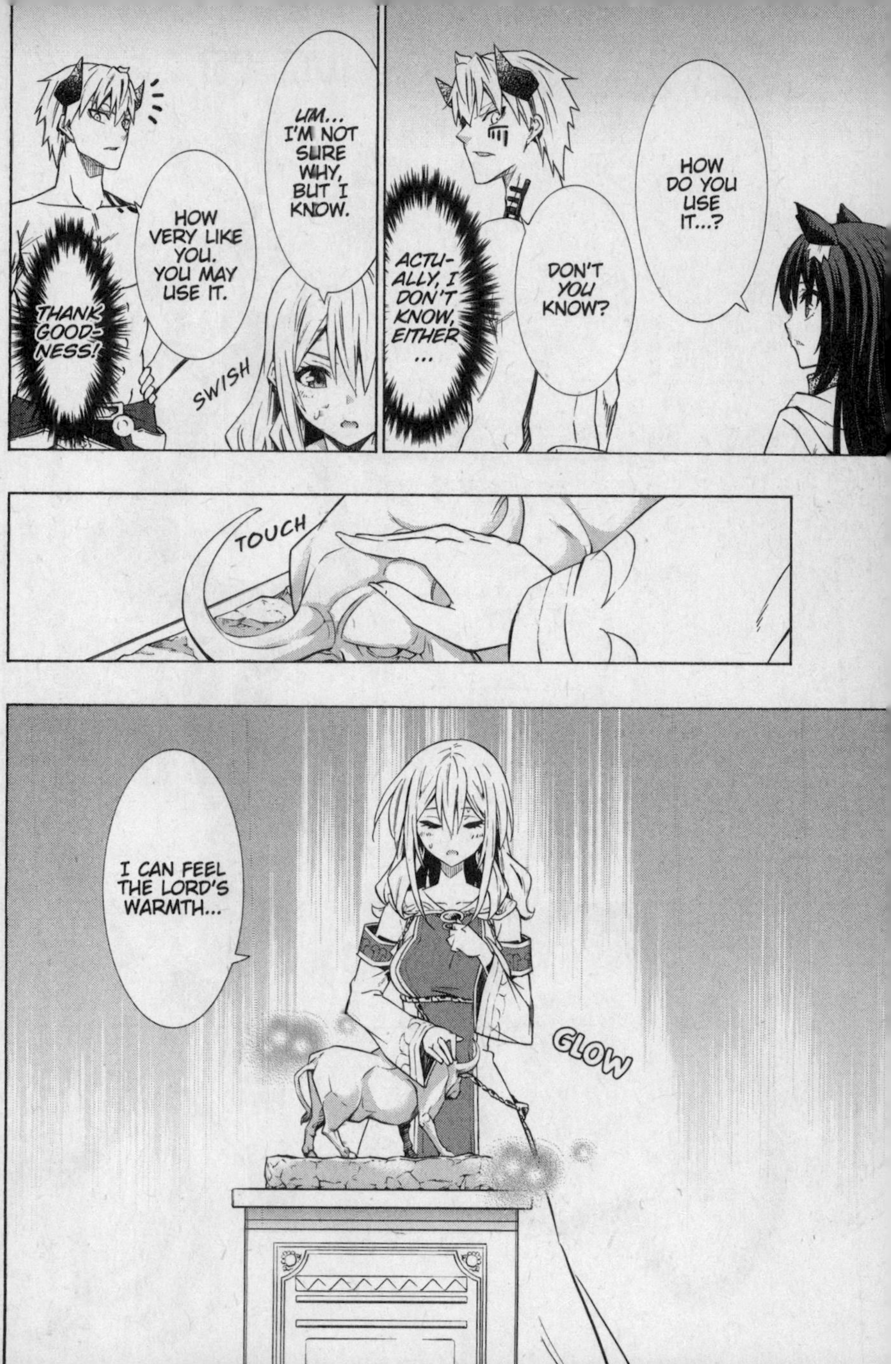
HOW DO YOU USE IT...?
DON'T YOU KNOW?
ACTU-ALLY, I DON'T KNOW, EITHER...
UM... I'M NOT SURE WHY, BUT I KNOW.
HOW VERY LIKE YOU. YOU MAY USE IT.
THANK GOOD-NESS!
SWISH
TOUCH
I CAN FEEL THE LORD'S WARMTH...
GLOW

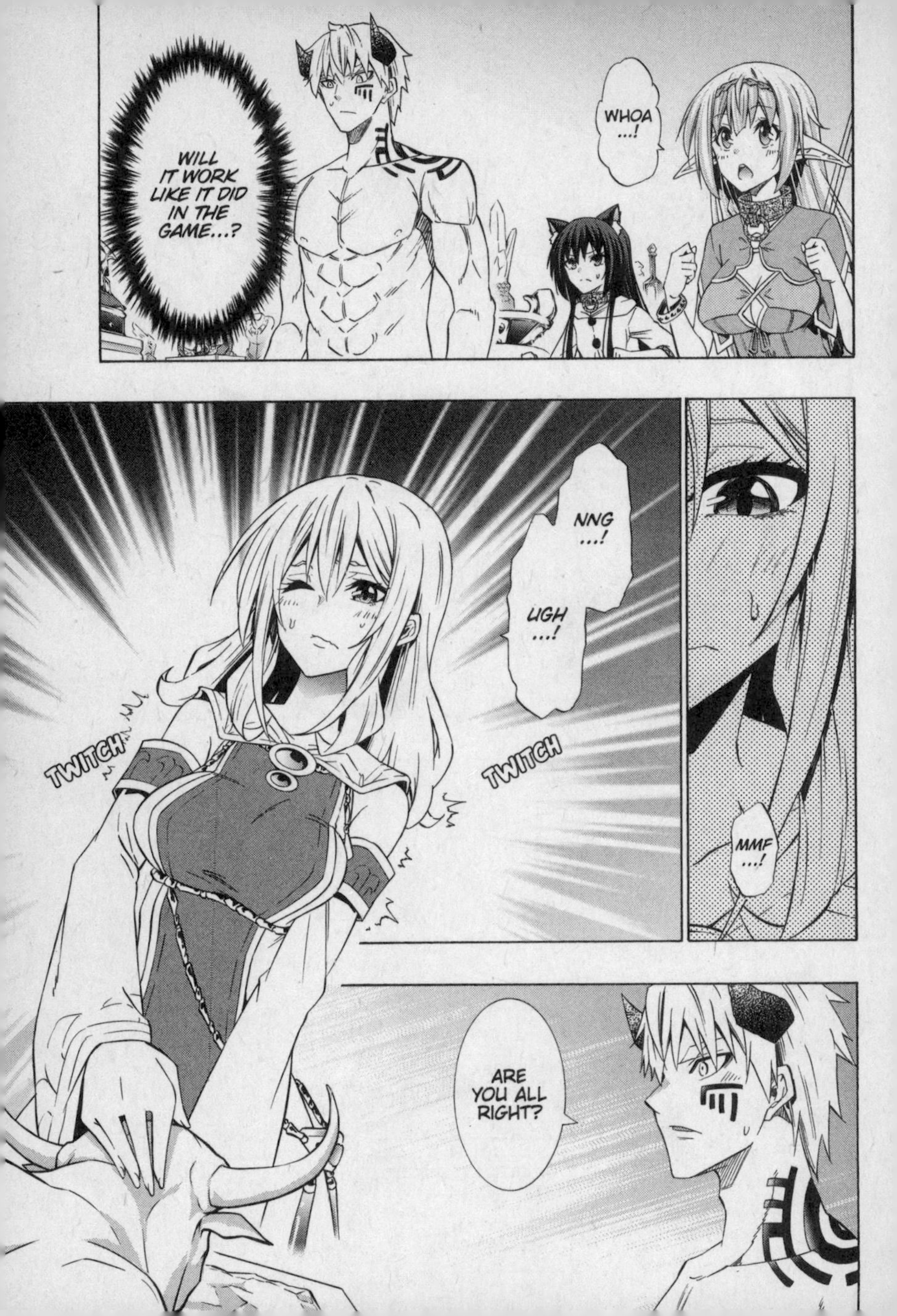
WHOA ...!
WILL IT WORK LIKE IT DID IN THE GAME...?
MMF ...!
ARE YOU ALL RIGHT?
NNG ...!
UGH ...!
TWITCH
TWITCH

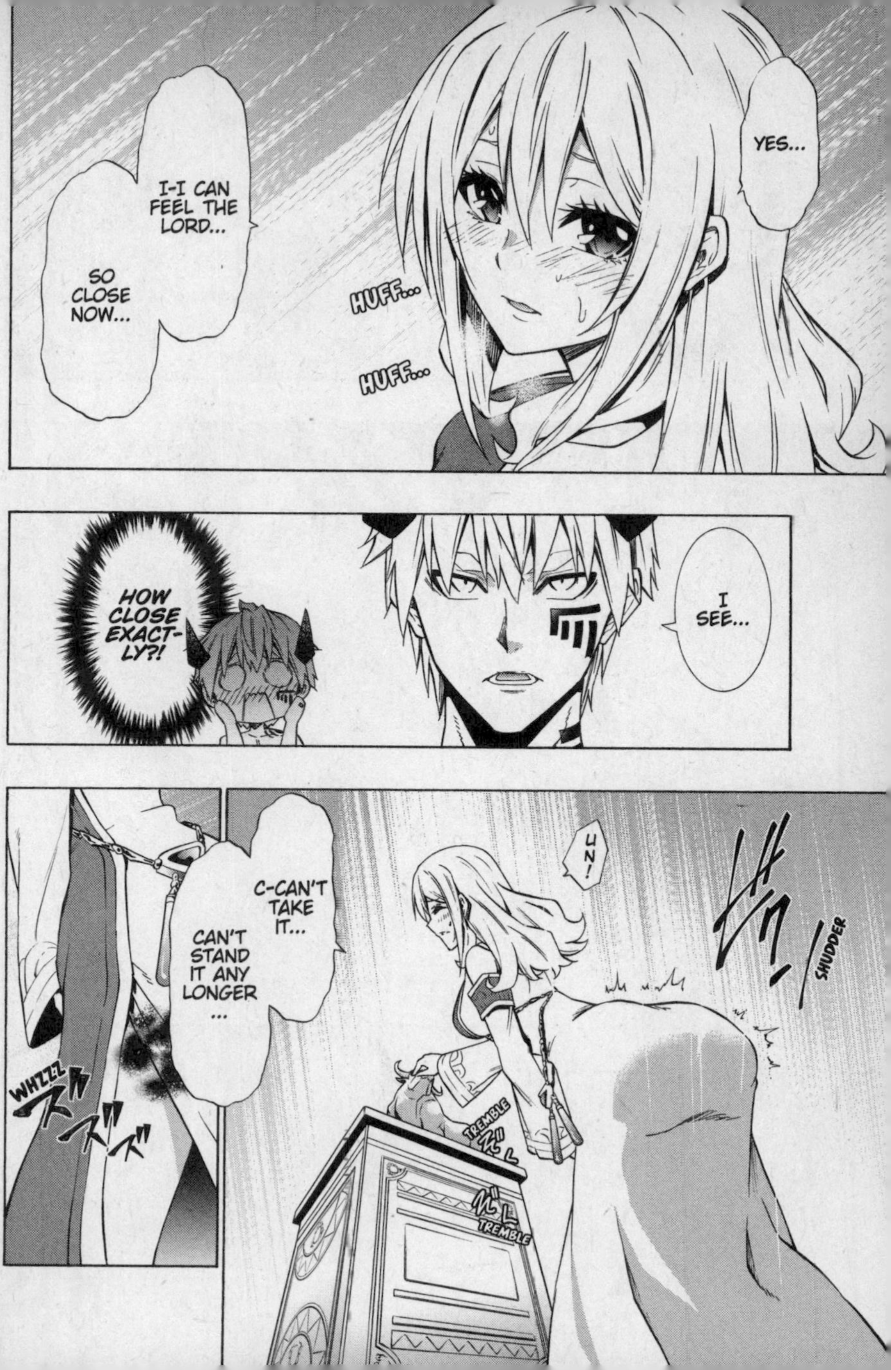
YES...
HUFF...
HUFF...
I-I CAN FEEL THE LORD...
SO CLOSE NOW...
I SEE...
HOW CLOSE EXACTLY?!
SHUDDER
UN!
C-CAN'T TAKE IT...
CAN'T STAND IT ANY LONGER...
TREMBLE
TREMBLE
WHZZZ

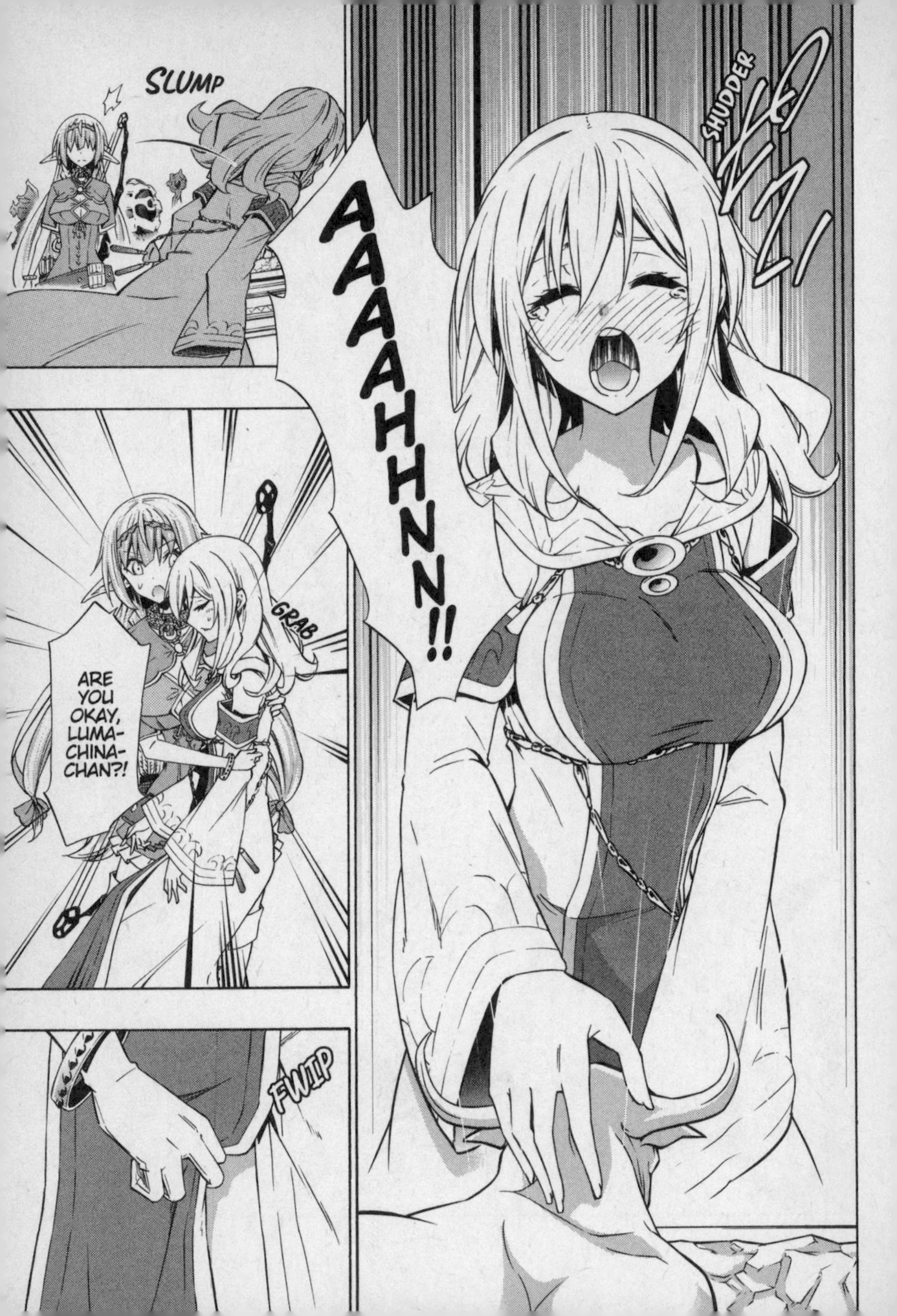
SHUDDER
AAAAHHNN!!
SLUMP
ARE YOU OKAY, LUMA-CHINA-CHAN?!
GRAB
FWIP

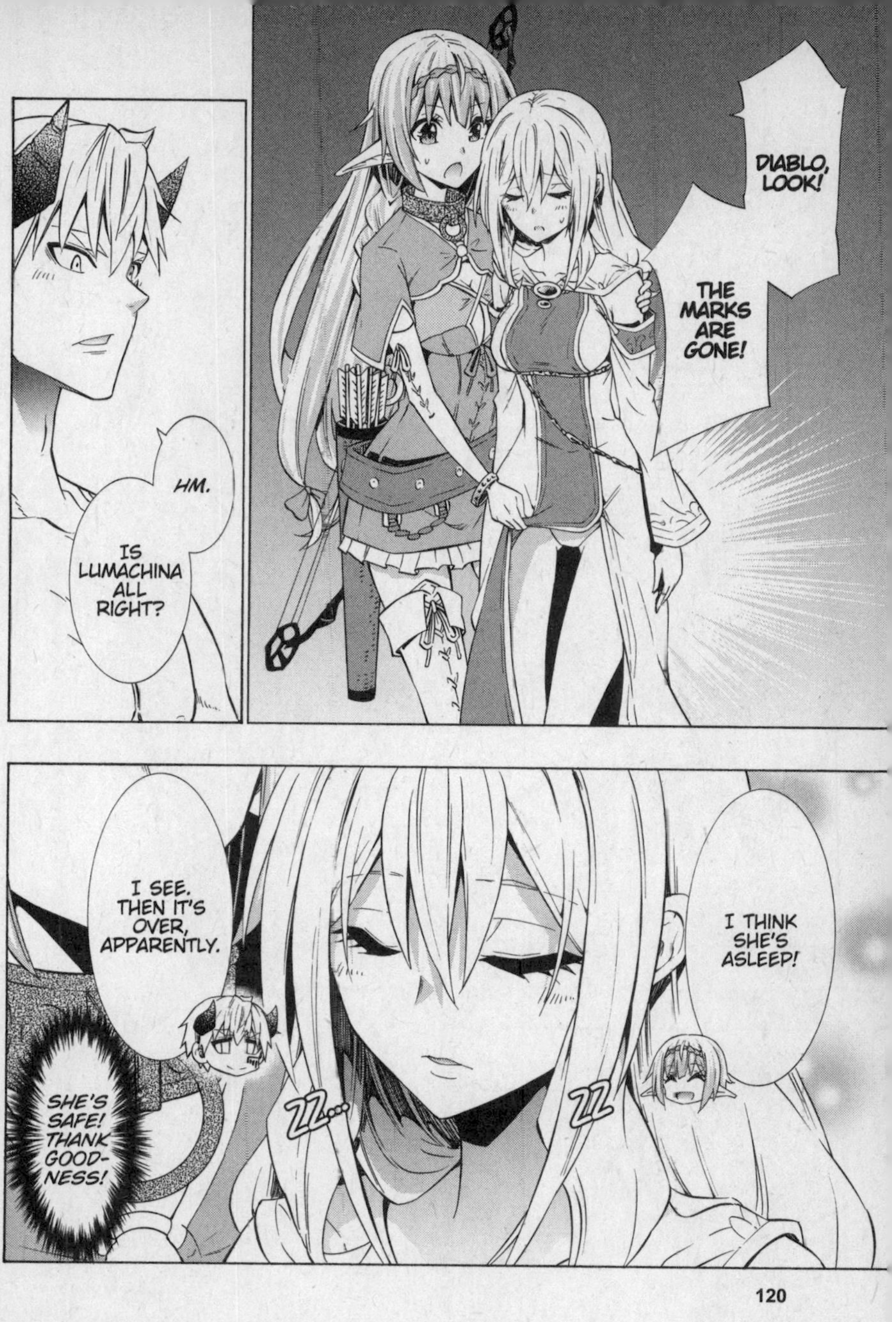
DIABLO, LOOK!
THE MARKS ARE GONE!
HM.
IS LUMACHINA ALL RIGHT?
I THINK SHE'S ASLEEP!
I SEE. THEN IT'S OVER, APPARENTLY.
ZZ
ZZ...
SHE'S SAFE! THANK GOOD-NESS!

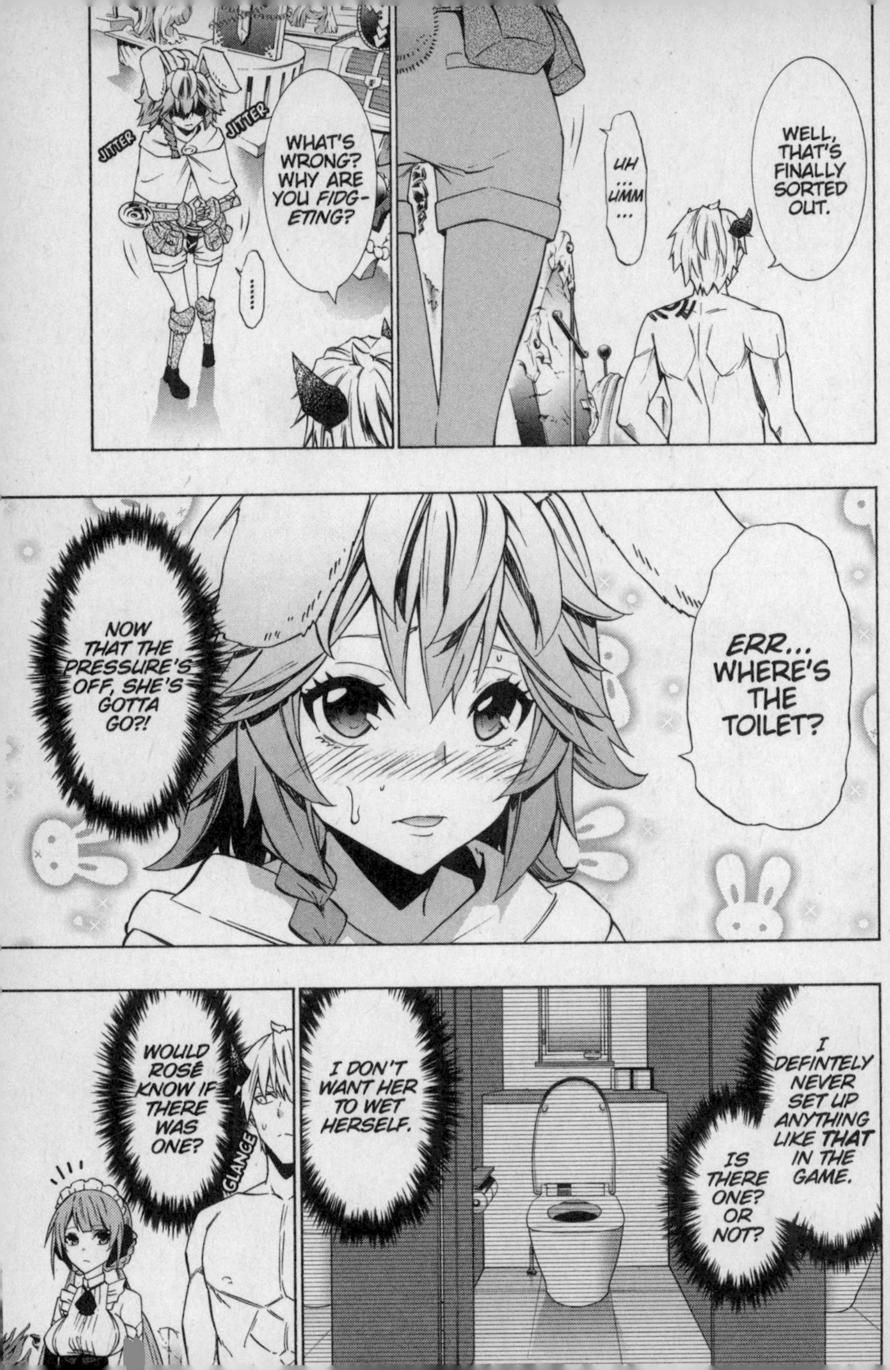
WELL, THAT'S FINALLY SORTED OUT.
UH... UMM...
JITTER
JITTER
WHAT'S WRONG? WHY ARE YOU FIDGETING?
......
ERR... WHERE'S THE TOILET?
NOW THAT THE PRESSURE'S OFF, SHE'S GOTTA GO?!
I DEFINTELY NEVER SET UP ANYTHING LIKE THAT IN THE GAME.
IS THERE ONE? OR NOT?
I DON'T WANT HER TO WET HERSELF.
WOULD ROSÉ KNOW IF THERE WAS ONE?
GLANCE

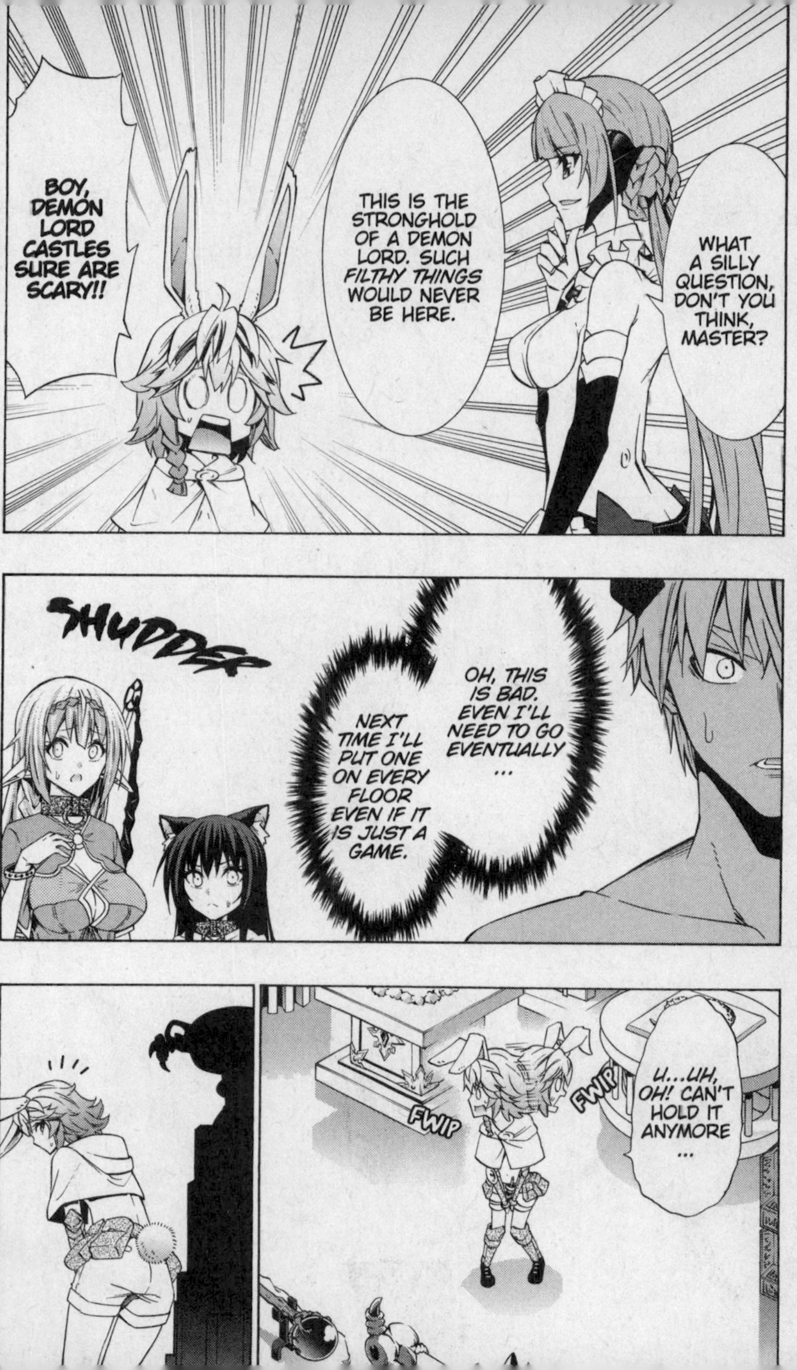
WHAT A SILLY QUESTION, DON'T YOU THINK, MASTER?
THIS IS THE STRONGHOLD OF A DEMON LORD. SUCH *FILTHY THINGS* WOULD NEVER BE HERE.
BOY, DEMON LORD CASTLES SURE ARE SCARY!!
OH, THIS IS BAD. EVEN I'LL NEED TO GO EVENTUALLY ...
NEXT TIME I'LL PUT ONE ON EVERY FLOOR EVEN IF IT IS JUST A GAME.
SHUDDER
U...UH, OH! CAN'T HOLD IT ANYMORE ...
FWIP
FWIP

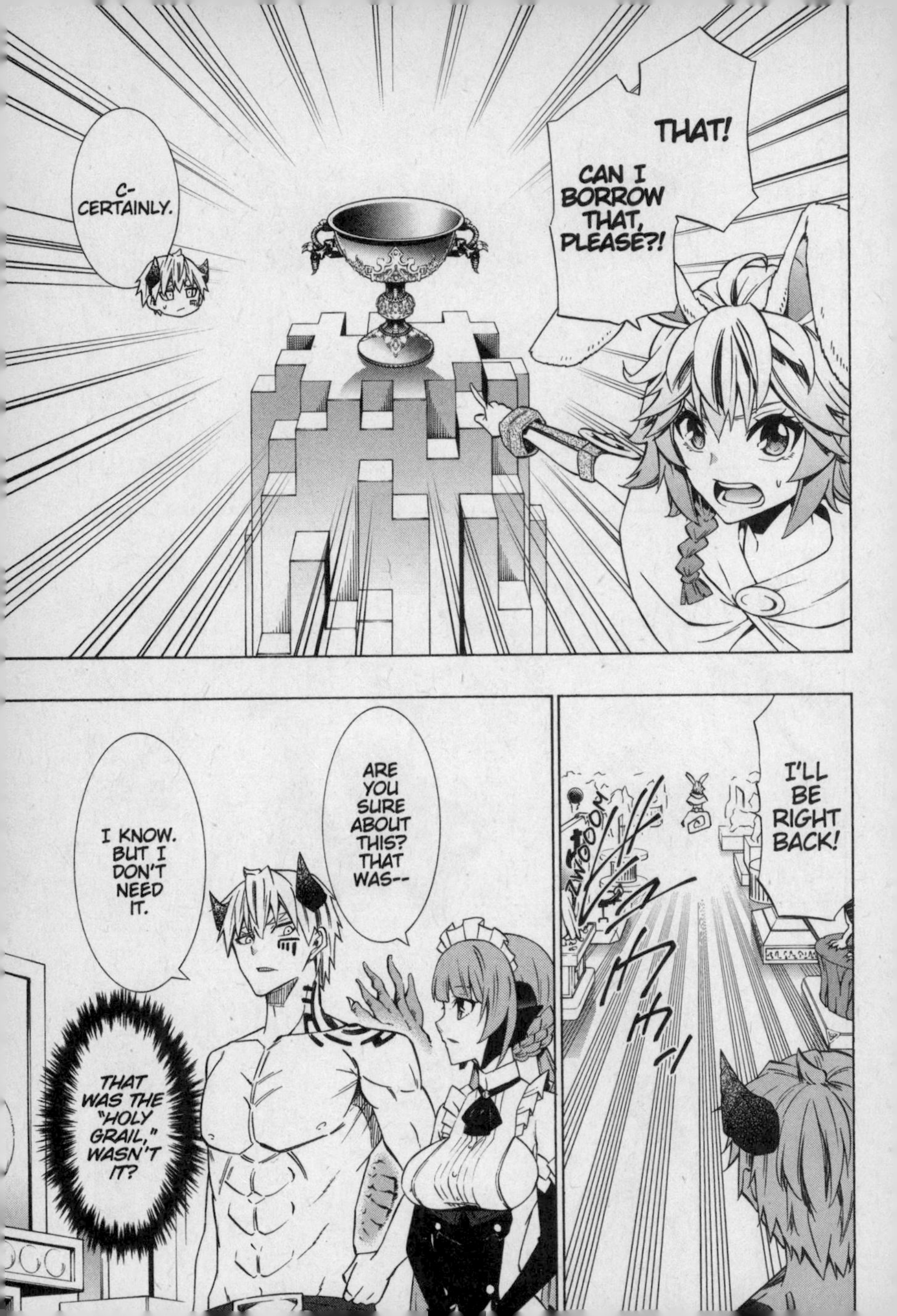
THAT!
CAN I BORROW THAT, PLEASE?!
C-CERTAINLY.
I'LL BE RIGHT BACK!
ZWOOOOM
ARE YOU SURE ABOUT THIS? THAT WAS--
I KNOW. BUT I DON'T NEED IT.
THAT WAS THE "HOLY GRAIL," WASN'T IT?

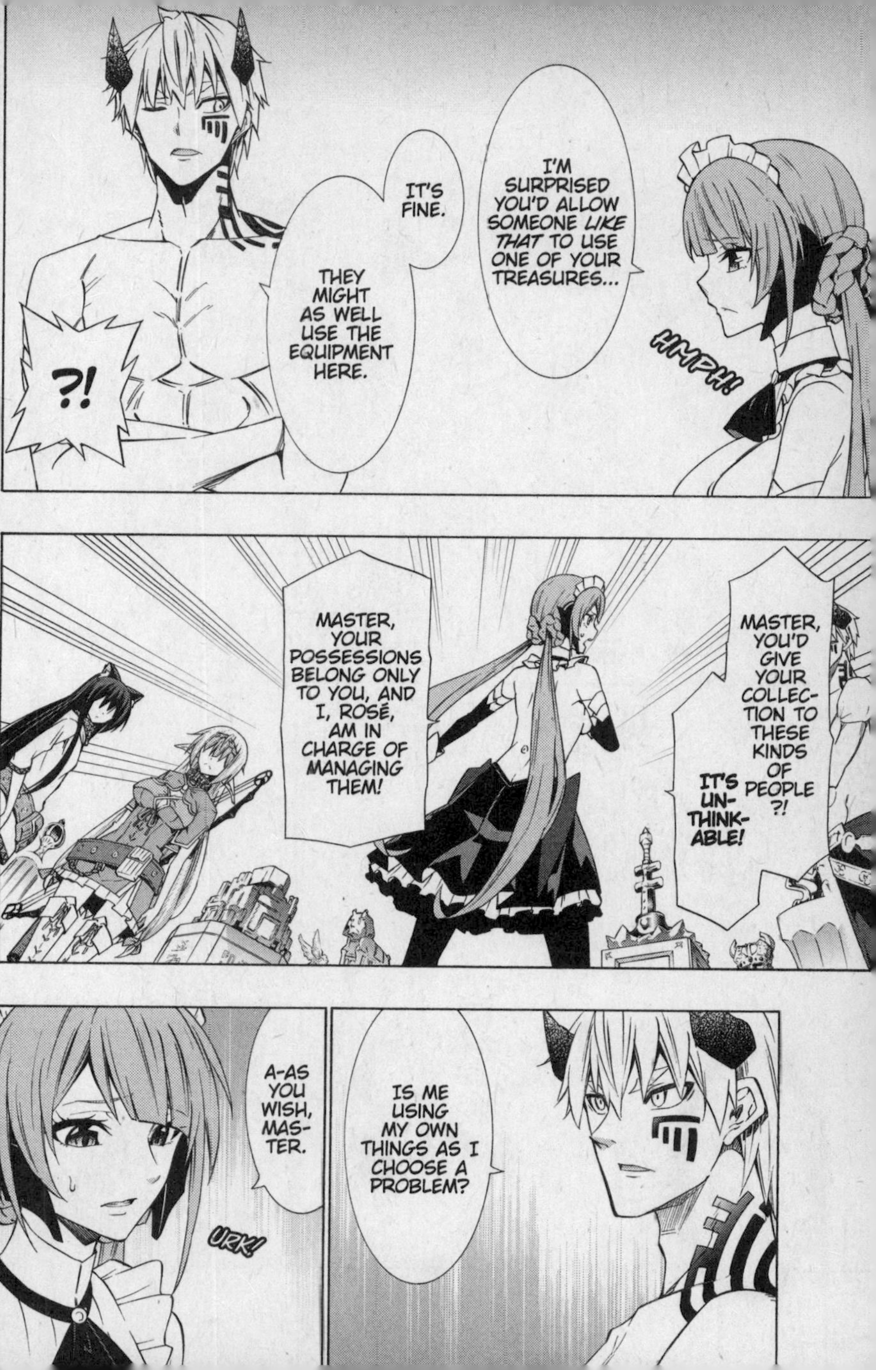
I'M SURPRISED YOU'D ALLOW SOMEONE LIKE THAT TO USE ONE OF YOUR TREASURES...
HMPH!
IT'S FINE.
THEY MIGHT AS WELL USE THE EQUIPMENT HERE.
?!
MASTER, YOU'D GIVE YOUR COLLECTION TO THESE KINDS OF PEOPLE?!
IT'S UNTHINKABLE!
MASTER, YOUR POSSESSIONS BELONG ONLY TO YOU, AND I, ROSÉ, AM IN CHARGE OF MANAGING THEM!
IS ME USING MY OWN THINGS AS I CHOOSE A PROBLEM?
A-AS YOU WISH, MASTER.
URK!

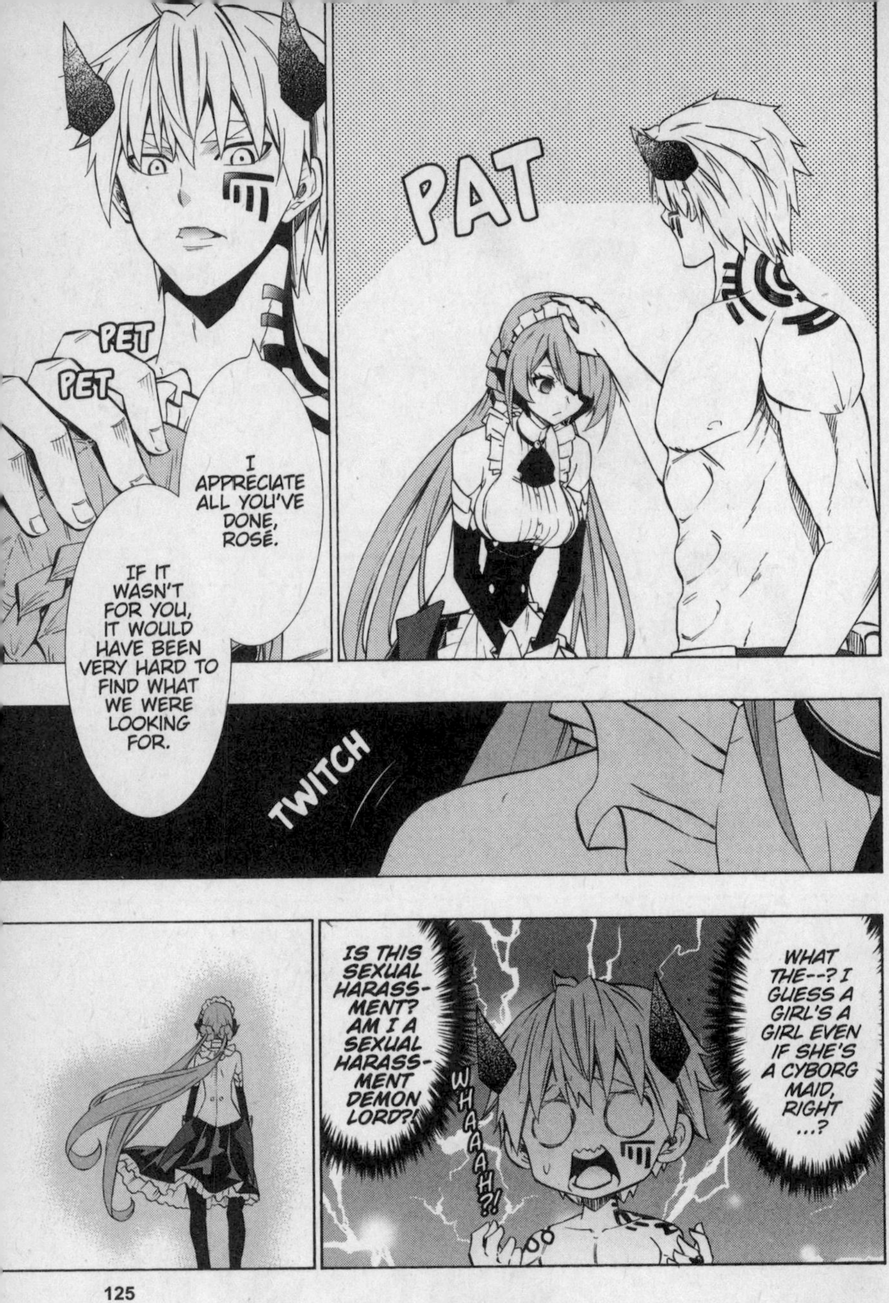
PAT
PET
PET
I APPRECIATE ALL YOU'VE DONE, ROSÉ.
IF IT WASN'T FOR YOU, IT WOULD HAVE BEEN VERY HARD TO FIND WHAT WE WERE LOOKING FOR.
TWITCH
WHAT THE--? I GUESS A GIRL'S A GIRL EVEN IF SHE'S A CYBORG MAID, RIGHT ...?
IS THIS SEXUAL HARASS-MENT? AM I A SEXUAL HARASS-MENT DEMON LORD?!
WHAAAAH?!

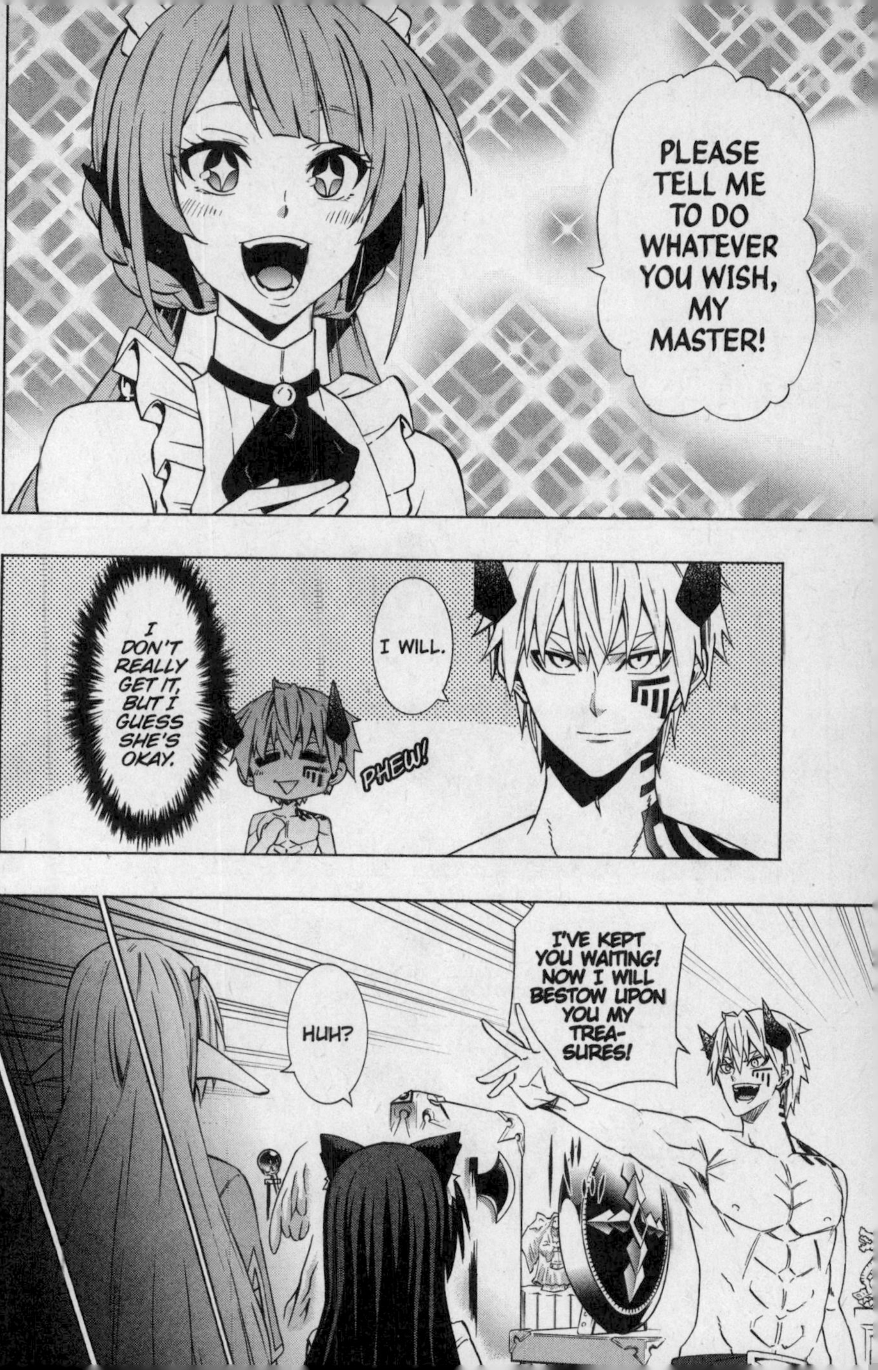
PLEASE TELL ME TO DO WHATEVER YOU WISH, MY MASTER!
I WILL.
I DON'T REALLY GET IT, BUT I GUESS SHE'S OKAY.
PHEW!
I'VE KEPT YOU WAITING! NOW I WILL BESTOW UPON YOU MY TREA-SURES!
HUH?

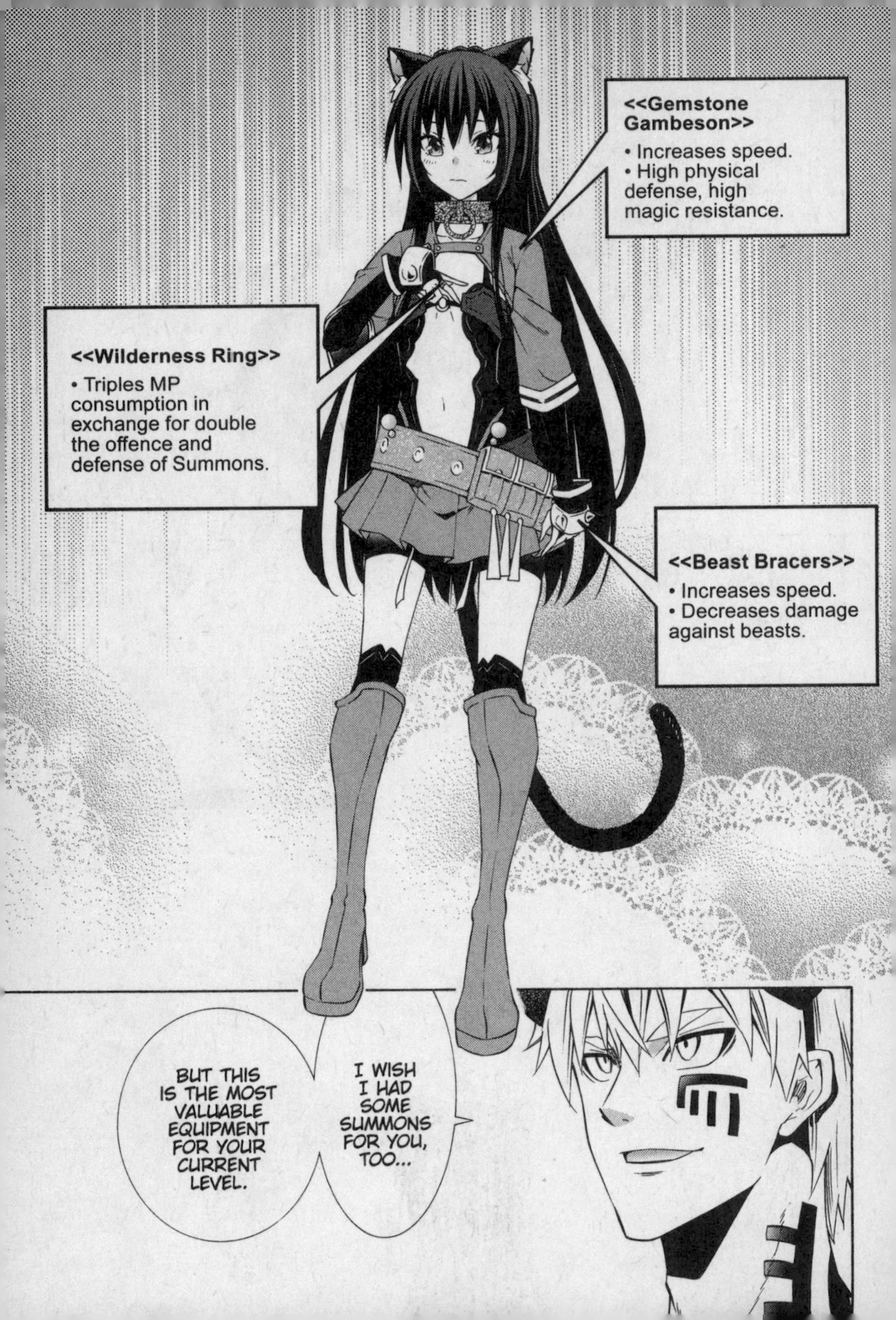

<<Gemstone Gambeson>>
• Increases speed.
• High physical defense, high magic resistance.
<<Wilderness Ring>>
• Triples MP consumption in exchange for double the offence and defense of Summons.
<<Beast Bracers>>
• Increases speed.
• Decreases damage against beasts.
I WISH I HAD SOME SUMMONS FOR YOU, TOO...
BUT THIS IS THE MOST VALUABLE EQUIPMENT FOR YOUR CURRENT LEVEL.

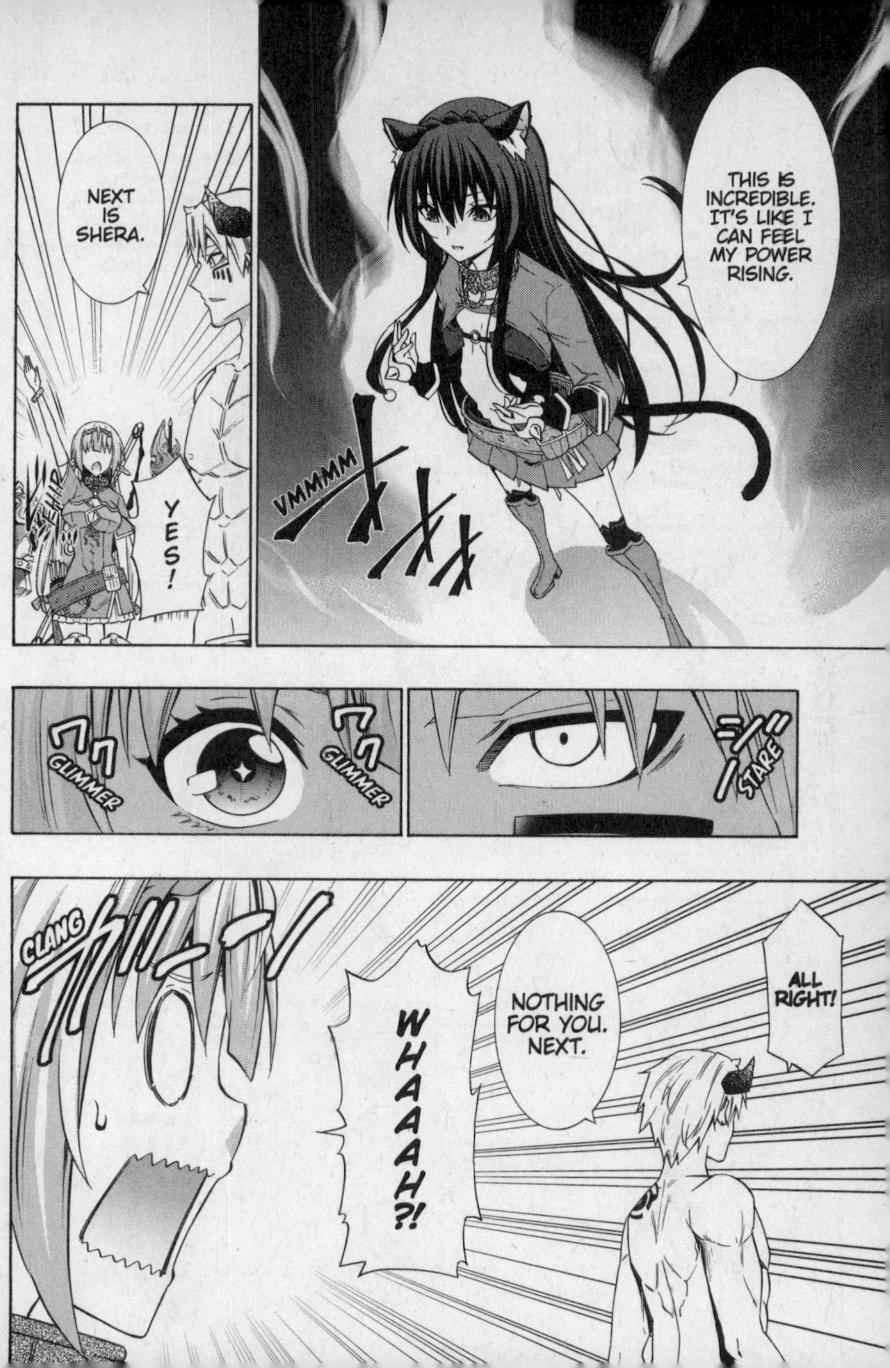

THIS IS INCREDIBLE. IT'S LIKE I CAN FEEL MY POWER RISING.
VMMMM
NEXT IS SHERA.
YES!
STARE
GLIMMER
GLIMMER
ALL RIGHT!
NOTHING FOR YOU. NEXT.
WHAAAAH?!
CLANG

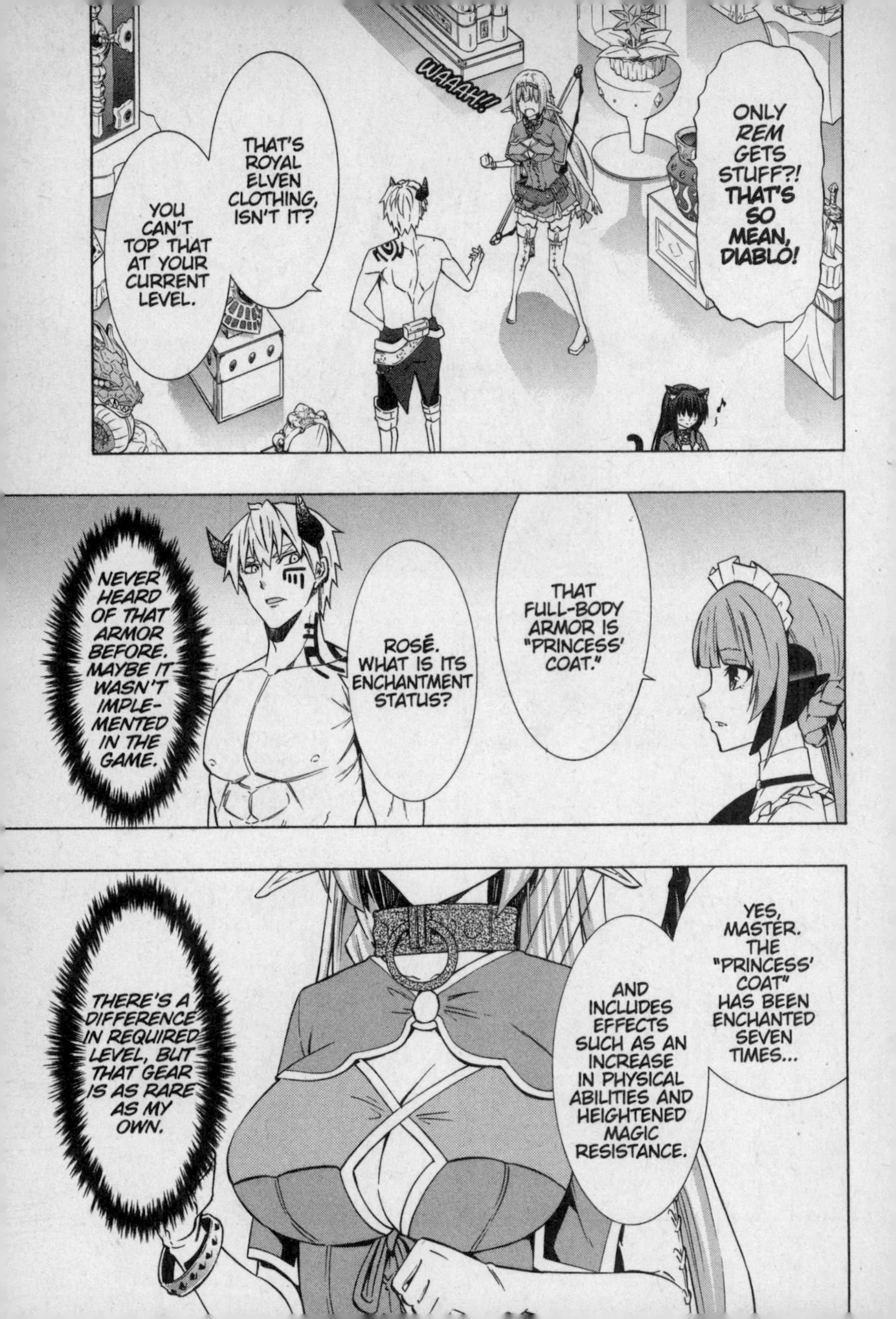
ONLY REM GETS STUFF?! THAT'S SO MEAN, DIABLO!
WAAAAH!!
THAT'S ROYAL ELVEN CLOTHING, ISN'T IT?
YOU CAN'T TOP THAT AT YOUR CURRENT LEVEL.
THAT FULL-BODY ARMOR IS "PRINCESS' COAT."
ROSÉ. WHAT IS ITS ENCHANTMENT STATUS?
NEVER HEARD OF THAT ARMOR BEFORE. MAYBE IT WASN'T IMPLE-MENTED IN THE GAME.
YES, MASTER. THE "PRINCESS' COAT" HAS BEEN ENCHANTED SEVEN TIMES...
AND INCLUDES EFFECTS SUCH AS AN INCREASE IN PHYSICAL ABILITIES AND HEIGHTENED MAGIC RESISTANCE.
THERE'S A DIFFERENCE IN REQUIRED LEVEL, BUT THAT GEAR IS AS RARE AS MY OWN.

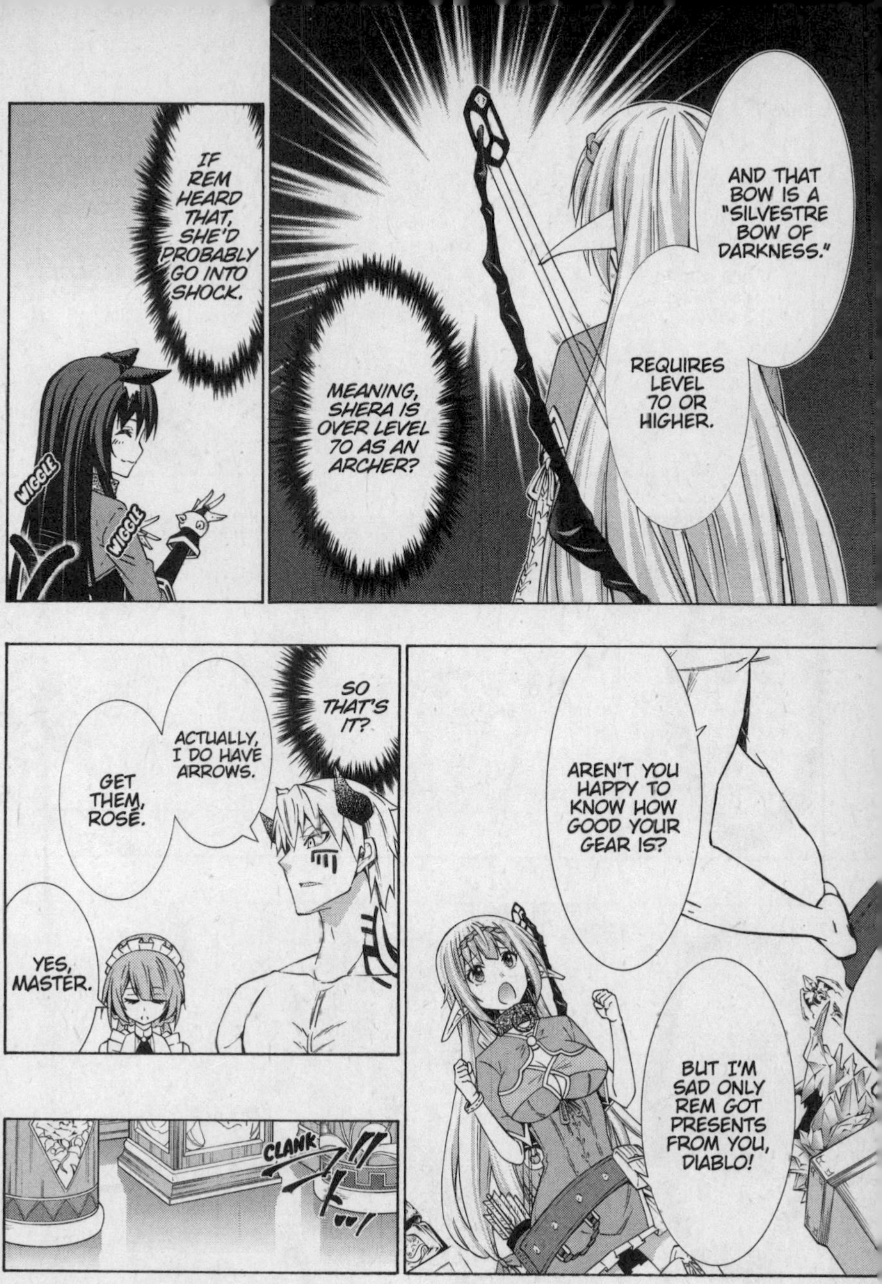
AND THAT BOW IS A "SILVESTRE BOW OF DARKNESS."
REQUIRES LEVEL 70 OR HIGHER.
MEANING, SHERA IS OVER LEVEL 70 AS AN ARCHER?
IF REM HEARD THAT, SHE'D PROBABLY GO INTO SHOCK.
WIGGLE
WIGGLE
AREN'T YOU HAPPY TO KNOW HOW GOOD YOUR GEAR IS?
BUT I'M SAD ONLY REM GOT PRESENTS FROM YOU, DIABLO!
SO THAT'S IT?
ACTUALLY, I DO HAVE ARROWS.
GET THEM, ROSÉ.
YES, MASTER.
CLANK

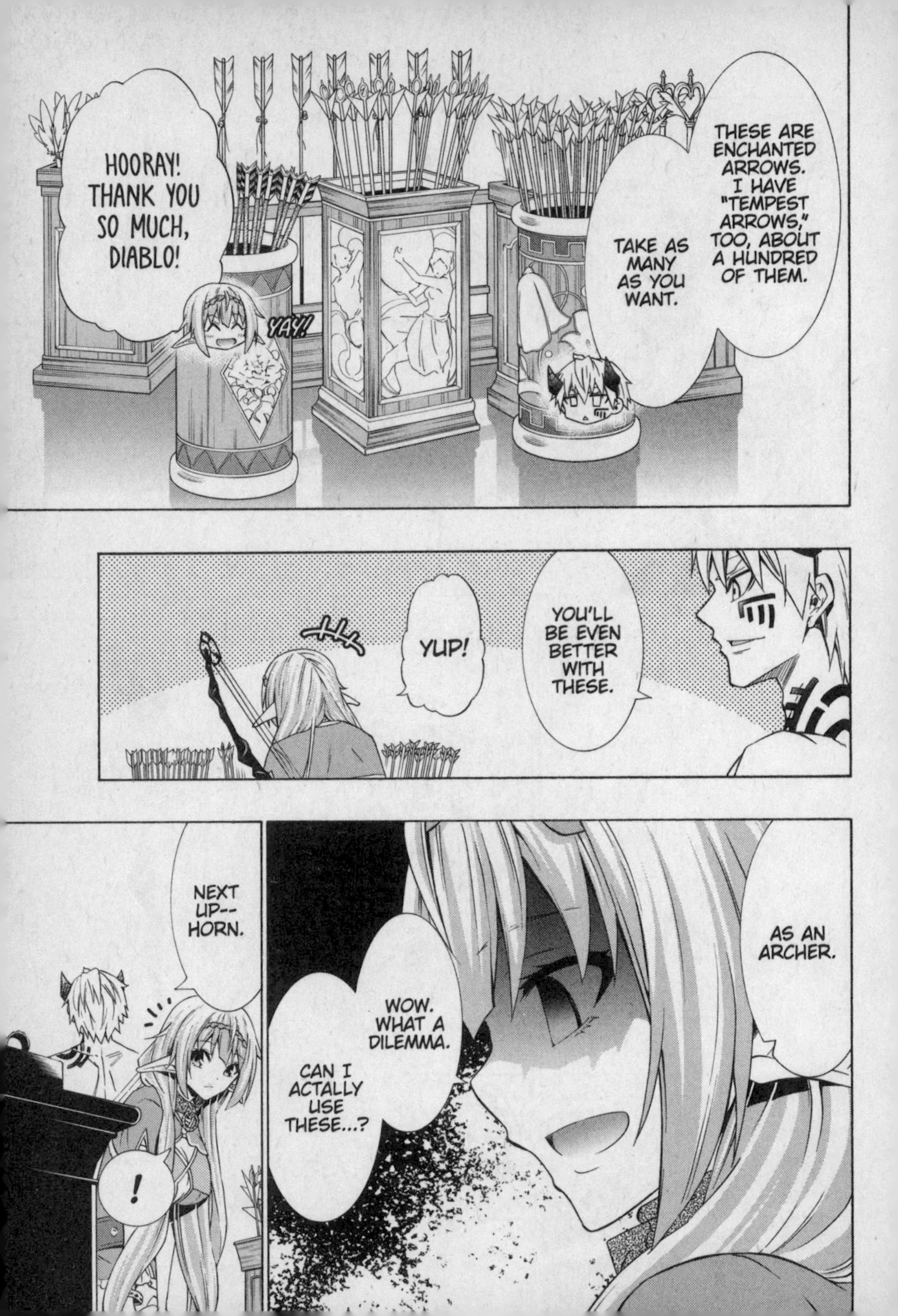
THESE ARE ENCHANTED ARROWS. I HAVE "TEMPEST ARROWS," TOO, ABOUT A HUNDRED OF THEM.
TAKE AS MANY AS YOU WANT.
HOORAY! THANK YOU SO MUCH, DIABLO!
YAY!
YOU'LL BE EVEN BETTER WITH THESE.
YUP!
AS AN ARCHER.
WOW. WHAT A DILEMMA.
CAN I ACTALLY USE THESE...?
NEXT UP-- HORN.
!

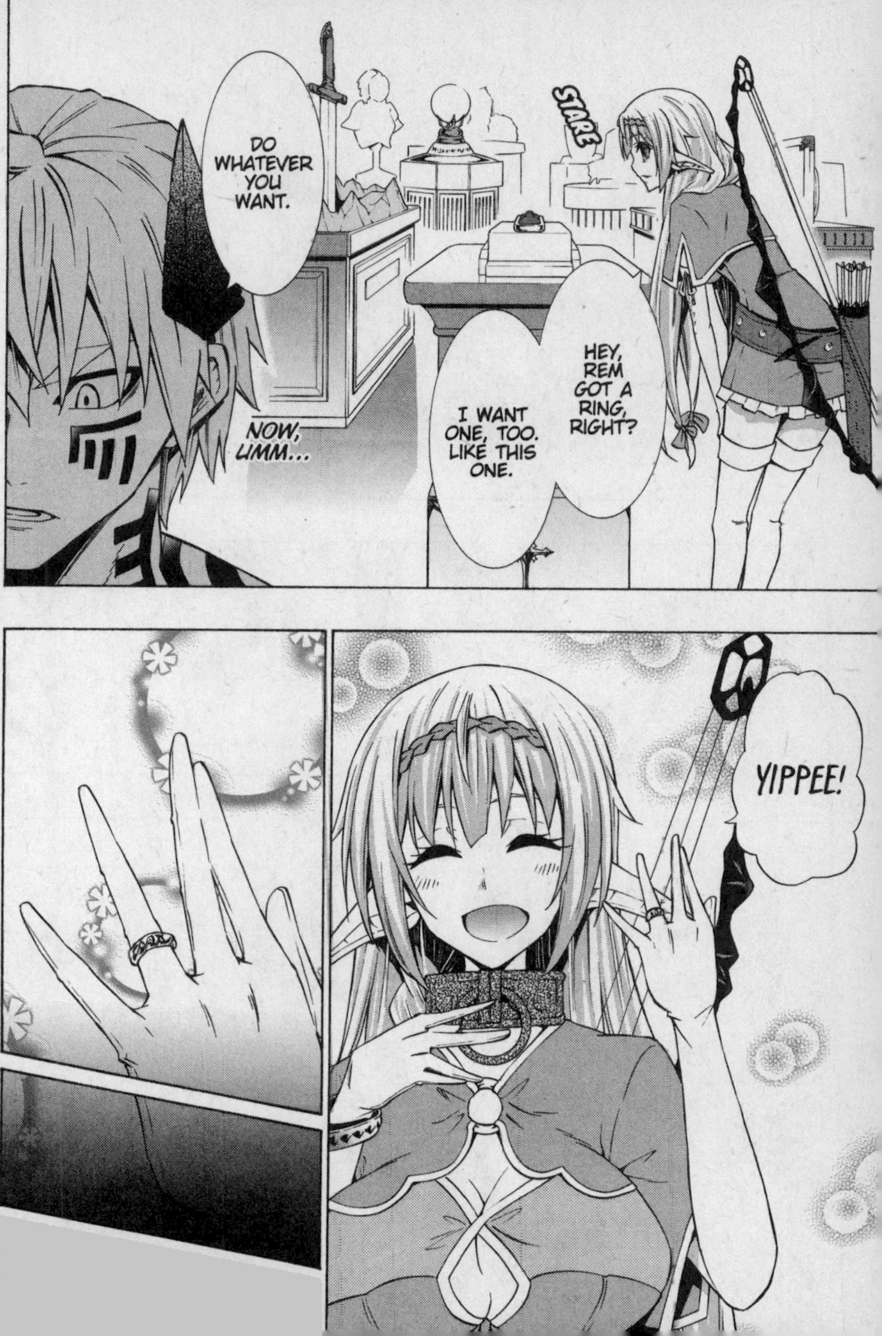
STARE
HEY, REM GOT A RING, RIGHT?
I WANT ONE, TOO. LIKE THIS ONE.
DO WHATEVER YOU WANT.
NOW, UMM...
YIPPEE!

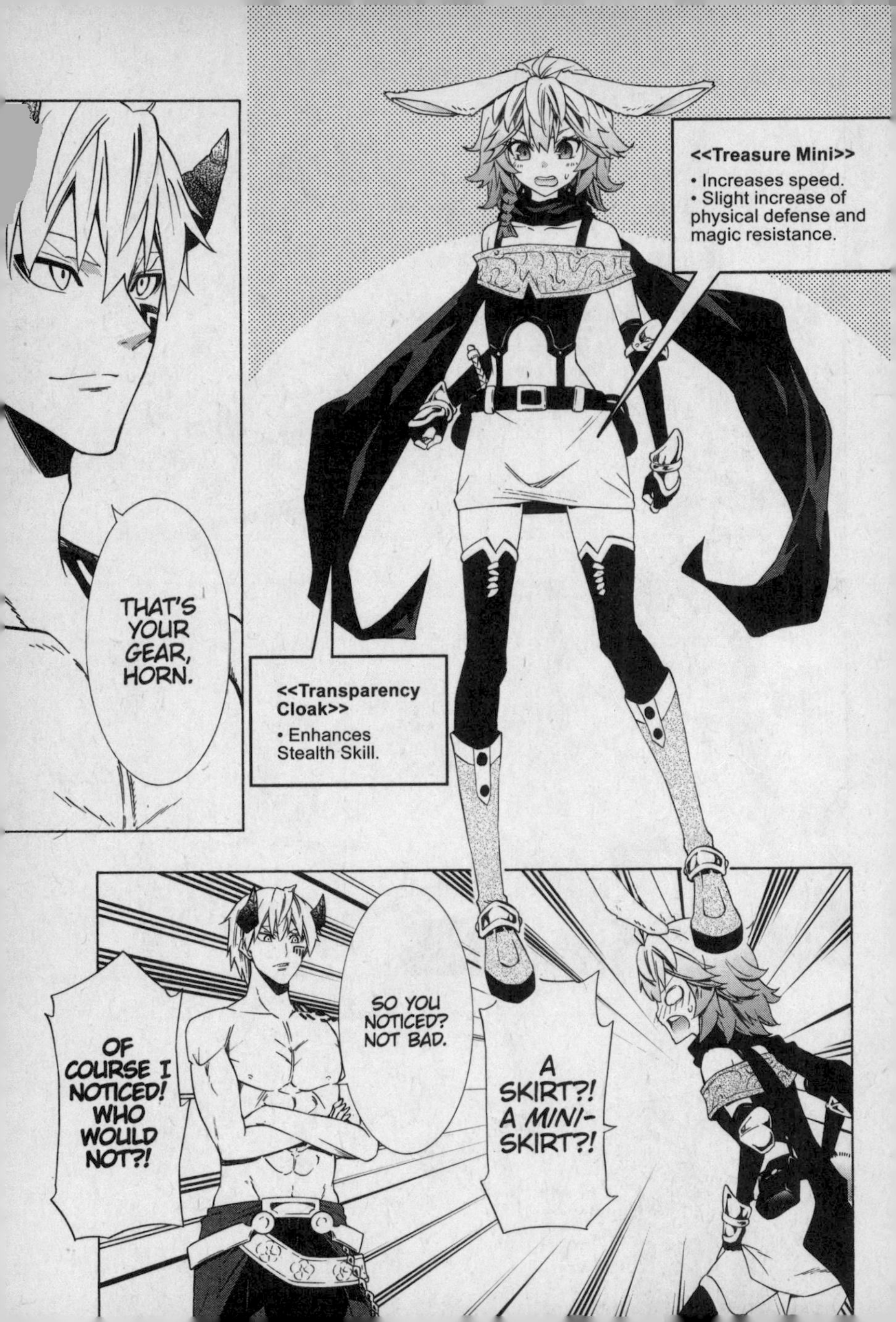
<<Treasure Mini>>
• Increases speed.
• Slight increase of physical defense and magic resistance.
<<Transparency Cloak>>
• Enhances Stealth Skill.
THAT'S YOUR GEAR, HORN.
A SKIRT?! A MINI-SKIRT?!
SO YOU NOTICED? NOT BAD.
OF COURSE I NOTICED! WHO WOULD NOT?!

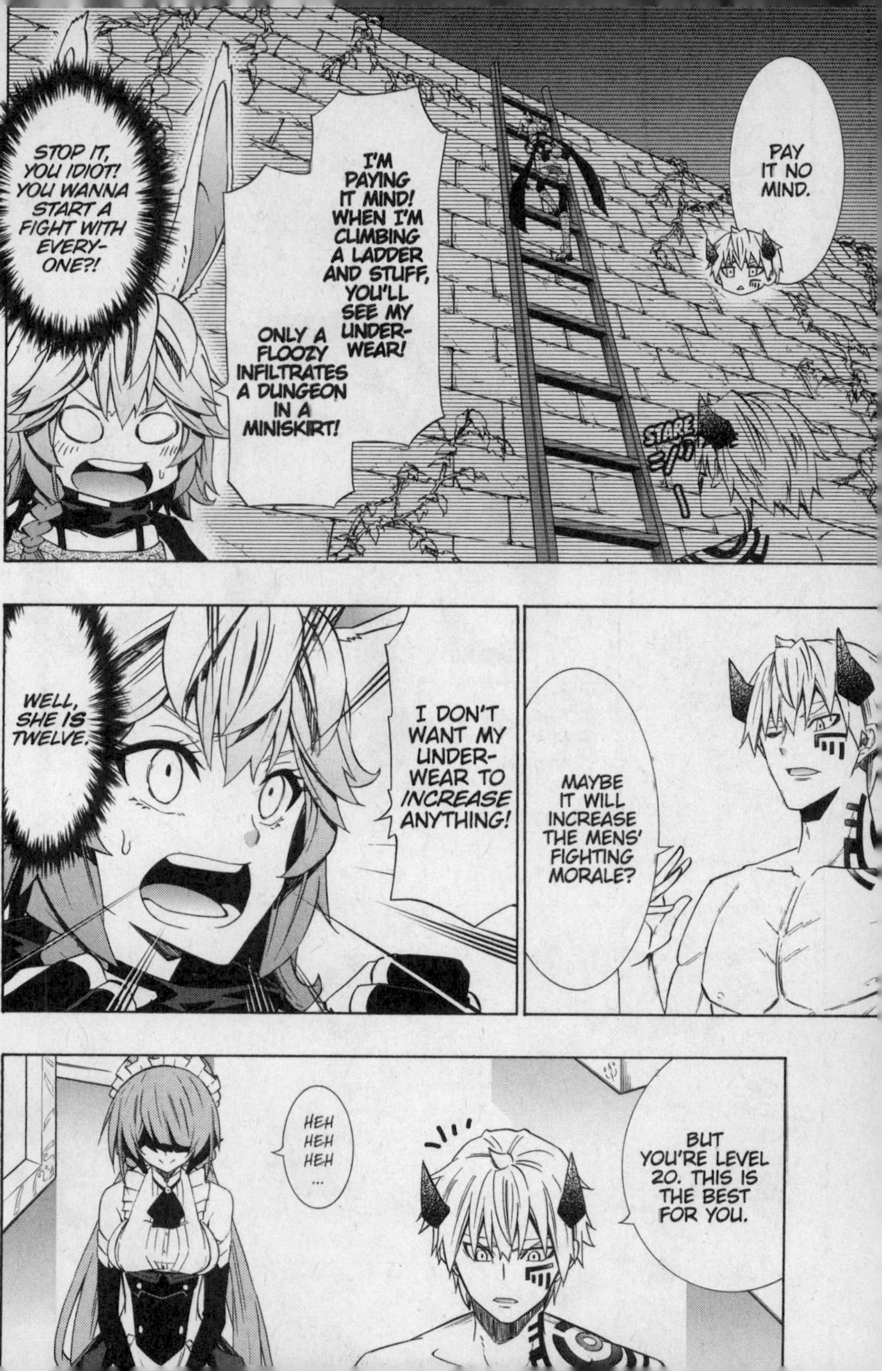
PAY IT NO MIND.
STARE
I'M PAYING IT MIND! WHEN I'M CLIMBING A LADDER AND STUFF, YOU'LL SEE MY UNDERWEAR!
ONLY A FLOOZY INFILTRATES A DUNGEON IN A MINISKIRT!
STOP IT, YOU IDIOT! YOU WANNA START A FIGHT WITH EVERY-ONE?!
MAYBE IT WILL INCREASE THE MENS' FIGHTING MORALE?
I DON'T WANT MY UNDER-WEAR TO *INCREASE* ANYTHING!
WELL, SHE IS TWELVE.
BUT YOU'RE LEVEL 20. THIS IS THE BEST FOR YOU.
HEH HEH HEH ...

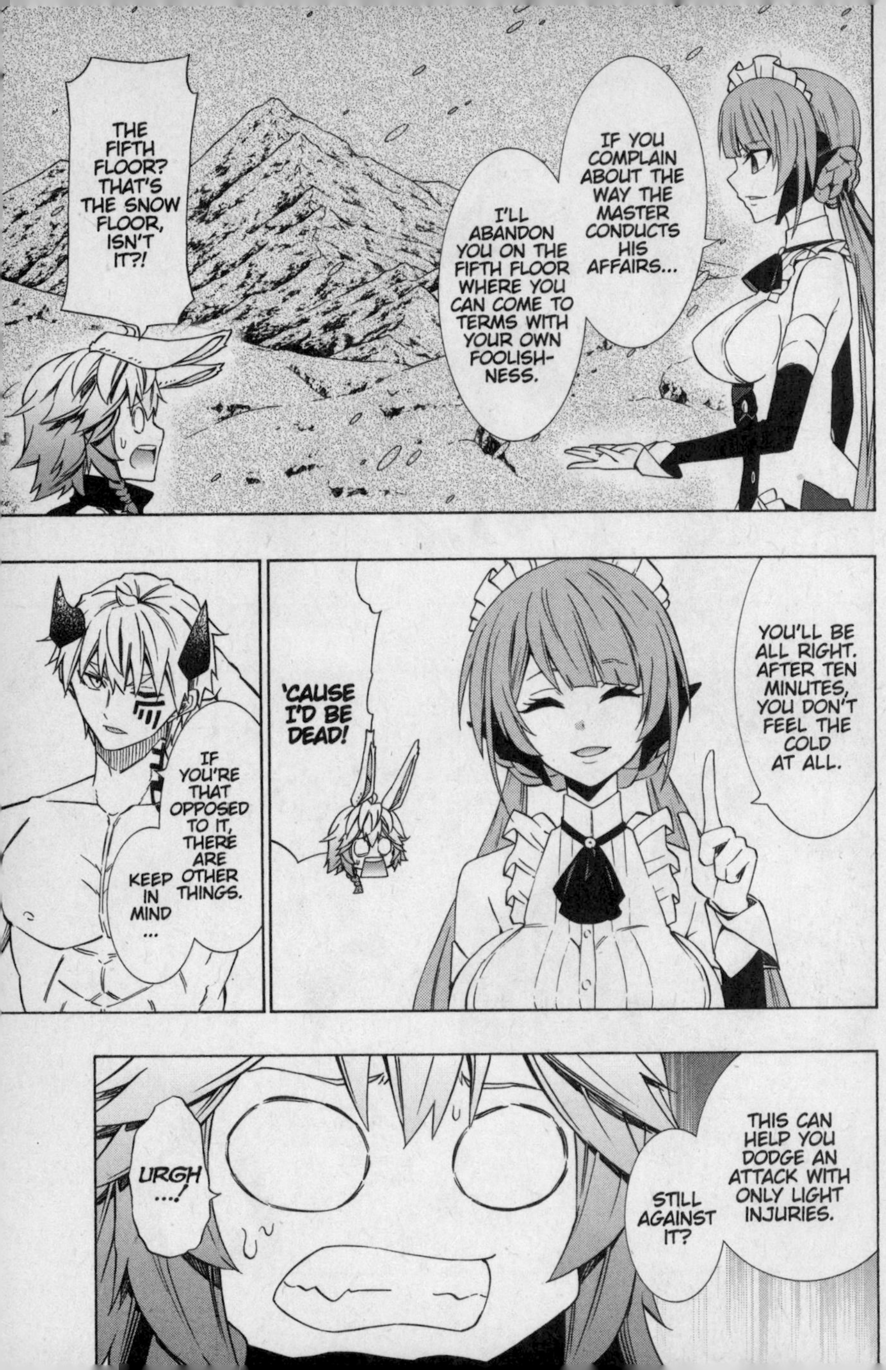
IF YOU COMPLAIN ABOUT THE WAY THE MASTER CONDUCTS HIS AFFAIRS...
I'LL ABANDON YOU ON THE FIFTH FLOOR WHERE YOU CAN COME TO TERMS WITH YOUR OWN FOOLISH-NESS.
THE FIFTH FLOOR? THAT'S THE SNOW FLOOR, ISN'T IT?!
YOU'LL BE ALL RIGHT. AFTER TEN MINUTES, YOU DON'T FEEL THE COLD AT ALL.
'CAUSE I'D BE DEAD!
IF YOU'RE THAT OPPOSED TO IT, THERE ARE OTHER THINGS.
KEEP IN MIND ...
THIS CAN HELP YOU DODGE AN ATTACK WITH ONLY LIGHT INJURIES.
STILL AGAINST IT?
URGH ...!

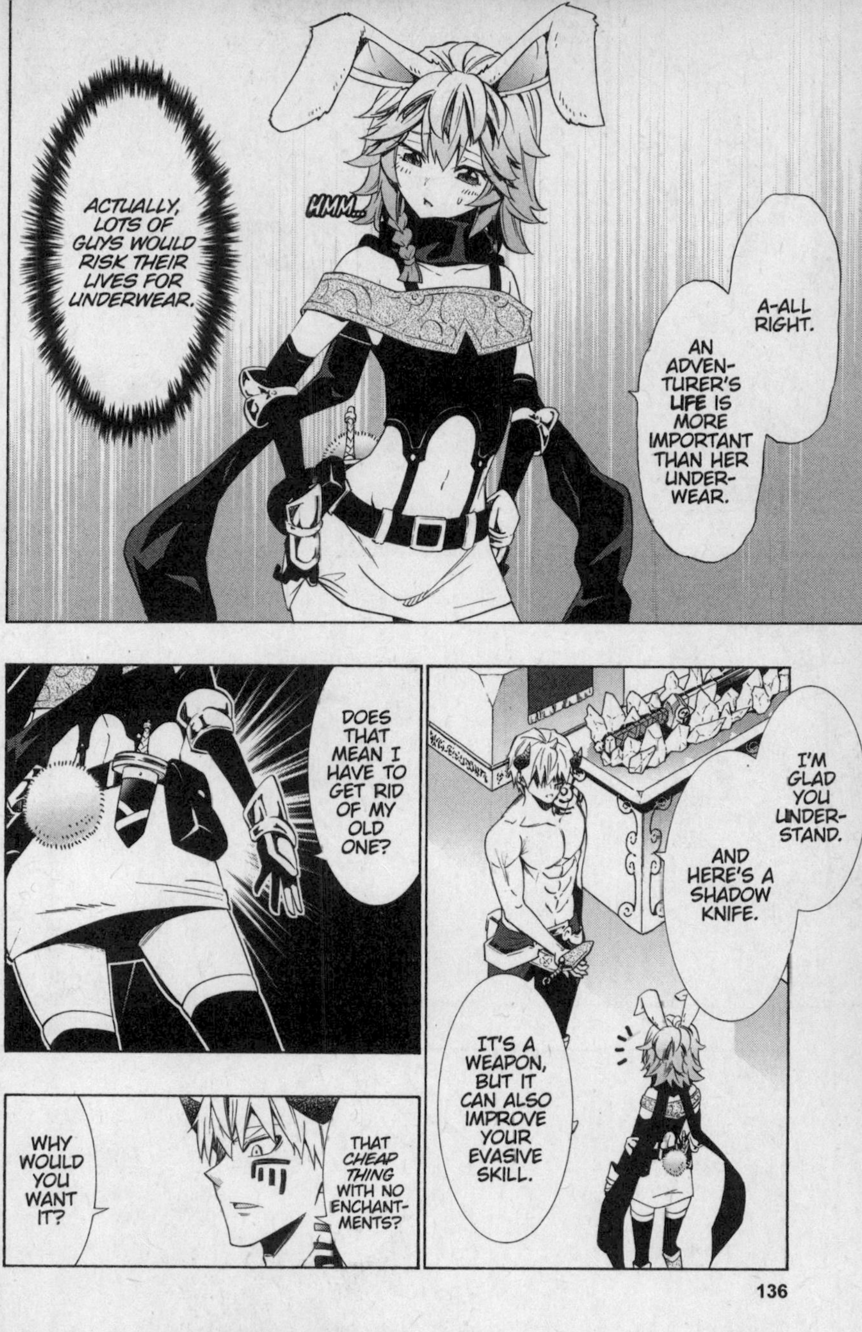
A-ALL RIGHT.
AN ADVENTURER'S LIFE IS MORE IMPORTANT THAN HER UNDERWEAR.
HMM...
ACTUALLY, LOTS OF GUYS WOULD RISK THEIR LIVES FOR UNDERWEAR.
I'M GLAD YOU UNDERSTAND.
AND HERE'S A SHADOW KNIFE.
IT'S A WEAPON, BUT IT CAN ALSO IMPROVE YOUR EVASIVE SKILL.
DOES THAT MEAN I HAVE TO GET RID OF MY OLD ONE?
THAT CHEAP THING WITH NO ENCHANTMENTS?
WHY WOULD YOU WANT IT?

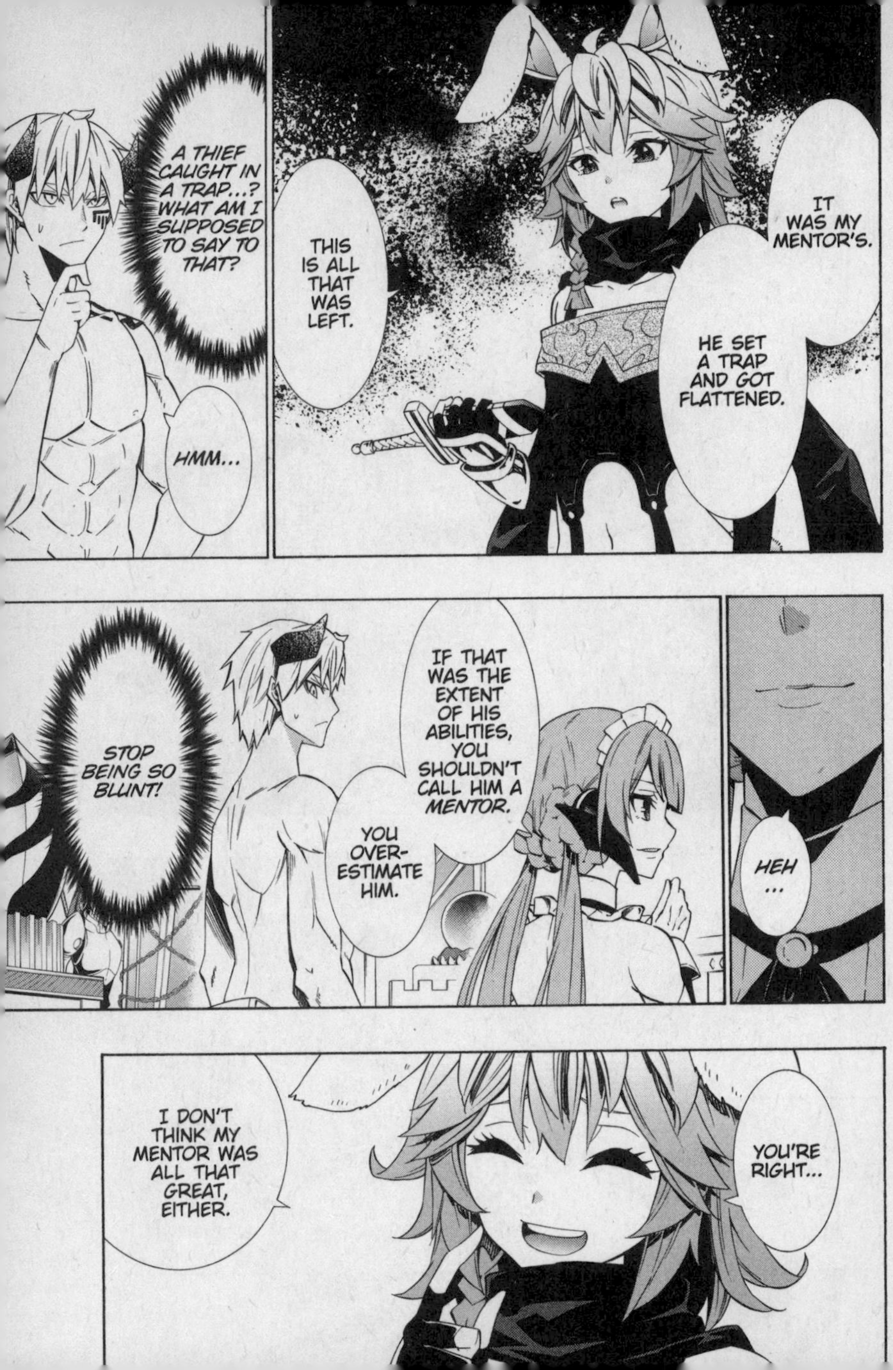
IT WAS MY MENTOR'S.
HE SET A TRAP AND GOT FLATTENED.
THIS IS ALL THAT WAS LEFT.
A THIEF CAUGHT IN A TRAP...? WHAT AM I SUPPOSED TO SAY TO THAT?
HMM...
HEH...
IF THAT WAS THE EXTENT OF HIS ABILITIES, YOU SHOULDN'T CALL HIM A MENTOR.
YOU OVER-ESTIMATE HIM.
STOP BEING SO BLUNT!
YOU'RE RIGHT...
I DON'T THINK MY MENTOR WAS ALL THAT GREAT, EITHER.

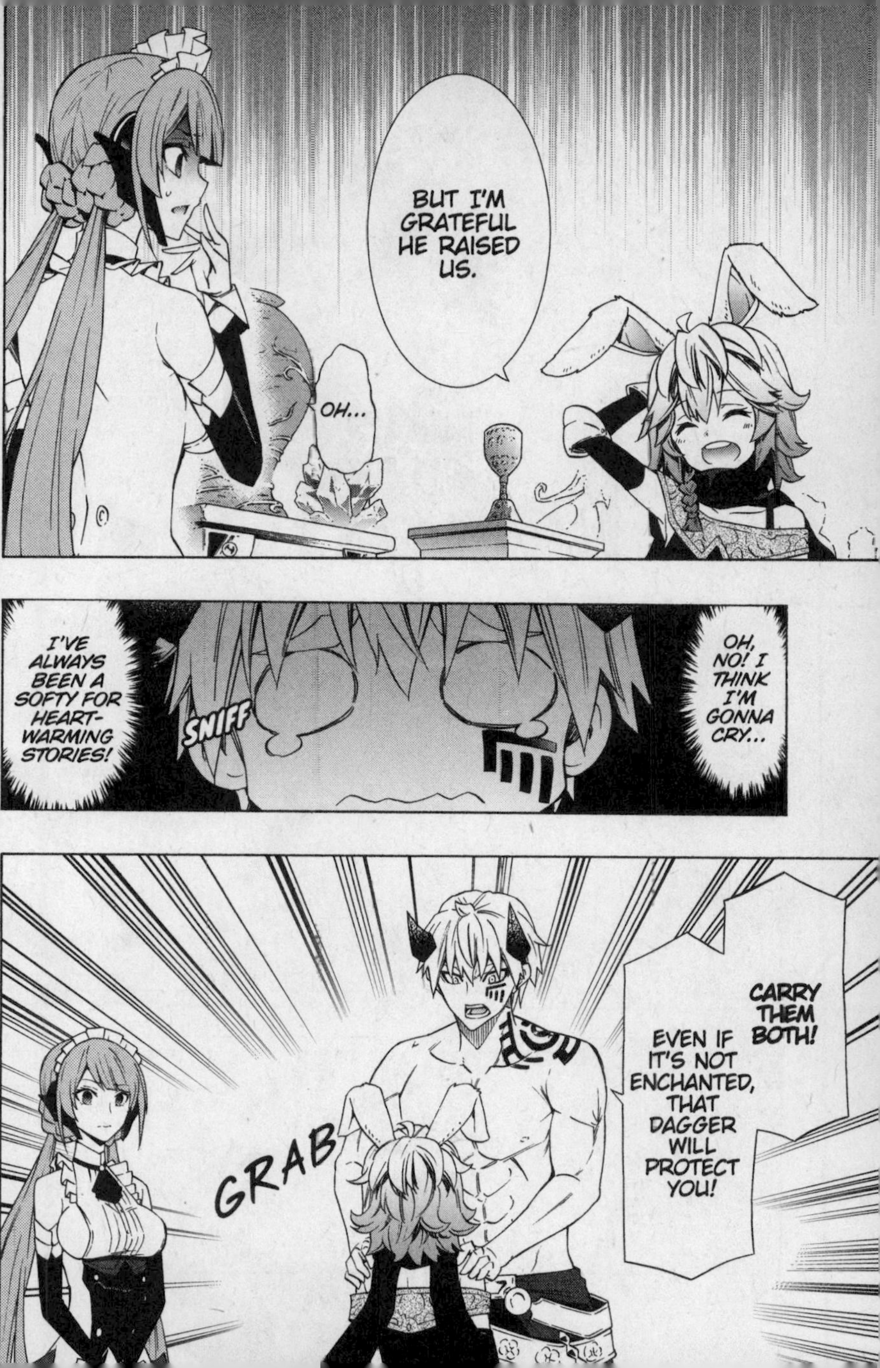
BUT I'M GRATEFUL HE RAISED US.
OH...
OH, NO! I THINK I'M GONNA CRY...
SNIFF
I'VE ALWAYS BEEN A SOFTY FOR HEART-WARMING STORIES!
CARRY THEM BOTH!
EVEN IF IT'S NOT ENCHANTED, THAT DAGGER WILL PROTECT YOU!
GRAB

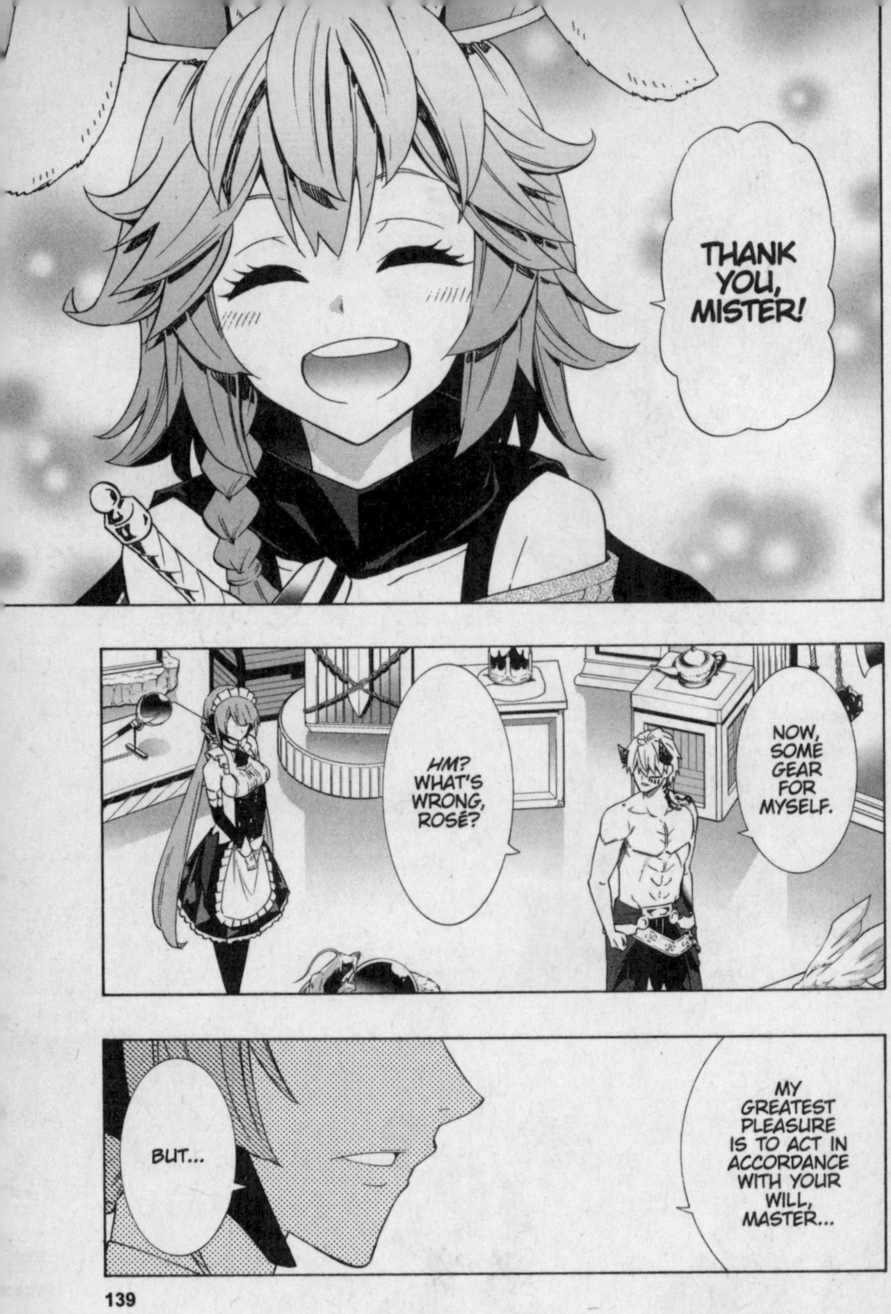
THANK YOU, MISTER!
NOW, SOME GEAR FOR MYSELF.
HM? WHAT'S WRONG, ROSÉ?
MY GREATEST PLEASURE IS TO ACT IN ACCORDANCE WITH YOUR WILL, MASTER...
BUT...

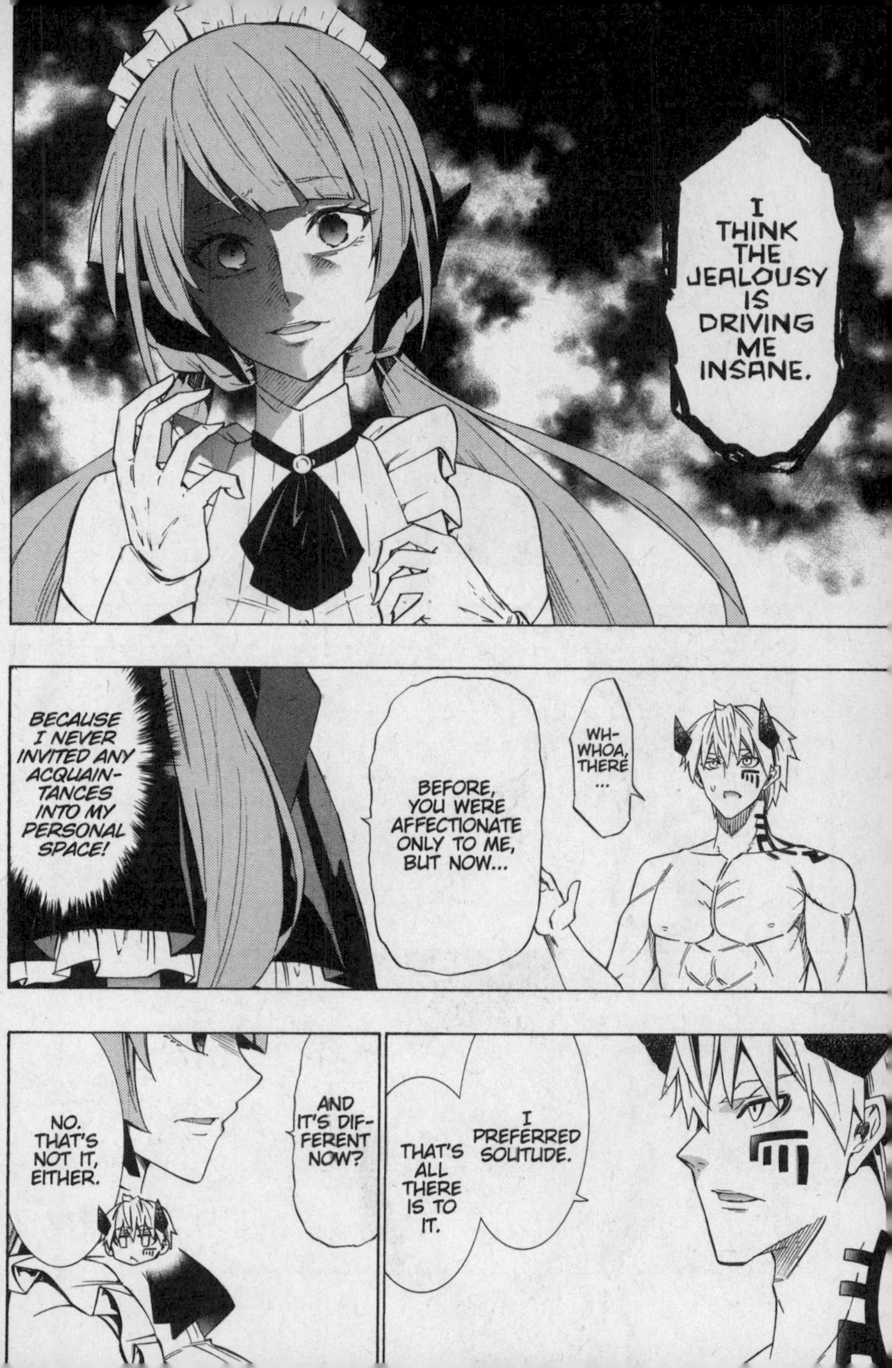
I THINK THE JEALOUSY IS DRIVING ME INSANE.
WH-WHOA, THERE...
BEFORE, YOU WERE AFFECTIONATE ONLY TO ME, BUT NOW...
BECAUSE I NEVER INVITED ANY ACQUAINTANCES INTO MY PERSONAL SPACE!
I PREFERRED SOLITUDE.
THAT'S ALL THERE IS TO IT.
AND IT'S DIFFERENT NOW?
NO. THAT'S NOT IT, EITHER.

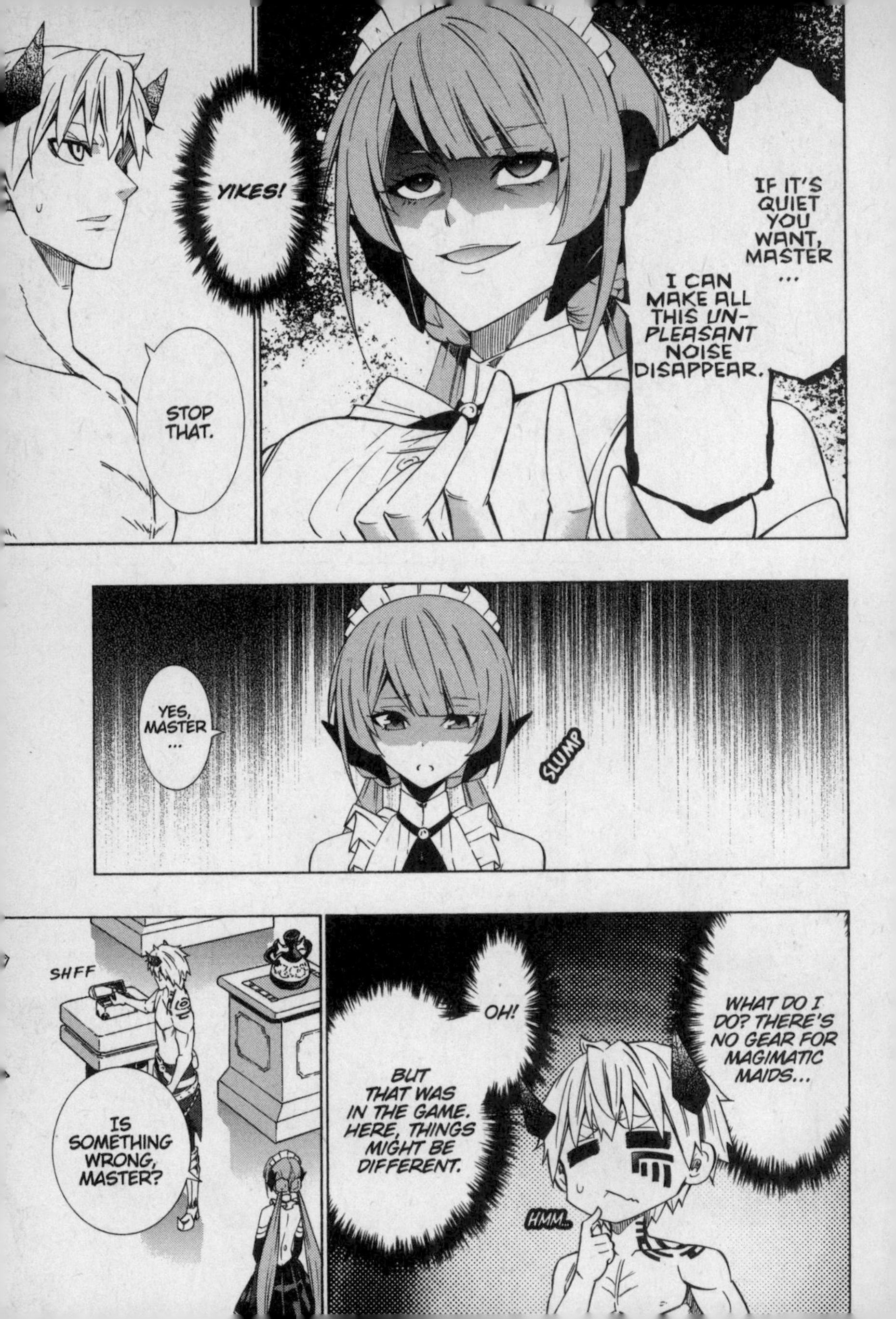
IF IT'S QUIET YOU WANT, MASTER...
I CAN MAKE ALL THIS UN-PLEASANT NOISE DISAPPEAR.
YIKES!
STOP THAT.
YES, MASTER...
SLUMP
WHAT DO I DO? THERE'S NO GEAR FOR MAGIMATIC MAIDS...
OH!
BUT THAT WAS IN THE GAME. HERE, THINGS MIGHT BE DIFFERENT.
HMM...
SHFF
IS SOMETHING WRONG, MASTER?

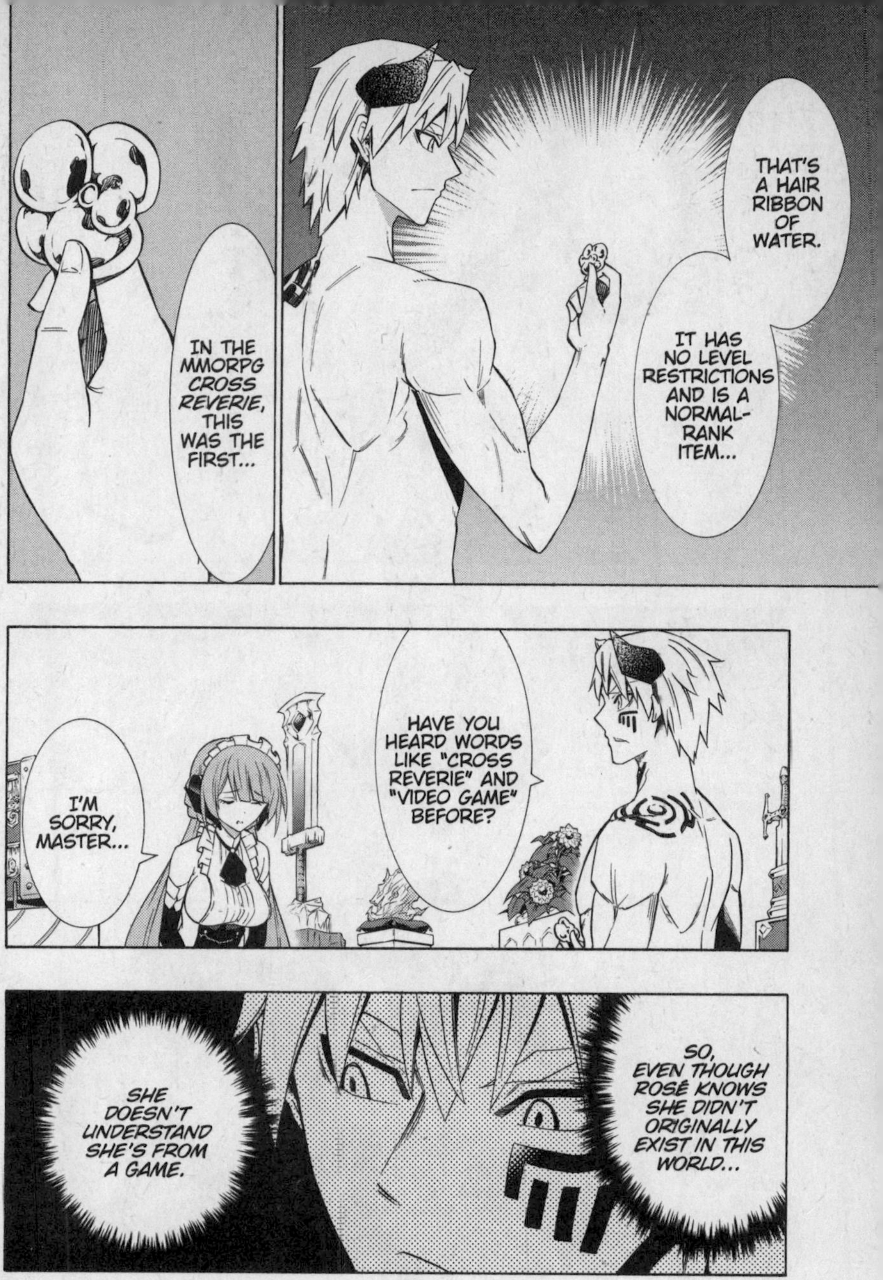
THAT'S A HAIR RIBBON OF WATER.
IT HAS NO LEVEL RESTRICTIONS AND IS A NORMAL-RANK ITEM...
IN THE MMORPG *CROSS REVERIE*, THIS WAS THE FIRST...
HAVE YOU HEARD WORDS LIKE "CROSS REVERIE" AND "VIDEO GAME" BEFORE?
I'M SORRY, MASTER...
SO, EVEN THOUGH ROSÉ KNOWS SHE DIDN'T ORIGINALLY EXIST IN THIS WORLD...
SHE DOESN'T UNDERSTAND SHE'S FROM A GAME.

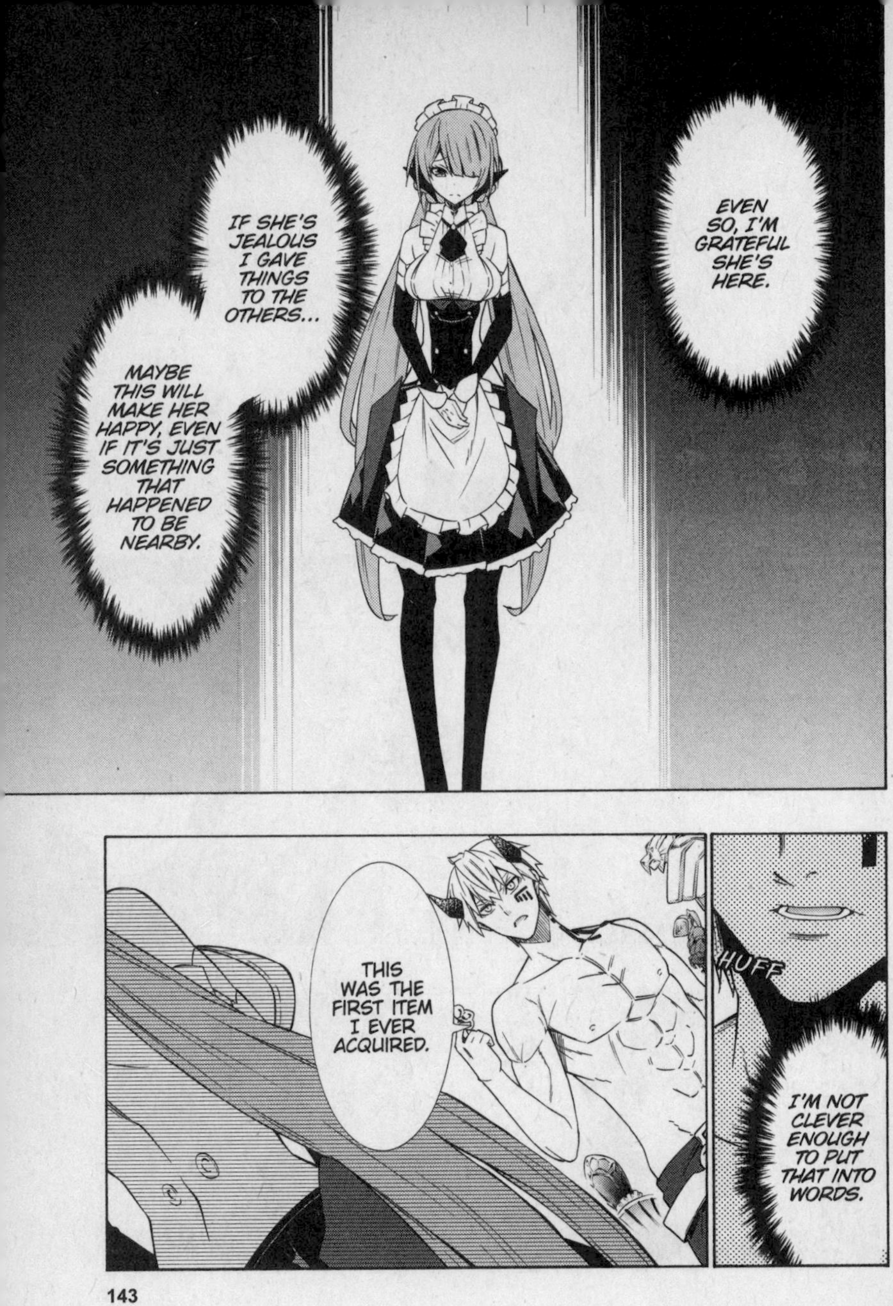
EVEN SO, I'M GRATEFUL SHE'S HERE.
IF SHE'S JEALOUS I GAVE THINGS TO THE OTHERS...
MAYBE THIS WILL MAKE HER HAPPY, EVEN IF IT'S JUST SOMETHING THAT HAPPENED TO BE NEARBY.
HUFF
I'M NOT CLEVER ENOUGH TO PUT THAT INTO WORDS.
THIS WAS THE FIRST ITEM I EVER ACQUIRED.

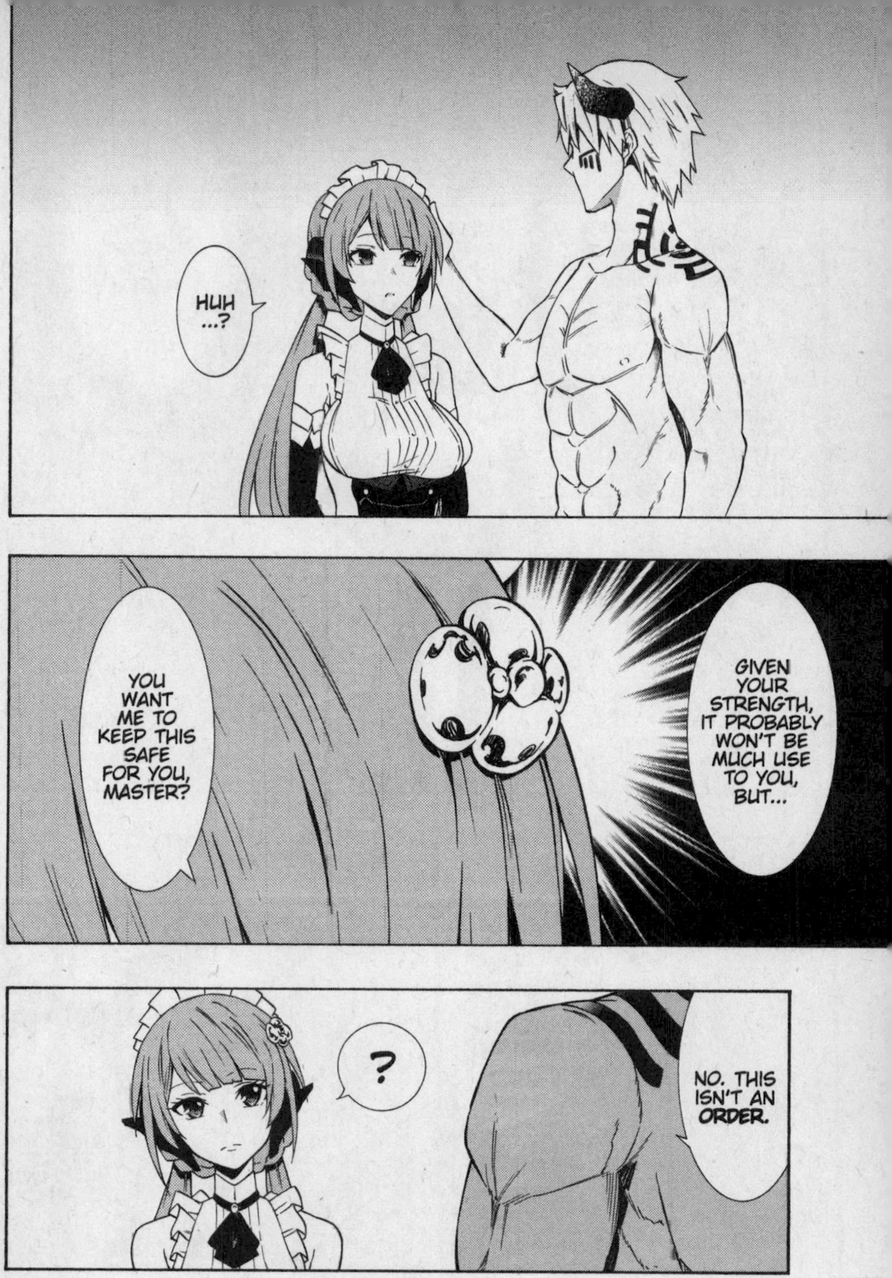
HUH ...?
GIVEN YOUR STRENGTH, IT PROBABLY WON'T BE MUCH USE TO YOU, BUT...
YOU WANT ME TO KEEP THIS SAFE FOR YOU, MASTER?
NO. THIS ISN'T AN ORDER.
?

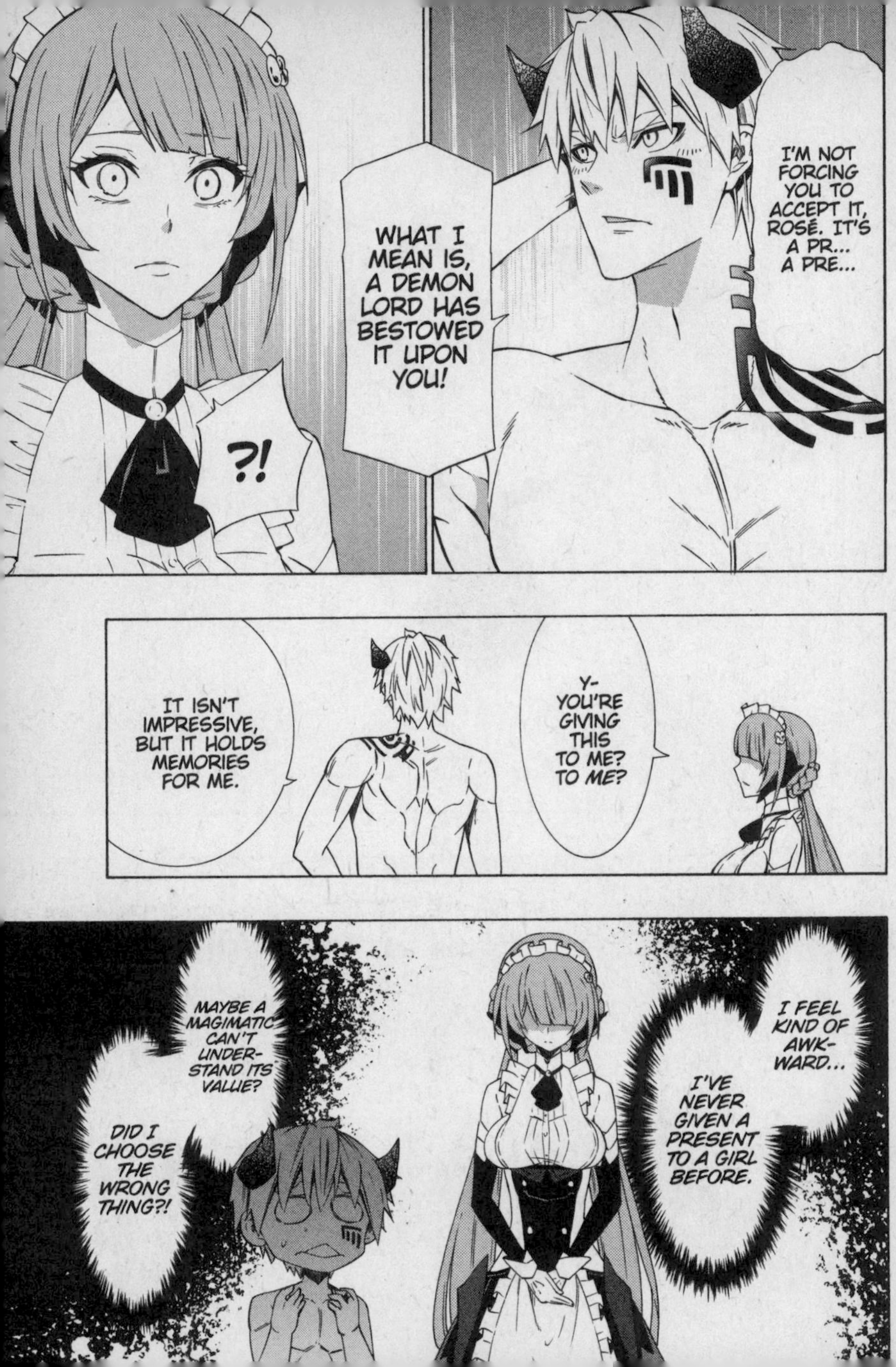
I'M NOT FORCING YOU TO ACCEPT IT, ROSÉ. IT'S A PR... A PRE...
WHAT I MEAN IS, A DEMON LORD HAS BESTOWED IT UPON YOU!
?!
Y- YOU'RE GIVING THIS TO ME? TO ME?
IT ISN'T IMPRESSIVE, BUT IT HOLDS MEMORIES FOR ME.
I FEEL KIND OF AWK-WARD...
I'VE NEVER GIVEN A PRESENT TO A GIRL BEFORE.
MAYBE A MAGIMATIC CAN'T UNDER-STAND ITS VALUE?
DID I CHOOSE THE WRONG THING?!

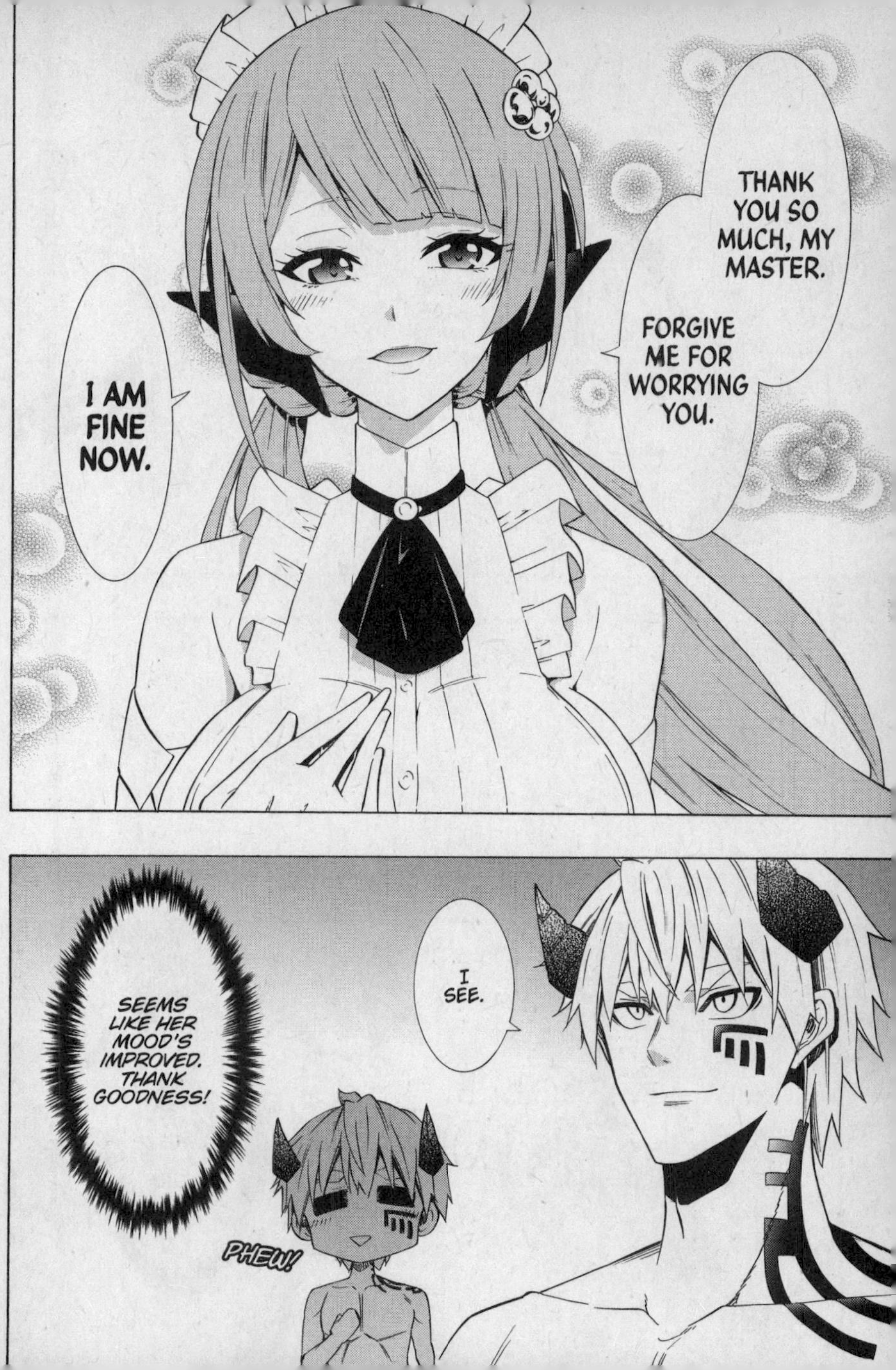
THANK YOU SO MUCH, MY MASTER.
FORGIVE ME FOR WORRYING YOU.
I AM FINE NOW.
I SEE.
SEEMS LIKE HER MOOD'S IMPROVED. THANK GOODNESS!
PHEW!

HOW NOT
TO SUMMON A
DEMON LORD

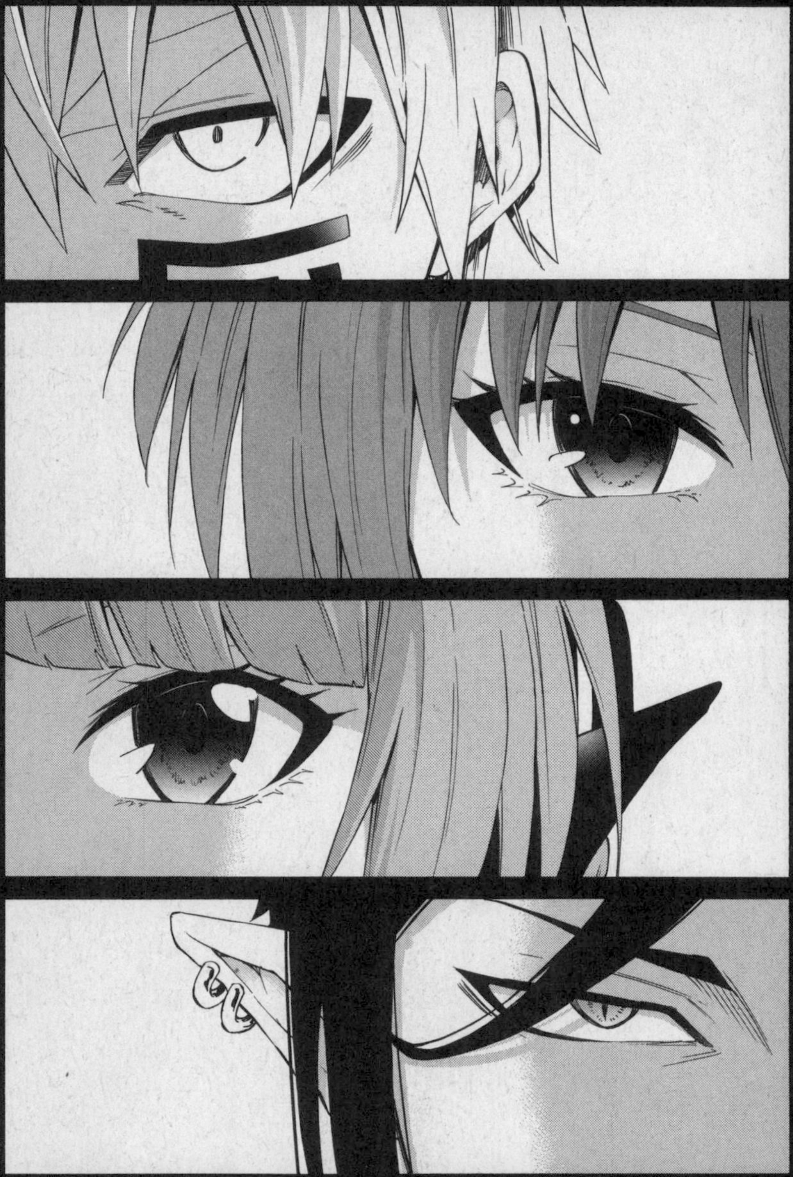

59 TRYING OUT NEW EQUIPMENT II

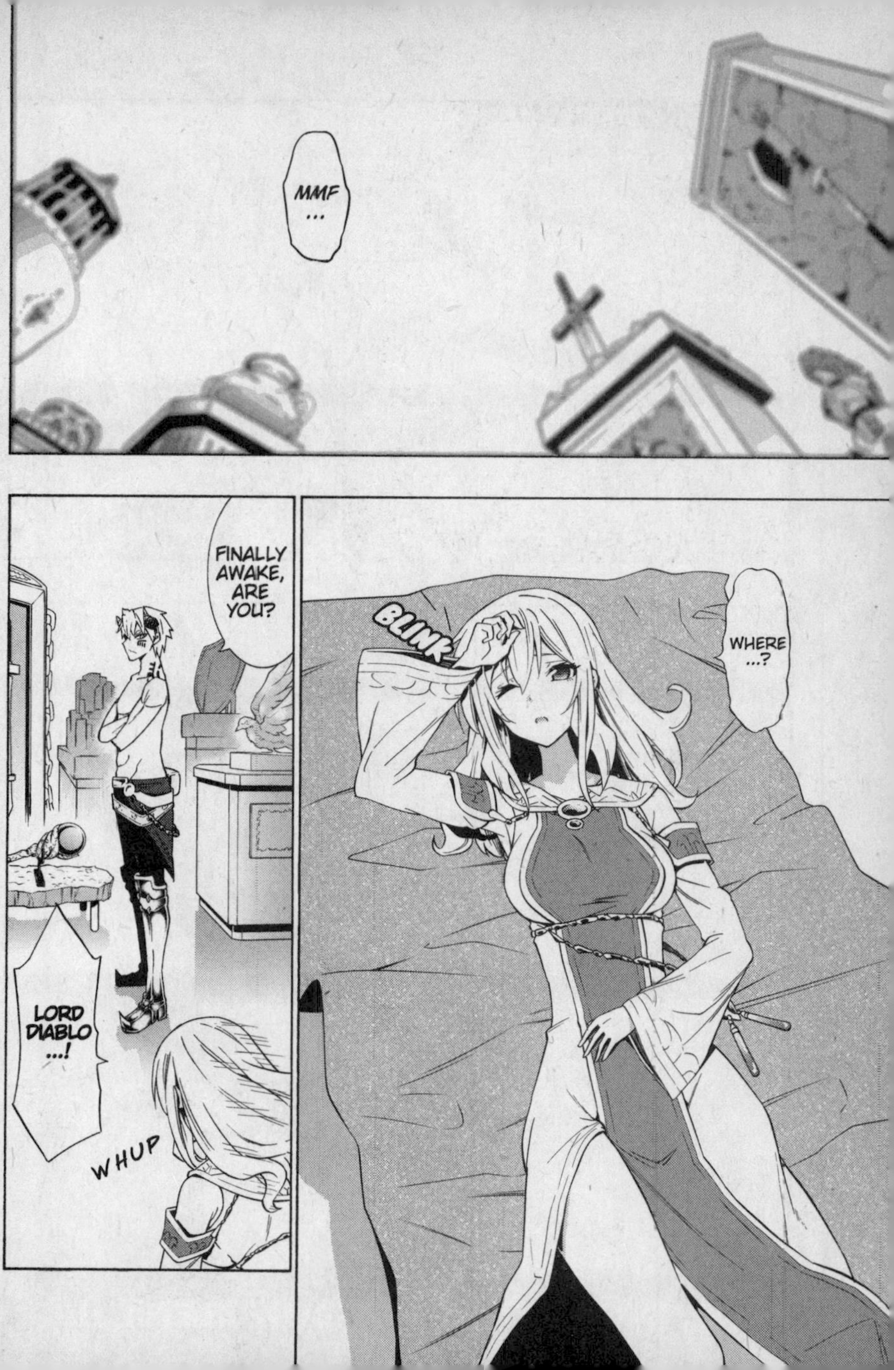
MMF ...
WHERE ...?
BLINK
FINALLY AWAKE, ARE YOU?
LORD DIABLO ...!
WHUP

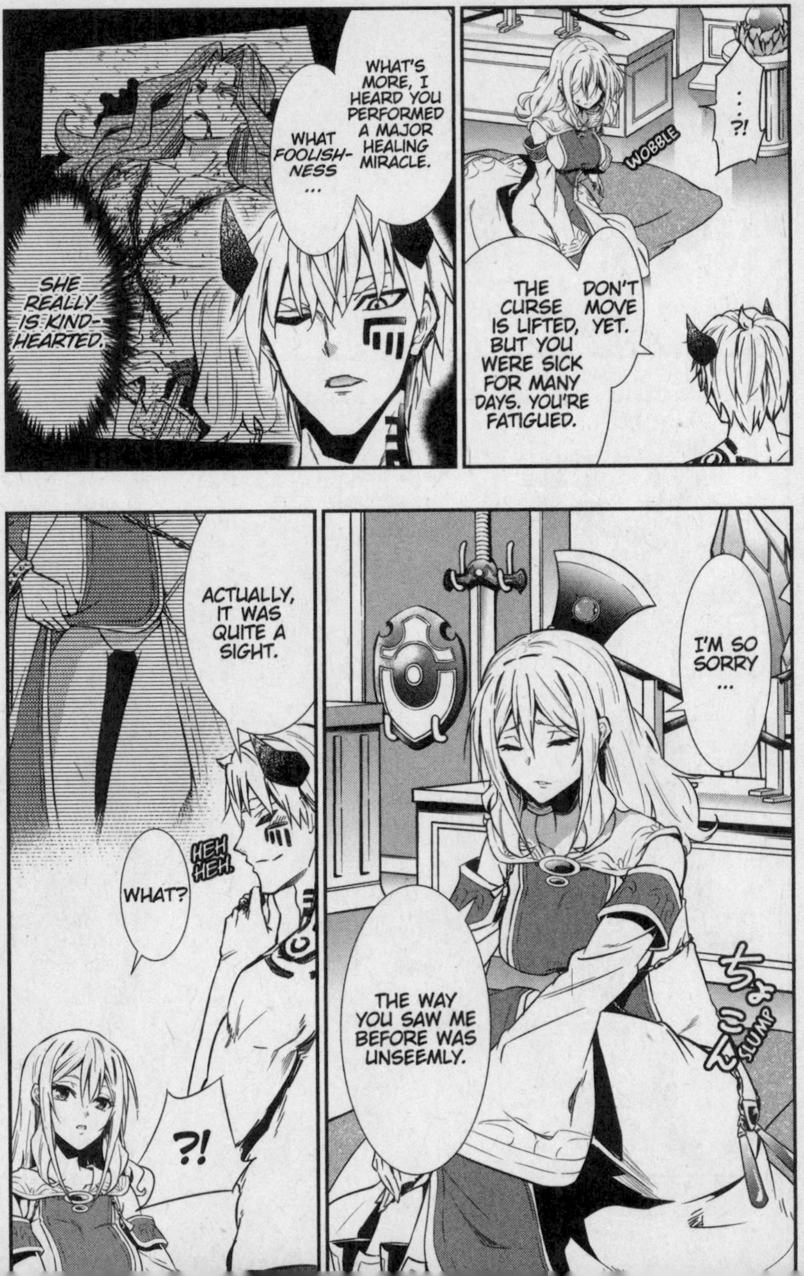
...?!
WOBBLE
DON'T MOVE YET.
THE CURSE IS LIFTED, BUT YOU WERE SICK FOR MANY DAYS. YOU'RE FATIGUED.
WHAT'S MORE, I HEARD YOU PERFORMED A MAJOR HEALING MIRACLE.
WHAT FOOLISHNESS...
SHE REALLY IS KIND-HEARTED.
I'M SO SORRY...
ちょこん
SLUMP
THE WAY YOU SAW ME BEFORE WAS UNSEEMLY.
ACTUALLY, IT WAS QUITE A SIGHT.
HEH HEH.
WHAT?
?!

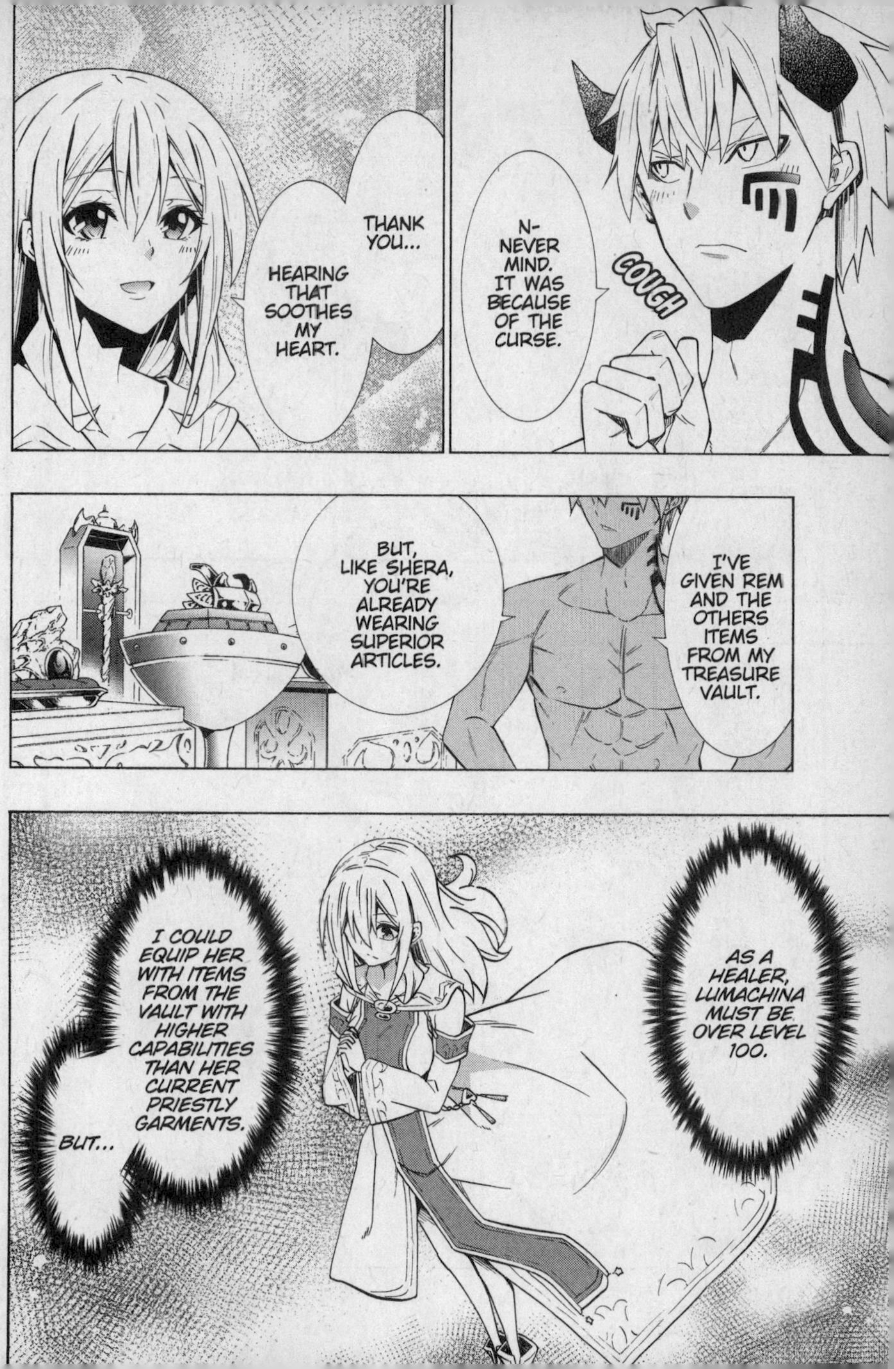
N- NEVER MIND. IT WAS BECAUSE OF THE CURSE.
COUGH
THANK YOU...
HEARING THAT SOOTHES MY HEART.
I'VE GIVEN REM AND THE OTHERS ITEMS FROM MY TREASURE VAULT.
BUT, LIKE SHERA, YOU'RE ALREADY WEARING SUPERIOR ARTICLES.
AS A HEALER, LUMACHINA MUST BE OVER LEVEL 100.
I COULD EQUIP HER WITH ITEMS FROM THE VAULT WITH HIGHER CAPABILITIES THAN HER CURRENT PRIESTLY GARMENTS.
BUT...

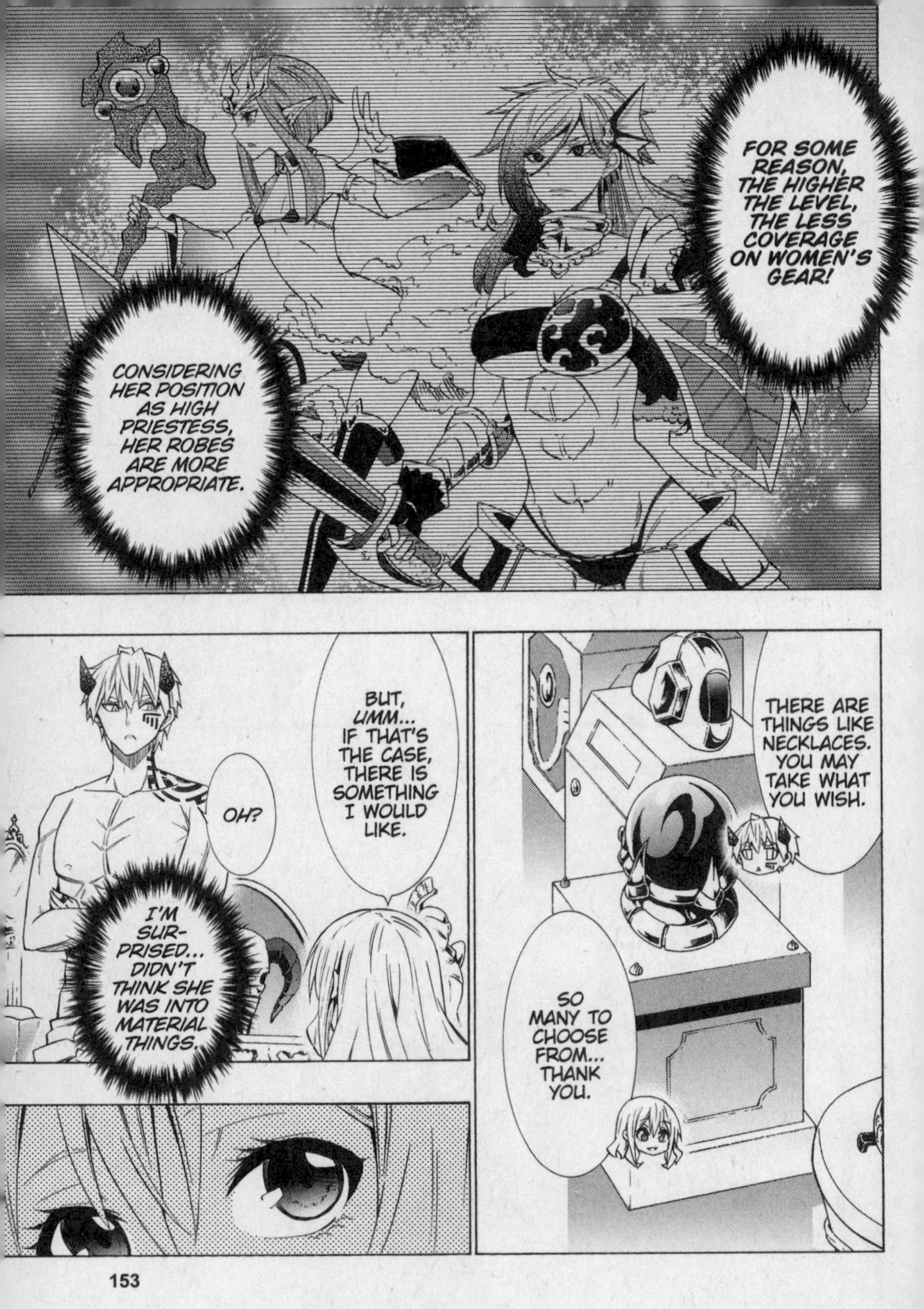
FOR SOME REASON, THE HIGHER THE LEVEL, THE LESS COVERAGE ON WOMEN'S GEAR!
CONSIDERING HER POSITION AS HIGH PRIESTESS, HER ROBES ARE MORE APPROPRIATE.
THERE ARE THINGS LIKE NECKLACES. YOU MAY TAKE WHAT YOU WISH.
SO MANY TO CHOOSE FROM... THANK YOU.
BUT, UMM... IF THAT'S THE CASE, THERE IS SOMETHING I WOULD LIKE.
OH?
I'M SUR-PRISED... DIDN'T THINK SHE WAS INTO MATERIAL THINGS.

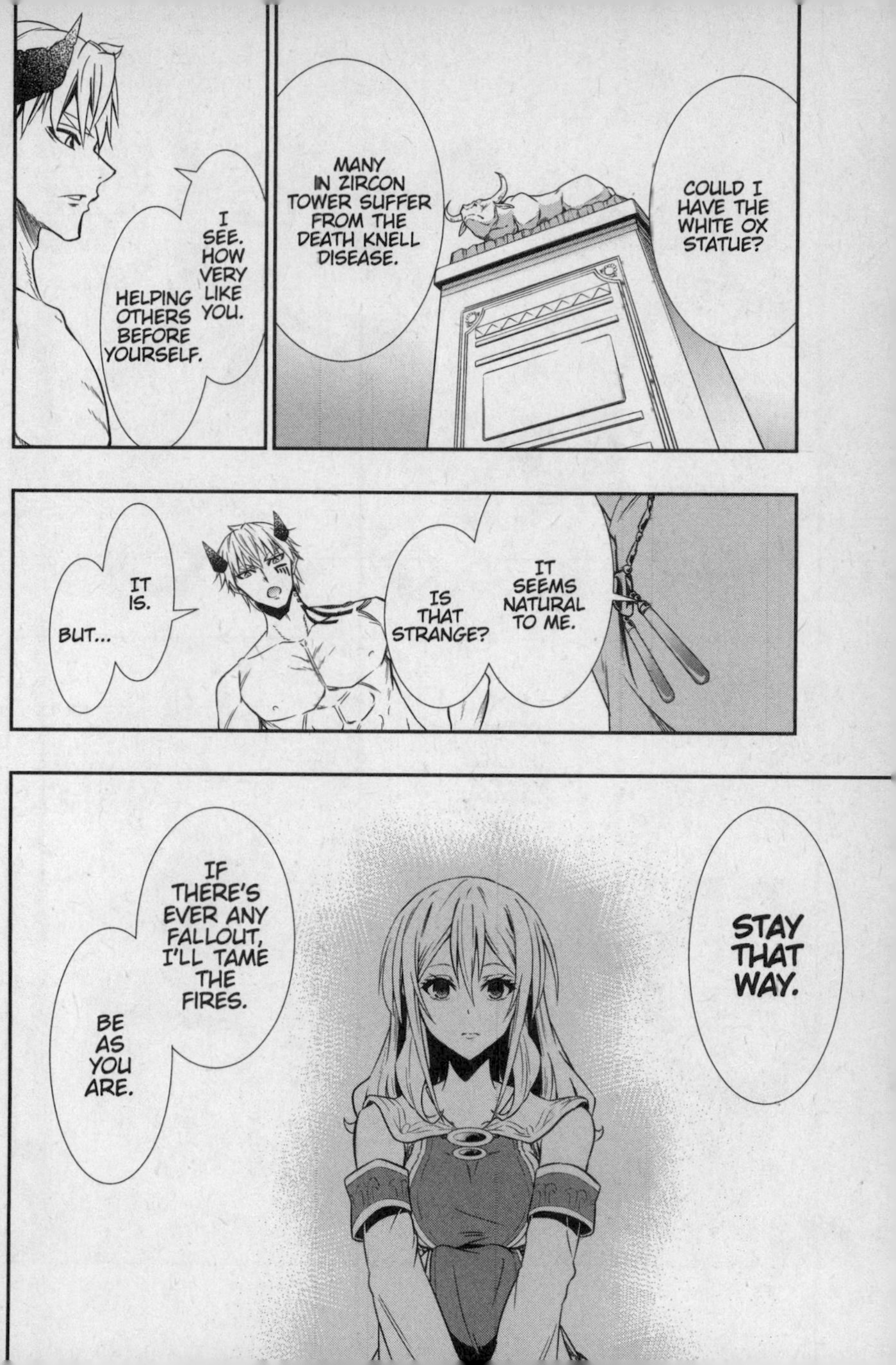
COULD I HAVE THE WHITE OX STATUE?
MANY IN ZIRCON TOWER SUFFER FROM THE DEATH KNELL DISEASE.
I SEE. HOW VERY LIKE YOU.
HELPING OTHERS BEFORE YOURSELF.
IT SEEMS NATURAL TO ME.
IS THAT STRANGE?
IT IS.
BUT...
STAY THAT WAY.
IF THERE'S EVER ANY FALLOUT, I'LL TAME THE FIRES.
BE AS YOU ARE.

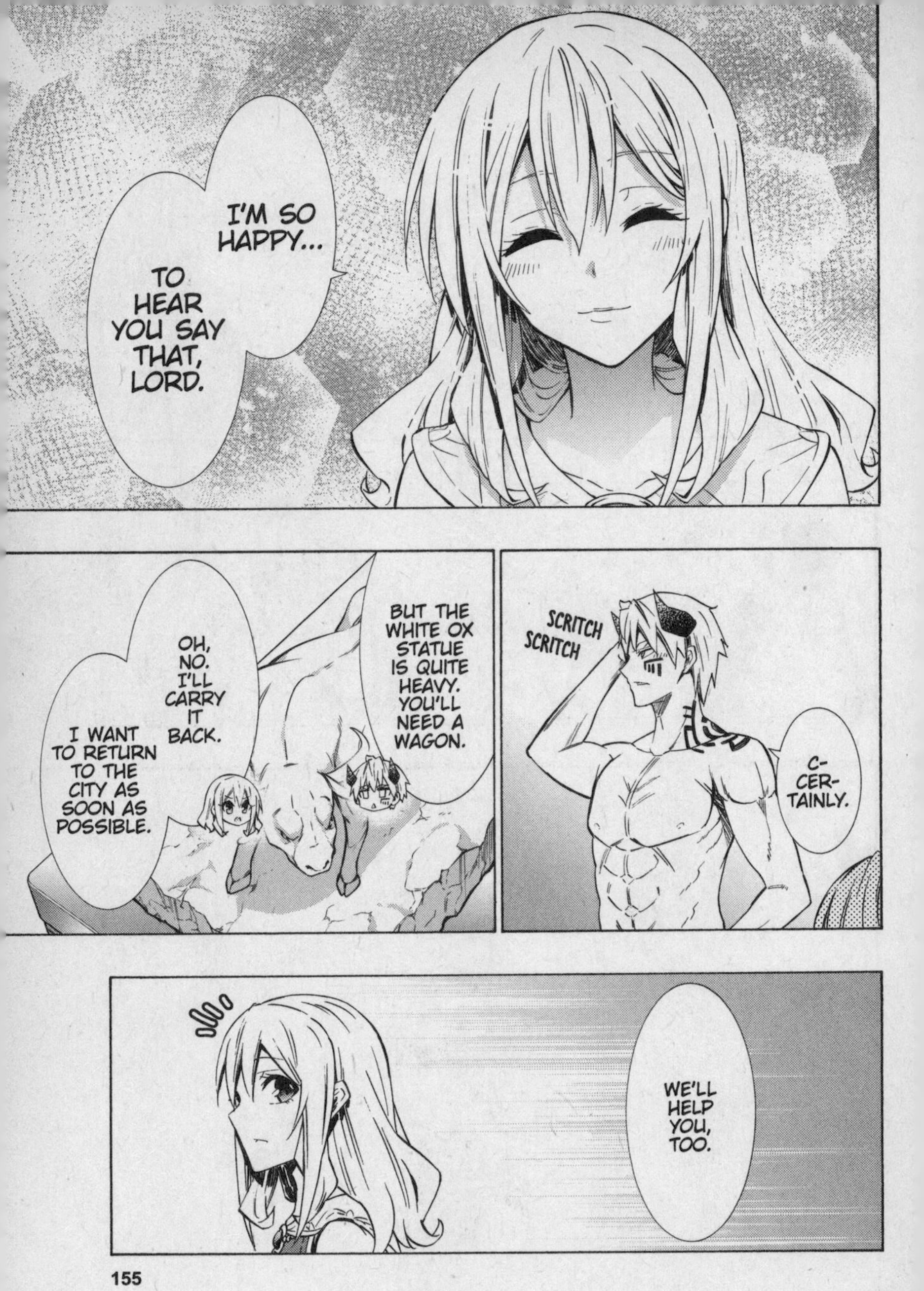
I'M SO HAPPY...
TO HEAR YOU SAY THAT, LORD.
SCRITCH SCRITCH
C-CERTAINLY.
BUT THE WHITE OX STATUE IS QUITE HEAVY. YOU'LL NEED A WAGON.
OH, NO. I'LL CARRY IT BACK.
I WANT TO RETURN TO THE CITY AS SOON AS POSSIBLE.
WE'LL HELP YOU, TOO.

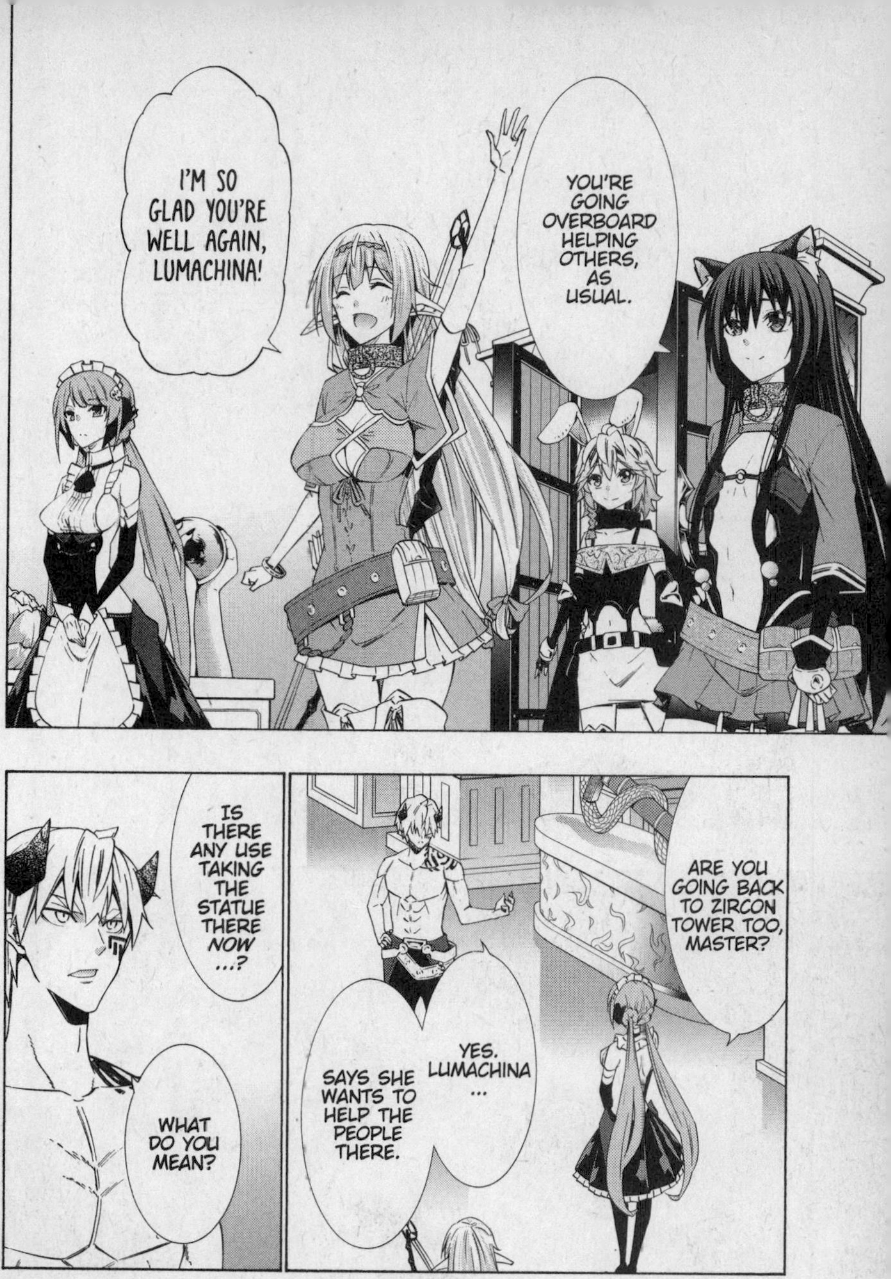
YOU'RE GOING OVERBOARD HELPING OTHERS, AS USUAL.
I'M SO GLAD YOU'RE WELL AGAIN, LUMACHINA!
ARE YOU GOING BACK TO ZIRCON TOWER TOO, MASTER?
YES. LUMACHINA ...
SAYS SHE WANTS TO HELP THE PEOPLE THERE.
IS THERE ANY USE TAKING THE STATUE THERE *NOW* ...?
WHAT DO YOU MEAN?

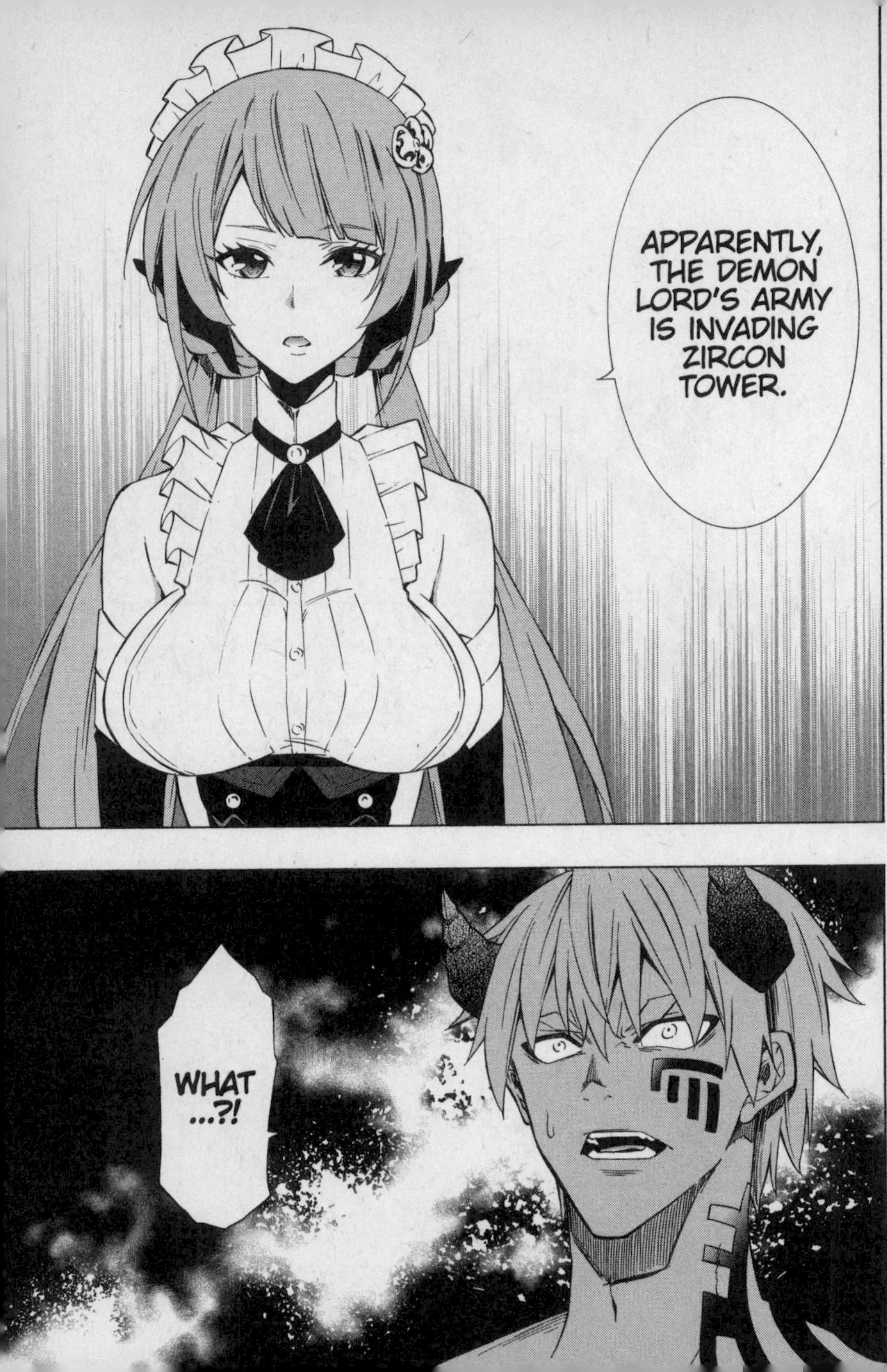
APPARENTLY, THE DEMON LORD'S ARMY IS INVADING ZIRCON TOWER.
WHAT ...?!

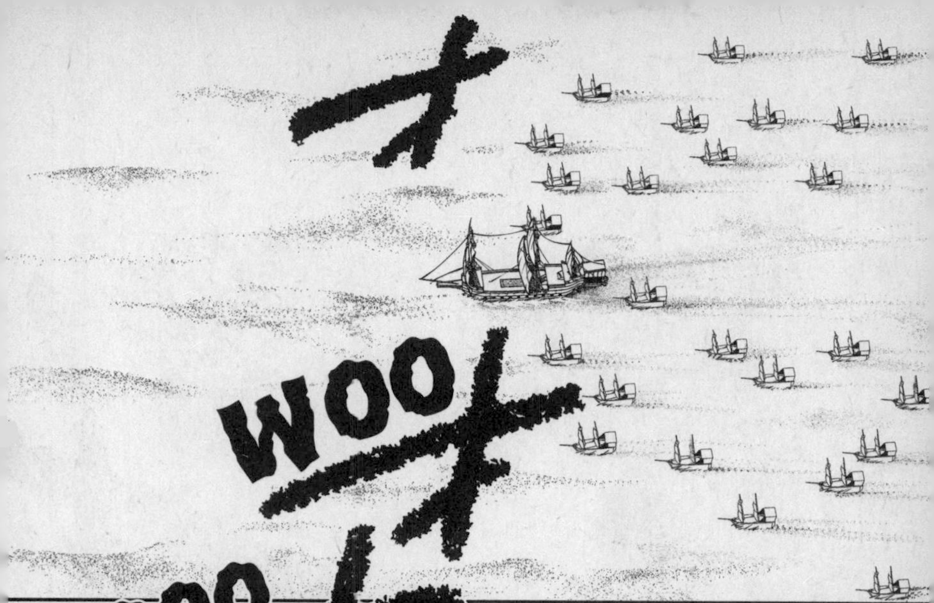
WOO
OOO
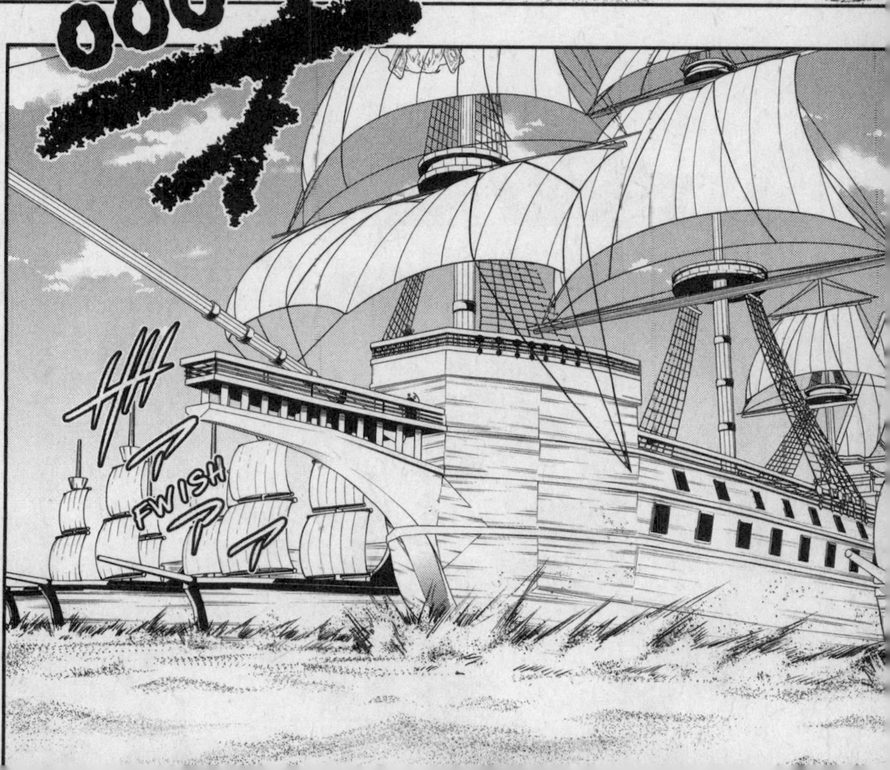
FWISH

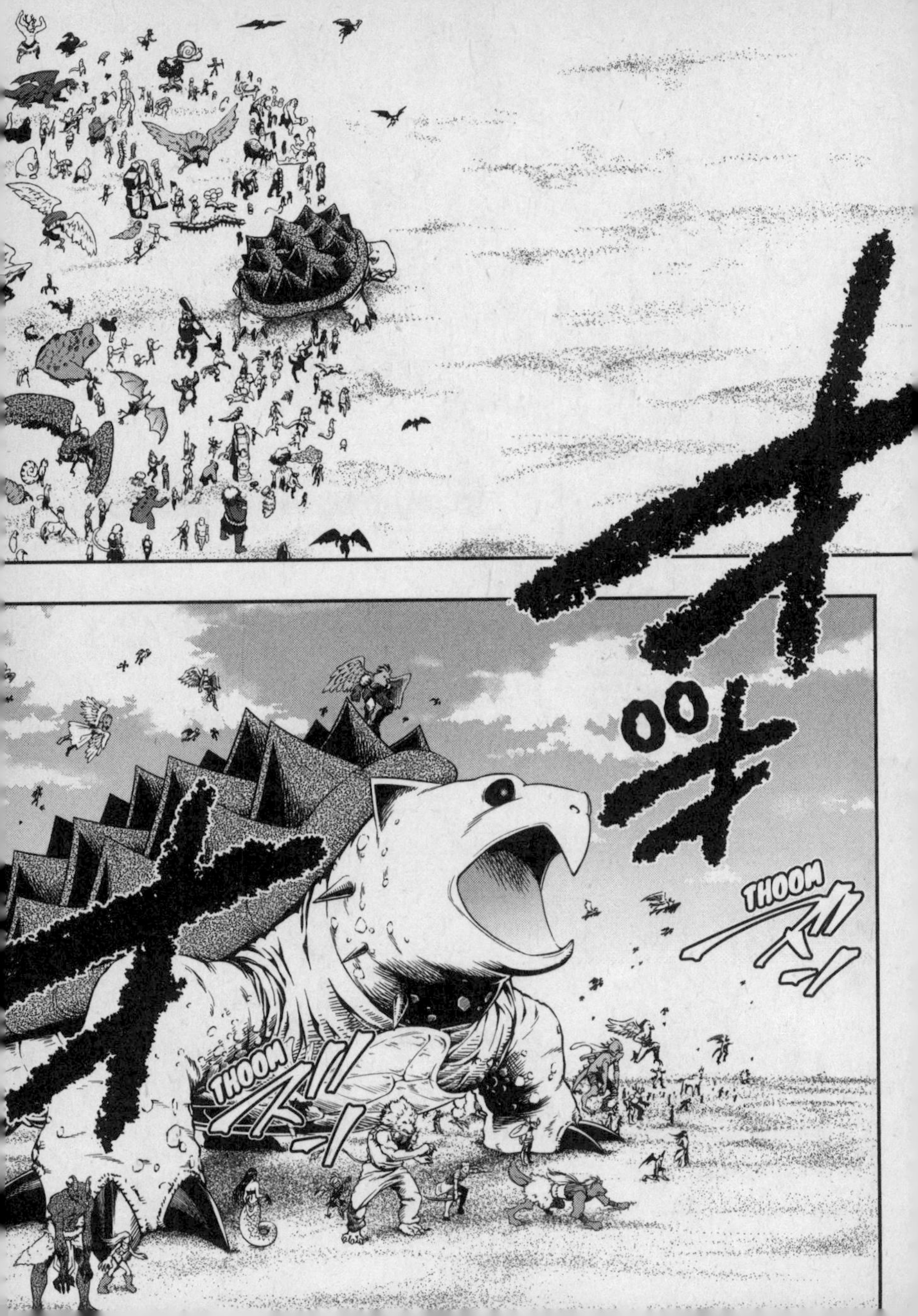
THOOM
THOOM

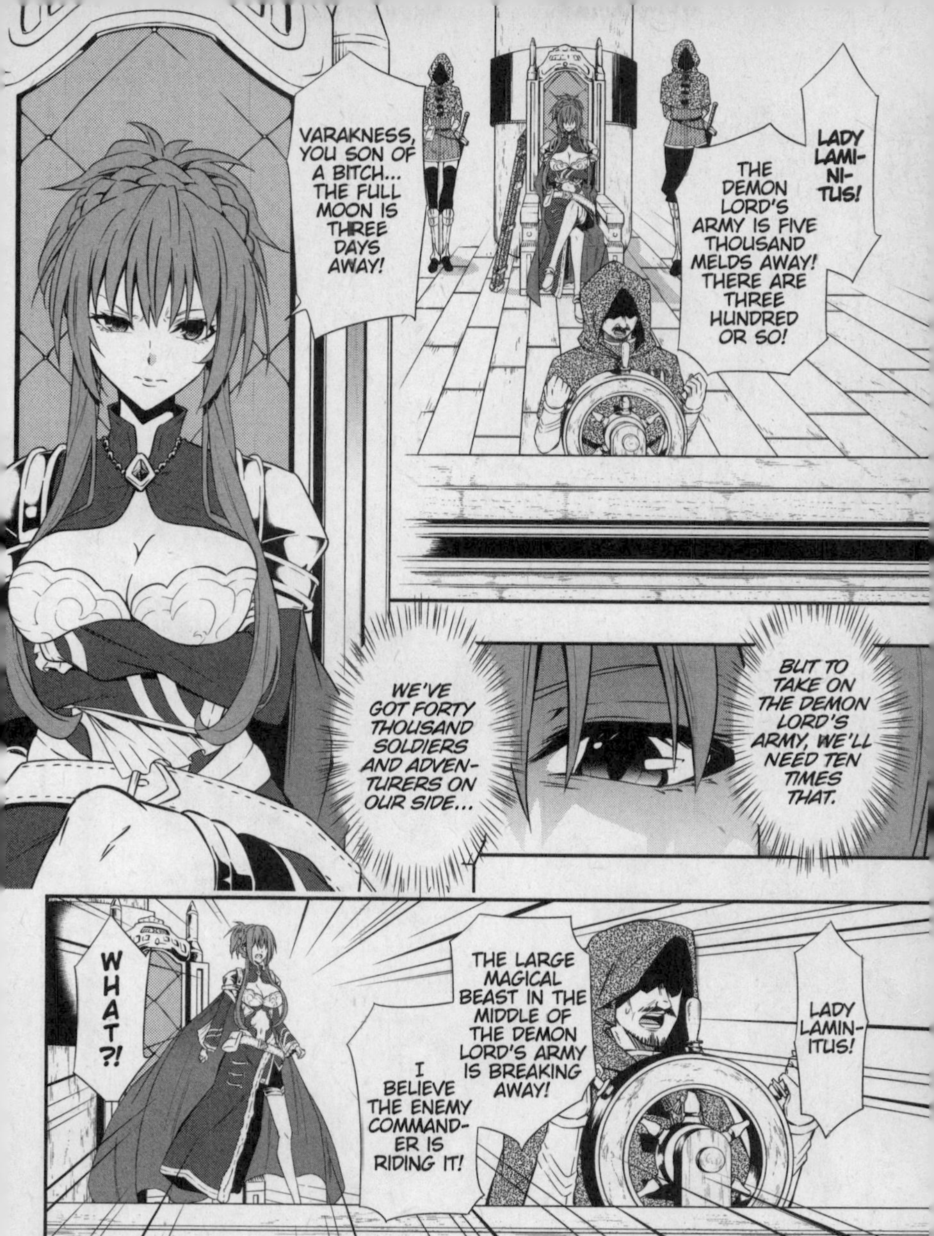
LADY LAMI-NI-TUS!
THE DEMON LORD'S ARMY IS FIVE THOUSAND MELDS AWAY! THERE ARE THREE HUNDRED OR SO!
VARAKNESS, YOU SON OF A BITCH... THE FULL MOON IS THREE DAYS AWAY!
BUT TO TAKE ON THE DEMON LORD'S ARMY, WE'LL NEED TEN TIMES THAT.
WE'VE GOT FORTY THOUSAND SOLDIERS AND ADVEN-TURERS ON OUR SIDE...
LADY LAMIN-ITUS!
THE LARGE MAGICAL BEAST IN THE MIDDLE OF THE DEMON LORD'S ARMY IS BREAKING AWAY!
I BELIEVE THE ENEMY COMMAND-ER IS RIDING IT!
WHAT?!

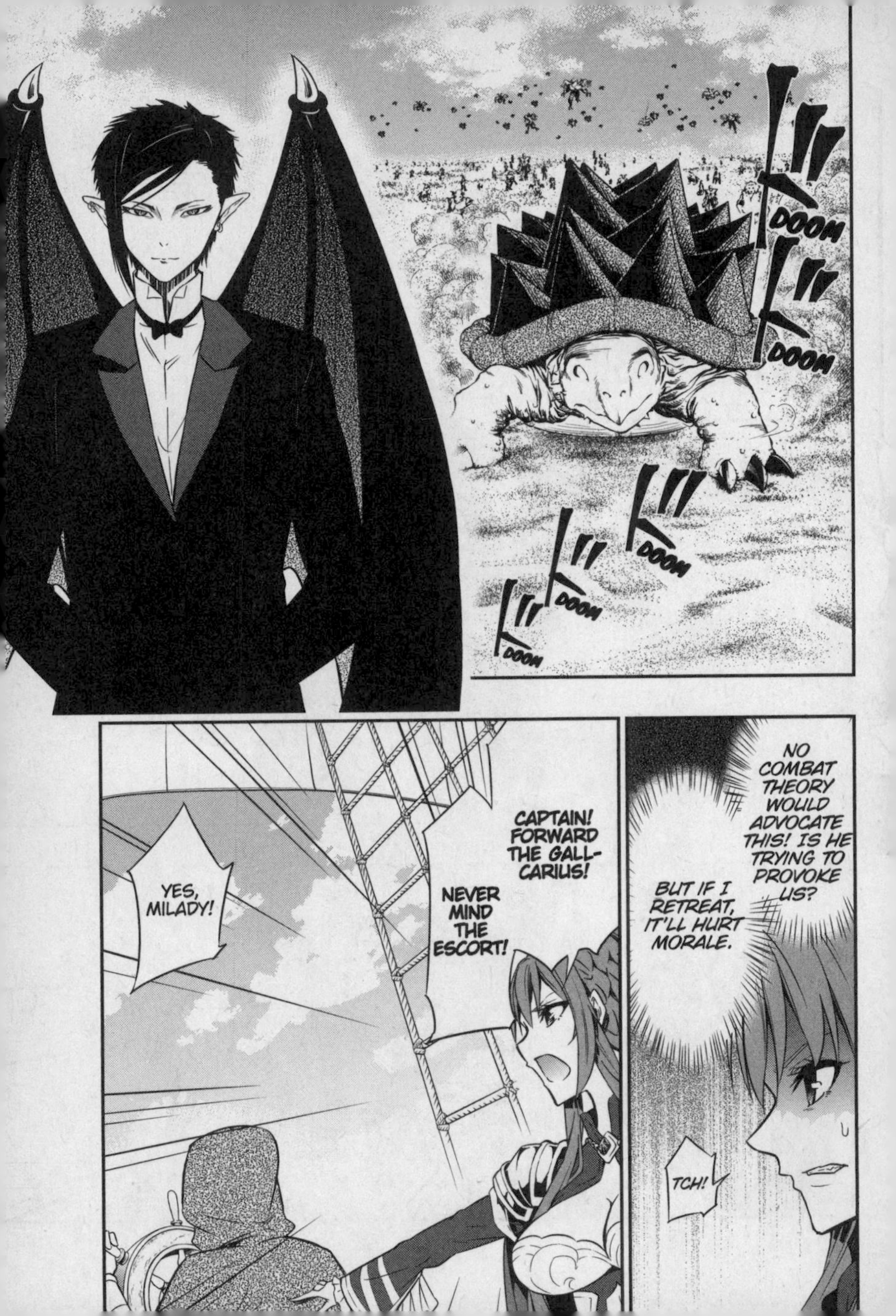
DOOM
DOOM
DOOM
DOOM
DOOM
NO COMBAT THEORY WOULD ADVOCATE THIS! IS HE TRYING TO PROVOKE US?
BUT IF I RETREAT, IT'LL HURT MORALE.
TCH!
CAPTAIN! FORWARD THE GALL-CARIUS!
NEVER MIND THE ESCORT!
YES, MILADY!

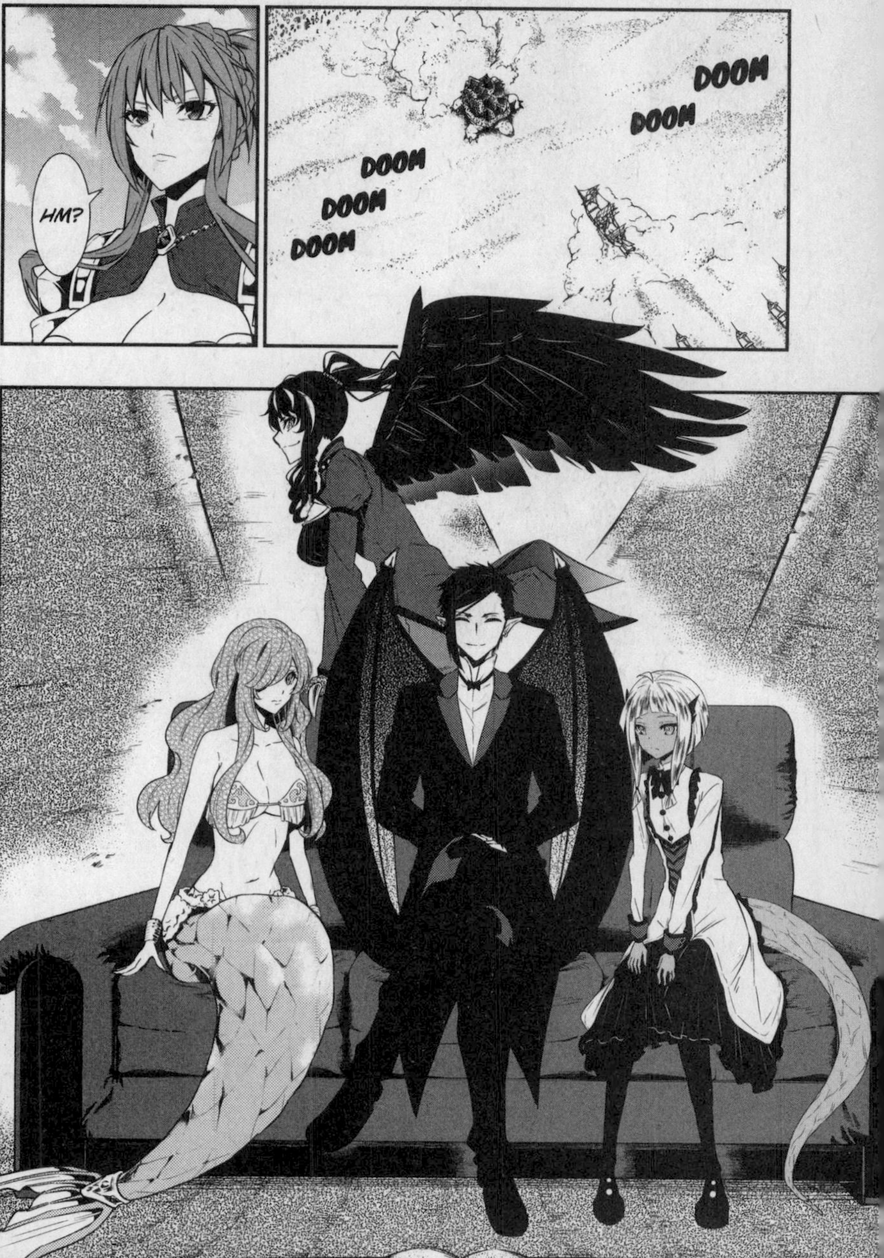
DOOM
DOOM
DOOM
DOOM
DOOM
HM?

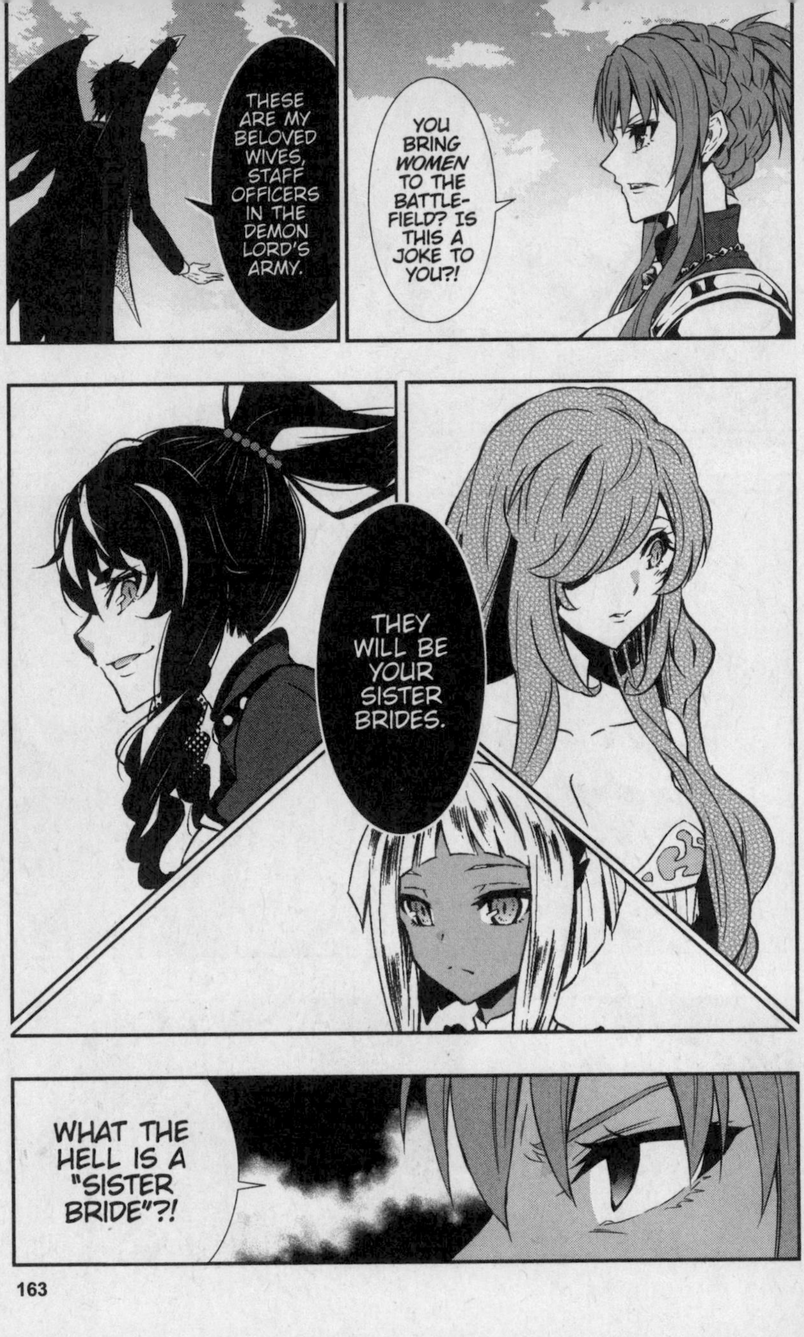
YOU BRING *WOMEN* TO THE BATTLE-FIELD? IS THIS A JOKE TO YOU?!
THESE ARE MY BELOVED WIVES, STAFF OFFICERS IN THE DEMON LORD'S ARMY.
THEY WILL BE YOUR SISTER BRIDES.
WHAT THE HELL IS A "SISTER BRIDE"?!

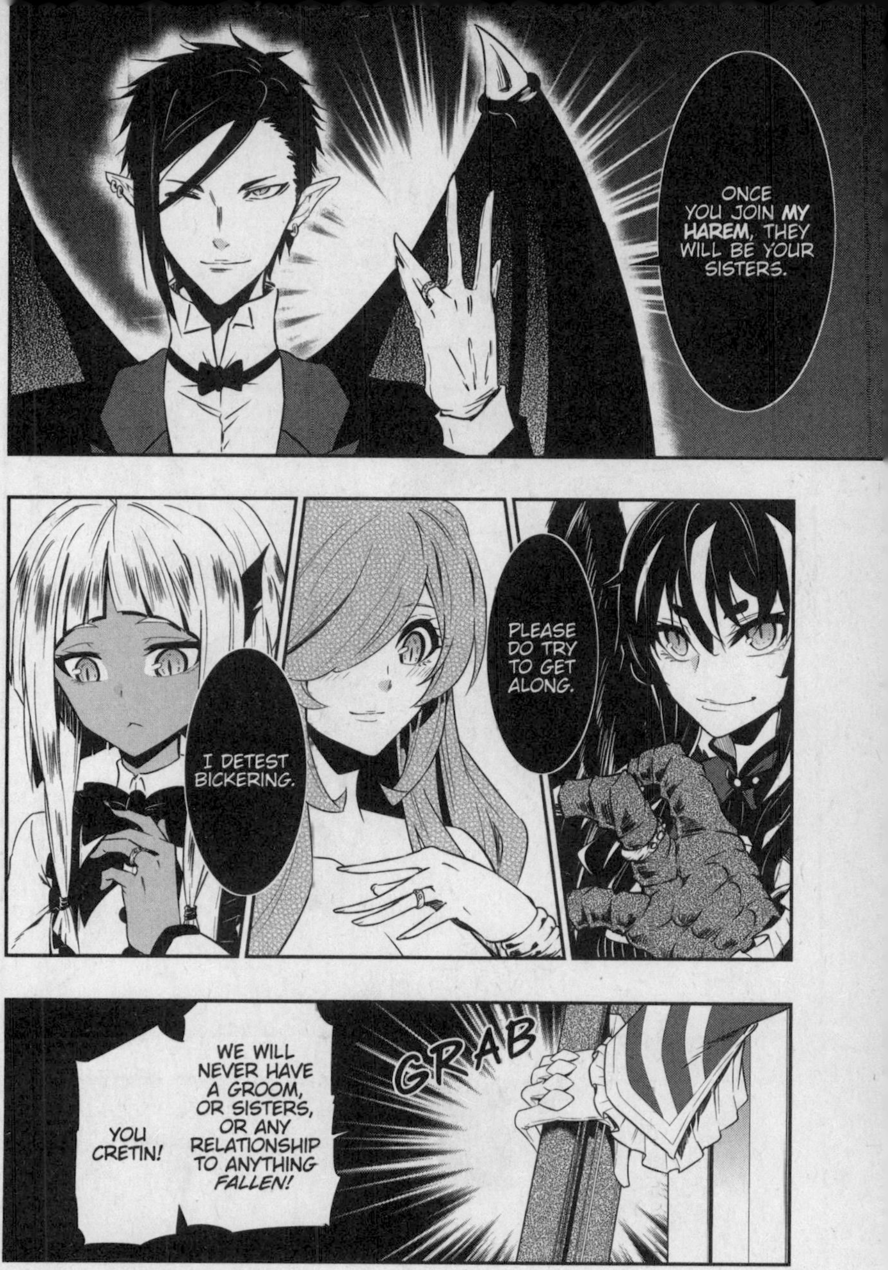
ONCE YOU JOIN **MY HAREM**, THEY WILL BE YOUR SISTERS.
PLEASE DO TRY TO GET ALONG.
I DETEST BICKERING.
GRAB
WE WILL NEVER HAVE A GROOM, OR SISTERS, OR ANY RELATIONSHIP TO ANYTHING *FALLEN!*
YOU CRETIN!

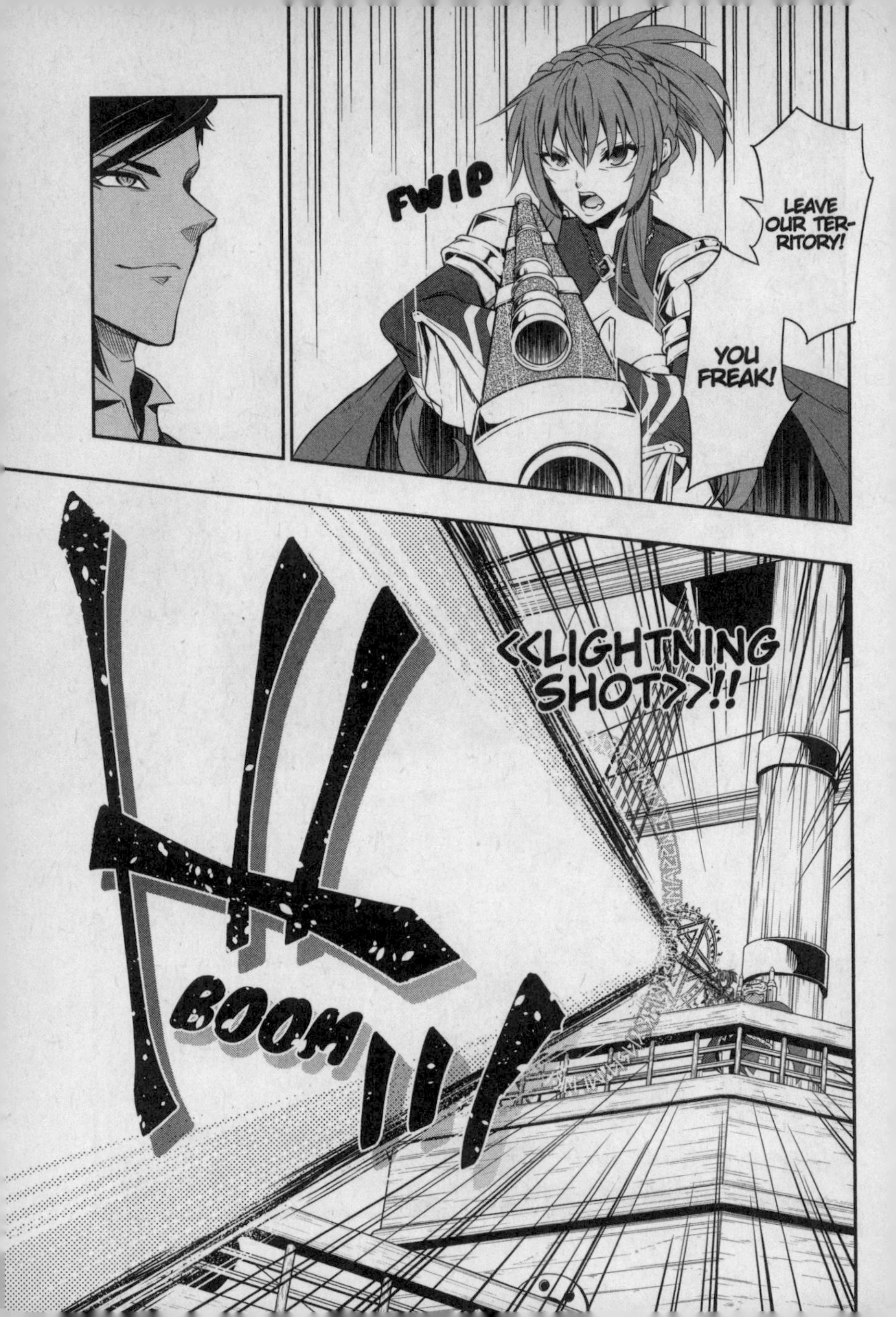
LEAVE OUR TER-RITORY!
YOU FREAK!
FWIP
<<LIGHTNING SHOT>>!!
BOOM

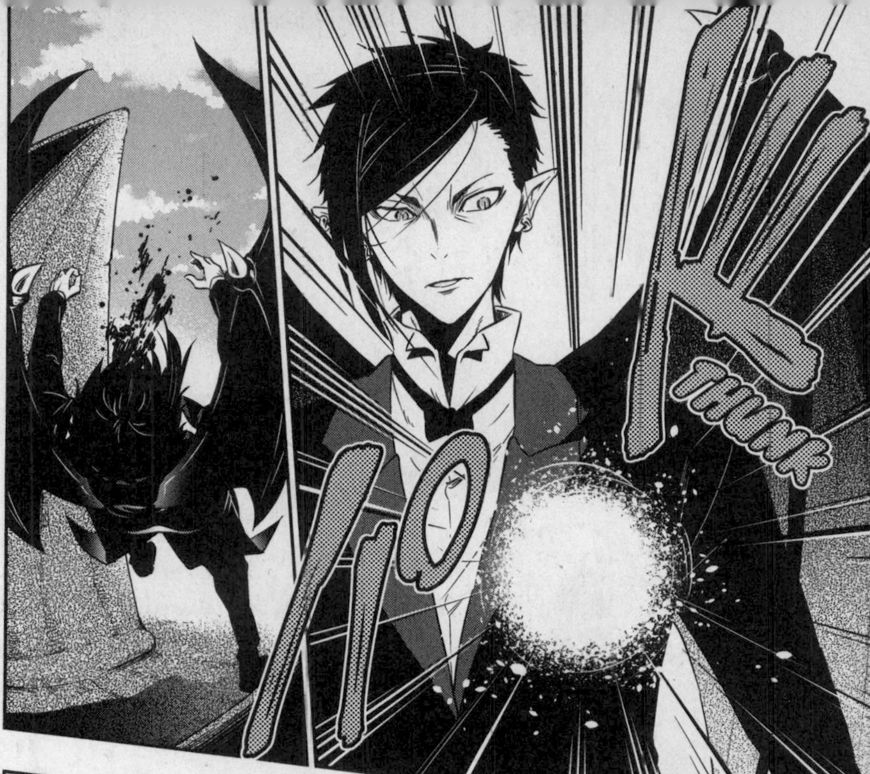
THUNK

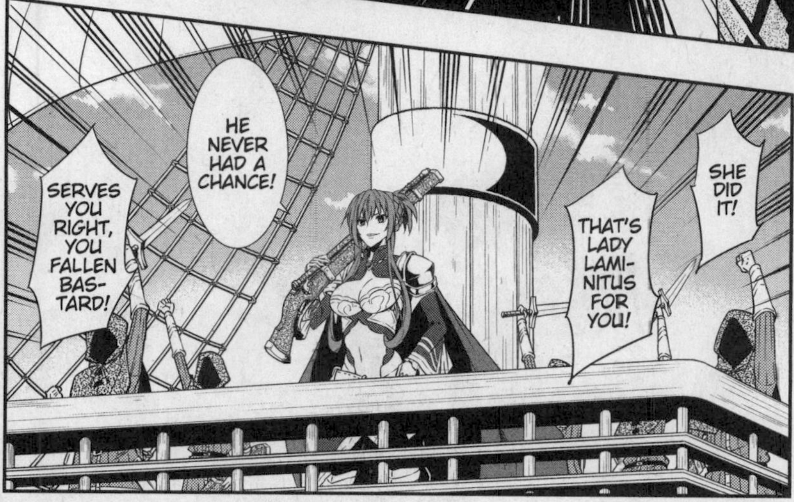
SHE DID IT!
THAT'S LADY LAMINITUS FOR YOU!
HE NEVER HAD A CHANCE!
SERVES YOU RIGHT, YOU FALLEN BASTARD!

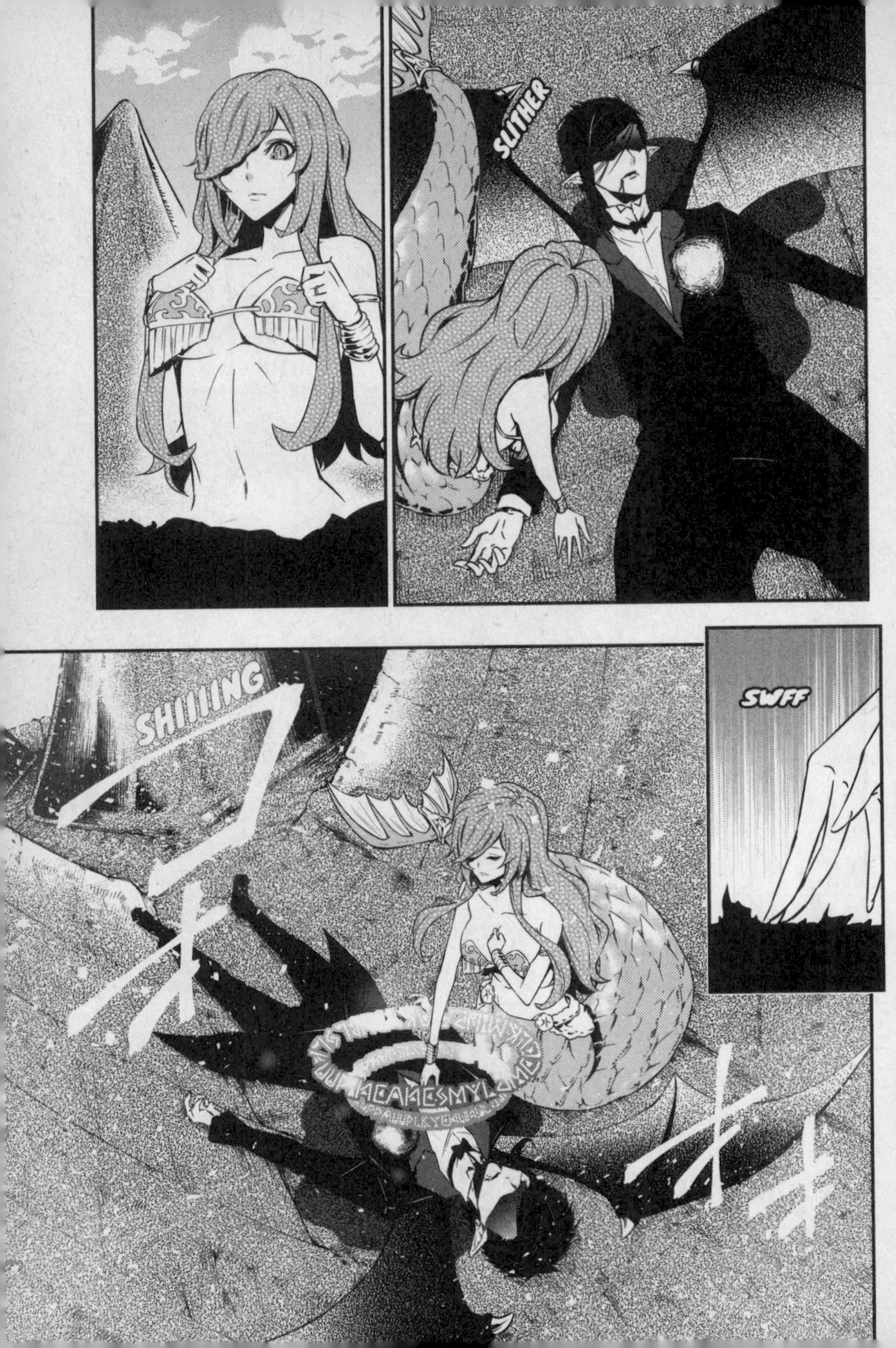
SLITHER
SWFF
SHIIIING

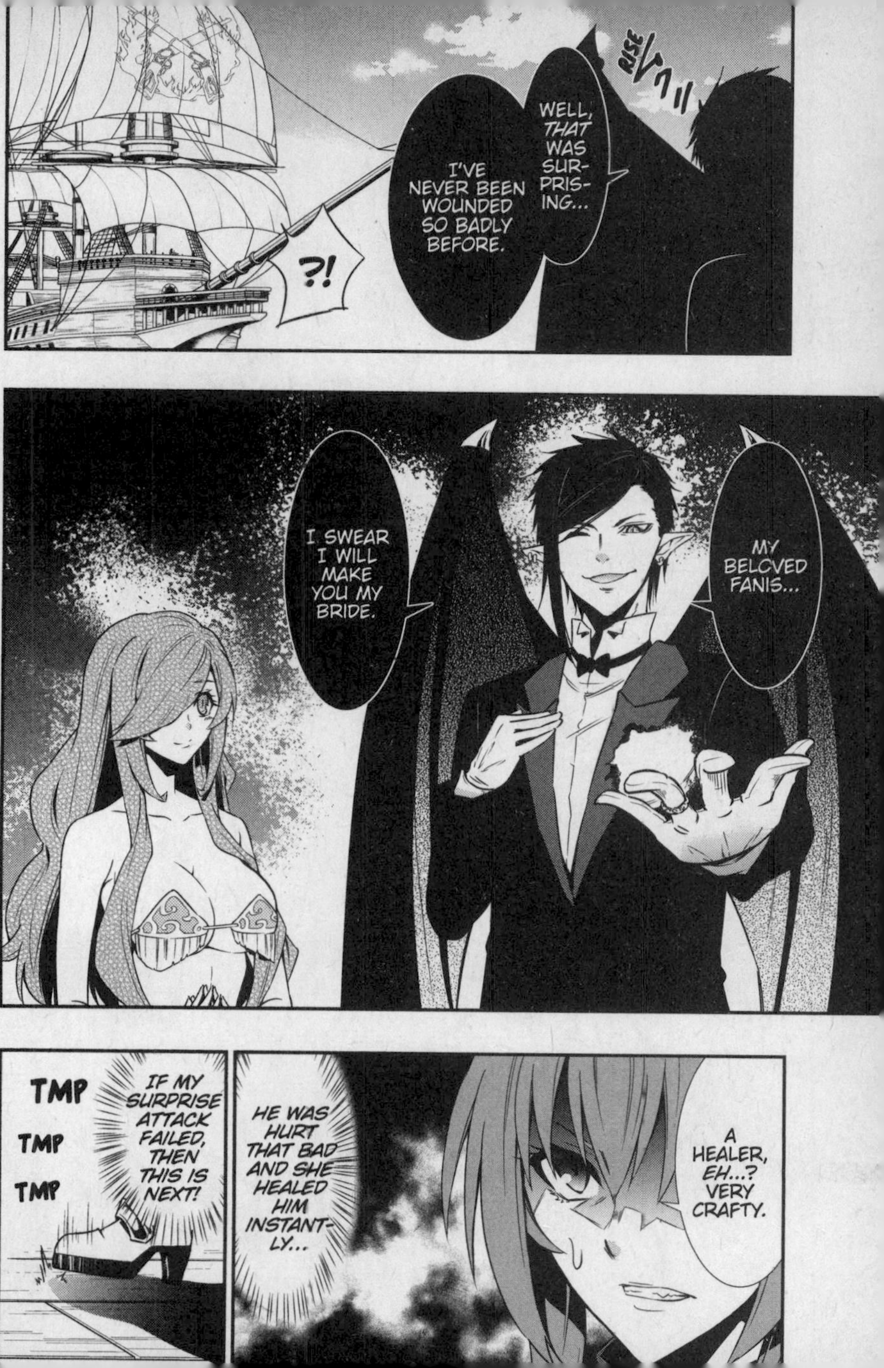
RISE
WELL, THAT WAS SURPRISING...
I'VE NEVER BEEN WOUNDED SO BADLY BEFORE.
?!
MY BELOVED FANIS...
I SWEAR I WILL MAKE YOU MY BRIDE.
A HEALER, EH...? VERY CRAFTY.
HE WAS HURT THAT BAD AND SHE HEALED HIM INSTANTLY...
IF MY SURPRISE ATTACK FAILED, THEN THIS IS NEXT!
TMP
TMP
TMP

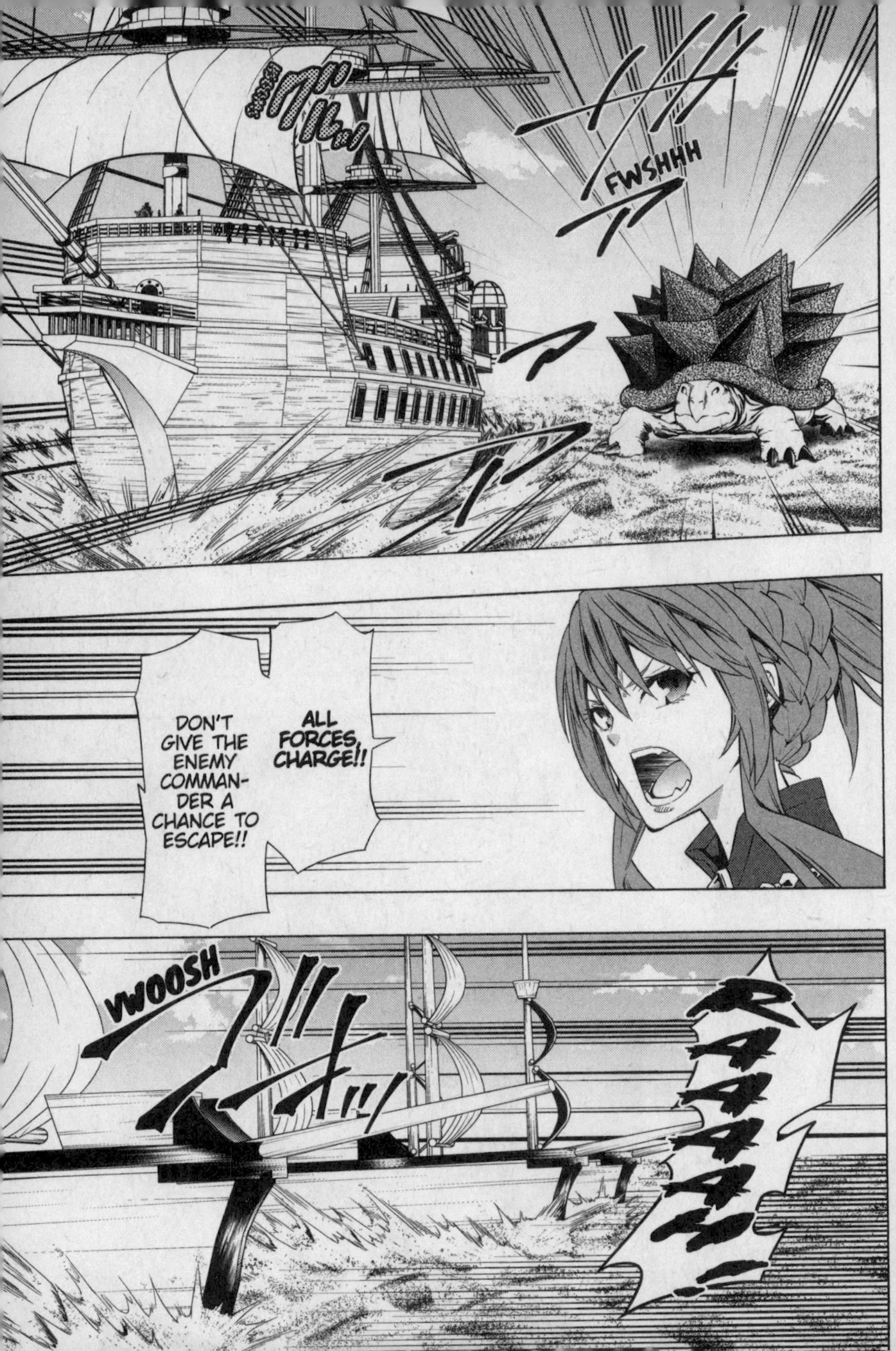
FWSHHH
ALL FORCES, CHARGE!!
DON'T GIVE THE ENEMY COMMANDER A CHANCE TO ESCAPE!!
RAAAAH!!
VWOOSH

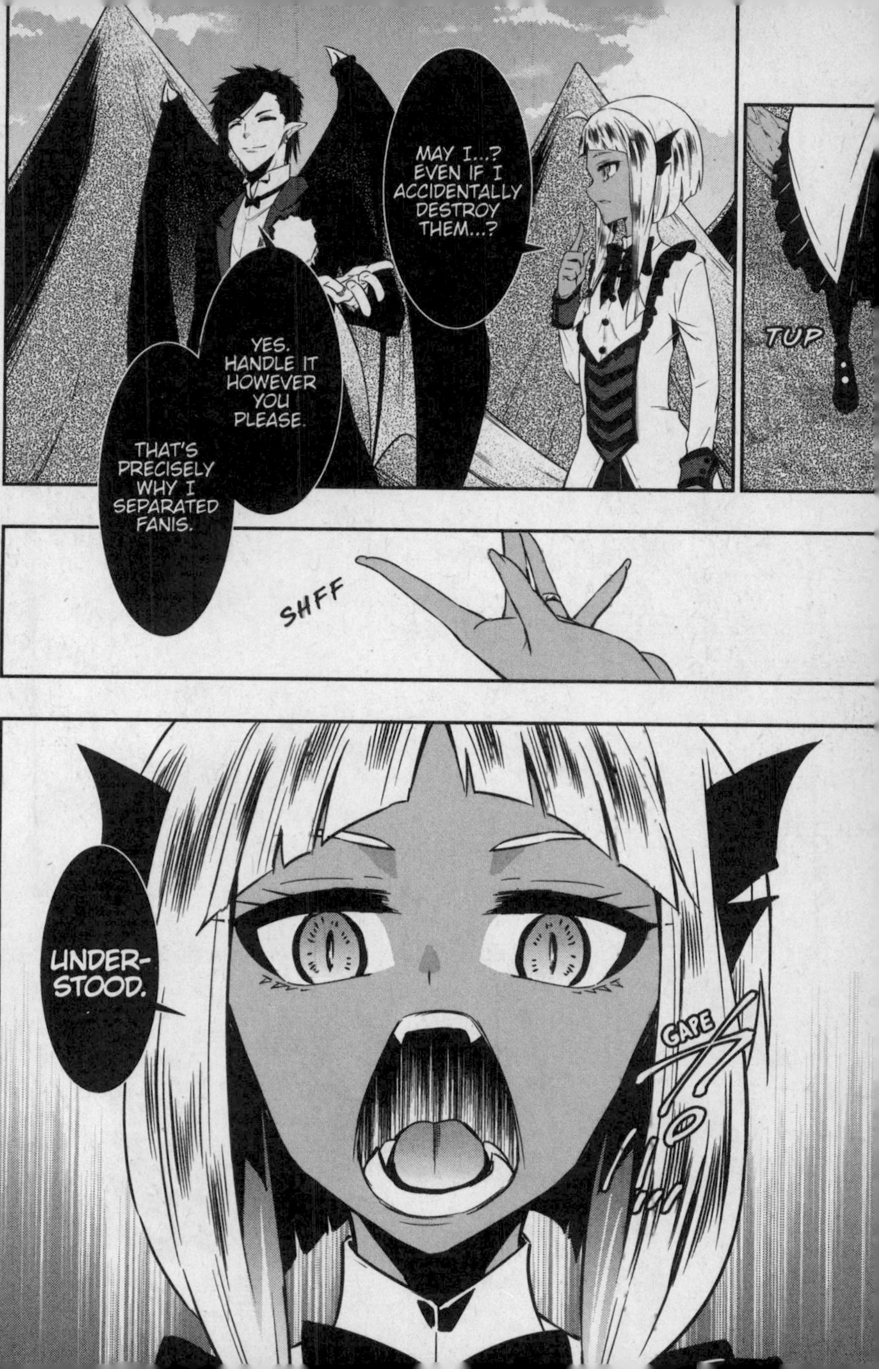
TUP
MAY I...? EVEN IF I ACCIDENTALLY DESTROY THEM...?
YES. HANDLE IT HOWEVER YOU PLEASE.
THAT'S PRECISELY WHY I SEPARATED FANIS.
SHFF
UNDER-STOOD.
GAPE

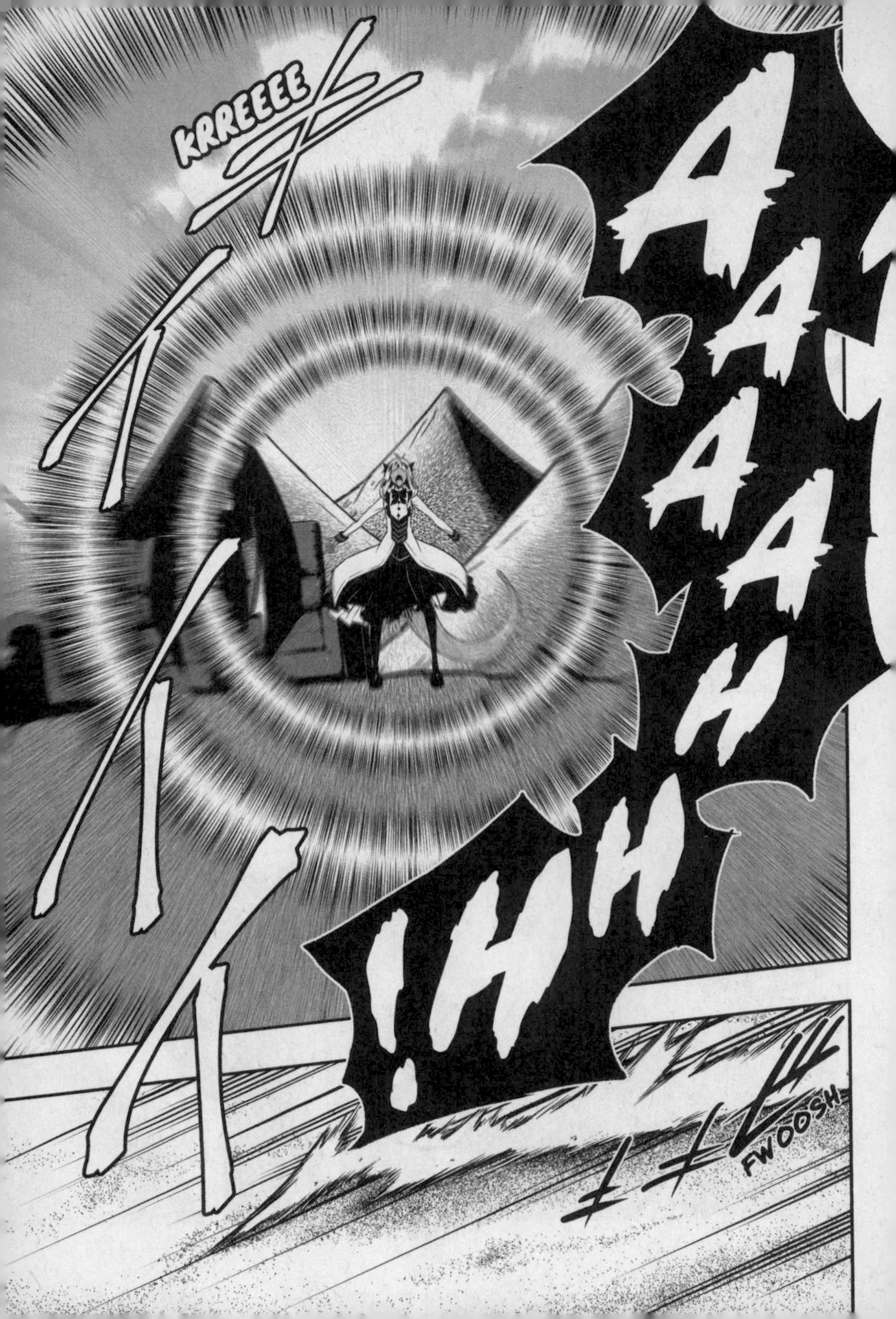

KRREEEE
AAAAAAHHHH!!
FWOOSH

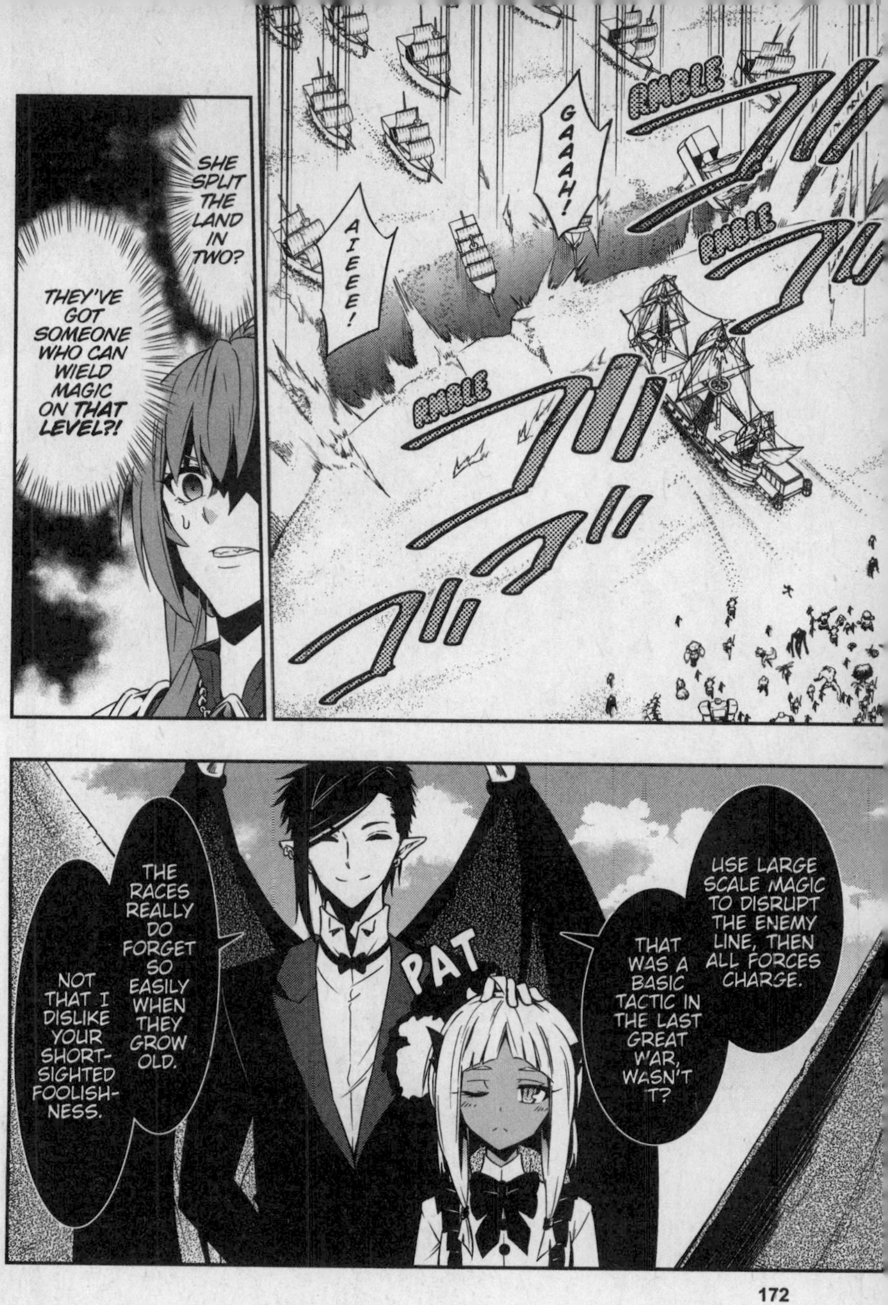
RMBLE
RMBLE
GAAAAH!
AIEEEE!
RMBLE
SHE SPLIT THE LAND IN TWO?
THEY'VE GOT SOMEONE WHO CAN WIELD MAGIC ON THAT LEVEL?!
USE LARGE SCALE MAGIC TO DISRUPT THE ENEMY LINE, THEN ALL FORCES CHARGE.
THAT WAS A BASIC TACTIC IN THE LAST GREAT WAR, WASN'T IT?
PAT
THE RACES REALLY DO FORGET SO EASILY WHEN THEY GROW OLD.
NOT THAT I DISLIKE YOUR SHORT-SIGHTED FOOLISHNESS.

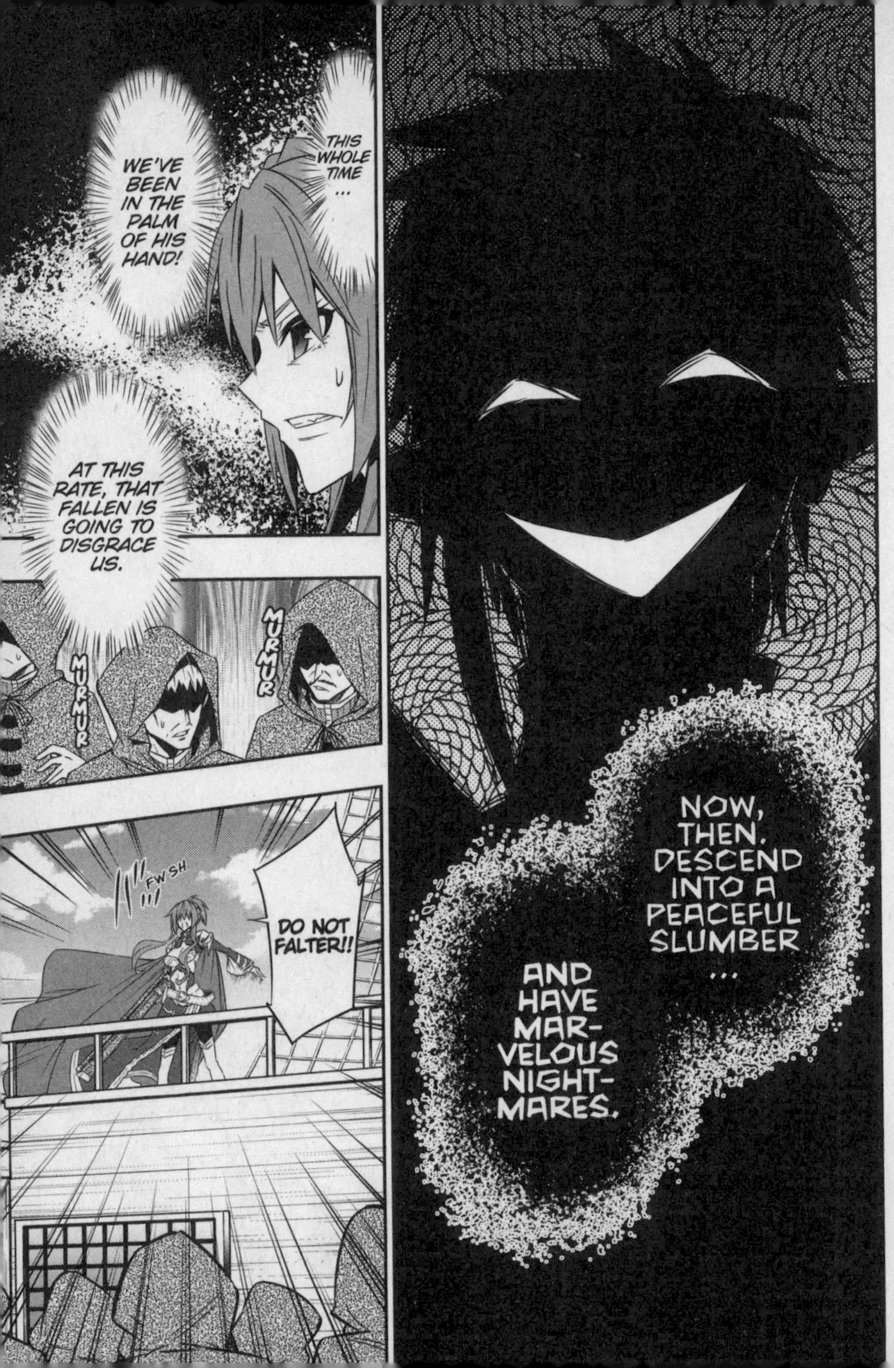
NOW, THEN. DESCEND INTO A PEACEFUL SLUMBER...
AND HAVE MARVELOUS NIGHTMARES.
THIS WHOLE TIME...
WE'VE BEEN IN THE PALM OF HIS HAND!
AT THIS RATE, THAT FALLEN IS GOING TO DISGRACE US.
MURMUR
MURMUR
FWSH
DO NOT FALTER!!

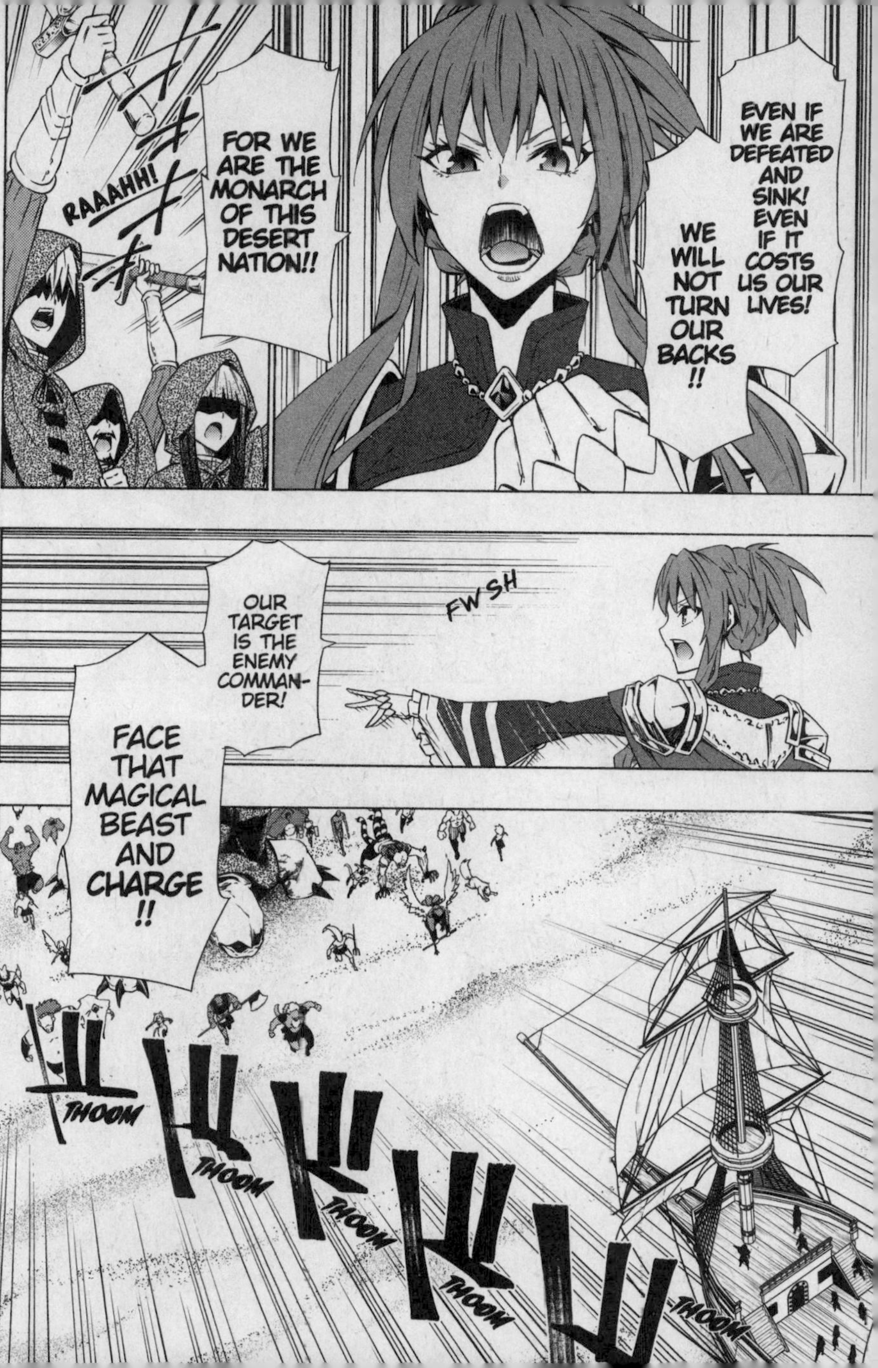
EVEN IF WE ARE DEFEATED AND SINK! EVEN IF IT COSTS US OUR LIVES!
WE WILL NOT TURN OUR BACKS!!
FOR WE ARE THE MONARCH OF THIS DESERT NATION!!
RAAAHH!
FWSH
OUR TARGET IS THE ENEMY COMMANDER!
FACE THAT MAGICAL BEAST AND CHARGE!!
THOOM
THOOM
THOOM
THOOM
THOOM
THOOM

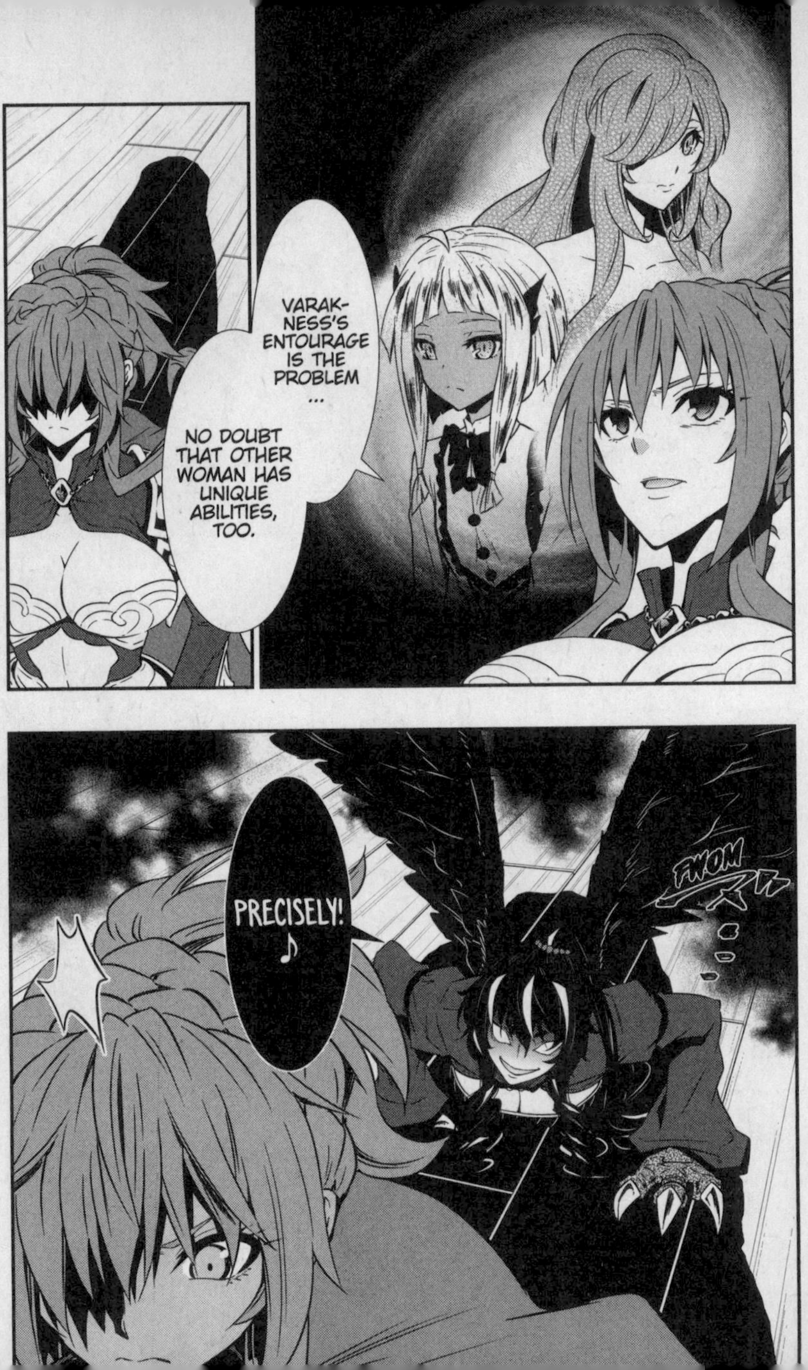
VARAKNESS'S ENTOURAGE IS THE PROBLEM ...
NO DOUBT THAT OTHER WOMAN HAS UNIQUE ABILITIES, TOO.
FWOM
PRECISELY! ♪

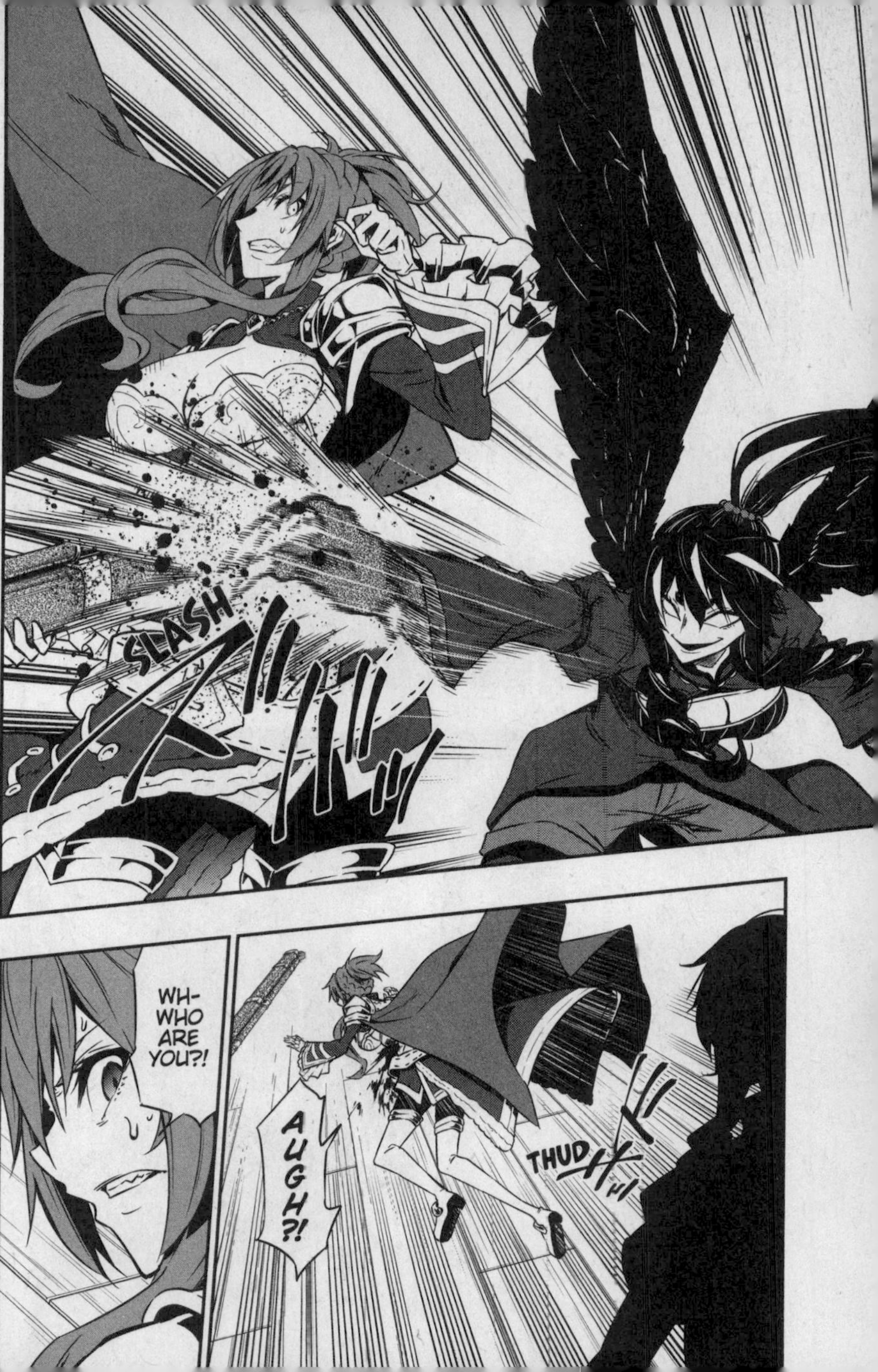
SLASH
AUGH?!
THUD
WH- WHO ARE YOU?!

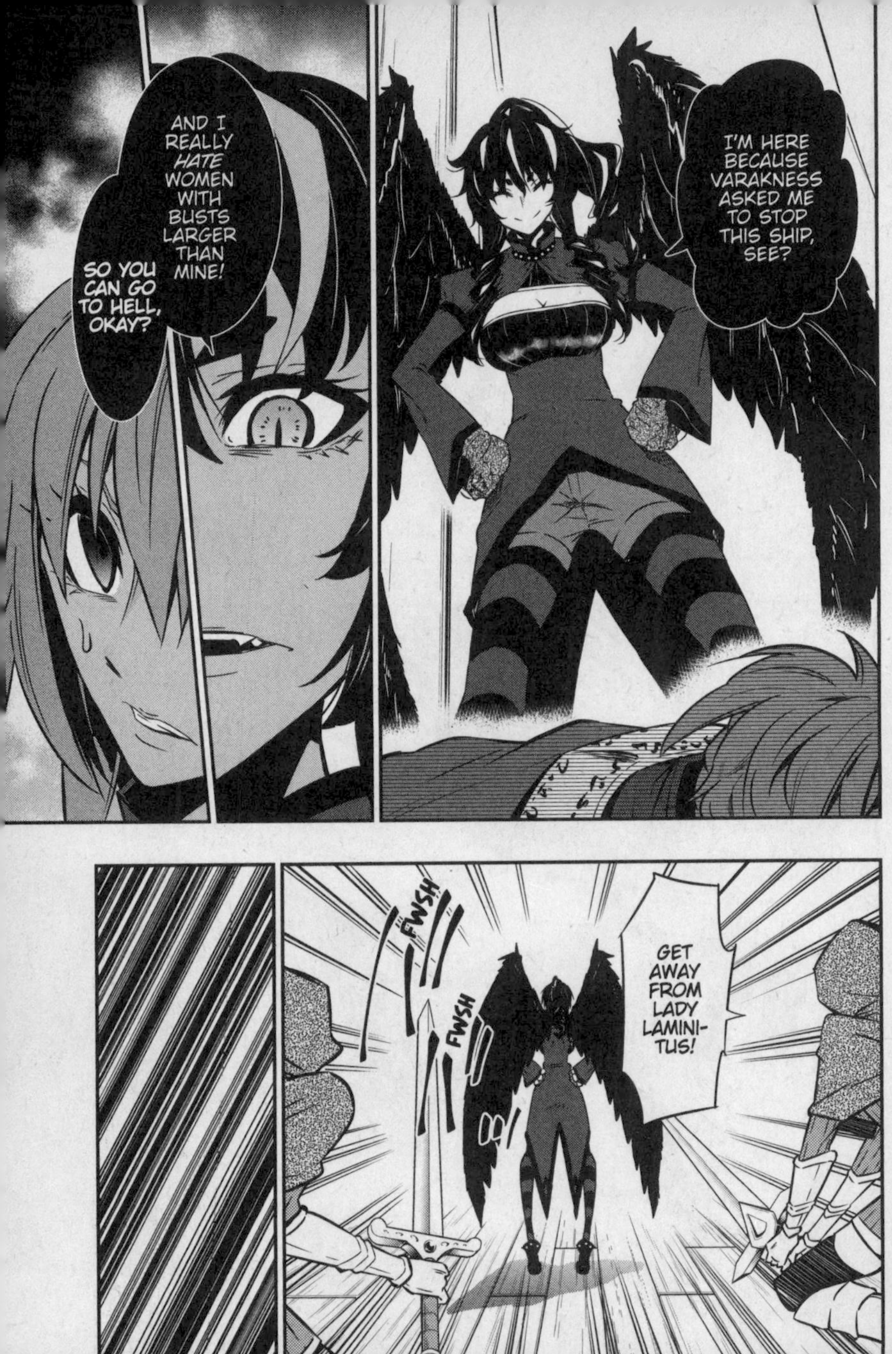
I'M HERE BECAUSE VARAKNESS ASKED ME TO STOP THIS SHIP, SEE?
AND I REALLY *HATE* WOMEN WITH BUSTS LARGER THAN MINE!
SO YOU CAN GO TO HELL, OKAY?
GET AWAY FROM LADY LAMINI-TUS!
FWSH!
FWSH

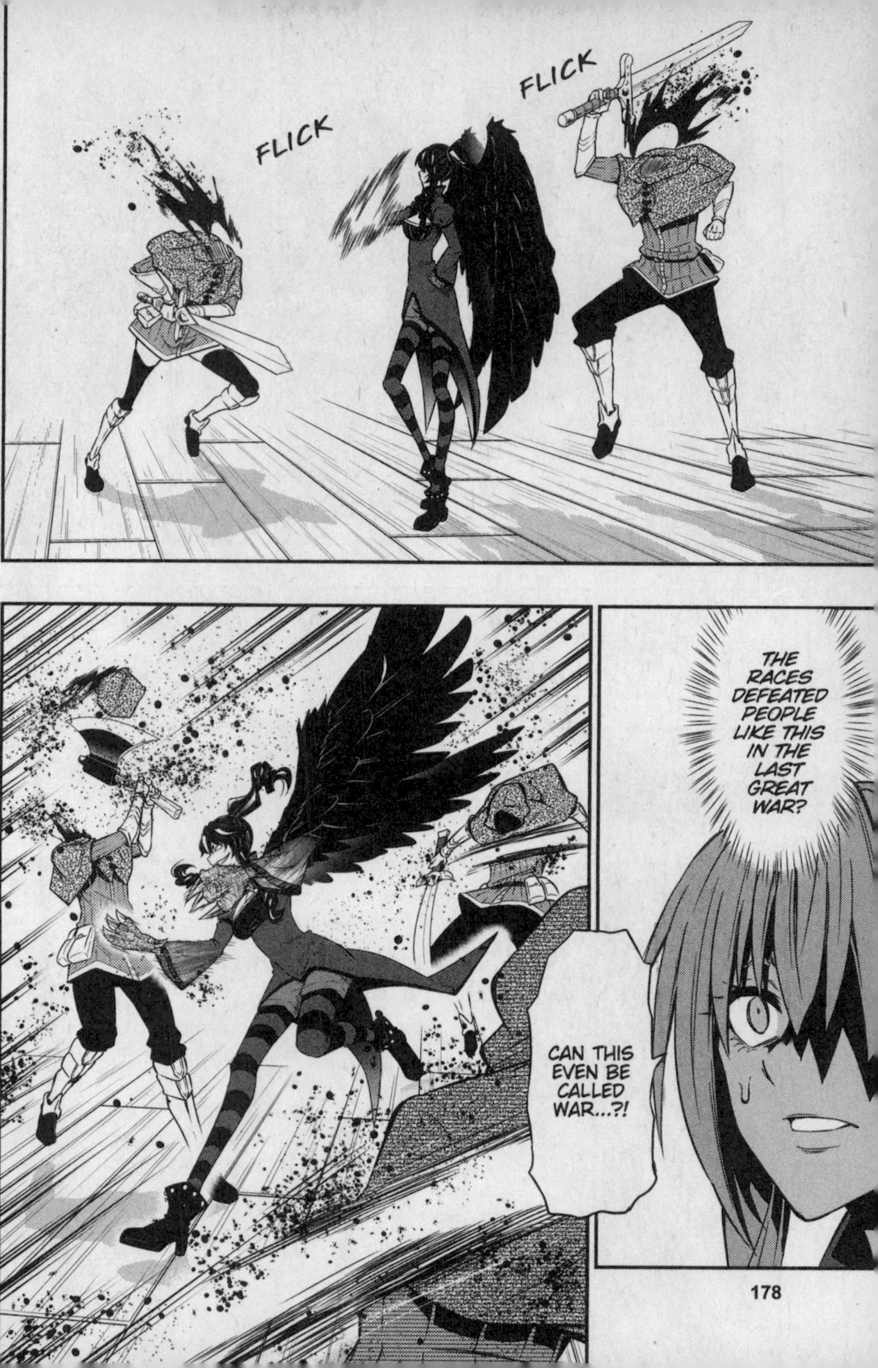
FLICK
FLICK
THE RACES DEFEATED PEOPLE LIKE THIS IN THE LAST GREAT WAR?
CAN THIS EVEN BE CALLED WAR...?!

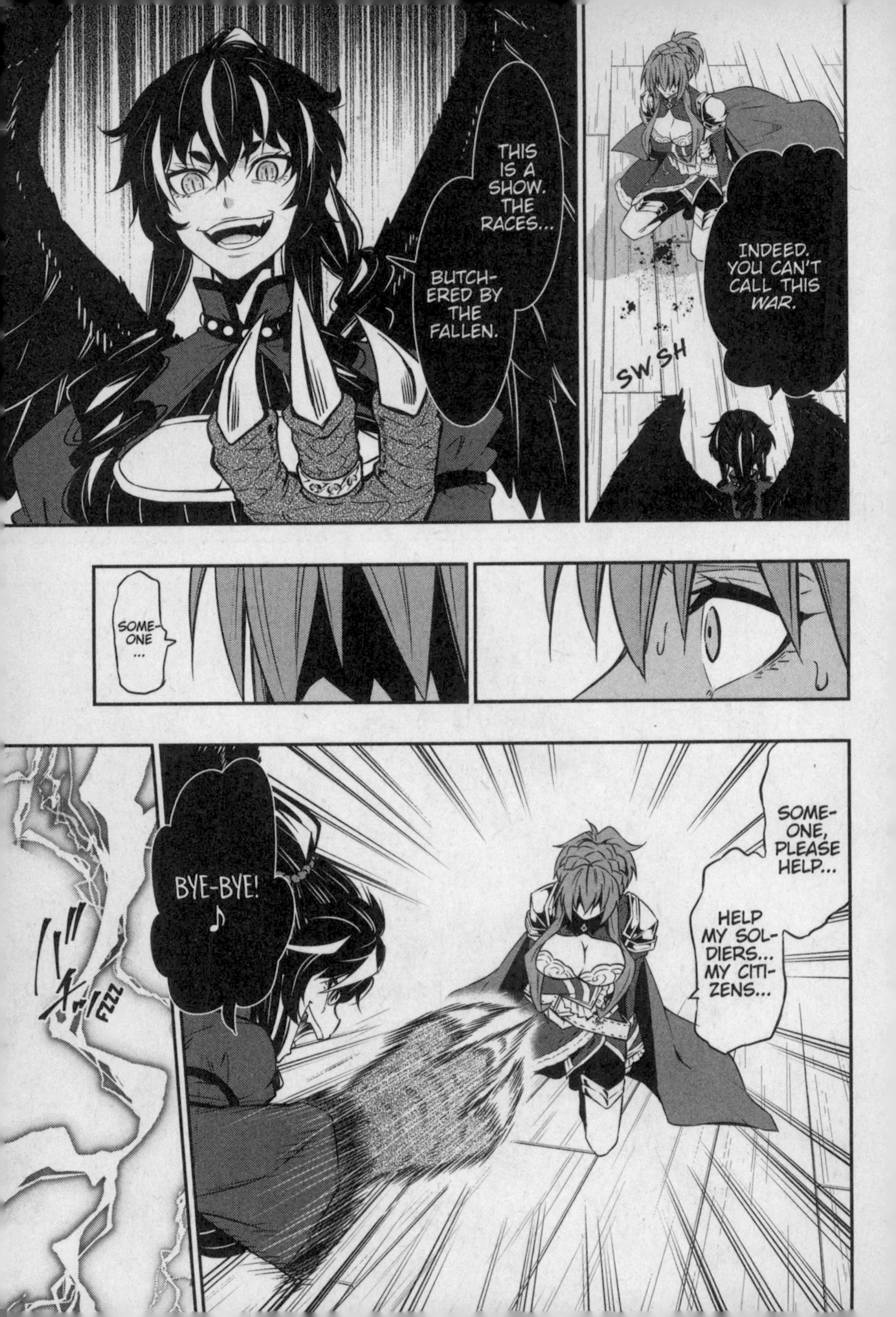
INDEED. YOU CAN'T CALL THIS WAR.
SWSH
THIS IS A SHOW. THE RACES...
BUTCHERED BY THE FALLEN.
SOME-ONE...
SOME-ONE, PLEASE HELP...
HELP MY SOLDIERS... MY CITIZENS...
BYE-BYE! ♪
FZZZ

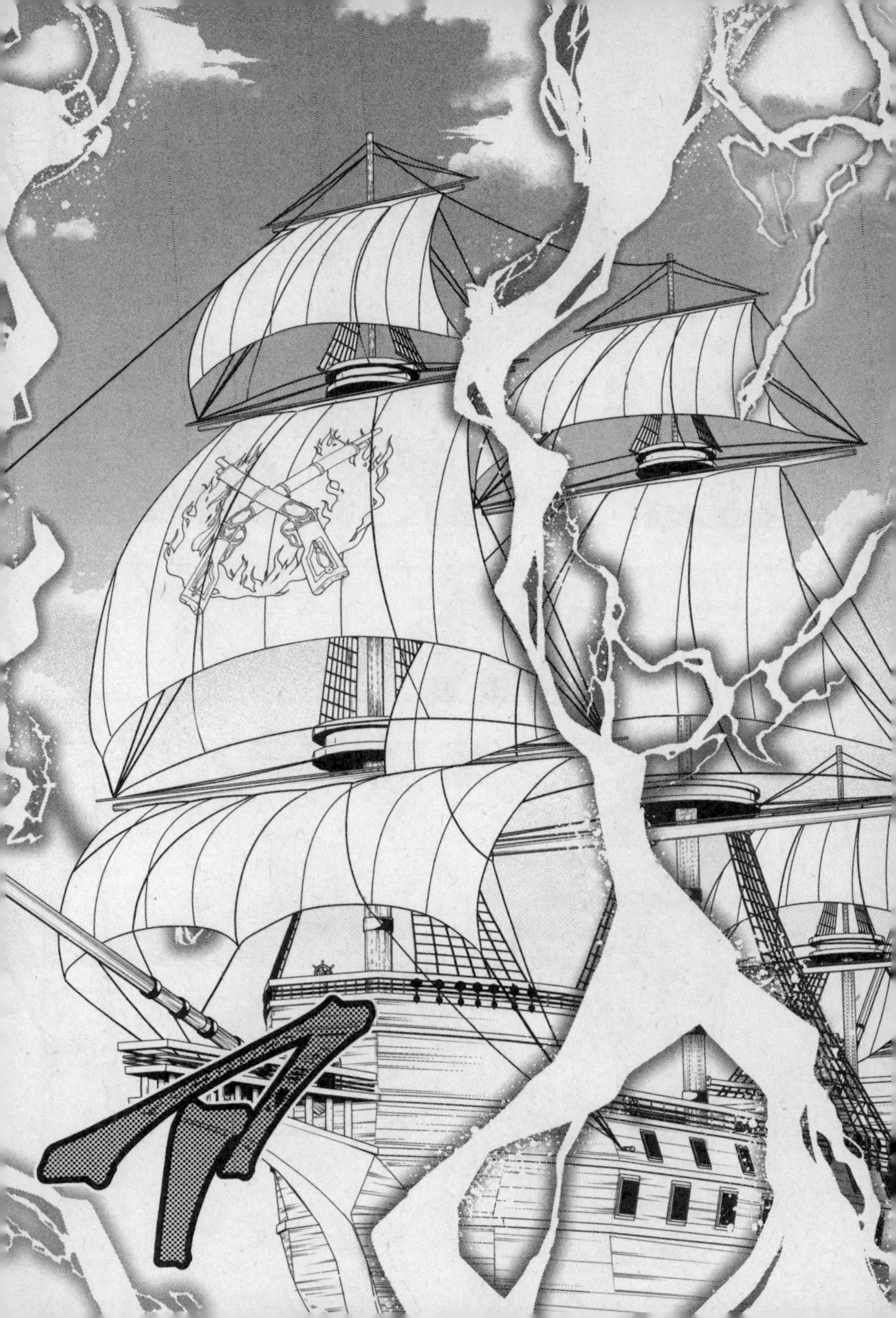

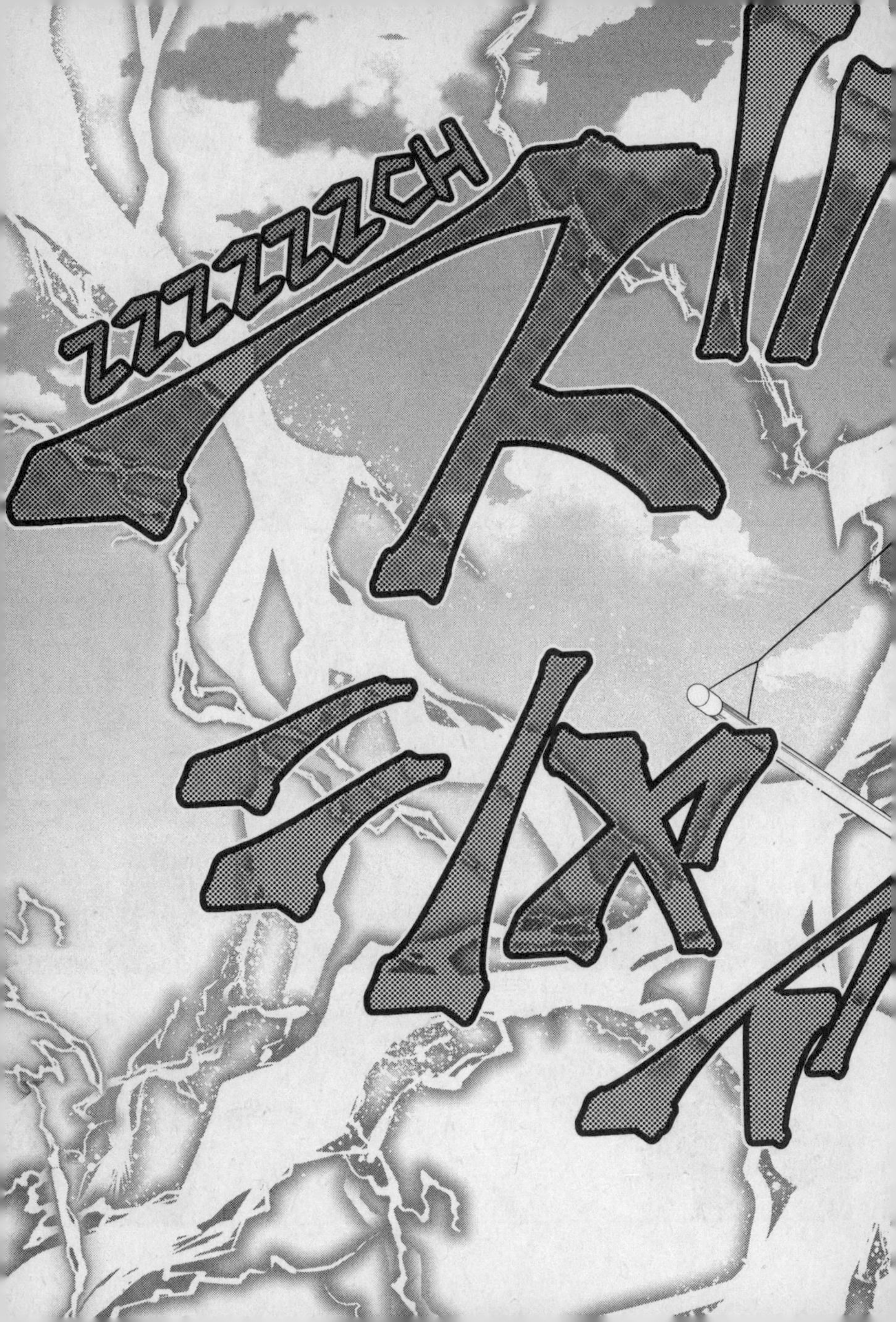
ZZZZZZZZCH

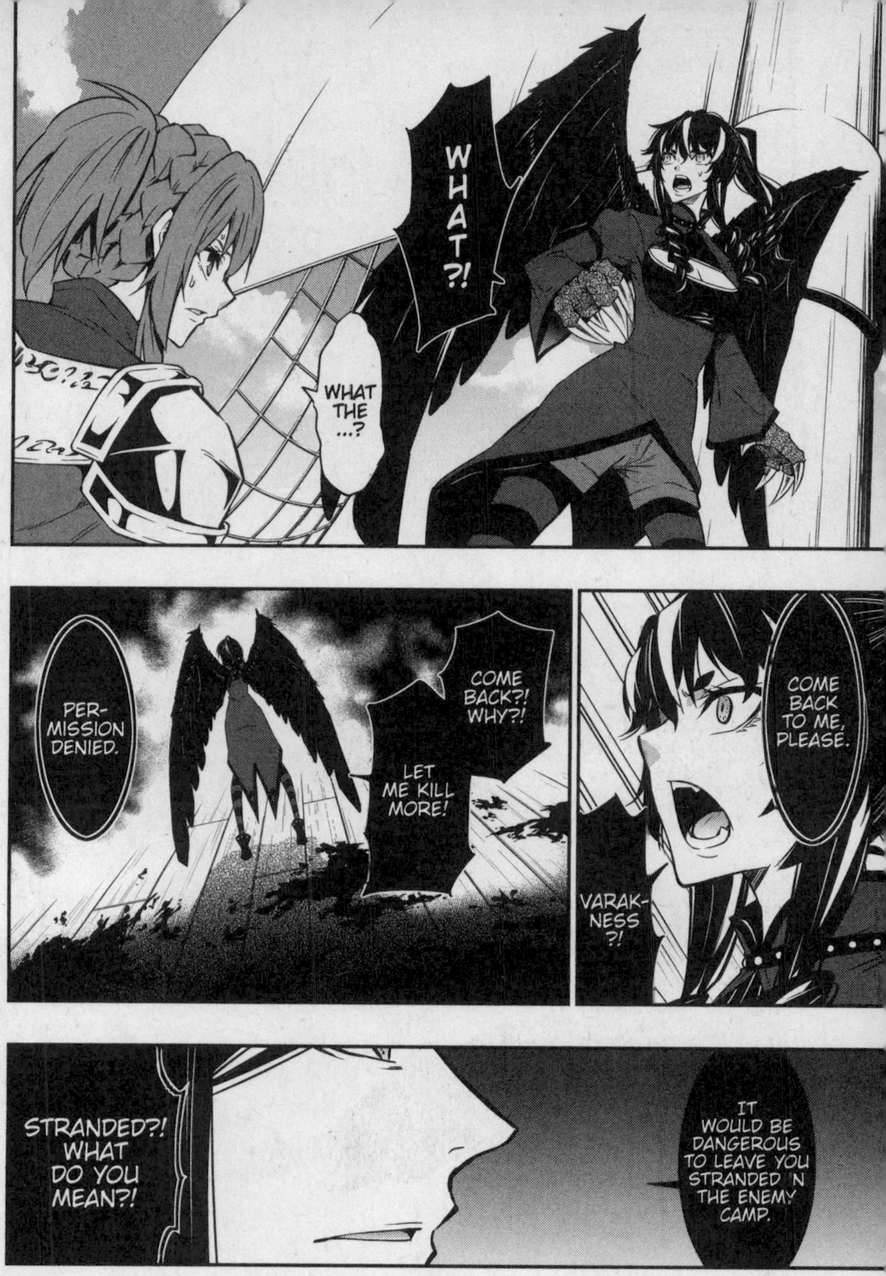
WHAT?!
WHAT THE ...?
COME BACK TO ME, PLEASE.
VARAKNESS?!
COME BACK?! WHY?!
LET ME KILL MORE!
PERMISSION DENIED.
IT WOULD BE DANGEROUS TO LEAVE YOU STRANDED IN THE ENEMY CAMP.
STRANDED?! WHAT DO YOU MEAN?!

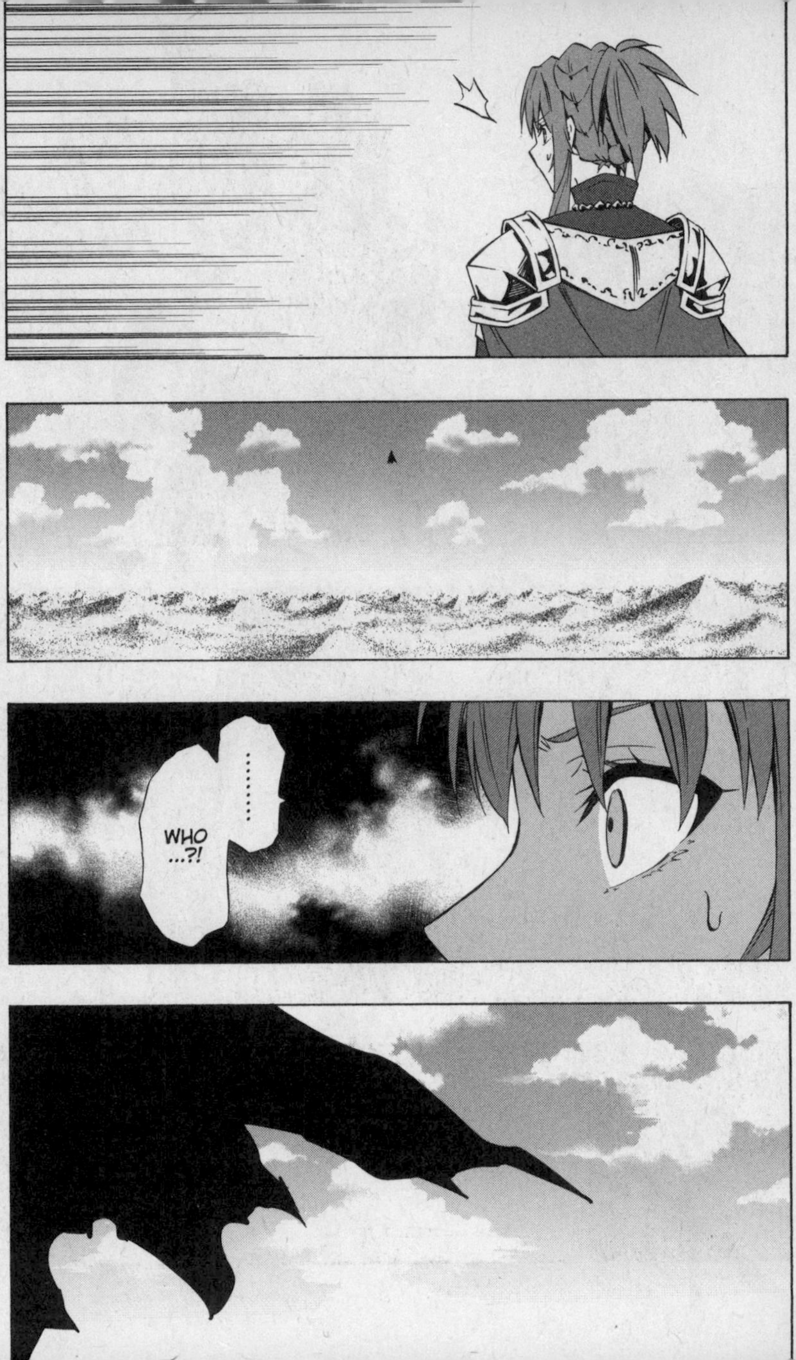
....
WHO ...?!

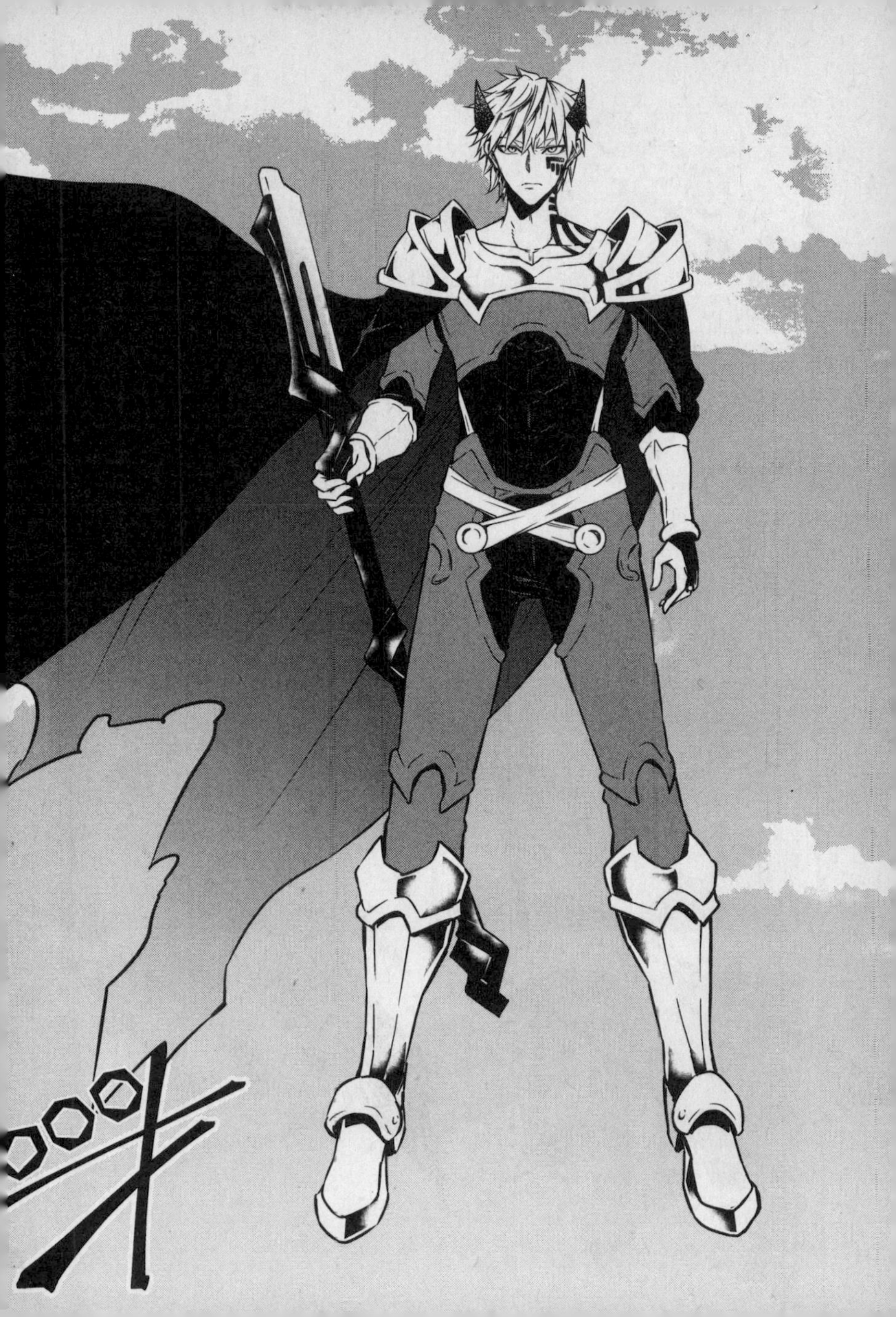

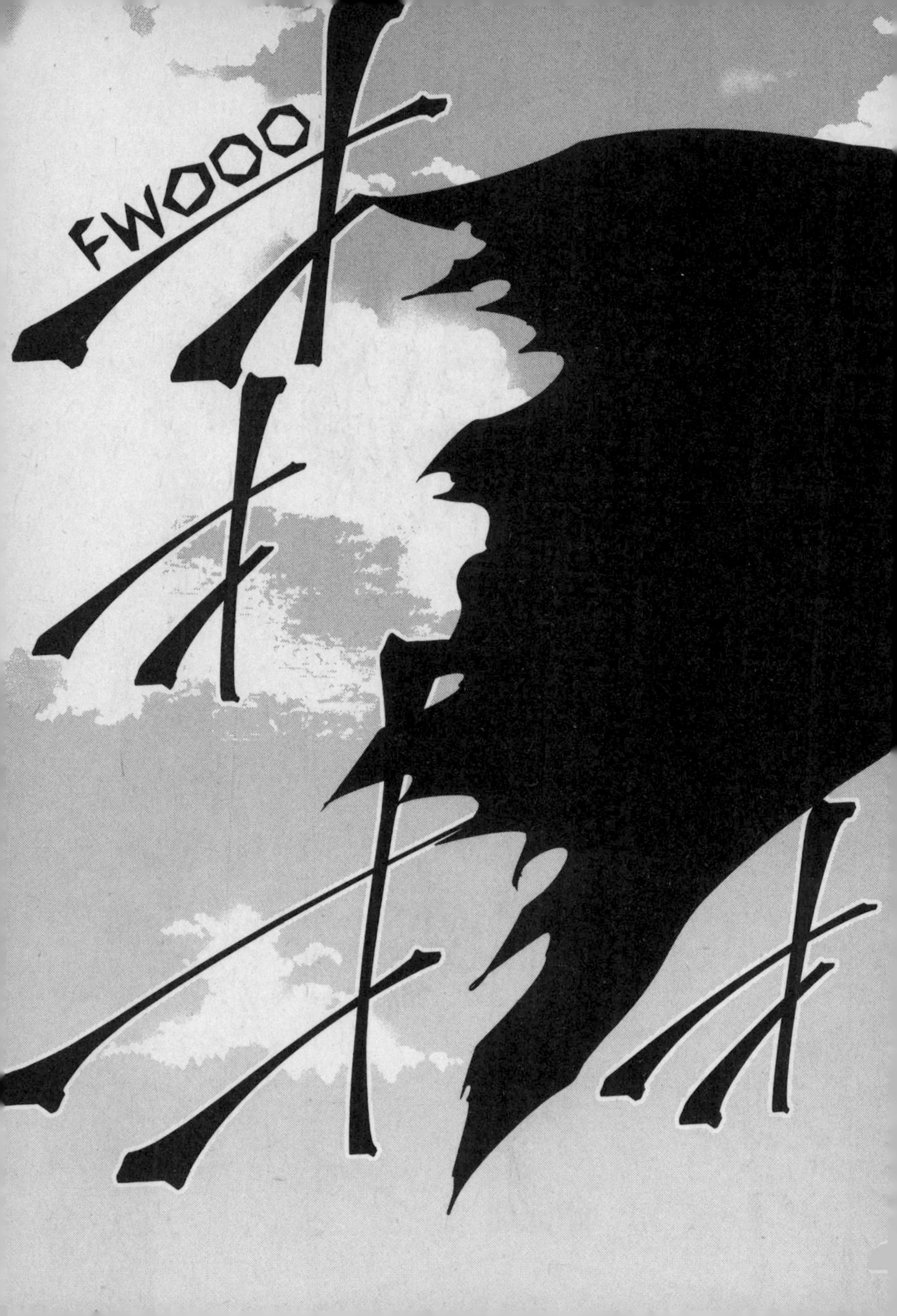
FWOOO

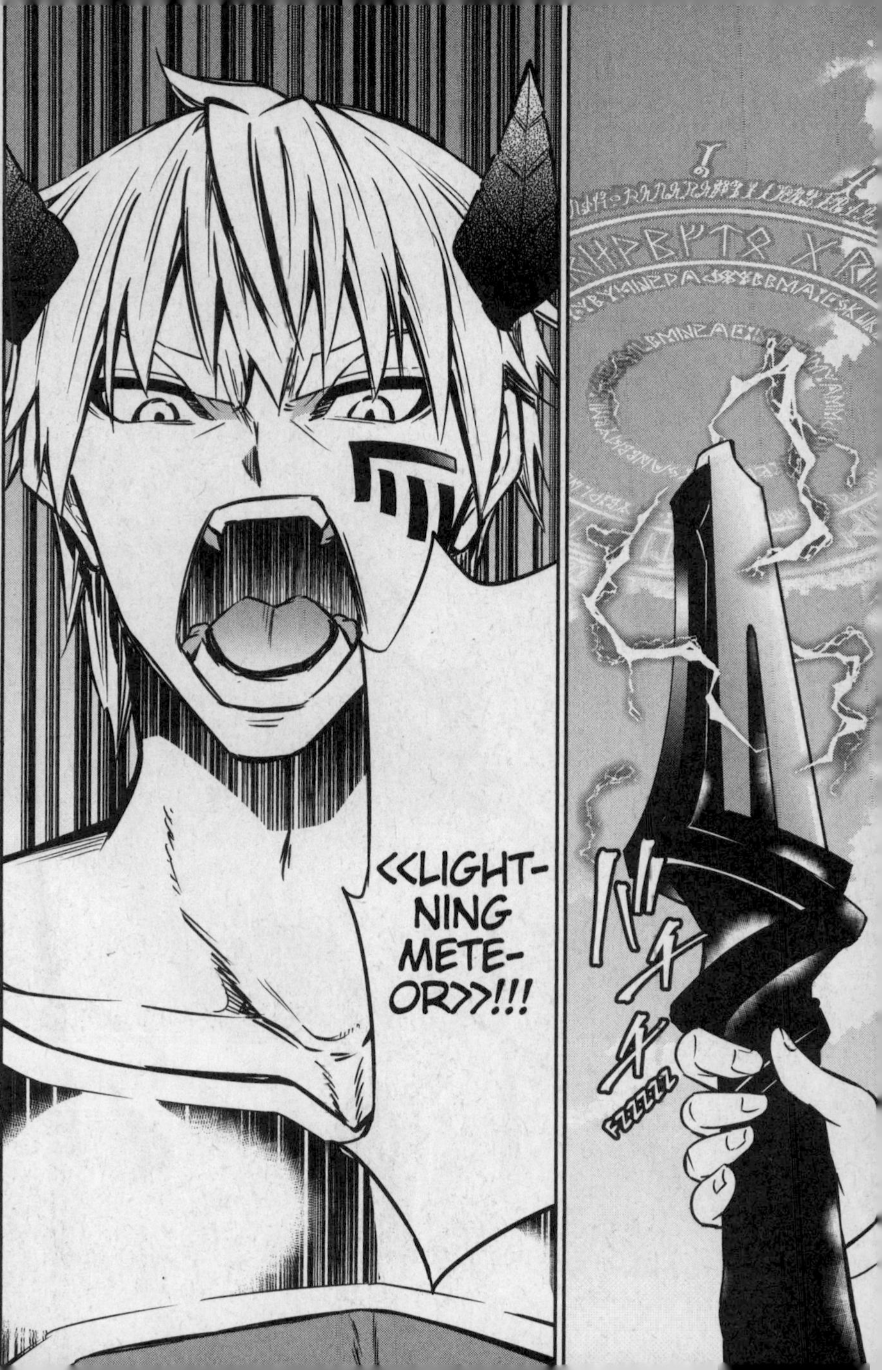
バチチ
FZZZZZZ
<<LIGHTNING METEOR>>!!!

HOW *NOT*
TO SUMMON A
DEMON LORD

to be continued...

DIABLO'S RAGE!

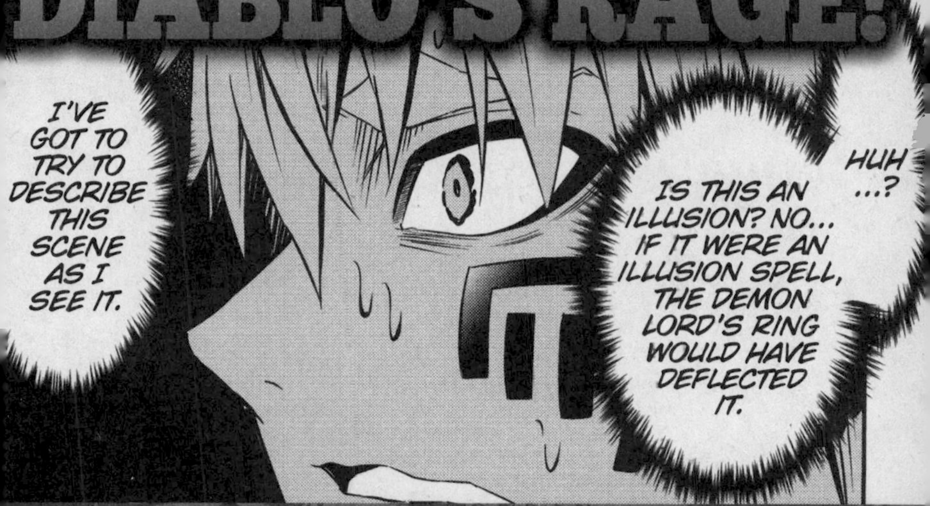
HUH ...?
IS THIS AN ILLUSION? NO... IF IT WERE AN ILLUSION SPELL, THE DEMON LORD'S RING WOULD HAVE DEFLECTED IT.
I'VE GOT TO TRY TO DESCRIBE THIS SCENE AS I SEE IT.

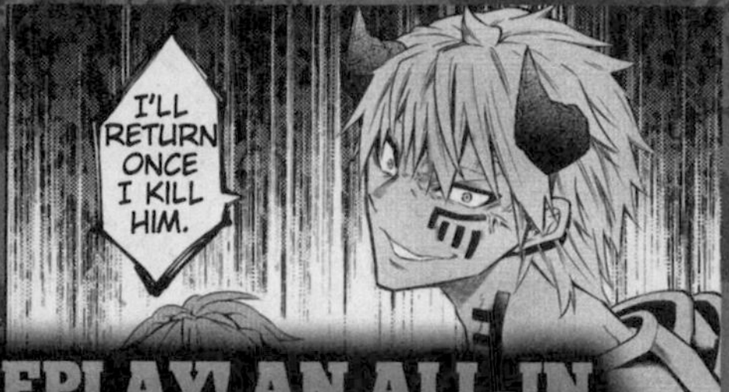
I'LL RETURN ONCE I KILL HIM.

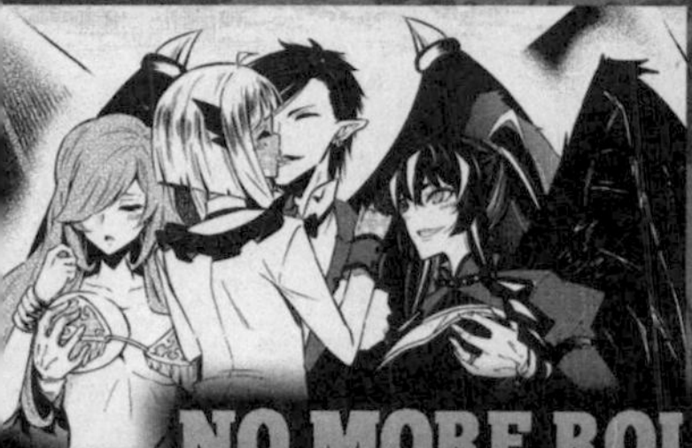

NO MORE ROLEPLAY! AN ALL-IN, UNPARALLELED DEMON LORD ARRIVES!!

HOW NOT TO SUMMON A DEMON LORD

STORY

After Diablo and the others upgrace their gear in the dungeon ard hurry to the battlefielc, they witness Varakness do the unforgivable. Corsumed by a rage like never before, Diablo loses himself. The true Demon Lord arrives!!

13

Story: Yukiya Murasaki

Art: Naoto Fukuda

Character Design: Takahiro Tsurusaki

COMING SOON!!

SPECIAL THANKS FOR VOLUME 12

YUKIYA MURASAKI

TAKAHIRO TSURUSAKI

«ASSISTANTS»
DAIKI HARAGUCHI
YUU TAKIGAWA
MASUMI HIGASHITANI
DAISUKE MIYAKOSHI
MINA ITAGAKI

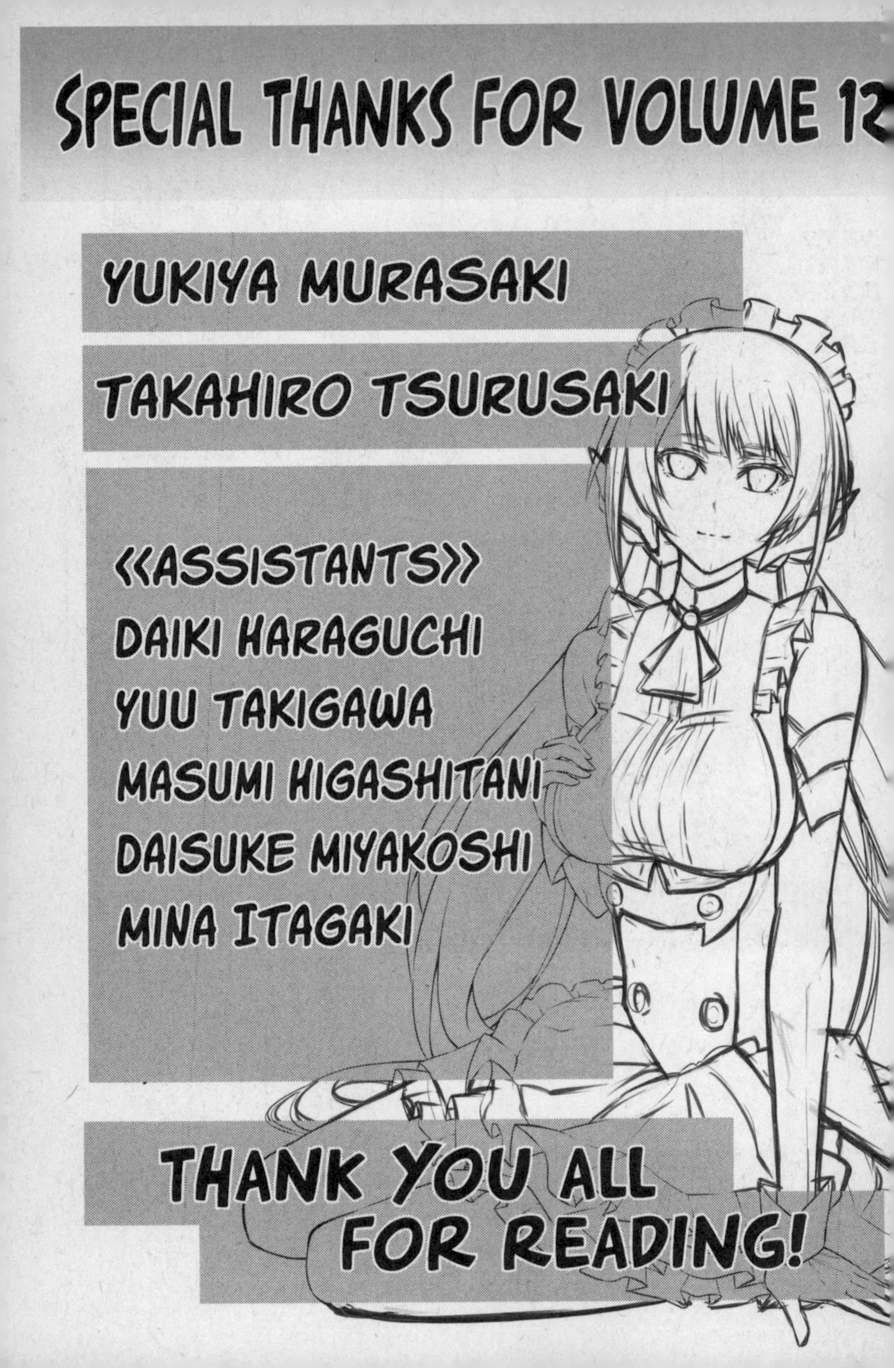

THANK YOU ALL FOR READING!

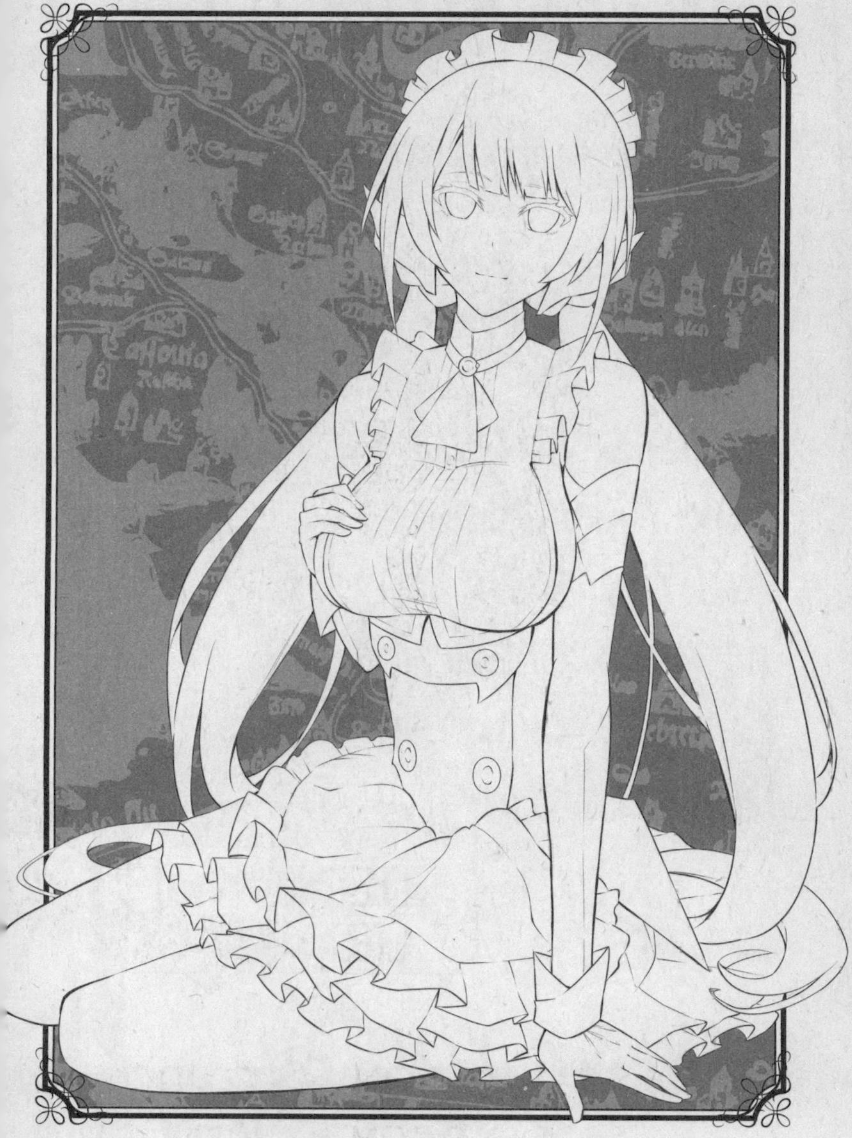

HOW NOT TO SUMMON A DEMON LORD
OMEG

SEVEN SEAS ENTERTAINMENT PRESENTS

HOW NOT TO SUMMON A DEMON LORD

VOLUME 12

story by YUKIYA MURASAKI art by NAOTO FUKUDA

TRANSLATION
Kumar Sivasubramanian

ADAPTATION
Lora Gray

LETTERING AND RETOUCH
Christa Miesner

COVER DESIGN
Kris Aubin

PROOFREADER
Dawn Davis
Stephanie Cohen

EDITOR
Kristiina Korpus

PREPRESS TECHNICIAN
Rhiannon Rasmussen-Silverstein

PRODUCTION MANAGER
Lissa Pattillo

MANAGING EDITOR
Julie Davis

ASSOCIATE PUBLISHER
Adam Arnold

PUBLISHER
Jason DeAngelis

First published in Japan in 2020 by Kodansha Ltd., Tokyo.
Publication rights for this English edition arranged through Kodansha Ltd., Tokyo.

Seven Seas press and purchase enquiries can be sent to Marketing Manager Lianne Sentar at press@gomanga.com. Information regarding the distribution and purchase of digital editions is available from Digital Manager CK Russell at digital@gomanga.com.

ISBN: 978-1-64827-289-9

Printed in Canada

First Printing: October 2021

10 9 8 7 6 5 4 3 2 1

FOLLOW US ONLINE: *www.sevenseasentertainment.com*

READING DIRECTIONS

This book reads from ***right to left***, Japanese style. If this is your first time reading manga, you start reading from the top right panel on each page and take it from there. If you get lost, just follow the numbered diagram here. It may seem backwards at first, but you'll get the hang of it! Have fun!!

1
2
3
4
5
6
7
8
9

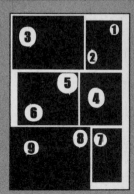

HOW *NOT* TO SUMMON A DEMON LORD CHARACTERS

INTRODUCTIONS

Race: Demon
Level: 150

Self-proclaimed Demon Lord from another world.

Thanks to the "Magic Deflection" effect of the Demon Lord's Ring, which Diablo received in-game, Rem and Shera's Enslavement Ritual backfired. Now *they're* the ones with Enslavement Collars. In the real world, Diablo was unpopular, didn't have a way with words, and couldn't interact with other people to save his life. But in this world, he's tall, handsome, and practically invincible! He still doesn't have a way with words, but he manages to make it through tough situations by acting like a Demon Lord.

Diablo (Sakamoto Takuma)

STORY

Takuma Sakamoto is an elite gamer in the fantasy MMORPG *Cross Reverie*. He is so overwhelmingly strong that he is known as the "Demon Lord." One day, he's summoned to a world nearly identical to the game by two girls: Shera, an Elf; and Rem, a Pantherian. Thanks to a pair of Enslavement Collars, Takuma Sakamoto—now Diablo—has control over the girls...but he really sucks at talking to other people!! To hide this, Diablo begins behaving like his Demon Lord persona from the game. While demonstrating his power, built up through skills he acquired by playing *Cross Reverie*, Diablo sets out on an adventure with Shera and Rem.

After an appearance by the Demon Lord's high commander Varakness, Laminitus begins to suspect that Diablo is the Lord in question. To prove his innocence and save Lumachina from the Death Knell disease, Diablo and his party head to a dungeon that he built himself to retrieve a particular item. However, Paladin Gewalt awaits them, intent on killing Lumachina. His attempt is thwarted when Horn protects Lumachina and is plunged into a raging stream, taking Gewalt with him! Without hesitation, Diablo dives in after them!

HOW NOT TO SUMMON A DEMON LORD

DEMON LORD

12

Story
YUKIYA MURASAKI

Art
NAOTO FUKUDA

Character Design
TAKAHIRO TSURUSAKI